...ed Time Model for Felony Case Disposition

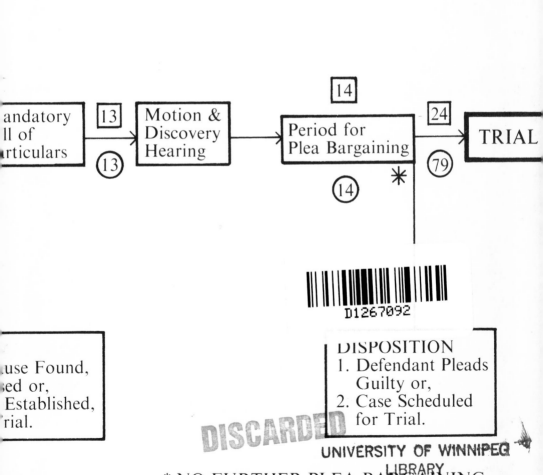

| andatory ll of rticulars | [13] 13 (circled) | Motion & Discovery Hearing | | Period for Plea Bargaining | [14] 14 (circled) | [24] 79 (circled) | TRIAL |

* (asterisk)

use Found, ed or, Established, rial.

DISPOSITION
1. Defendant Pleads Guilty or,
2. Case Scheduled for Trial.

* NO FURTHER PLEA BARGAINING.
TRIAL DATE SCHEDULED ON CHARGE.

JUSTICE IS THE CRIME

PRETRIAL DELAY IN FELONY CASES

LEWIS KATZ
LAWRENCE LITWIN
RICHARD BAMBERGER

THE PRESS OF
CASE WESTERN RESERVE UNIVERSITY
Cleveland & London
1972

Justice Is the Crime was originally prepared as a report to the National Institute of Law Enforcement and Criminal Justice of the Law Enforcement Assistance Administration. The fact that the National Institute of Law Enforcement and Criminal Justice furnished financial support to the activity described in this publication does not necessarily indicate the concurrence of the Institute in the statements or conclusions contained herein.

To Brett and her mother

ACKNOWLEDGMENTS

The authors gratefully acknowledge the research assistance of the following individuals: Frederick Anthony, Michael Banta, Glenn Berman, Charles Bloom, Thomas Brigham, Mary Lou Conlin, Michael Cyphert, Paul Dutton, Margaret Foster, Nelson Genshaft, Karl Herold, Vilma Kohn, Joyce Neiditz, Larry Sokol, Edward Tetelman, Maynard Thomson, Ralph Tyler, Jerome Weiss, Richard Whitney, Robert Woodside; and the secretarial work of Lucy Muttillo.

The authors convey further gratitude to the judges, prosecutors, defense attorneys, court administrators, defendants, and probation officers who were of assistance in preparing this report; and particularly the judges and administrators of the Cuyahoga Court of Common Pleas who facilitated our compiling of local court statistics.

CONTENTS

The Bail Bondsman
Elimination of Money Bail
A Reasonable Response

Delay and Its Abuse
Motions Practice and Delay
Discovery: Basic Problems
Discovery: Present Status for the Defendant
Discovery: Present Status for the Prosecution
Discovery and the Avoidance of Trials
What Should Be Discoverable?
Plea Bargaining
The Defense and Plea Bargaining
The Role of Judges in Plea Bargaining
Reform of Plea Bargaining

JUSTICE IS THE CRIME

INTRODUCTION

In New York City a defendant charged with the attempted rape of a four-year-old child was permitted to plead guilty to attempted assault. The tearful prosecutor was prodded into agreeing to this plea because of the great backlog of cases facing the court.[1] In the same city, thirteen Black Panthers were tried and acquitted on all counts of a conspiracy indictment. The case had lasted for twenty-five months, thirteen of those months in courtrooms, and the cost of the case was estimated at over two million dollars.[2] While the Panther trial plodded along, prisoners in city detention centers rioted to protest the delay in bringing their cases to trial.[3]

In Cleveland a man jailed for ten months on a nonbailable offense was acquitted by a jury after only forty-five minutes of deliberation. Two days before the trial was to begin, the prosecutor reduced the charge. Had the defendant originally been held on the reduced charge he would have been eligible for release on bond.[4] During the time he was in jail he was assaulted and beaten, and he had to be hospitalized for his injuries.

A San Francisco trial judge was censured by the California Supreme Court for the "slap on the wrist" sentences given to three defendants who pleaded guilty to rape charges and for his conduct towards the victim of the rape. Two of the defendants were subsequently arrested and charged with an attempted murder and burglary in which five shots were fired at a police officer.[5]

Almost two decades ago a committee headed by the late Mr. Justice Robert Jackson wrote: "There is widespread doubt that existing criminal procedures can be relied upon either adequately to protect society or to protect the individual accused."[6] The widespread doubt has not been elimi-

---

1. Mills, *I Have Nothing to Do with Justice,* LIFE, Mar. 12, 1971, at 57, 64.
2. N. Y. Times, May 14, 1971, at 20, col. 7.
3. N. Y. Times, Oct. 2, 1970, at 1, col. 3; Oct. 4, 1970, at 1, col. 8.
4. Cleveland Press, Feb. 23, 1971, § A, at 4, col. 5.
5. San Francisco Examiner, Jan. 21, 1971, at 6, col. 4; San Francisco Chronicle, Jan. 21, 1971, at 8, col. 1.
6. ABA Special Committee on the Administration of Criminal Justice,

1

nated; in fact it has now reached epidemic proportions.

Across the country the American criminal justice system is a failure. Too frequently defendants are detained or released, tried or not tried, imprisoned or put on probation, for the wrong reasons. In every urban center, cases can be found where defendants got off too easily, where some were detained who never should have been charged, and where excessive time was spent on a few cases instead of being more valuably utilized in processing those defendants who waited.

As a result of the inability of the criminal justice system to protect the community from crime and its meting out of injustices to particular defendants caught in the system, the glare of publicity has focused attention upon the criminal courts. The last decade ended with the criminal justice system, the courts, and law enforcement agencies in the center of a political campaign that added little understanding to the problems. The new decade has begun with newspaper, magazine, and television studies that examine the inadequacies of the criminal justice system.

Concurrently, the American public has lost confidence in the criminal justice system. Strangely, that loss of confidence appears on all sides of the polarized society and includes both those who believe that the courts are protecting criminals and those who argue that the courts are guarding the status quo through their dispersal of a brand of justice which seeks only to ensure social control at the expense of emerging groups. The doubts Mr. Justice Jackson alluded to, about the inability of the system to protect either the society or the accused, have developed into open hostility, and the courts have become the focal point of the dissatisfaction. Today, judges and lawyers, managers of the justice apparatus, share the doubts; but more importantly, they share a growing concern about the inadequacy of the system and evidence a growing determination to set it right.[7]

The problem in the system is the inordinate amount of time that elapses between the time an arrest occurs and final disposition is made of the case. During the period pending a disposition, the defendant is either free on the street and a symbol to others of the inability of the criminal justice system to protect the community from crime, or he is detained in jail and becomes a person who is being punished without having been convicted of a crime.

The courts are filled with criminal cases that never seem to end. No longer are the courts able to hear criminal cases judiciously and speedily. The great number of cases makes delay inherent: courts are battling simply

---

Criminal Justice: The Vital Problem of the Future, 39 A.B.A.J. 743 (1953) [hereinafter cited as *The Vital Problem*].
7. *See* Chief Justice Warren Burger's first Address on the State of the Judiciary. N. Y. Times, Aug. 11, 1970, at 24, col. 4.

to stay even and not fall farther behind. When the chief administrative judge of the Brooklyn Division of the New York Supreme Court resigned because of frustration, he said, "Right now, quantity, not quality, has become the gauge of a good judge."[8]

Some people would blame the Supreme Court and its decisions in the past twenty years for the problems of the criminal justice system. But as a result of those decisions, safeguards that protect the rights of defendants have been added at every step of a criminal prosecution. Under the stewardship of Chief Justice Earl Warren the Supreme Court attempted to transform the constitutional ideal of due process into a living reality. The Warren Court came to grips with the American dream and tried, as far as the criminal justice system was concerned, to translate that dream into the reality of a fair trial for every American citizen. One of the most noted state jurists of this century has described this as a process of putting flesh and blood on our ideals, a difficult task and not always a comfortable process.[9]

In essence what the Warren Court did was to require that the Constitution be injected into most aspects of police and judicial involvement with an individual citizen.[10] The Court further tried to ensure that the poor, when involved in the criminal justice process, received fair handling equal to that dispensed to the citizen with ample financial resources.[11] By emphasizing individual rights, the Court undoubtedly increased the amount of time necessary to dispose of a criminal case and broadened the opportunities for guilty individuals to avoid justice. But Justice Jackson, who was never accused of protecting criminals and was a hard-liner on law and order even before that was an issue, maintained that "no system can fully safeguard the innocent without affording loopholes through which some guilty persons will escape."[12]

The goal of the criminal justice system must be to strike a proper balance between safeguarding the innocent and prosecuting and convicting the guilty. The role of the Supreme Court is to determine whether the procedures used in arriving at a conviction in an individual case are constitutionally valid; thus by its very nature the Court is precluded from creating that balance. The task of creating a workable criminal justice system must fall to the state legislatures and those courts within each state that have the

---

8. N. Y. Times, May 23, 1971, § 1, at 46, col. 2.

9. Comment by Justice Walter V. Schaefer, 54 KY. L J. 521 (1966).

10. *See, e.g.,* Pointer v. Texas, 380 U. S. 400 (1965); Escobedo v. Illinois, 378 U. S. 478 (1964); Mapp v. Ohio, 367 U. S. 643 (1961).

11. *See, e.g.,* Gideon v. Wainwright, 372 U. S. 335 (1963); Griffin v. Illinois, 351 U. S. 12 (1956).

12. *The Vital Problem, supra* note 6, at 743.

power to make rules for the efficient management of their own courts. The task must fall to the states because they have the power to reorder their own criminal justice systems and to create a system that is both constitutional and workable.[13]

The American philosophy of justice has been that the more procedures there are, the more likely it is that the defendant will be treated fairly. At the same time, each legislative session writes new crimes into the criminal codes and has made the criminal process the dumping ground for all of society's problems irrespective of whether those problems should be properly treated as crimes. Consequently, criminal courts throughout the country have more cases than can be intelligently handled, and these cases move slowly through the maze of legal procedures towards disposition.

Delay has become the byword of the justice system. Part of that delay is inherent in the system, as a consequence of its myriad stages. The rest of the delay is created by the participants in the system in the belief that delay serves their cause. The need for drastic overhaul and reform is obvious. The criminal justice system is close to the breaking point; the name itself is a euphemism for a structure that is neither systematic nor capable of dispensing justice. A trial by jury, guaranteed by the Constitution of the United States, is not even remotely possible for all persons accused of serious crimes in any American urban community.[14] There are too many defendants and not enough courtrooms, judges, prosecutors, defense attorneys, or willing jurors. The guilty defendant believes, probably correctly, that if he waits long enough, the prosecutor, if only to avoid going to trial, will be almost willing to let the defendant determine his own sentence.

The delay that is thus created affects the entire system and everyone who comes in contact with it. Especially harmed by the delay is the innocent defendant who has criminal charges and the threat of a prison sentence hanging over his head. He may be pressured into dealing, and possibly even to pleading guilty to a lesser offense, particularly if he is in jail and either is denied bail or is unable to raise the money to meet his bail. He learns that if he has no prior criminal record and pleads guilty he is likely to be released immediately. If he demands his constitutional right to trial and persists in

---

13. The power of the United States Supreme Court with respect to state criminal procedure begins and ends with the Constitution. Responsibility for the day-to-day management of state courts rests with the states.

14. The Constitution has been held to guarantee a jury trial to each person charged with a criminal offense carrying a potential penalty greater than six months in jail. Duncan v. Louisiana, 391 U. S. 145 (1968); Baldwin v. New York, 399 U. S. 66 (1970).

his plea of not guilty, he will remain in jail until the prosecutor and his attorney can take the case to trial.

To make both equal and speedy justice a reality, the apparatus and its existing procedures must first be examined to determine whether they are capable of fulfilling these goals. Equal justice for all should not mean an identical opportunity for defendants to avoid answering and paying the penalty for their crimes. Equal justice requires that defendants, their victims, and the community be treated fairly, irrespective of their wealth and influence. Justice is not served when guilty people are permitted to evade punishment or when the rights of accused persons, whether guilty or innocent, are ignored. Somehow, our efforts must be harnessed so that the goals of fairness and swift justice can each be met.

The legislatures that tackle the morass in the courts will find that delay is the greatest problem and that greater fairness will naturally flow if the delay between arrest and disposition can be alleviated. The purpose of this book is to analyze the pretrial criminal procedures and show how each of these procedures contributes to delay. In so doing, we will pay particular attention to the original due process goals of each of the procedures: whether they currently fulfill those aspirations and whether, in fact, each of the procedures is essential to the due process, or fairness, model. Upon identification of the problem areas, we will recommend changes that we believe will materially alter the drift towards greater delay, yet preserve the due process ideal which remains one of America's fragile links to humanism.

1/ THE ORIGINS
OF THE AMERICAN
CRIMINAL
JUSTICE SYSTEM

STATE v. JOHNSON: A CASE HISTORY

Some of the procedures of an American criminal prosecution can be traced back ten centuries in Anglo-American history. Prior to a discussion of the evolution of the criminal justice system, it is probably best to consider a case that demonstrates how that system is working today.

Ralph Johnson[1] was arrested at his home in a suburb of Cleveland on April 13, 1970. He was charged with the intentional stabbing of the man with whom he shared the house. At the time of the arrest Johnson, who is black, was unemployed and was preparing to leave to attend school in the South. Johnson is a transplanted Southerner and has no family in the Cleveland area. He had no prior criminal record.

Johnson claims that on the evening of the stabbing he was upstairs in his room when he heard noise and scuffling in the rooms below. He went downstairs, found that his roommate had been stabbed but was still alive, and ran next door, where he asked the neighbor to call the police and an ambulance. "I rode with the police to the hospital," he later reported, "and there the police started asking me questions. Then a detective asked me to accompany him to the police station. When I got to the police station, the detective just pointed his finger and said, 'I charge you.' "[2]

When told that he was under arrest, Johnson asked the detective why.

---

1. Ralph Johnson is not the defendant's real name.
2. All the following quotations are from a conversation between Ralph Johnson and Professor Lewis R. Katz recorded at Case Western Reserve University Law School on April 29, 1971.

He told me I was the most likely suspect in the case. That's all. He proceeded to fingerprint me and everything. After he fingerprinted me he took me to a little card on the board and told me to read it which was informing me of my rights. The detective then read the card to me. I asked for an attorney because I knew one I could call, but they didn't give me an attorney. There was nothing said. There was a continuation of processing. Everything they were doing was in such a rush that they practically paid no attention to the things that I was saying. And that was it.

The following morning, April 14, Johnson appeared before a judge in the municipal court of the suburb in which he had been arrested. He had been charged with intentional stabbing.[3] At that time, the record shows, Johnson was informed of his rights, and a preliminary hearing was scheduled.

They took me to court the next day. I don't recall whether the judge informed me of my rights. I was wearing handcuffs until the time when the bailiff or whoever it was called my name. There was a gentleman there who was prosecuting and he charged me at that point with stabbing with intent. They went through the process. I wasn't paying too much attention because, to tell the truth, I was afraid and I didn't exactly know what they were doing and what was going on at the time.

Intentional stabbing is not a capital offense and Johnson was eligible for release on bail. His description of how the municipal court judge set bail is instructive.

I talked and the judge asked me questions. Then what got me was the detective who arrested me and was in court with me walked around to the judge and whispered something in his ear. After that the detective came around and stood with me and the judge set the bail at $5,000. The judge asked me if I could make the bond. I had some money but it was in check form at home, and nobody could go in the house and get it from what I understood. So therefore, I had to stay in jail, and the judge continued my case.

The preliminary hearing to ascertain probable cause was set for April 22, but it was continued to May 4, "with the consent of both parties." On April 23, the victim of the stabbing died, and Johnson was charged with first degree murder, a nonbailable offense. On April 27, the prosecutor filed a motion to dismiss the stabbing charge. A preliminary hearing was held May

---

3. OHIO REV. CODE § 2901.23 (Page 1954). The statutory penalty is one to twenty years.

6 on the murder charge, and at its conclusion the defendant was bound over to the grand jury.

> When the date rolled around for me to appear, the detectives came and got me and I appeared, but the hearing was rescheduled. I never consented to anything, postponement or otherwise. After this I was informed that the person had died and that they charged me with murder. When I appeared for the preliminary hearing I had this attorney appointed by the court. This gentleman was peculiar. I sat down and talked with him and when he got in court he didn't say or do anything. He just did nothing. I said, My goodness! I wanted to know what was going on, because when we stepped in court I never seen an attorney who was defending a person, *supposed to be defending a person,* go and become chummy and shake hands and everything with the prosecutor and everybody else. I mean it's all right to remain on friendly terms with them, but I think the way he was going at it they knew more than I knew and he knew something more too. It seems as if I'd been put on rails and I was getting ready to be shipped. The police, a doctor from the hospital, and a coroner were the only witnesses at the hearing. My attorney maybe asked them one or two questions. I'm no attorney but I would have asked more questions in more depth and detail than the ones that he asked. Then from there the judge, after everything, bound me over to the grand jury. This was while I was still learning about the process because I never been in any trouble before and never had to go through anything like that. From there I was taken to the county jail.

Johnson was indicted for first degree murder by the grand jury on June 12. At his arraignment on June 18, the court determined that Johnson was indigent and appointed two attorneys to handle his case. The plea of not guilty was entered at the arraignment.

> I didn't know about the grand jury indictment until I received it. As far as I know, the only evidence presented was by the prosecutor, and as far as I'm concerned it seems as if a person is being tried at that particular moment while not being there. Anyway, at my arraignment hearing, my name was called off, and the indictment was read. I was asked if I understood the indictment and I said yes, as far as reading it, but as far as anything else concerning the indictment, no. The judge told me that I could give no plea so he entered a plea of not guilty. The judge also said I was entitled to attorneys and an attorney should be present, but at the time I had no attorney, so he said that he would appoint me an attorney and that attorney should be in contact with me in the next week or two and these are his words. I believe it was almost three weeks later that I saw an attorney. We had a nice

conversation because I told him that I was putting my confidence in him. I knew he was appointed by the courts and indications to me are that a person appointed by the courts to some degree are subject to that court, but I told him that I was putting my confidence in him to a point that I wanted him to defend me. I knew, because the judge told me, that I was entitled to two attorneys since the case was murder. I didn't see the second attorney for some time, but I received a couple of letters from him to let me know that he was working.

During the period between the arraignment on June 18 and the impaneling of the jury for trial on February 16, a motion for a bill of particulars, a motion to review and produce hospital records, and a motion to suppress the dying declaration of the victim were filed. The last was filed on February 10, one day after the pretrial conferences began. While arguing on the motion to suppress, the prosecutor admitted he could not prove the premeditation element of first degree murder; when the judge ruled that the charge could not go to trial, the prosecutor amended the indictment to second degree murder. The amended indictment made Johnson eligible for bail, but he was not released. On February 16 the jury was impaneled and the trial began.

Throughout this period I saw my attorney quite often and many times I called he was right down. I was told both attorneys were going to file motions but I never knew exactly what those motions were, because I put my complete confidence in them. I think I learned they were only trying to get me for second degree murder at the pretrial conferences which ran into the trial. I really didn't know what was happening then because I didn't understand what they were saying as far as the legal terms they were using and all that. Then I remember the trial starting when the jury was sworn in. No one ever told me I could get bail when the charge was changed. I sure didn't think I could get bail then. But I could have gotten somebody to bail me out, if I had been told.

After a week-long trial, the jury found Johnson not guilty. He had spent ten and a half months in jail.

The accused was subjected to extensive pretrial procedures that prolonged the time necessary for disposition of the case. As a result of a common history and the requirements set forth in the Constitution, similar procedural formalities are common to all justice systems in the states. Thus, the length of time that the Johnson case required prior to a determination of guilt or innocence is not unusual.

Although there is no question that the tremendous increase in the number of criminal cases contributes significantly to the delay in terminating a case, there is also reason to believe that the system itself, with its many procedural steps, is a further catalyst in the creation of delay. Certainly there are specific procedural steps that are necessary to protect the individual's constitutional rights, but other procedures may have outlived their usefulness. In order to understand how our system is supposed to work and why it is perhaps not suited to the needs of the twentieth century, there must be an understanding of both how the institutions have developed through absorption from the English system and how the founders of this country intended these institutions to function in a frontier society which dictated a more primitive system of criminal justice.

THE HISTORICAL APPROACH

The society in which the English justice system evolved was totally different from the one in which we live. Today massive police departments, capable of sophisticated scientific investigation, are charged with the responsibility of securing the safety of our communities. Further, a public prosecutor doggedly pursues the community interest of enforcing the law against those who are accused of violating it. These institutions were not originally part of the English justice system. But because of the creation of these additional tools to assist in the obtaining of justice, the states have been able to reorganize and restructure the procedural stages of a criminal prosecution to better suit the needs and goals of each state. Consequently, there is variation from state to state in the manner in which an accused moves through the pretrial system, but rather than pointing out the minute differences, the ensuing material will first analyze the various pretrial stages and then show how they work in modern practice.

GRAND JURY AND INFORMATION

In order to punish wrongdoers, there was a need for some procedure to initiate criminal action. Once a private citizen or local official became cognizant of a crime, in order to initiate criminal charges and bring wrong-doers before the bar of justice the services of the grand jury were invoked.

The grand jury can be traced to Rome (ca. A.D. 350–450),[4] but it appeared in England in the tenth century.[5] King Henry II, in 1166, provided

---

4. Whyte, *Is the Grand Jury Necessary?*, 45 VA. L. REV. 461, 463 (1959) [hereinafter cited as Whyte].

5. Coates, *The Grand Jury, the Prosecutor's Puppet: Wasteful Nonsense of Criminal Jurisprudence,* 33 PA. B. ASS'N. 311 (1962) [hereinafter cited as Coates]. The Assize of Clarendon, 1166, which established the

for the use of the grand jury in all courts under his control.[6] He ordered the royal sheriff to summon "twelve men of the neighborhood, or village, to declare the truth"[7] and to report to the royal sheriff or justices the names of those persons who were believed to have committed crimes.[8] The twelve men, either knights or other freemen, acted not as judges but as accusers or witnesses. Usually the grand jury called no witnesses and took no testimony.[9] Indictments were returned on the basis of the common knowledge of the community or the personal knowledge of the members of the grand jury. After gathering and reviewing the facts surrounding a crime, the grand jury was justified in bringing an indictment only if there was "sufficient cause to call upon the party to answer" the charge.[10]

Since it was designed to function solely as a public prosecutor in the interest of the Crown, the original grand jury deliberated in public.[11] In the thirteenth and early fourteenth centuries at least some members of the grand jury always served on the petit jury that tried the defendant.[12] An acquittal of the defendant by the same citizens who had found enough evidence to hold him for trial often brought the wrath of the judges down upon the jurors in the form of a jail sentence.[13]

When the grand and petit juries were separated, the independence of the grand jury began to be asserted. To protect the grand jurors and the persons they were considering from the threat of oppression by the Crown, the concept of secrecy was developed.[14] In the fourteenth century, the practice

---

first true grand jury, was based not on Anglo-Saxon law but upon Frankish inquests as adopted in Normandy. L. ORFIELD, CRIMINAL PROCEDURE FROM ARREST TO APPEAL 137–39 (1947) [hereinafter cited as ORFIELD].

6. Coates, *supra* note 5, at 311.
7. Kaufman, *The Grand Jury: Its Role and Its Powers,* 17 F.R.D. 331, 332 (1955) [hereinafter cited as Kaufman].
8. Kuh, *The Grand Jury Presentment: Foul Blow or Fair Play?,* 55 COLUM. L. REV. 1103, 1106 (1955) [hereinafter cited as Kuh]. The person accused could then defend himself by swearing to his denial and submitting to the ordeal by water.
9. Note, *The Grand Jury as an Investigatory Body,* 74 HARV. L. REV. 590 (1960–1961).
10. Coates, *supra* note 5, at 312.
11. Calkins, *Grand Jury Secrecy,* 63 MICH. L. REV. 455, 456 (1965) [hereinafter cited as Calkins].
12. ORFIELD, *supra* note 5, at 138–39.
13. *Id.* at 139.
14. Calkins, *supra* note 11, at 458.

developed of taking testimony, and the grand jury adopted the policy of hearing witnesses in private. The secrecy and eventual taking of testimony in private excluded representatives of the Crown; in this manner, the grand jury became an institution that was protective of the rights of the individual and immune from governmental pressures which sought an indictment against a private citizen. The independence of the grand jury became one of the most decisive factors in protecting individual liberty and looking into official misdeeds. Later, when fear of governmental coercion diminished, a representative of the Crown was admitted while testimony was taken so that the indictment could be framed in the proper manner.[15]

As the protector of individual freedom, the grand jury also exercised investigatory authority over public officials. Grand jury reports were used to publicize the misconduct of royal officers in England;[16] and later, in the colonies, the grand jury report was used widely to investigate matters of public concern.[17] In order to conduct these investigations, the grand jury was empowered to compel the attendance and testimony of witnesses and was able to grant varying degrees of immunity from prosecution in return for information.[18]

Given its importance in assuring the protection of individual rights from governmental abuse, it is no surprise that the founders of the American colonies incorporated the grand jury into the justice system developed for the emerging nation. In a society where communities were small enough so that everyone knew all the local residents and knew everyone else's business, and in a society that had not yet developed police and prosecutors charged with investigating and initiating criminal charges, the grand jury was the logical institution. It filled the needs of seventeenth- and eighteenth-century America. By the time the framers of the Bill of Rights adopted the right

---

15. *Id.*

16. Kuh, *supra* note 8, at 1109. Sidney and Beatrice Webb have set forth specific instances of early grand jury inquiries into misconduct of royal officials. S. & B. WEBB, ENGLISH LOCAL GOVERNMENT FROM THE REVOLUTION TO THE MUNICIPAL CORPORATION ACT: THE PARISH AND THE COUNTY 448–56 (1906).

17. Kuh, *supra* note 8, at 1110. The grand jury practice of issuing reports on matters of public concern was followed in the American colonies. Grand juries in New Jersey rendered reports on matters of public affairs as early as 1680. *In re* Camden County Grand Jury, 10 N. J. 23, 41–44, 89 A.2d 416, 426–28 (1952).

18. Scigliano, *The Grand Jury, The Information, and the Judicial Inquiry,* 38 ORE. L. REV. 303, 304 (1958) [hereinafter cited as Scigliano]. Immunity was offered in cases involving public corruption or conspiracy. *Id.*

to a grand jury indictment as a part of the Constitution it had already enjoyed a venerable past in the colonies. For example, Virginia, which adopted the grand jury system as a result of royal decree, recreated the original notion of the grand jury in America. Virginia colonists were notified six months in advance that they were to be called for service on a grand jury and were charged during the ensuing six months to be on the lookout for crime.[19] Thus, the grand jury in colonial Virginia indicted solely upon those facts within the knowledge of each individual juror.[20]

During the latter part of the eighteenth century, the grand jury came under attack: in England by Jeremy Bentham and in the colonies by his disciple Edward Livingston.[21] By this time the grand jury had expanded to the extent that it could investigate not only private crime but also political and administrative misconduct. Those who favored retention of the grand jury wanted the investigation of all serious crimes to remain in the hands of the people. Bentham argued that the grand jury should be limited to reviewing whether a prosecutor had presented sufficient evidence and testimony to justify holding a suspect for a particular crime. This is essentially the way the grand jury functions in the United States today.

In 1846, the United States Congress, by statute, made the calling of a federal grand jury discretionary with the presiding judge, except in capital offenses.[22] Additionally the Supreme Court, in 1884, refused to include a grand jury as a sine qua non of Fourteenth Amendment due process in the states.[23] Following this ruling, several Western states when designing their justice systems recognized the grand jury as an anachronism. Some restricted the number of situations in which a grand jury could be convened or wrote their constitutions to allow the legislature to "abolish, limit, change or amend" the existing grand jury system. Nebraska and Colorado did

---

19. Whyte, *supra* note 4, at 470.

20. *Id.* at 471. "After 1705, instead of making a presentment on the knowledge of one grand jury member, no presentment could be made unless on the information of two members of that body." *Id.*

21. Younger, *The Grand Jury Under Attack,* 46 J. CRIM. L.C. & P.S. 26, 28 (1955–1956) [hereinafter cited as Younger]. Jeremy Bentham (1748 –1832) was an English legal reformer who believed a professional prosecutor could perform grand jury functions more efficiently and less expensively. Edward Livingston (1764–1836) was an American disciple of Bentham. Livingston codified Louisiana's criminal laws. The Livingston Code limited the grand jury to reviewing and ruling upon the indictments submitted to them. *Id.*

22. *Id.* at 31; 1 Stat. 119 (1790), U. S. CONST. amend. V.

23. Hurtado v. California, 110 U. S. 516 (1884).

subsequently abolish the grand jury.[24] It is clear that the purpose for which the grand jury was originally conceived, that of maintaining the peace and security of the community by investigating wrongdoing and initiating charges against offenders, is today better served by efficient and highly trained police departments and public prosecutors. Its role as the carrier of the bright torch of freedom protecting individuals from government harassment has likewise been curtailed by the dominant role played by modern prosecutors in the grand jury proceedings.[25] With the prosecutor selecting the cases that the grand jury is to consider and presenting the evidence that he wishes the grand jury to hear, the grand jury has become little more than an appendage to do his bidding. Ideally the grand jury should further act as a check on abuse by the prosecutor in charging persons with crimes. If the grand jury's major purposes have been preempted over the years, and its minor function of checking abuses can be better performed by another existing procedural step such as the preliminary hearing, then perhaps the delay brought about by the grand jury as a procedural step becomes unnecessary.[26]

Since the Norman Conquest, the English have used, in addition to the grand jury, two other types of accusations: accusation by a private person and accusation by information.[27] In the former, a private individual who had been aggrieved by the criminal act of another could swear out a complaint charging that person with the commission of a crime. The accused would be brought before the justice of the peace, who would hold a hearing to determine whether the complaint was sufficient to detain the accused for trial. At this hearing the accused was entitled, if he chose, to attempt to clear himself by calling witnesses and presenting evidence. Identical to the practice in England, private citizens in the American colonies were authorized to appear before a magistrate and swear out a complaint against another citizen.[28] In Virginia, this procedure had considerable popularity because the private citizen was entitled to a percentage of the fine levied against a person who was convicted as a result of this charging method.[29]

Other procedures were developed in the colonies to circumvent the grand

24. Younger, *supra* note 21, at 39.
25. L. HALL, Y. KAMISAR, W. LaFAVE & J. ISRAEL, MODERN CRIMINAL PROCEDURE 791 (3rd ed. 1969).
26. *See* Chapter 3 concerning charging.
27. ORFIELD, *supra* note 5, at 137.
28. 2 Z. SWIFT, A SYSTEM OF THE LAWS OF THE STATE OF CONNECTICUT 377 (1796) [hereinafter cited as SWIFT].
29. A. SCOTT, CRIMINAL LAW IN COLONIAL VIRGINIA 52 (1930) [hereinafter cited as SCOTT].

jury procedure. Connecticut authorized individual jurors to act independently of the full grand jury and to swear out a complaint charging that an individual had probably committed a crime.[30] Courts subsequently initiated the practice of commissioning private attorneys to originate criminal action, a technique untested by the English. The commissioning of a private attorney is the antecedent of today's prosecuting attorney and has its origin in the continental European inquisitorial procedure, a system that the colonies otherwise substantially rejected.[31] The prosecutor's counterpart in the French inquisitorial system is the *juge d'instruction,* an official with the dual function of judge and police officer.[32] The concept provided at its nucleus a person solely charged with representing the community's interest. There were few lawyers on the frontier, and the need for a representative of the government to be present was highlighted by the great distances between the capitals of the colonies and their outlying settlements. As could be expected, the creation on the frontier of an office staffed by a law-trained official did produce imbalances. The familiarity of the prosecutor with the law and the niceties of juries and judges put the defendant in a criminal case at a disadvantage because few attorneys were available to represent the accused.[33]

The attorneys could bring charges in the form of an information, the third accusatorial technique carried over from the English. The specific origin of the criminal information is unclear. Evidence exists from the reign of Edward I that the king through his legal representatives, the sejeant of treason or the sejeant of felony (forerunners of the modern prosecutor), accused persons of felony or misdemeanor offenses in the Court of the Star Chamber and thus avoided the grand jury.[34] In this way the king used the

---

30. SWIFT, *supra* note 28, at 375.
31. F. HELLER, THE SIXTH AMENDMENT TO THE CONSTITUTION OF THE UNITED STATES, A STUDY IN CONSTITUTIONAL DEVELOPMENT 21 (1969) [hereinafter cited as HELLER].
32. R. MOLEY, OUR CRIMINAL COURTS 37 (1930) [hereinafter cited as MOLEY]. The *juge d'instruction* is the titular or assistant judge of first instance, appointed to make preliminary examinations for a period of three years. In criminal cases it is the duty of the *juge d'instruction* to discover all the evidence pointing to the existence of the crime and to identify the perpetrator. *Id.* at 37.
33. HELLER, *supra* note 31.
34. 2 F. POLLOCK & F. MAITLAND, THE HISTORY OF ENGLISH LAW 662 (2d ed. 1968). The Star Chamber was not the only court using informations. The Court of the King's Bench also used informations but only in misdemeanor cases. Since the king used various court officers to represent him, justices, sheriffs, or attorneys could bring an information. The information procedure was eventually misused by Crown

information to control those who might oppose or criticize him. For instance, after grand juries twice refused to indict colonist John Peter Zenger for criminal libel, the Crown's governor charged Zenger by information.[35] Increasingly, with the diminished importance of the grand jury, the public prosecutor would use the information as a substitute for the grand jury indictment.[36] This development was paralleled in the state constitutions, which in the nineteenth century almost exclusively required grand jury indictment but which by the early twentieth century had been modified in some states to permit information in felony prosecutions.[37]

In practice, the information is filed by the prosecuting officer when the accused has been bound over for trial following a preliminary hearing.[38] In the preliminary hearing, the judge performs the old grand jury function of determining the existence of probable cause. This requires him to find that a crime has probably been committed and that the accused is the probable offender. In most jurisdictions, an information may not be filed unless a judge is convinced that probable cause exists.[39] The effect of the use of an information, in lieu of indictment, is to eliminate the time normally spent awaiting return of an indictment from the grand jury. Although the information procedure removes the potential check that the grand jury has upon a prosecutor, the judge must still have made a probable cause determination at the preliminary hearing, which minimizes the possibilities of prosecutorial abuse. In some jurisdictions an information may be used to charge a defendant even though there is no preliminary hearing, in which case there is no review of the charge until trial. The information procedure has the potential for disposing of cases with greater speed than the grand jury without sacrificing fairness. Consequently, the trend is towards its more frequent use in felony cases.

---

officials through malicious prosecutions. This abuse was remedied by the statute of 4 Will. & Mary, c. 18 (A. D. 1692), which forced the Master of the Crown Office into a proceeding with a magistrate. 1 J. STEPHEN, A HISTORY OF THE CRIMINAL LAW OF ENGLAND 294–97 (1883) [hereinafter cited as STEPHEN].

35. HEARTMAN, JOHN PETER ZENGER AND HIS FIGHT FOR FREEDOM OF THE AMERICAN PRESS, *cited in* Kuh, *supra* note 8, at 1109.

36. Scigliano, *supra* note 18, at 304–5.

37. *Id.* at 305. An information is a written accusation of crime preferred by a public prosecuting officer, without the intervention of a grand jury. Historically, in England, informations were employed in misdemeanors whereas felonies were required to be prosecuted by indictment. *Id.*

38. *See* Chapter 3 concerning charging.

39. Scigliano, *supra* note 18, at 305.

BAIL

Whether the eventual accusation is made by indictment or information, the prosecution today generally begins when a police officer at the "scene" makes an arrest. Shortly after the arrest the accused will make an initial appearance before a magistrate. The magistrate will inform him of his rights and will, unless the charge is nonbailable, set bail. The effect of setting bail is to enable a person to obtain his release from legal custody with the accompanying understanding that he later appear as ordered before the appropriate court.

The historical origins of the concept of bail are obscure. Some experts believe the concept is derived from the English institution of hostageship, where the party (hostage) was held "until the promise of a certain person was fulfilled or a certain consequence achieved."[40] If the promise was not kept, according to some scholars, the hostage-surety would submit himself personally to the disappointed party;[41] according to others, the hostage-surety would forfeit his property to the disappointed party.[42] The other frequently noted origin of the concept of bail is the ancient English law of debt. This law required that someone accused of a wrongful act assure payment to reimburse the injured party in case the alleged wrongdoer was found guilty.[43] A third party would guarantee payment to the victim if liability was-established, and if the debtor could not pay, the third party was ultimately responsible for payment.[44]

Whatever its source, bail was a necessary response to the very real problems of feudal times. In those days, the system of law and order was administered by traveling magistrates whose visits to a particular region were infrequent and irregular. During these intervals, the local sheriffs bore the responsibility of prisoner custody. Since the jails were hardly escape-proof and prisoner care was expensive, it was desirable to avoid imprisoning an accused if the sheriff could be certain of his appearance at trial. Sheriffs could avoid prisoner detention if a third party, perhaps a friend or relative of the defendant, would assume personal responsibility for the defendant's later trial appearance.[45] Frequently, the sheriff exercising his expansive discretionary power would allow a prisoner to be placed in the provisional

---

40. R. GOLDFARB, RANSOM: A CRITIQUE OF THE AMERICAN BAIL SYSTEM 22 (1965) [hereinafter cited as RANSOM].
41. 2 F. POLLOCK & F. MAITLAND, THE HISTORY OF ENGLISH LAW 588 (1895) [hereinafter cited as 2 POLLOCK & MAITLAND].
42. *Id.* at 589–90.
43. RANSOM, *supra* note 40, at 23.
44. *Id.*
45. *Id.* at 23–24. *See* 2 POLLOCK & MAITLAND, *supra* note 41, at 582.

custody of a surety. Should the defendant who had been released to a surety fail to show up on the date of the trial, the surety might be imprisoned[46] or might be required to pay a sum of money to the sheriff.[47]

Since there were no formal standards to be applied by the sheriffs in deciding whether to release on bail, it became a decision subject to arbitrariness and abuse. To combat this, Parliament, in 1275, enacted the Statute of Westminster I,[48] listing crimes that were and were not bailable and imposing fines upon the sheriffs if the standards were not obeyed.[49] Later in the thirteenth century, justices of the peace replaced the sheriffs as grantors of bail.[50] Toward the end of the fifteenth century (1486), another act was passed that made it necessary for two justices to agree on bail for certain prisoners.[51] This practice apparently led to situations of collusion between the two justices and the prisoner. To counteract these tacit agreements, a law requiring a preliminary hearing was enacted. When a prisoner was released on bail under this statute, his deposition, a testimony given in response to interrogatories, was taken and submitted to the court.[52]

To understand the significance of three additional statutes applicable to bail, it is necessary to consider them in the historical context of the Magna Carta. The Magna Carta as early as 1215 provided as follows: "No freeman shall be taken, or imprisoned, or disseised, or outlawed or exiled, or in any way destroyed, nor will we go upon him, nor will we send upon him, except by the legal judgement of his peers or by the law of the land."[53] In the famous seventeenth-century case, *Darnel's Case*,[54] certain persons were imprisoned by order of the king on unstated grounds. The defendants brought a habeas corpus action, but the court agreed with the prosecution that the Magna Carta provision quoted above did not apply to pretrial incarceration. This resulted in an irreconcilable dilemma. If the grounds for imprisonment were not enumerated, the defendant, according to the result in *Darnel,* could be imprisoned without bail prior to trial because the Magna Carta was inapplicable. The Statute of Westminster I was also inapplicable since it listed bailable and nonbailable crimes and could not be invoked unless a

---

46. 2 POLLOCK & MAITLAND, *supra* note 41, at 582.
47. Note, *The Bail System: Is It Acceptable?,* 29 OHIO ST. L. J. 1005, 1006–7 (1968) [hereinafter cited as *The Bail System*].
48. 3 Edw. 1, c. 15 (1275).
49. RANSOM, *supra* note 40, at 26.
50. Note, *Bail: An Ancient Practice Reexamined,* 70 YALE L. J. 966, 967 (1961) [hereinafter cited as *Bail: An Ancient Practice*].
51. 3 Hen. 7, c. 3 (1486), *cited in* STEPHEN, *supra* note 34, at 236.
52. ORFIELD, *supra* note 5, at 101–4.
53. 14 ENCY. BRIT. 577 (1968).
54. 3 How. St. Tr. 1 (1627).

defendant was charged with a specific offense. The Petition of Rights,[55] which required that grounds for detention be specified, was passed in 1628 to resolve this conflict. Thus more than four hundred years after the Magna Carta was forced from King John, the protection of the Magna Carta was extended to pretrial imprisonment.

Further meaning was imputed to the Magna Carta in 1676 because of a case in which bail had been refused to a defendant imprisoned for three months on bailable charges.[56] Protest over this treatment led to the passage of the Habeas Corpus Act,[57] which penalized judges who refused to grant bail where the offense charged was bailable. This practice, however, led to still another abuse, and more patchwork was required. As they could no longer refuse bail with impunity, some judges responded by imposing prohibitively high bail in certain felonies. This is still a common practice in modern American courts. The problem was attacked in the English Bill of Rights, [58] which was enacted by Parliament as William and Mary ascended the throne in 1689. The English Bill of Rights provided that excessive bail ought not to be required (nor excessive fines imposed, nor cruel and unusual punishment inflicted).[59] This law provided the model that the colonies were to use in drafting the Eighth Amendment to the new Constitution. Additional laws in nineteenth-century England permitted the justices to exercise discretion in admitting to bail anyone accused of a felony, while certain misdemeanors were bailable as of right.[60]

Because of the mobility of its people and its expanding frontiers, colonial America followed a different path in developing a bail practice. The English system of bail-surety emphasized the personal responsibility of the surety to produce the defendant at trial. The surety was invariably a friend or relative. The mobile colonists, on the other hand, developed comparatively few family ties or friends. Since a personal guarantee was unreliable in the new world, a purely monetary bail system was substituted for the surety approach.[61]

Congress first gave serious consideration to bail in Section 33 of the Judiciary Act of 1789,[62] which described bail as an absolute right in non-

---

55. 3 Car. 1, c. 1 (1627).

56. Jenkes Case, 6 How. St. Tr. 1190 (1676).

57. 31 Car. 2, c. 2 (1679).

58. 1 W. & M. Sess. 2, c. 2 (1688).

59. Foote, *The Coming Constitutional Crisis in Bail: I,* 113 U. PA. L. REV. 959, 965–68 (1965) [hereinafter cited as Foote].

60. ORFIELD, *supra* note 5, at 101–4.

61. Note, *Bail in the United States: A System in Need of Reform,* 20 HASTINGS L. J. 380 (1968).

62. 1 Stat. 73 (1789).

capital federal offenses. Two years later, the Eighth Amendment protection against excessive bail was adopted. The effect of these independent actions was to give the right to bail a statutory origin and the protection against excessive bail a constitutional basis. This conceptual distinction engendered no problems among its creators, but courts subsequently considering bail have had to remain cognizant of the distinction.

The development of the English and American bail systems is thus a study in contrast. The English began with legislation setting forth specific standards and progressed to authorizing the exercise of judicial discretion in granting bail.[63] In the United States, on the other hand, the state constitutions and federal statutes gave a defendant an absolute right to bail "except for capital offenses."[64]

The historical development of bail does not disclose any influence that bail can have in slowing the disposition of a criminal case. Whether the accused is or is not on bail may be a significant factor, however, in determining an attorney's efforts to move the case through the justice system.[65] Consequently, as the historical development of the other procedural steps is discussed, it should be remembered that there are two classes of individuals being dealt with—those on bail and those detained. The system approaches these two groups with varying degrees of urgency: whether a defendant is in jail or on bail has a tremendous effect on the time required for disposition as well as on the result in the case.

PRELIMINARY HEARING

After arrest and before action by a grand jury, an accused in most states is entitled to a preliminary hearing. Indictment by the grand jury prior to the date set for the preliminary hearing will negate the right. There are two important distinctions between the preliminary hearing and the grand jury procedures. First, unlike the grand jury indictment, which may precede arrest, the preliminary hearing will always follow an arrest.[66] Second, while the grand jury proceeding is ex parte (that is, an accused has no right to be present or heard, to be represented by counsel, to present evidence, or to question his accusers), the preliminary hearing is an adversary proceeding. The defendant at a preliminary hearing has the right to appear, to be represented by counsel, to cross-examine the state's witnesses, and to produce his own. These distinctions point to an ecclesiastical, rather than an

---

63. Foote, *supra* note 59, at 968–73.

64. *The Bail System, supra* note 47, at 1007.

65. *See* Chapter 4 concerning bail.

66. Note, *The Preliminary Hearing—an Interest Analysis,* 51 Iowa L. Rev. 164 (1966) [hereinafter cited as *An Interest Analysis*].

English law, origin of the preliminary hearing.[67] The preliminary hearing can be observed evolving from an embryonic beginning in Roman times as an accusatory technique, through its use by the Roman Catholic Church, and subsequently to its codification in the French Ordonnance Criminelle of 1498.[68]

The Ordonnance operated in the following inquisitorial manner. After receiving a civilian or prosecutor's complaint of a crime, the French magistrate began an investigation to assure himself that a crime had been committed. If convinced, he then began a secret investigation to discover the identity of the criminal. He used recorded statements of witnesses and any other means of investigation his ingenuity fashioned.[69] When a suspect had been identified, he was ordered to appear before the magistrate for questioning. The questioning occurred in secret and without counsel,[70] and was the defendant's first notice of an accusation. Witnesses were asked to reappear, and their depositions were read to the accused in their presence. At this point, the defendant could object to the statements which he was hearing for the first time, but he still had no right to counsel. If the evidence was sufficiently probative of guilt, the magistrate was required to convict the defendant. Only at this point, with the defendant adjudged guilty, did the case go to trial, and then only for sentencing. The purpose of the French procedure was to construct an airtight case. Relying heavily upon the findings of the preliminary hearing, the trial court privately reexamined the defendant, who was again without counsel.[71] Then the court would impose sentence.

The first such English procedure, also inquisitorial in nature, was the coroner's inquest, remnants of which persist even today. The coroner, upon learning of an unnatural death, questioned representatives from the four

---

67. Ploscowe, *The Development of Present-Day Criminal Procedures in Europe and America,* 48 HARV. L. REV. 433, 447 (1935) [hereinafter cited as Ploscowe].

68. *Id.* at 449.

69. *Id.* at 450. The French call this the *period de l'instruction,* covering the gathering of evidence and the formulation of the state's case for trial. The method of investigation varies, depending on the crime committed and the circumstances under which it is discovered. MOLEY, *supra* note 32, at 37.

70. Moley states that the defendant was informed of both his right to remain silent and his right to counsel prior to interrogation. In exceptional circumstances the judge questioned the accused without informing him of his rights. MOLEY, *supra* note 32, at 38.

71. Ploscowe, *supra* note 67, at 451–52.

townships nearest the place where the death had occurred.[72] He could compel witnesses to testify under oath and could bind them over for trial, should he decide a felony had been committed.[73] In 1324, when the office of justice of the peace was created, the justice was not required to conduct a preliminary hearing; nevertheless, it is likely that a justice conducted some sort of preliminary examination to determine probable cause.[74] A justice of the peace served in the capacity of detective, arresting officer, and, if he decided the accused should stand trial, principal witness.[75] By the mid-1500s, two statutes had been enacted that required a justice of the peace to examine the defendant and prosecution witnesses.[76] Defendants were permitted neither to confront these witnesses nor to see their depositions.[77] Evidence against the defendant was put in writing, and the witnesses could be required to appear for trial.[78] This was a closed and secret system, with the magistrate playing the role of prosecutor and arresting officer,[79] as well as presiding over the preliminary hearing and appearing at trial as principal witness for the state. This biased system created a distinct disadvantage for the defendant.

By the nineteenth century, with the emergence of a professional police force, a separation of functions became apparent.[80] The justice of the peace assumed the role of judge, and the preliminary hearing became accusatorial rather than inquisitorial. The police did the interrogating, and the use of physical brutality to obtain confessions was not uncommon.[81] In 1836, the Prisoner's Counsel Act allowed defendants to see depositions that could be used against them. In 1848, another law required prosecution witnesses to testify at the preliminary hearing in the defendant's presence and allowed

---

72. *An Interest Analysis, supra* note 66, at 165.
73. *See* F. NICHOLS, BRITTON 7–8 (1901). The sheriff's powers were very great in the 1100s and the king viewed the sheriff with some suspicion. To alleviate the fears of the king, another official who could check the sheriff's power and safeguard the royal interest was appointed. Thus, the coroner became a recognized figure by the beginning of the twelfth century. 1 W. S. HOLDSWORTH, A HISTORY OF ENGLISH LAW 82 (3rd ed. 1922) [hereinafter cited as HOLDSWORTH].
74. MOLEY, *supra* note 32, at 15.
75. *Id.* at 15–16.
76. 1 & 2 Phil. & M., c. 13 (1554).
77. Ploscowe, *supra* note 67, at 458–59.
78. ORFIELD, *supra* note 5, at 54–55.
79. *Id.* at 55–58.
80. *Id.* at 56–57.
81. *Id.* at 62–64.

a defendant to make statements and to call witnesses in his own behalf.[82] But it was not until 1930 that a defendant could be assigned counsel at the preliminary hearing, and then only in exceptional circumstances.[83]

It is not clear whether the preliminary hearing was also used in the colonies and later in the states as an inquisitorial tool.[84] In Connecticut, for example, by the end of the eighteenth century, magistrates could not examine the accused during the preliminary hearing, although defendants were permitted to present their own witnesses to counter adverse testimony.[85] Virginia followed a similar pattern but, in felony cases, added the Examining Court to the fact-finding process. Here, the justice of the peace would examine the defendant, take his statement and the statements of witnesses (not under oath), and commit the defendant to the general court. Then, within five to ten days after the hearing before the justice of the peace, he would order the sheriff to convene an Examining Court consisting of laymen. At this session, witnesses could be subpoenaed, the defendant could cross-examine them, and the defendant himself could be examined. These examinations were without oath. In this way, the lay Examining Court could sift out and screen cases, saving the general courts both time and money. If the case was considered triable, the justice could either bind over the defendant to the grand jury or remand him to stand trial for his life. If the case was uncertain or if the defendant requested, he could immediately be given his punishment, usually the whipping post, and be discharged.[86] This latter alternative was frequently used. It had the advantage to the defendant of being quick and cheap, since a prisoner had to pay his own upkeep in jail. The immediate punishment also protected the defendant from further prosecution and a possible death penalty.[87]

Today, the preliminary hearing operates primarily for the benefit of the accused. Its object is to prevent hasty and oppressive prosecutions, to avoid unwarranted trials, and to discover whether or not there are substantial grounds on which to base a prosecution.[88] It has also developed into a discovery device, enabling the defense to learn the state's case. The judicial officer rules only on the probability of the defendant's guilt or innocence.[89]

---

82. *Id.* at 55–56.
83. *Id.* at 57. Now the accused has the right to appointed counsel at the preliminary hearing, for it is considered a critical stage of the criminal process. Coleman v. Alabama, 399 U. S. 1 (1970).
84. MOLEY, *supra* note 32, at 20.
85. SWIFT, *supra* note 28, at 390.
86. SCOTT, *supra* note 29, at 59–61.
87. *Id.* at 61–62.
88. Thies v. State, 178 Wis. 98, 103, 189 N. W. 539, 541 (1922).
89. ORFIELD, *supra* note 5, at 68.

The state's burden of proof is minimal: it need establish only a prima facie case to hold the accused for further grand jury action.[90] In practice, then, the preliminary hearing will result in the defendant's discharge only when the state has failed either to show that a crime has been committed or to produce evidence linking the defendant with the crime.[91] The preliminary hearing does serve to record and preserve witness testimony for future use at trial.[92] Since the hearing is held soon after the suspect's arrest, the chances that a witness will disappear or be intimidated by the accused are lessened.[93] By means of a preliminary hearing, the accused is informed of the nature of the state's case against him and, knowing this, can raise defenses and refute the charges.[94] Thus the preliminary hearing is an invaluable step in the process, but its purposes occasionally overlap those of the grand jury. Where this overlap occurs, the case is exposed to unnecessary delay that can be eliminated without sacrificing the legitimate interests of either the state or the defendant.

ARRAIGNMENT

After the grand jury returns an indictment or a prosecutor files an information, the next step on the long road to trial is the arraignment. At the arraignment the prisoner is called before the trial court and informed of the charges against him. He is required to plead to those charges. The arraignment of today has its origins in eighteenth-century English law. At that time, the prisoner was called to the bench to answer the charges against him in the indictment. After the indictment was read to him, the prisoner had three alternatives. He could "stand mute," confess, or make one of several pleas.[95]

If he stood mute, it meant either that he had not answered at all or that he had introduced a defense outside the scope of the indictment. If he made no answer, the potential consequences of which he was forewarned, a special jury had to be convened to determine whether he was capable of answering or not. If this special jury decided he could have replied, he was convicted. If, on the other hand, he was really unable to respond, the trial

---

90. Comment, *Preliminary Hearings in Pennsylvania: A Closer Look,* 30 U. Pitt. L. Rev. 481, 498–99 (1968–1969).

91. *Id.* at 498.

92. *An Interest Analysis, supra* note 66, at 171.

93. *Id.*

94. *Id.* at 176.

95. 4 Blackstone, Commentaries on the Law of England, 321–24 (1807) [hereinafter cited as Blackstone].

proceeded as if he had pleaded not guilty.[96]

A defendant might confess. In capital cases, a special kind of confession called an approvement was available to the defendant. In this type of confession, the defendant not only confessed to the indictment but also accused someone else of the crime, while asking that he, the accuser, be pardoned. If the person accused was found guilty, the defendant was pardoned; if not, the defendant was convicted. Since this procedure lent itself to the accusation of many innocents, it fell into disfavor and disuse.[97]

A defendant could also challenge the propriety of the charges without answering them directly. By the eighteenth century he could object to the jurisdiction of the court or contend that even if the facts were true as alleged, they did not constitute an offense.[98] Further, he was entitled to contest formal inadequacies in the indictment[99] or enter special pleas going to the merits of the charge and demonstrating why he should not be tried.[100]

---

96. *Id.* at 323–39.

97. *Id.* at 329–31.

98. *Id.* at 333–34.

99. *Id.* at 334–35.

100. By the eighteenth century there were four broad types of pleas available. The defendant, without answering any of the allegations in the indictment, could *plead to the jurisdiction* if he believed that the court receiving the indictment lacked jurisdiction to hear the case.

The defendant could demur if he believed that the charges, even if true, did not constitute a felony. This plea placed a point of law in issue. Some judges felt that the defendant was in effect admitting the truth of the charges and should be convicted, while other judges contended that the defendant should still be permitted to plead the general issue.

Thirdly, the defendant could offer a *plea of abatement* if his name or title was improperly recorded in the indictment. This plea was merely a delaying technique, since the defendant was required to indicate the flaw in the indictment so that it could be amended and the proceedings resumed.

Special *pleas in bar* went to the merits of the indictment and set forth reasons why the defendant should not be tried. Pleas of *former acquittal* or *former conviction* were based on the common law rule that no man should be placed in jeopardy of losing his life more than once for the same offense. A *plea of former attainder* was used by a defendant who had previously been convicted of any felony, for in the law's eyes a defendant could lose his life only once, and he would have already forfeited his property after the first conviction. This plea, however, was inapplicable if the prior conviction had been reversed, or if the defendant had been pardoned, or if the case had involved an

Of course, the defendant had the option of pleading not guilty. Formerly called a *plea to the general issue,* this was the only plea on which a defendant could receive his final judgment and thus the only plea from which the death penalty could be directly inflicted. A defendant accused of a felony had to plead not guilty before he could put special defenses into evidence. Thus, where there was disagreement as to the defendant's guilt, an issue of fact was joined, and the case went to trial.[101]

The arraignment has changed little over the centuries. It remains essentially the same procedure that was developed in eighteenth-century England. Considering that its basic function is to formally apprise the defendant of the charges leveled against him, little is accomplished that has not previously been done at the time of arrest, the preliminary hearing, or the grand jury hearing if the defendant was called as a witness. Granted, it is a time for taking pleas and raising motions before the court, but neither requires a court appearance. More recently, it has become the time when indigents accused of felonies are accorded their right to counsel and when an attorney is appointed to represent the defendant for all subsequent proceedings. Although recent Supreme Court decisions mandate the appointment of counsel at much earlier stages of the criminal prosecution, a court appearance is hardly necessary to determine whether the defendant is able to retain counsel or whether to appoint counsel. It is only when the prosecution originates with the grand jury, and there are no earlier preliminary procedures, that the arraignment serves any purpose, and even then it serves only as a formal beginning. Thus the arraignment looms as another repetitive step contributing to delay in the process.

RIGHT TO COUNSEL

While the right to be represented by an attorney in serious prosecutions is an accepted fact of life today, it was not always so. Historically, counsel was available only to those accused of misdemeanors. Persons charged with felonies or treason were denied this assistance.[102] This was due in part to the political climate of the feudal period and the attendant weakness of the central government. The government needed every advantage to best its

---

accusation of treason. It also did not apply if the defendant was charged in the second crime as a principal and where his conviction as principal was a prerequisite to bringing any accessories to trial. Lastly, the plea of *pardon* could be offered. This was in effect a guilty plea coupled with an attempt to avoid any punishment. *Id.* at 335–37.

101. *Id.* at 338–40.

102. *Id.* at 354–55. Only where a point of law required debate was the accused permitted counsel. *Id.* at 355.

enemies, and denial of counsel was but one way to accomplish this.[103] The political stability that resulted from the revolution of 1688 against James II was accompanied in 1695 by an act of Parliament which permitted counsel to be retained or appointed by the court in cases of high treason.[104] The courts also used their discretion to permit attorneys to argue points of law in other felony cases. By the close of the eighteenth century, counsel was permitted to conduct the entire defense, except for addressing the jury at trial's end, which was the exclusive privilege of the king's counsel.[105]

Early in the nineteenth century, English law was amended to permit all criminal defendants to retain counsel.[106] In practice, lawyers occasionally gave free legal service to indigents in felony cases.[107] But not until the Poor Prisoner's Defense Act of 1903 did impoverished felony defendants achieve the right to free legal aid.[108] And yet this right was by no means absolute, for the prisoner had to first explain his defense to the judge. The judge would then decide whether or not to appoint counsel for him.[109] Generally, except for defendants accused of murder, most requests were denied.[110] In 1930, the ineffective earlier law was replaced by the new Poor Prisoner's Defense Act, which gave an indigent accused of murder an unqualified right to counsel.[111] In other felony cases, the decision whether or not to provide counsel was entirely in the court's discretion.[112] Many of the problems inherent in this latter act were resolved in 1949 with the Legal Aid and Advice Act, which provided for the assigning of counsel to indigents in noncapital felonies.[113]

The colonies initially gave greater recognition to the defendant's right to be represented at trial by counsel. Rhode Island provided this right as early as 1660.[114] Pennsylvania's law had a three-stage development, beginning in 1701, when a defendant received the same privilege of witness and counsel

---

103. HOLDSWORTH, *supra* note 73, at 196.
104. By singling out these defendants, some measure of protection was afforded controversial members of Parliament who were charged with high treason. 7 & 8 W. 3, c. 3, Sess. 1 (1695).
105. W. BEANEY, THE RIGHT TO COUNSEL IN AMERICAN COURTS 8–10 (1955) [hereinafter cited as BEANEY].
106. 6 & 7 W. 4, c. 114, Sess. 1 (1836).
107. BEANEY, *supra* note 105, at 10–12.
108. 3 Edw. 7, c. 38, Sess. 1 (1903).
109. BEANEY, *supra* note 105, at 12–13.
110. ORFIELD, *supra* note 5, at 362 n. 72.
111. 20 & 21 Geo. 5, c. 32 (1930).
112. BEANEY, *supra* note 105, at 13.
113. 12 & 13 Geo. 6, c. 51 (1949).
114. BEANEY, *supra* note 105, at 17–18.

as the prosecution had. In 1718, the Pennsylvania legislature extended to certain serious felonies the right to have counsel appointed by the court,[115] and fifty years later authorized court-appointed counsel in all felonies.[116] Other statutory variations existed: in South Carolina, which in 1731 gave the defendant a right to retain counsel for murder, treason, felonies, and other capital offenses;[117] in Virginia and Delaware, which authorized counsel in all capital cases upon the defendant's request;[118] and in Connecticut, which appointed counsel without a request by the defendant, if the defendant was operating under a handicap.[119] The English rule that assistance of counsel was a matter of judicial discretion persisted in the remaining colonies.[120] As the colonies made the transformation to statehood and new states were born, the law changed and the constitutions of all states but Virginia affirmed a criminal defendant's right to be represented at trial by someone else.[121] Even in Virginia, the due process clause of the Constitution was judicially interpreted as granting the right to counsel.[122]

But the American experience involved two avenues of development—state and federal. In the federal courts, the Sixth Amendment to the United States Constitution echoed the Judiciary Act of 1789[123] and granted assistance of counsel to an accused "in all criminal prosecutions."[124] As a result of the Federal Crimes Act of 1790, appointment of counsel for indigent defendants in all capital cases became mandatory in federal courts.[125] State courts also faced the problem of right to counsel and their duty to appoint an attorney if a defendant could not afford one. Most state courts interpreted their constitutions as not imposing an overall duty to appoint counsel for the poor,[126] although all states required—either by statute, constitution, or judicial interpretation—appointment of counsel in capital cases.[127] Not

---

115. *Id.* at 16.

116. *Id.* at 16–17.

117. *Id.* at 17.

118. *Id.* at 16–17.

119. *Id.* at 16. The handicap warranting automatic appointment of counsel was the inability of the defendant to understand the applicable law or to plead properly to the charge. SWIFT, *supra* note 28, at 392.

120. BEANEY, *supra* note 105, at 18.

121. *Id.* at 80.

122. *Id.* at 89.

123. 1 Stat. 73, 92 (1789).

124. Betts v. Brady, 316 U. S. 455 (1942).

125. 1 Stat. 112, 119 (1790), *reenacted as* 18 U. S. C. 563 (1940).

126. BEANEY, *supra* note 105, at 82–83.

127. *Id.* at 86, 138.

until the landmark decision of *Gideon v. Wainwright*[128] in 1963 did the Supreme Court apply the Sixth Amendment to the states through the Fourteenth and declare that a state must provide counsel to all indigents accused of serious crimes. The Supreme Court has only now agreed to decide whether there is an absolute right to counsel for persons accused of misdemeanors.[129]

The right to counsel has thus become an integral part of the criminal process. The expansion of this right has injected an attorney into a greater number of cases and has given the attorney an extremely influential role in controlling the speed of case disposition and the destiny of the criminal court docket. Consequently, an attorney who believes delay to be in his or his client's interest can, in the absence of statutory or judicial restraints, slow a case considerably.

RIGHT TO A SPEEDY TRIAL

Essential to the effective operation of the entire criminal justice system is the concept that criminal cases should be dispatched within a reasonable time. Although only recently has there been extensive public clamor concerning the importance to the accused and the state of the prompt disposition of criminal cases, it is a right which was first mentioned in the Magna Carta[130] and evoked concern in thirteenth-century England. At that time justice was dispensed by traveling justices of the peace whose route took them to a village only three times each year. Although cases coming before the justices were disposed of quickly,[131] a prisoner apprehended shortly after the justice had moved on to his next destination could still have a four months' wait in jail.

In order to give some meaning to the speedy trial right and to avoid unjustified delays, the Writ of Habeas Corpus became prominent and subject to frequent use. Originating in the chancery courts of fourteenth-century England and used to bring before the court persons already in the

---

128. 372 U. S. 335 (1963).

129. Argersinger v. Hamlin, 236 So. 2d 442 (Fla. 1970), *cert. granted,* 401 U. S. 908 (1971). The issue in *Argersinger* is whether the right to appointed counsel extends to misdemeanors and petty offenses carrying a penalty of less than six months. The case was argued before the Supreme Court in December, 1971.

130. "We will sell to no man, we will not deny or defer to any either justice or right." *Magna Carta,* c. 29 (c. 40 of King John's Charter of 1215) (1225), *translated and quoted in* COKE, THE SECOND PART OF THE INSTITUTES OF THE LAWS OF ENGLAND 45 (5th ed. 1797).

131. *Id.* at 43.

sheriff's custody, it compelled the government to produce the person being detained and to present the reason for the prolonged detention.[132] By the 1600s the court was using the Writ to inquire into the legality of a detention and to order the prisoner's release if the detention was found to be unlawful.[133] Despite this expanded use, case law dictated that the Writ was inapplicable to an order by the king to imprison a defendant,[134] until Parliament enacted the Petition of Rights,[135] which specified that the Crown could no longer imprison arbitrarily and without lawful cause.[136] Some fifty years later (1679), the Habeas Corpus Act[137] strengthened the Writ by providing for both a speedy judicial inquiry into any detention on a criminal charge and a speedy case disposition for those awaiting trial.[138] Thus, the Writ became the means by which a prisoner could raise the question of unlawful detention and safeguard those rights granted him by the Magna Carta.[139]

Colonial America embraced the speedy trial concept as part of its common law heritage. This right was formalized in the Constitution's Sixth Amendment and found its way into most state constitutions.[140] The Writ of Habeas Corpus, on the other hand, had a more difficult time achieving

---

132. D. MEADOR, HABEAS CORPUS AND MAGNA CARTA: DUALISM OF POWER AND LIBERTY (1966) [hereinafter cited as HABEAS CORPUS]. *See also* Cohen, *Habeas Corpus Cum Causa—the Emergence of the Modern Writ*—I, 18 CAN. B. REV. 10, 13 (1940). In the fifteenth century *habeas corpus cum causa* was used to enforce "privilege"; clergy, legislators, and ministers could only be indicted in certain courts. If such an individual was put in jail by another court, a superior court would issue *habeas corpus cum causa* to release him. HABEAS CORPUS at 11. *See also* Jenks, *The Story of the Habeas Corpus,* 18 LAW. Q. REV. 64, 69–73 (1902). Habeas corpus was next used by the common law courts to control the equity and special royal courts. The common law judges were able to release those committed by other courts. HABEAS CORPUS at 12.

133. *Id.* By this time the writ had become compartmentalized into several forms; the most important form was *habeas corpus ad subjeciendum,* used in criminal cases.

134. *See* note 132 *supra.*

135. 3 Car. 1, c. 1 (1627).

136. *Id.*

137. 31 Car. 2, c. 2 (1679).

138. 4 W. S. HOLDSWORTH, A HISTORY OF ENGLISH LAW 82 (3rd ed. 1923).

139. HABEAS CORPUS, *supra* note 132, at 28–31.

140. *See, e.g.,* DEL. CONST. art. 1, § 7 (1792); MASS. CONST. Part 1, art. XI (1779); R. I. CONST. art. 1, § 10 (1842); CONN. CONST. art. 1, § 8 (1818). *See generally* Appendix B.

acceptance.[141] In 1692, colonial Massachusetts tried to adopt the English Habeas Corpus Act of 1679, but the English Crown blocked the effort with its veto power. South Carolina successfully adopted the Habeas Corpus Act that same year, and Virginia had the Act conferred on it at the turn of the century by proclamation of Queen Anne. Other colonies apparently used the Writ without any specific authorization to do so.[142]

The continued existence of the Writ was assured with the enactment of the United States Constitution.[143] Although not affirmatively authorizing habeas corpus, the Constitution denied Congress the power to suspend it except under extraordinary circumstances. Initially, the federal writ applied only to those imprisoned under federal authority,[144] but in 1867 it was extended to state prisoners.[145] Since state constitutions already provided for a habeas corpus act, the prisoner could now seek the writ in both state and federal courts.

Habeas corpus and enforcement of the right to a speedy trial have been the traditional means by which a defendant has sought to assure himself of the shortest time between his arrest and the final disposition of his case. However, since the use of the writ and the enforcement of the speedy trial right are elective and are used only where a party believes their use is in his own interest, these tools cannot be relied upon to provide the system with the means to achieve swift and fair justice for both the state and the defendant. Assuming, then, that speedier justice is necessary, additional means must be sought to speed up the process and thus assure the survival of the criminal justice system.

CONCLUSION

The American pretrial criminal system is the outgrowth of institutions that originated on the Continent and in England and were adapted to suit the peculiar needs of a mobile frontier society. The pretrial process reflects a profound awareness of the need to protect an individual from arbitrary government prosecution. The system is, however, fraught with considerable duplication of procedure which has the effect of stretching out the time from arrest to trial. The reason for the duplication becomes evident when one recalls that the initial system was originally self-contained in the grand

---

141. Oaks, *Habeas Corpus in the States—1776–1865,* 32 U. CHI. L. REV. 243, 247 (1965).
142. HABEAS CORPUS, *supra* note 132, at 28–31.
143. U. S. CONST. art. 1, § 9.
144. HABEAS CORPUS, *supra* note 132, at 35–38.
145. 14 Stat. 385 (1867).

jury's duties of investigating, determining probable cause, charging an individual with a crime, and submitting a prepared case for trial. As American society became more complex, so did the criminal justice system. A sophisticated police-prosecutorial system was developed to investigate crimes and identify individuals to be charged. The prosecutor was given a right to charge by information, in lieu of a grand jury indictment, and the preliminary hearing became the vehicle through which a probable cause determination was made. Although it might be expected that with these former grand jury functions now being accomplished at other stages of the process the grand jury would be eliminated, this has not generally been the case. Moreover, this is just one area of the process in which excessiveness has not been controlled. The American way has been to increase steps rather than to refine or dispense with stages that no longer fulfill a valid purpose.

The historical reasons for aspects of the criminal justice system are in many instances no longer valid. Old traditions, once supported by persuasive reasons, now make the system the enemy of defendants like Ralph Johnson. Johnson was a victim of history, for he had to wait while procedures that had long since outlived their usefulness were exhausted. Adopted to protect his rights, these stages served only to delay his ultimate right to vindication. Ralph Johnson languished in jail for ten months, waiting for the system to follow its circuitous, maze-like path to the conclusion of acquittal. The screening effect that the pyramid of duplicated procedures is intended to have failed to protect Johnson from prosecution, and the procedures greatly delayed ultimate resolution of the charge. The imposition of historic institutions on a modern society for which they were not designed and are not suited acts to delay the determination of guilt, not to improve its quality.

The system has been receptive to expansion at various levels but has been extremely reluctant to relieve itself of unnecessary procedures that have firm historical roots. A system designed for effectiveness in colonial America may need substantial modification to operate adequately in the twentieth century. It is society's inability to confront this reality which has contributed to the problem of court delay today. The direction must be away from blind devotion to historical tradition and towards a fair and equitable enforcement of the speedy trial right through a refined system subject to reasonable controls.

2/ DELAY IN
THE COURTS

In all criminal prosecutions, the accused shall enjoy the right to a speedy ... trial.... U. S. CONST. amend. VI.

The right to a speedy trial is guaranteed to every United States citizen by the Sixth Amendment, and in 1967 the United States Supreme Court held that the federal right applied to the states through the Fourteenth Amendment.[1] That a speedy trial heads the list of trial rights enumerated in the Sixth Amendment is no accident, since without a trial or the threat of trial there can be no justice,[2] only unproved accusations hanging over a defendant's head. Further, justice that is delayed is more prone to error when the case is finally tried than is justice administered while the facts surrounding an incident are fresh in the minds of those involved.[3] Despite society's need and the constitutional mandate for swift justice, in the last decade courts have had increasing difficulty assuring a speedy trial to all persons charged with a criminal offense. The reality of this statement does not become apparent until one realizes just how inadequate the actual court performance is when measured against reasonable time guidelines for case disposition.

MINIMUM ACCEPTABLE STANDARDS FOR PROSECUTION OF A CRIME AND THE REALITIES OF DELAY

The President's Commission on Law Enforcement and Administration of Justice, created by executive order in July, 1965, was born of the need to recognize and investigate the challenge of crime in this country.[4] With

1. Klopfer v. North Carolina, 386 U. S. 213 (1967).
2. "Justice delayed is not only justice denied, it is justice circumvented, justice mocked, and the system of justice undermined." Speech by President Nixon, National Conference of the Judiciary, in Williamsburg, Virginia, Mar. 11, 1971.
3. Delay creates the possibility that witnesses will die or disappear and that memories will fade. Ponzi v. Fessenden, 258 U.S. 254, 264 (1922).
4. Exec. Order No. 11, 236, 3 C. F. R. 329 (Supp. 1964–1965).

35

the assistance of other government agencies, the Commission analyzed, among other areas, the problems of the police, courts, and corrections and recommended many programs directed at controlling crime in this society —among them, the revitalization of the judicial process. The Commission thus recognized that to control crime and turn the tide against an ever increasing crime rate, the courts and the entire justice system must be rescued from a moribund state.

The Commission realized that time was one of the key ingredients of the process. The most effective system, they acknowledged, would be one that dealt with alleged criminals within a reasonable time after the commission of a crime and an arrest. Towards this end, the Commission developed a Model Timetable, which proposed two sets of maximum intervals permissible between specific steps in a criminal prosecution. The shorter intervals were designed to serve defendants who are ineligible for or unable to make bail. The longer intervals were made applicable to those persons free during the period between arrest and trial, since their need for a speedy trial is less urgent.

The Model Timetable provides that an accused person should be brought to trial within eighty-one days of his arrest, if he is free during this interval, and within seventy-one days of his arrest, if he is held in jail.[5] These figures do not represent an ideal that would be desirable to strive for but are the Commission's concerted judgment of what is necessary and what is workable:

> Making allowance for needed flexibility, however, it is possible to establish standards that emphasize the court's ability to deal efficiently with its business, that distinguish between needless and necessary delay, and that provide a reference for court management.[6]

Moreover, the Commission fashioned a formula for the maximum time intervals between each of the stages of a criminal prosecution leading up to a trial or a plea of guilty. They also developed a timetable for the maximum period that should elapse between conviction and sentencing of an offender. According to their recommendations, there is no reason why a criminal case cannot be disposed of within three months, irrespective of whether the defendant is free on bail or in jail. The three-month figure does not include

---

5. THE PRESIDENT'S COMMISSION ON LAW ENFORCEMENT AND ADMINISTRATION OF JUSTICE, TASK FORCE REPORT: THE COURTS 86–87 (1967) [hereinafter cited as TASK FORCE: THE COURTS].

6. THE PRESIDENT'S COMMISSION ON LAW ENFORCEMENT AND THE ADMINISTRATION OF JUSTICE: THE CHALLENGE OF CRIME IN A FREE SOCIETY 155 (1967) [hereinafter cited as THE CHALLENGE OF CRIME IN A FREE SOCIETY].

the time actually spent in trial, but so few cases ever get to trial that the three-month figure applies to over 70 percent of the felony cases in any given court.[7] No recommended number of days could be developed for actual trials because they vary depending on the charge and the amount and complexity of evidence. In other words, for the overwhelming number of cases, the three-month figure should apply; for those few cases that go to trial, the number of trial days should be added to the three months.

We set out to compare the Model Timetable with the existing situation. Few cities provide statistics that lend themselves to comparison with the recommendations of the Commission, and little information of a comprehensive nature has been published. To supplement the existing data, we took a sampling of the cases in the Court of Common Pleas, the court of general jurisdiction in Cleveland, Ohio. The sample consisted of 1,616 persons charged with felonies in that court, representing more than one-half of the 1968 criminal docket for the court.[8]

The primary finding from these statistics and from other available information indicates that on the average urban courts take almost three times longer to dispose of a criminal case than the President's Commission recommended as necessary. Among our sample, the average number of days elapsing between the arrest of a defendant and the disposition of his case (whether by conviction, a not guilty verdict, or dismissal) was 245. This total elapsed time is not atypical. A study of 1968 criminal cases in South Bend, Indiana, indicated that the average case required 252 days from arrest to final resolution.[9] In Philadelphia, Pennsylvania, available data indicated that those cases resolved in June, 1970, averaged 205 days and those concluded in December, 1970, required 170 days.[10] The Commission recom-

---

7. D. NEWMAN, CONVICTION: THE DETERMINATION OF GUILT OR INNOCENCE WITHOUT TRIAL 3 n. 1 (1966) [hereinafter cited as NEWMAN, CONVICTION]. About 90 percent of all criminal cases are resolved without going to trial. Although the percentage of guilty pleas in any jurisdiction depends on what crimes are tabulated, if felonies alone are used as the basis of calculation the percentage of guilty pleas is in the range of 70–85 percent.

8. The year 1968 was chosen because many cases require more than one year to complete and that was the most recent nearly complete year. For a more elaborate discussion of the study of the criminal cases in Cuyahoga County, see Appendix A.

9. Data received from Leslie Foschio, Assistant Dean, University of Notre Dame Law School, based upon a study conducted by Notre Dame University.

10. Data received from John Michael Willmann, Deputy Court Administrator for Public Information and Planning, and Larry Polansky,

mended that the case of a jailed defendant be disposed of, including sentencing, in a maximum of 92 days or within no more than 102 days if a defendant is free on bail.[11]

Fewer than one-third of the cases involving defendants detained in the Cuyahoga County jail were disposed of within the recommended period. More than two-thirds of the defendants, whether guilty or not, endured from three months to more than one year in jail because they were unable to raise bail or were ineligible for bail. The figures are even more disconcerting for those defendants who were free on bail. Fewer than 10 percent of the cases were disposed of within ninety days, and 35 percent of the defendants who were free on bail were involved in cases that extended for more than one year. Table 1 shows the breakdown of the sample, depending upon defendant's status, in jail or on bail.

TABLE 1. AMOUNT OF TIME FROM ARREST TO DISPOSITION
DEPENDING ON JAIL/BAIL STATUS

INTERVAL	DEFENDANTS IN JAIL: PERCENTAGE OF CASES DISPOSED OF	DEFENDANTS ON BAIL: PERCENTAGE OF CASES DISPOSED OF
Within 90 days	28.3%	6.6%
From 3 to 6 months	35.6%	22.0%
From 6 months to 1 year	32.0%	35.7%
Over 1 year	4.1%	35.7%
Total	100.0%	100.0%

The vast differences in time, depending upon whether the defendant is in jail or free on bail, would tend to support two theses. First, those cases involving defendants held in custody are scheduled by courts as soon as possible, to avoid unnecessary time in jail. Second, the accompanying effect of slowing disposition for those defendants who are free of restraint is

---

Chief Deputy Court Administrator, Research and Data Processing, Philadelphia, Pennsylvania [hereinafter cited as Willmann & Polansky].

In New York City, during 1969, the average felony case required 4.29 appearances and consumed 13.1 weeks in Manhattan Criminal Court. However, approximately 25 percent of the cases were required to proceed to New York State Supreme Court for final adjudication. Of the cases that went to the state supreme court, 7.34 weeks were spent in Manhattan Criminal Court on the average. JENNINGS, THE FLOW OF THE ARRESTED ADULT DEFENDANTS THROUGH THE MANHATTAN CRIMINAL COURT IN 1968 AND 1969 (New York City Rand Institute, 1971) 12, 47–49 [hereinafter cited as RAND REPORT].

11. TASK FORCE: THE COURTS, *supra* note 5, at 86–87.

welcomed by their attorneys, who contend that the longer the case drags on the better the outcome will be for the defendant.[12] Although more than two-thirds of the cases involving jailed defendants were disposed of within six months, over 70 percent of the cases where the defendant was free on bail took more than six months, and more than one-third took more than one year to be completed. A similar picture of delay exists in state courts throughout the nation, and the situation is not much better in the federal courts. Figures from 1968 in the federal district courts within the jurisdiction of the United States Court of Appeals for the Second Circuit indicated that 46.6 percent of the criminal cases had been pending over a year; and in the federal district covering most of Manhattan the percentage of cases

---

12. A questionnaire was sent to 232 defense attorneys in eighteen cities throughout the country. In each city the questionnaire was sent to a cross section of the criminal defense bar. Eighty-six responses were received. The average respondent has been practicing law for 15.6 years but has been specializing in criminal law for 12.8 years. One-half of the respondents who are now defense attorneys obtained experience as criminal lawyers working as either state or local prosecutors, United States Attorneys, or public defender or legal aid attorneys. Forty-six percent of the respondents estimated that they spend 50 to 100 percent of their time defending alleged felons. Forty-four percent of the respondents estimated that they spent less than 10 percent of their time defending alleged misdemeanants. Thirty-six percent of those who responded said that 50 to 100 percent of their income resulted from defending those accused of felonies; only three respondents did not answer the questions about income. Although half of the responses show that 10 to 50 percent of the attorney time is spent defending clients who retained counsel, most of the respondents (70 percent) indicated that less than 10 percent of their time is spent defending clients whose cases are assigned to the attorney by the court. Retainers paid to the criminal defense attorney are determined according to the criminal offense involved, the number of days spent in court, and the client's ability to pay.

An overwhelming number of the responses, 81 percent, indicated that in their cities the cases of defendants in jail awaiting trial because of inability to afford bail were scheduled prior to those cases in which a defendant was free on bail. In Atlanta, Fort Worth, Houston, Philadelphia, Pittsburgh, and Washington, D.C., the respondents did not all agree as to whether such a scheduling preference existed in their city. Consequently, the lawyer may be misguided or unaware of the best way to obtain a speedy trial for his client because he is unaware of scheduling practices.

Better than 50 percent of the responses indicated that delay benefited the defendant who was free on bail and better than 64

pending over a year was 57.3 percent.[13] State courts generally present an even bleaker picture. Former Senator Joseph D. Tydings reported on three states: New Jersey had 175 cases pending between two and three years; Kansas had 178 cases pending from one to three years; and New Mexico had 772 cases that had awaited trial for more than twelve months, as of January, 1970.[14]

Moreover, the median time between arrest and disposition continues to increase unabated.[15] In the District of Columbia, cases culminating in trial

---

percent of the responses indicated that delay improves the defendant's position in plea negotiations [hereinafter cited as QUESTIONNAIRE].

13. Brief for the Association of the Bar of the City of New York and the Lawyers Committee for Civil Rights Under Law as Amicus Curiae at 3–4, United States *ex rel.* Frizer v. McMann, 437 F.2d 1312 (2d Cir. 1971).

   However, note the progress in the federal courts in the Southern District of New York. Through careful screening, removal of old cases, bringing others to trial, and use of a new individual assignment system giving prime responsibility for each case to one particular judge, the courts have succeeded in reducing a backlog of some seven hundred criminal cases and have significantly reduced the number of pending civil cases. N. Y. Times, Mar. 15, 1971, at 28, col. 1.

14. Tydings, *Improving Archaic Judicial Machinery,* 57 A.B.A.J. 154, 155 (1971).

15. *Cf.* N. Y. Times, May 28, 1971, at 37, col. 6.

   For the first time in recent years, the Criminal Courts of New York City have begun to dispose of more cases than they receive and to make inroads on the backlog of cases.

   From Jan. 1 to April 30, 1971, . . . the courts in the five boroughs disposed of 89,935 cases and handled 85,612 arraignments or new cases.

   Efforts to increase efficiency have also made it possible for the judges to cut the number of pending cases from 59,406 to 39,573. The improved results, according to some judges, are due to the development of all-purpose courts which handle a broad range of actions in criminal cases, and to earlier probation reports in youthful offender situations. This permits prosecutors to screen more cases before filing a complaint, providing for earlier preliminary hearings and making more courtroom space available. *Id.* One weakness attributed to the all-purpose courts in New York City is that the judges do not stay in that part but continue to be rotated into other parts of the Criminal Court.

   According to Judge Joel Tyler, however, the statistics are improved

required a median of 5.5 months for resolution in 1965,[16] but 10.1 months in 1968.[17] Similarly, those cases that were disposed of without a trial averaged 4.5 months in 1965,[18] but by 1968 this time had increased to 8.8 months.[19] These figures indicate an alarming twofold increase in the median times for criminal case disposition. Ohio publishes figures disclosing the time between indictment and disposition in felony cases. This time period does not take into consideration the time spent in preliminary procedures. Although the compilation considers all state courts including rural courts where no backlog exists, the median time between indictment and disposition in all Ohio courts still rose from slightly over two months in 1964[20] to 5.8 months in 1969.[21]

DELAY BETWEEN SPECIFIC PRETRIAL PROCEDURES

Management of the earliest phases of a criminal case rests with the prosecutor's office and the municipal court in which the case is first filed. Responsibility for delay in the trial court, during the preliminary stages from arrest to arraignment, rests likewise with the prosecutors and the

---

because judges are being evaluated based on their ability to move the caseload. Good judges are those who are able to handle the most cases. Judges know that if they do not move cases they will be reassigned to Traffic Court. The emphasis is on quantity. Interview with Judge Joel Tyler, New York City Criminal Court, in New York City, June 1, 1971.

16. THE PRESIDENT'S COMMISSION ON LAW ENFORCEMENT AND ADMINISTRATION OF JUSTICE, TASK FORCE REPORT: SCIENCE AND TECHNOLOGY 202 (1967) [hereinafter cited as SCIENCE AND TECHNOLOGY].
17. *Breakdown of the Courts in America,* U. S. NEWS & WORLD REPORT, Mar. 10, 1969, at 58 [hereinafter cited as *Breakdown*].
18. SCIENCE AND TECHNOLOGY, *supra* note 16.
19. *Breakdown, supra* note 17.
20. REPORT OF THE PRESIDENT'S COMMISSION ON CRIME IN THE DISTRICT OF COLUMBIA 258 (1966) [hereinafter cited as DISTRICT OF COLUMBIA].
21. OHIO DEPARTMENT OF MENTAL HYGIENE AND CORRECTION, OHIO JUDICIAL CRIMINAL STATISTICS 5 (1969).
    During the year ending June 30, 1970, a criminal case in Pittsburgh consumed, on the average, 6.59 months from the time of the indictment until final disposition. SIXTH ANNUAL REPORT: COURT OF COMMON PLEAS OF ALLEGHENY COUNTY, PENNSYLVANIA 9.

originating courts.[22] Any blame, however, must be tempered with a realization that neither the prosecutors nor the courts are in total control of their case calendars. Responsibility for the time elapsing from the arrest of a suspect to the presentment of the charges against him in court, and then to the preliminary hearing, may also be shared by the defendants who seek continuances for the purpose of obtaining counsel.[23] A defendant's attorneys may also set up procedural roadblocks to delay a case, particularly if they must still collect their fee.[24] Nonetheless, the responsibility for moving

---

22. In Baltimore, David Earl Moore was indicted on February 6, 1971. Although the defendant was in jail, the indictment was not served by the prosecutor or other court official until April 8, 1971.

   In some instances the court is unable to force the department of corrections to produce the proper defendant at the appropriate time. In Boston, on April 12, 1971, a preliminary procedure for Robert Zachari was delayed because the prosecutor did not know the defendant was in jail. After it was learned that the defendant was in jail, there was a delay until the defendant was brought from the jail. When it was learned that the defendant did not have counsel, the case was continued for three weeks.

   In Cleveland, preliminary procedures may be delayed if a defendant is in the Warrensville workhouse. If an attorney wishes to confer with his client in the downtown courthouse, it may take two to three weeks for the department of correction to make the arrangements. If the attorney goes to the workhouse to see the client, half the attorney's day may be lost.

23. In New York, one year after his arrest and after numerous delays, George Colcloughley again demanded a new attorney. Eventually the defendant was found guilty of the charges against him. N. Y. Times, Dec. 6, 1970, § 1A, at 1, col. 1.

   In Boston, on April 12, 1971, the defendant in *Commonwealth v. Watkins* wanted to change his attorney at the arraignment. The defendant's first attorney, Mr. Skeels, had represented the defendant on a previous charge; since the defendant was found guilty he felt that another attorney could possibly do a better job on this case. The case was continued for seven days, at which time new counsel was to be appointed.

24. QUESTIONNAIRE, *supra* note 12. Almost 80 percent of the responses indicated that defense attorneys engage in pretrial delay for the purpose of collecting fees.

   The courts have a legitimate interest in assuring that attorneys who represent defendants in criminal cases are paid. In addition, it is known that after conviction the defendant loses interest in paying the attorney's fees. Steps should be taken so that defense attorneys cannot

the case rests with the prosecutor and the court; and if these early proceedings are to progress at a more reasonable pace, then the prosecutors and the municipal court judges will be forced to exert the pressure.

The President's Commission recommended that the time interval between arrest and the preliminary hearing should range from four to eight days,[25] which is a far cry from the realities of the existing procedural process. Probable cause, the standard of proof required at preliminary hearings, is not an exacting standard and does not require a great deal of case preparation by the prosecuting attorney. In many cities, the prosecutor simply does not have any time to prepare for the preliminary procedure.[26] He receives the police file and talks with the police officers and other witnesses immediately prior to the scheduled hearing.[27] A random sample of cases in the year 1969 in Dayton, Ohio, indicated that preliminary hearings were held in 30 percent of the cases; but among our sample only one out of every six cases involved a preliminary hearing.[28] The number of

---

delay a case indefinitely to obtain a fee. Further, there should be some means to insure that a defendant cannot delay a case by refusing to pay his attorney. If a judge learns of a request for a delay because of the client's nonpayment of fee, the judge should investigate the defendant's ability to pay the fee and the reasonableness of the fee. Such an inquiry may also reduce the situations in which further crime is committed to pay legal fees. TASK FORCE: THE COURTS, *supra* note 5, at 86. *See generally* Banfield & Anderson, *Continuances in the Cook County Criminal Courts,* 35 U. CHI. L. REV. 259, 265 (1968) [hereinafter cited as *Continuances in Cook County*].

25. TASK FORCE: THE COURTS, *supra* note 5, at 86–87.
26.   A normal caseload consists of some 300 cases per day. During a one hour period in which Mr. Frazer [a prosecutor] was present on Oct. 14, 1970, he handled some 30 cases. . . . The appearance of the defendant before the judge for arraignment is the first time that a District Attorney has general knowledge of the case before him. He relies heavily on the complaining witness or the arresting officer, who stands at his side during the arraignment. N. Y. Times, Nov. 18, 1970, at 52, col. 1.
27. On April 8, 1971, a Baltimore, Maryland, judge expressed his discontent with the manner in which the prosecutor had prepared his case in *State v. Nelson.* The judge commented: "Counsellor, you can't base your case on what is in the police report alone."
28. Two random samples of 1969 cases in Dayton, Ohio, were made under the direction of John Kessler of the Pilot Cities Project. Interview with John Kessler, in Dayton, Ohio, Jan. 28, 1971 [hereinafter cited as Kessler].

days between the arrest of the accused and the preliminary hearing is presented in Table 2.

TABLE 2. NUMBER OF DAYS BETWEEN ARREST AND
PRELIMINARY HEARING

NUMBER OF DAYS	NUMBER OF DEFENDANTS	PERCENTAGE
1–10	84	32.8%
11–25	87	34.0%
26–50	69	26.9%
Over 50	16	6.3%
Total	256	100.0%

Other cities make use of various techniques to keep the period between arrest and preliminary hearing at a minimum. The municipal court administrator in Minneapolis, Minnesota, indicated that a defendant may make a demand for a preliminary hearing and it will usually be held within six days of arrest, if the defendant is incarcerated; but if he is free on bail, a thirty-day maximum applies.[29] Boston's assistant assignment commissioner indicated that similar time standards are followed in that city.[30] In Pittsburgh and Philadelphia, however, a court rule dictates that the preliminary hearing be held within ten days of arrest.[31] Attempts to control the time by statute or court rules are simply not succeeding, however, and the delay is considerably greater than the four to eight days recommended by the Commission.

Once the preliminary hearing is concluded, only the grand jury indictment remains before the defendant is formally charged in a court with trial jurisdiction. Many states have sought to eliminate this step in the procedure and to replace the grand jury indictment by an information filed by the

29. Letter from S. Allen Friedman, Municipal Court Administrator, Hennepin County Courthouse, Minneapolis, Minnesota, April 5, 1971.
30. Interview with Leo Manning, Assistant Assignment Commissioner, in Boston, April 13, 1971 [hereinafter cited as Manning].
31. PA. R. CRIM. P. 119. The preliminary hearing must be held no sooner than three nor more than ten days after the preliminary arraignment, which occurs within close proximity of the arrest. Letter from Charles Starrett, Jr., Administrator of the Court of Common Pleas, Pittsburgh, Pennsylvania, April 5, 1971.

   Despite a statutory requirement in Ohio that no continuance shall extend for more than ten days unless the state and the accused agree to a further delay, the Cleveland statistics indicate infrequent compliance with this rule. See OHIO REV. CODE § 2937.21 (Page Supp. 1970).

prosecutor, but Ohio retains the procedure and makes waiver of it by a defendant a cumbersome matter. In Cuyahoga County the general rule is to indict (only 15 of the 1,616 cases in our sample proceeded on information).[32] Defendants do not contribute to the delay between preliminary hearing and the return of an indictment or a no bill (a finding by the grand jury that probable cause does not exist and the defendant should be discharged). Responsibility for ushering a case from the preliminary hearing and into the grand jury rests solely and squarely with the prosecutor. There can be only two reasons for delay at this juncture. Either the prosecutor has lost track of his witnesses after the preliminary hearing or there is an extensive backlog of cases requiring time for a case to reach the top of the list. Chicago has developed the practice of trying to take a case directly from the preliminary hearing into the grand jury, all in one day. This procedure ensures the prosecutor that his witnesses are present and available, and it also permits the witnesses to complete the preliminaries in one day. Thus, if the witness is a police officer, he will not be away from his beat twice; and if the witness is a private citizen, it means that he will not have to miss two, or parts of two, days' work.

The President's Commission recommended that the maximum time interval from the preliminary hearing to formal charging be three to seven days. This reasonable proposal again bears no resemblance to the actual figures. In Boston, the grand jury receives a case on the first Monday of the month following the preliminary hearing and indicts or returns a no bill within nine days.[33] In Philadelphia, defendants indicted in January, 1970, waited an average of thirty-three days from arrest, and those indicted in November experienced a fifty-five-day delay.[34] Table 3 presents the results of the study taken in Cuyahoga County.

TABLE 3. NUMBER OF DAYS BETWEEN PRELIMINARY HEARING AND THE RETURN OF AN INDICTMENT OR NO BILL

NUMBER OF DAYS	NUMBER OF DEFENDANTS	PERCENTAGE
1–10	10	3.9%
11–25	46	18.0%
26–50	146	57.0%
51–100	51	19.9%
Over 100	3	1.2%
Total	256	100.0%

32. In the Dayton study only 9 percent of the cases were prosecuted by way of information. Kessler, *supra* note 28.

33. Manning, *supra* note 30.

34. Willmann & Polansky, *supra* note 10.

Every stage of the entire preliminary procedure among our sample exceeds the time period recommended by the President's Commission. In the judgment of the Commission, the procedure from arrest to arraignment, when the defendant is presented with the formal charge returned by the grand jury, should be completed in 11 to 18 days. Including the time for a preliminary hearing, the average number of days in our sample between arrest and arraignment was 68 days. Suffering even greater delay was the typical defendant arraigned in Philadelphia in June or December of 1970. Philadelphia statistics indicate that the defendant arraigned in June had waited 110 days and the defendant arraigned in December had waited 95 days.[35]

Vast numbers of defendants in courts throughout the country waive their rights to a preliminary hearing, thereby eliminating the one preliminary stage which might be time-consuming. Although a constitutional argument could be made that the preliminary hearing is necessary to make meaningful the Fourth Amendment guarantee of freedom from unreasonable arrest, it is unlikely that the Supreme Court would accept this approach and cloak the preliminary hearing with constitutional sanctity. Consequently, whether there is or is not a preliminary hearing is by and large decided solely on the basis of state law. Among our sample of 1,616 cases, there were only 256 preliminary hearings. In over half of the cases, 901, the preliminary hearing was waived by the defendant; and in more than one-fourth of the cases, 459, the records indicate that the case originated on an original indictment returned by the grand jury without any preliminary procedure. The Dayton, Ohio, sample produced somewhat comparable results: 30 percent of the cases included a preliminary hearing, about one-half of the defendants waived the hearing, and 15 percent were proceeded against by original indictment.[36]

These cases were prosecuted prior to the United States Supreme Court's decision that a state must provide an attorney for indigent defendants at the preliminary hearing.[37] There is much evidence that the states have still not complied with that decision.[38] States have been able to avoid the necessity of providing counsel at the preliminary hearing by delaying the hearing until the grand jury takes final action.[39] This supplants the requirement for

35. *Id.*
36. Kessler, *supra* note 28.
37. Coleman v. Alabama, 399 U. S. 1 (1970).
38. *Coleman* was decided in June, 1970, but as of Nov. 23, 1970, counsel was not provided for indigents at preliminary hearings in Cleveland. Cleveland Press, Nov. 23, 1970, § B, at 9, col. 1.
39. One New York City prosecutor remarked that in homicide cases the state avoids the preliminary hearing and its attendant discovery for the

the preliminary hearing, and thus counsel need not be assigned. In any event, waivers came from indigent defendants who were not aware of the discovery value of preliminary hearings, or believed that it was fruitless to proceed in such a hearing without an attorney, or doubted the value of such a hearing and desired to expedite matters. Moreover, although the record in each case may show a waiver on the part of the defendant, he is generally without counsel, and there is no way to determine whether he in fact knew what he was doing.[40]

The waiver of a preliminary hearing should drastically shorten the time span between arrest and grand jury action. Our findings indicated that this did happen, but not often enough to blame the preliminary hearing for causing much of the delay. Where there was a preliminary hearing, the time span between arrest and arraignment on the indictment averaged sixty-eight days, as previously indicated, and in those cases where the record indicates that the defendant waived his right to a preliminary hearing, the average time span was reduced to fifty-one days. Table 4 indicates the number of days between arrest and arraignment, when the defendant waived a preliminary hearing.

TABLE 4. NUMBER OF DAYS BETWEEN ARREST AND
ARRAIGNMENT WHEN THE DEFENDANT WAIVED
A PRELIMINARY HEARING

NUMBER OF DAYS	NUMBER OF DEFENDANTS	PERCENTAGE
1–10	15	1.7%
11–25	51	5.7%
26–60	560	62.1%
61–100	262	29.1%
Over 100	13	1.4%
Total	901	100.0%

defense by going directly to the grand jury.

Defense Attorney Gilbert Rosenthal indicated that because a defendant is denied information about the state's case from a preliminary hearing, the defendant creates fantasy defenses. Interview with Gilbert Rosenthal, in New York City, Oct. 10, 1970.

The defendant can learn the strength of the state's case at the preliminary hearing because to establish probable cause, the prosecutor must present at least a bare outline of the state's case, including evidence from witnesses. Note, *Preliminary Hearing in the District of Columbia —an Emerging Discovery Device,* 56 GEO. L. J. 191, 193 (1967).

40. In New York City the Legal Aid Society handles about 80 percent of the more than 11,000 prisoners in the city jails. Recognizing that the society is unable to give the proper amount of time to each client, a

The question arises whether the benefits to the defendant, the state, or both, justify the amount of time that elapses between arrest and the beginning of formal proceedings, signified by the arraignment. Because the preliminary hearing is a valuable defense tool, and in many jurisdictions provides the only real opportunity for the defense to learn anything of the state's case, it should be more readily available to all defendants within a reasonable time.

A question also arises as to the real value of the grand jury. Lawyers all over the country doubt its worth, except as it helps to delay the ultimate resolution of a case.[41] One lawyer in Fort Worth reported that the local grand jury simply does not have time to consider any evidence beyond the police report and thus merely acts on the prosecutor's recommendation. This is the consensus of attorneys contacted throughout the nation. Our statistical sample showed only seventy-nine no bills in Cuyahoga County, and for all anyone knows, many or all of these may have been on the recommendation of the prosecutor. Further indications of this rubber-stamp effect came from the Dayton, Ohio, survey, which showed that the grand jury followed the prosecutor's suggestion for charging 64 percent of the time. Although a no bill was returned in 31 percent of the cases, it is likely that a substantial number were at the prosecutor's request.[42] If the grand jury is no longer able to protect the citizen from arbitrary government action, it has lost its reason for being. Instead of serving as a shield for the citizen, it provides the prosecutor with an opportunity to dodge responsibility by attributing prosecutions or the failure to prosecute to the grand jury. It becomes apparent that what the community needs is not protections for those charged with the management of the criminal justice system, but rather opportunities to spotlight responsibility, to highlight where the system is faltering, and to identify those with the responsibility to see that it does not falter at that stage. The line between faltering and total collapse may be a fine one, but the consequences to the society of a faltering justice system have already been significant; the consequences of collapse may be irreparable.

---

new program is being instituted to use trained personnel as ombudsmen to advise prisoners of their rights and to provide more continuous legal contact. N. Y. Times, June 1, 1971, at 27, col. 1. With the advice of such ombudsmen, the number of preliminary hearings waived may be reduced.

41. QUESTIONNAIRE, *supra* note 12. The survey indicated that in certain areas such as Buffalo, Newark, Philadelphia, Portland, and Washington, D.C., the grand jury itself is considered to be a major contributor to the delay that is clogging the court system.

42. Kessler, *supra* note 28.

Notwithstanding the time lost during the preliminary phases of a criminal case, the most substantial block of dead time occurs between the arraignment and a plea of guilty or the time of trial. Although this could be an invaluable period for case preparation, this is simply not what happens in our urban centers. The time pressures on both prosecutors and defense attorneys are such that little is actually done until shortly before the parties must go to trial.[43] The defense attorney with a hundred other legal matters pending gets around to each matter when it can no longer be deferred. The burdens on prosecutors are even more staggering. It is little wonder that prosecutors fail to push cases and instead permit the defense attorney to have partial control of the decision to bring a case to trial.[44] Generally, then, the prosecutor attends to only those cases where the defense attorney is finally ready to come to terms or where the case is acknowledged to be ready for trial.

Recognizing that a case requires extensive preparation to be ready for trial, and that the motions practice may involve a few weeks,[45] the maximum interval recommended by the President's Commission between arraignment and readiness for trial is sixty-three days. Our sample indicated that only 39.2 percent of the cases in Cuyahoga County went to trial or were resolved by a plea or dismissal within sixty days of the defendant's arraignment.[46] The figures and percentages in Table 5 may be used to compare our

---

43. On April 6, 1971, in Philadelphia, Judge Nix was not going to permit *State v. Zaltowsky,* an assault and battery case, to be continued. First, the defense attorney, Mr. Lipschultz, tried to get a continuance because the defendant had just been released from the hospital. Since the defendant was in court, the judge said that the case was going to proceed. The defense attorney then said that he was not prepared to go to trial. In despair, the judge conducted the examination of the witnesses.

44. In Boston, for example, the assistant prosecutors are part-time employees and their compensation is minimal. Nevertheless, they attempt to handle their burdensome caseload. Prosecutors are rarely concerned with one particular case; they want to move their total caseload.

45. One of the usual reasons given for delay is the wealth of pretrial motions. N. Y. Times, Sept. 17, 1970, at 49, col. 1.

46. In Los Angeles, in 1969, from the time of the filing of the information or indictment, a median time of 57 days elapsed before a dismissal resulted; a median time of 33 days elapsed before a guilty plea at the arraignment; a median time of 93 days elapsed before a guilty plea which followed the arraignment; a median time of 123 days elapsed before a jury trial; and a median time of 108 days elapsed before a nonjury trial. JUDICIAL COUNCIL OF CALIFORNIA, ANNUAL REPORT OF THE ADMINISTRATIVE OFFICE OF THE CALIFORNIA COURTS 122

sample with the sixty-three-day figure recommended by the President's Commission.

TABLE 5. NUMBER OF DAYS BETWEEN ARRAIGNMENT AND
THE BEGINNING OF TRIAL, OR THE ENTRY
OF A GUILTY PLEA OR A DISMISSAL

NUMBER OF DAYS	NUMBER OF DEFENDANTS	PERCENTAGE
1–3	128	7.9%
4–15	204	12.6%
16–30	174	10.8%
31–60	127	7.9%
61–90	77	4.8%
91–180	228	14.1%
181–270	252	15.5%
271–365	216	13.4%
366–485	90	5.6%
486–605	27	1.7%
606–730	12	.7%
Over 730	2	.1%
No bill–defendant discharged	79	4.9%
Total	1616	100.0%

Even if the most outlandishly prolonged cases are discounted because of the likelihood that the defendant made himself unavailable by jumping bail, the figures are nothing to be proud of. It must be kept in mind that the time which elapsed during the preliminary phases (an average of sixty-eight days if there was a preliminary hearing, or fifty-one days if there was no hearing) would have to be added to the figures in each of the categories in order to compute the total time from arrest to the beginning of trial or the entry of a plea.

What is perhaps most exasperating is that only 150 cases, less than 10 percent of the entire sample, actually went to trial. In Philadelphia, during 1970, over 50 percent of all dispositions resulted from either a judge or a jury trial.[47] Despite the fact that over 90 percent of the cases were disposed of without trials in Cleveland, the average length of time for all cases remained 245 days. The amount of time exhausted prior to a case actually

(1971). *See also* CRIME AND DELINQUENCY IN CALIFORNIA, REFER-ENCE TABLES SUPERIOR COURT PROSECUTIONS TABLE 16 (1969). The median time in Los Angeles between filing of the information and sentencing for all felonies was 3.0 months.

47. Willmann & Polansky, *supra* note 10. In New Jersey, about 20 percent of the cases are brought to trial. N. Y. Times, Sept. 17, 1970, at 80, col. 1.

going to trial did not significantly affect the totals for the entire sample. For even where the defendant pleaded guilty to the charge or to a lesser offense, in 23.6 percent of those cases (263 out of 1,156) the total number of days from arrest to disposition of the case amounted to more than one year.

There is a glimmer of hope in the statistics, in that only 5.9 percent of the defendants who were detained and not free on bail were involved in cases that lingered for more than one year. The percentage of cases involving defendants free on bail where the time exceeded a year was 35.7. While some claim this is due to the scheduling preference given to jailed defendants, others assert that this disparity exists because the jailed defendant is more likely to plead guilty earlier and face a more serious sentence than is his bailed counterpart, because of the pressures associated with the desire for freedom.

One disturbing figure is the incidence of dismissals occurring in cases that exceeded one year. In our sample, 13.4 percent of the cases were dismissed or nolled by the prosecutor, but nearly one-third of the dismissals or nolles occurred after the case had already been pending for a year.[48] The reasons for a dismissal or nolle varied all the way from the prosecutor's decision that the case was too weak to the decision not to pursue a defendant who was to be tried in another jurisdiction. Some of these cases undoubtedly involved situations where the defendant's delaying tactics wore the prosecution down until the evidence was no longer available. But some of these cases also involved defendants who did not desire the delay, because they were being held in jail. In effect, although the state eventually declined prosecution for any number of reasons, these defendants were punished without ever having been convicted of a crime. The Sixth Amendment right to a speedy trial must be elevated to a position where it can prevent this type of situation and can also secure adherence to time guidelines similar to those suggested by the President's Commission.

EFFECTS OF DELAY ON THE INDIVIDUAL AND SOCIETY AND THE NEED TO ENFORCE THE RIGHT TO A SPEEDY TRIAL

We rationalize the decision to deprive men of their freedom on the basis of three theories: (1) that certain criminals should be removed from society for our protection; (2) that incarceration of certain criminals will deter others from engaging in the same conduct; and (3) that certain criminals

---

48. In Philadelphia, during 1970, slightly less than 20 percent of all cases were disposed of because the charges were dismissed. Willmann & Polansky, *supra* note 10. In Dayton, 15.8 percent of the cases resulted in not guilty verdicts or dismissals. Kessler, *supra* note 28.

need rehabilitation before they resume their places in the free society. All three of these theories are highly suspect and riddled with paradoxes, and perhaps it is because judges are cognizant of this that only a paucity of convicted criminals are actually sentenced to prison.[49] Nevertheless, whatever rationale is used to imprison a particular defendant or class of defendants, it is weakened or totally defeated by extended delays prior to conviction.

Analyzing the first theory, it becomes apparent that it is in the community's interest to remove a person, as soon as possible, if he represents a threat to the community's physical security. To be imprisoned for an extended period, however, he must first be convicted beyond a reasonable doubt; while the convicting process goes on, the defendant may remain free, if eligible for bail. If he can raise bail[50] and obtain his freedom, at least for the lengthy period between arrest and conviction, the community is subjected to the possibility that he might commit other acts of physical violence. Protection that is deferred because the criminal justice system is unable to bring a particular defendant to trial for a year or more is of no value to those in the community who fall victim to the additional wrongful acts committed by the bailed defendant.

The second theory, that punishing wrongdoers will serve as a deterrent to others, has long been under attack. As a theory of punishment deterrence is premised on the socialization of men. Through witnessing the punishment of those who violate the community's codes, the theory proposes, we develop our own social and moral codes and learn to conform to society's laws. It has been charged that deterrence just does not work, that people who commit violent crimes under the strain of anguish and emotion simply do not think about the consequences nor will their punishment have any influence upon others like them in the population.[51] The seemingly ever

---

49. The report of the New York City Criminal Justice Coordinating Council found that only 32 percent of all persons arrested on felony or misdemeanor charges are found guilty of any charge. "And for the comparative handful that are convicted, the council concluded that 7.4 percent receive a sentence of more than a year, 50 percent less than a year, and the balance suspended sentences." N. Y. Times, Mar. 14, 1971, at 1, col. 6.

50. Of the estimated 52 percent of the people who are in jail but not convicted, 80 percent qualify for bail but cannot meet the cash requirement for release. *The Shame of the Prisons,* TIME, Jan. 18, 1971, at 48.

51. D. MOYNIHAN, THE REPORT OF THE NATIONAL COMMISSION ON THE CAUSES AND PREVENTION OF VIOLENCE 43, 45 (1969). "These crimes tend to be among intimates and acquaintances. Often the crime is provoked by the victim, and it is spontaneous. As a general rule, the

increasing crime rate[52] is cited to demonstrate that people are not concerned with the eventual legal consequences of their acts. What the denigrators of deterrence are unable to measure, however, is how many people would, but do not, commit crimes because of their concern with the possible consequences of their actions. Those who would dismiss deterrence because of the high crime rate fail to recognize that the reason for the high incidence of crime may lie not with the invalidity of the deterrence doctrine but with the way society reacts to crime and treats its offenders.[53] For people to be deterred by the way society treats offenders, punishment must follow swiftly upon the wrongful act and the apprehension of the wrongdoer. Instead, the public is treated to the spectacle of persons charged with crime remaining free for extended periods before the case is even called for trial.

Moreover, the community is witness to the spectacle of the accused delaying his case long enough to avoid answering for his wrongful act simply because witnesses lose interest and fail to appear for trial.[54] As a case drags on, witnesses tend to disappear, and those who do appear often forget

---

more serious the crime committed, the less chance it will be repeated."

52. "Overall crime increased in the nation 11% over 1969. However, the increase in crime between 1968 and 1969 was 12%, and 17% between 1967 and 1968. . . . Violent crimes which overall increased 12% during 1970 include robbery, up 17%; murder and aggravated assault, up 7%, and forcible rape, up 2%." Cleveland Plain Dealer, Mar. 29, 1971, at 1, col. 2.

Additionally, it should be noted that white-collar crime is increasing. The Attorney General of the United States testified before a Senate investigating committee that $500,000,000 in securities had been stolen in the last two years. N. Y. Times, June 9, 1971, at 1, col. 2. *See also* N. Y. Times, June 10, 1971, at 22, col. 3. For a discussion of white-collar crime *see generally* EDELHERTZ, THE NATURE, IMPACT AND PROSECUTION OF WHITE-COLLAR CRIME (Nat. Inst. of Law Enforcement and Criminal Justice 1970).

53. M. King, *Four Inmates Speak,* NEW REPUBLIC, July 4, 1970. Jack Griswald says in his book AN EYE FOR AN EYE: "Man, let me tell you, when you come out of a place like this, you hate everyone. You feel like you've been stomped on, and you're going to get back." *Id.* at 23. Eldridge Cleaver further remarked: "All society shows the convict its ass and expects him to kiss it." *Id.* at 23–24.

54. [T]he cases involving free defendants are repeatedly postponed because of lack of time and judges. As a result, many of the complainants, having lost a full day from their jobs on several occasions, finally become discouraged and do not show up to press their case . . . and that leads to outright dismissal of the defendant. N. Y. Times, Aug. 25, 1968, at 47, col. 1.

certain facts or tend to embellish what they actually saw. Moreover, the complainant and witnesses often appear only to find that the hearing or trial has been rescheduled and that they must reappear without any assurance the matter will be heard at the later time. A Philadelphia couple, owners of a retail store, were the victims of several armed robberies. The cases in which they were involved were postponed as many as two or three times, and they were compelled to make sixteen appearances prior to resolution of one case. Although the couple were willing to make these appearances in order to help convict the defendant,[55] few witnesses will make such sacrifices. Another Philadelphian, after waiting two full days for an armed robbery trial, vowed that he would not appear when subpoenaed again.[56] Witnesses are the lifeblood of the system. Without them, few wrongdoers would be brought to justice for their acts, nor would there be any evidence to present in criminal cases. And yet no consideration is given to their needs or to the inconvenience that having to appear in court may cause them.[57]

As for the third theory, all punishment, except where a person is sentenced to death or life imprisonment without possibility of parole, should be directed towards the rehabilitation of the offender. Unfortunately, there seems to be little confidence that rehabilitation can be accomplished through a jail term; a typical sentiment is: "If we send a man to jail we write him out of the human race. When he comes out of jail and does not commit another crime, it's an amazing thing."[58] Recidivist rates for persons who

---

55. N. Y. Times, Mar. 8, 1971, at 1, col. 3. *See also* R. F. Kennedy, *Crime in the Cities Improving the Administration of Criminal Justice,* 58 J. CRIM. L. 142 (1967); W. E. Burger, *Paradoxes in the Administration of Criminal Justice,* 58 J. CRIM. L. 428, 429 (1967); *Continuances in Cook County, supra* note 24; TASK FORCE: THE COURTS, *supra* note 5, at 90 (1963); THE CHALLENGE OF CRIME IN A FREE SOCIETY, *supra* note 6; *Justice on Trial,* NEWSWEEK, Mar. 8, 1971, at 46.

56. Interview with A. Kahn, in Philadelphia, April 6, 1971.

57. In *Commonwealth v. Stratford,* the defendant was accused of robbing Mr. C. Miller's store. At the trial before Judge Welch in Philadelphia, on April 5, 1971, the defense attorney wanted to make a motion to suppress the evidence. The prosecutor objected because of an agreement between the prosecutor and public defender, whereby the prosecutor is to be notified one day in advance whenever such a motion is to be made. Further, the prosecutor, knowing that the complaining witness had appeared on three previous occasions without testifying, stated, "The victim of crime should not be prejudiced by the defendant's motion to suppress." The court did not permit the defendant to make the motion to suppress the evidence.

58. LEAGUE OF WOMEN VOTERS OF MINNEAPOLIS, HENNEPIN COUNTY MUNICIPAL COURT 11 (1971).

pass through the criminal justice process and for those who are imprisoned[59] would indicate either that our methods of rehabilitation are based upon false premises or that we are not taking this goal seriously. The prisons have become stations where idle men are left to rot in bitterness and where the dream of rehabilitation is merely a dirty joke. Rod Beatty exemplifies the dilemma. He began by forging a $65 check, graduated to armed robbery, and is now a four-time loser. His greatest fear during imprisonment is his feeling that he will be unable to adapt when he is returned to society. The prison facility is not easing his fear with constructive assistance.[60] The problem is much the same in prisons everywhere. Until society is willing to provide additional funds to upgrade facilities, hire trained personnel, and provide follow-up care, rehabilitation as a workable and practiced ideal will remain unattainable.[61] But it is also equally clear that even if society makes the necessary and enormous investment, rehabilitation will be impeded if the inordinate delays between arrest and conviction persist. Rehabilitation is most effective when begun as close as possible to the criminal activity which necessitates the treatment. It is least effective when postponed so long

---

59. *The Shame of the Prisons,* TIME, Jan. 18, 1971, at 48–49. The rhetoric that jails are to rehabilitate and that punishment is individualized treatment to enable an individual to return to a normal existence is far from reality. Forty percent of all released inmates (75 percent in some areas) are recidivists. Such individuals will be reimprisoned within five years of their discharge, frequently for a more serious offense. *Id.* at 49.

   Justice is just an abstract theory for a large number of people who come in contact with the criminal process. It seems clear to me that the end result is that our prisons become factories for crime; that is, they actually increase the crime factor in our communities, add to the violence, add to the hostility and tensions and serve very little community purpose. Interview with William vanden Heuval, Chairman of the New York City Board of Corrections, 7 CRIM. L. BULL. 299 (1971) [hereinafter cited as William vanden Heuval].

60. *The Shame of the Prisons,* TIME, Jan. 18, 1971, at 48–49.

61. "Every time the police budget is raised—and it is quite often of late—the number of arrests increases, resulting in more jail inmates, more prosecutions, more trials, and more convictions. We have not improved or increased the court and corrections budgets commensurately." Clark, *Courts, Crime, Dollars and Justice,* N. Y. Times, Dec. 12, 1970, at 31, col. 3.

   We spend $850 million a year in the City of New York for our whole system of criminal justice, but 80 percent of that money is spent in the pre-arrest phase and then the courts and the prisons

that the wrongdoer is scarcely able to relate the treatment to his wrongful act.

No matter which theory is the cornerstone of punishment, each is at least partly dependent for success upon getting to the criminal offender without delay. Whether the emphasis is on protecting society, discouraging others from committing criminal acts, or restoring the offender, all are rendered of negligible value when inordinately delayed.

To the defendant who is denied his freedom during the period between arrest and trial, either because he is charged with a nonbailable offense or because he is unable to raise the bail, prolonged delay is disastrous.[62] He is confined to a holding institution, a county or city jail, which is usually among the worst penal institutions in this country. Often there is no distinction made in these jails between the accused, who comprise about 50 percent of the jail population throughout the country,[63] and the convicted, who have been sentenced to confinement within the jail or are there pending an appeal or transfer to a state penitentiary. These jails also frequently permit those charged with a minor offense to associate with those accused or already convicted of a serious crime. Often the youthful offender is thrown in with older, more experienced criminals.[64] Consequently, even the acquitted person is more capable of committing antisocial acts upon his release because of what he has learned during his confinement. Sanitation facilities are antiquated and the quality of the food is poor. Exercise facilities are virtual-

---

and the other groups that have to mete out our justice and to make the legal system work just don't have adequate resources. I think we have to reallocate the resources that are presently committed to the criminal justice system, put all the fragments together and then look at it as an entity. We must demand social productivity from the investment we're presently making. William vanden Heuval, *supra* note 59.

62. N. Y. Times, July 12, 1969, at 1, col. 6. Senator Sam Ervin said: "Such detention may cost him his job. It is detrimental to his family, and it subjects him to psychological and physical deprivations of jail life." *See also* TASK FORCE: THE COURTS, *supra* note 5, at 50; K. MENNINGER, THE CRIME OF PUNISHMENT 36; ABA PROJECT ON MINIMUM STANDARDS FOR CRIMINAL JUSTICE: STANDARDS RELATING TO PRE–TRIAL RELEASE (1968).

63. *The Shame of the Prisons,* TIME, Jan. 18, 1971, at 48.

64. On September 7, eighteen-year-old Ismial Nieves, awaiting trial at Cook County Jail for being truant from school, wrote his mother he could not stand the beatings he was taking from the other inmates. That night, someone set fire to Nieves' mattress and locked him in his cell. Nieves, who did not smoke and had no matches, was severely burned and died a few weeks later. Davidson, *The Worst I've Ever*

ly nonexistent and medical care is scarce. Visits are stringently limited.[65] Thus the environment in which the defendant is confined becomes a world of its own subject to mores and disciplines at variance with those of the free society. The rotting that the defendant endures while awaiting trial makes it more difficult for him to respond to any form of rehabilitative treatment. In the atmosphere of these detention facilities, eruptions of violent rioting are not uncommon. Although the immediate cause of the disturbances in

---

Seen, SATURDAY EVENING POST, July 13, 1968, at 17.

Unless the defendant is exceptionally adept at self-defense his experience could parallel that of Michael Tait in the Orleans Parish Prison in New Orleans. Built in 1929 to accommodate five hundred prisoners, the jail now houses eight hundred. A Justice Department consultant also noted that the jail's plumbing and heating systems were decrepit, the sanitary conditions "deplorable," and that fire protection was lacking. Last year he recommended that the building be abandoned at the earliest possible moment. Last September, Tait, a twenty-one-year-old pre-law student at the University of Maryland, was remanded to Parish Prison to await trial on a charge of carrying a concealed weapon. Like more than one million American offenders, he was unable to post bail of $500.

Tait was placed in a dormitory-style confinement with thirty to forty other inmates who were accused of everything from minor offenses to armed robbery and murder. Having been warned by a guard to avoid any fights, Tait reluctantly obeyed a cellmate's order to take a shower. When he emerged, he discovered his clothes had been taken; and when he got to his bunk he was given a severe beating. That was it, for the first night. For the next nine nights, Tait later reported, he was forced to submit to sexual acts by other inmates. At his trial he was fined $50 and released. *Prisons in Turmoil,* NEWSWEEK, Sept. 14, 1970, at 42.

See also K. MENNINGER, THE CRIME OF PUNISHMENT 28, 40; Mills, *I Have Nothing to Do with Justice,* LIFE, Mar. 12, 1971, at 62; *A Riot Against the Law's Delay,* NEWSWEEK, Aug. 24, 1970, at 19–21; THE CHALLENGE OF CRIME IN A FREE SOCIETY, *supra* note 6, at 163.

65. N. Y. Times, Jan. 7, 1971, at 1, col. 4. A federal census of city and county jails found that of the 3,300 jails in large communities, 85 percent have no recreational or educational facilities of any kind. About one-fourth have no facilities for visitors. The survey went on to report that in many instances all persons—accused persons, inmates, and juveniles—were placed in the same overcrowded, filthy cell. *Id.*

One large detention center that received wide publicity as the scene of jail riots in August and October, 1970, has opened recreational facilities for prisoners. The move was cited as "an example of how prison tensions could be eased." N. Y. Times, June 17, 1971, at 45, col. 4.

the New York House of Detention in October, 1970, was terrible overcrowding, the primary demand common to all was depicted by one inmate
who held a sign through his cell bars reading "No More Long Court
Dates."[66] Even suicides are not infrequent in these jails, and the only surprise is that they do not occur with greater frequency. Describing the
suicide of Julio Roldan, who had hanged himself while awaiting trial, the
New York City Board of Correction categorized his detention as having
"succeeded only in deranging him."[67]

Society thus casts those who are accused of a crime and confined pending
a determination of guilt into a world void of reality. Within this unreal
world of county jails are defendants who will be acquitted, defendants
whose cases will be dismissed, and defendants who will be found guilty. The
innocent are subjected to the same inhumanity and brutality as the guilty;
all offenders, even the most guilty ones, deserve protection from these
indignities. Every day that a person is confined in one of these institutions
compounds the dehumanization process. Every hour increases his chances
of being sexually brutalized and reinforces his disillusionment and
bitterness.[68] These prisoners are the primary victims of delay, for they are

66. N. Y. Times, Oct. 11, 1970, at 80, col. 2.
67. N. Y. Times, Nov. 18, 1970, at 1, col. 7. Roldan and a friend, Roberto
    Lemus, both members of a youth gang known as the Young Lords,
    were arrested on October 13, 1970. At the arraignment the next day,
    they were charged with the attempted arson of an apartment building.
    Because of the nature of the offense and the potential danger to life,
    bail was set at $1,500. Roldan was taken that day to the Manhattan
    House of Detention, the Tombs. Although visibly upset with the chain
    of events, he was not put in a cell designed for observation of agitated
    defendants. On October 16 he committed suicide in his cell. *Id.* at 52,
    col. 7.
       The judiciary was partially blamed for the death because of the
    summary proceedings prior to incarceration in the Tombs. *Id.* at 1,
    col. 1. A release on recognizance report (ROR) was not prepared for
    Roldan, as he was not being represented by the Legal Aid Society. This
    report gives the judge at the arraignment some background on the
    defendant for purposes of determining a more realistic bail figure.
       If a defendant is privately represented (as Mr. Roldan was), the
    irony is that an ROR report is not prepared. The defendant's attor-
    ney is expected to make the argument that his client should be
    released on his own recognizance. The transcript in the Roldan
    arraignment shows that his attorney never had a chance to make
    an argument for his immediate release pending trial. *Id.* at 52, col.
    1.
68. If a prisoner happens to be rich, a guard may sell him a girlish

subject to prolonged detention while clogged courts hear cases that originated at earlier dates.[69]

Many courts provide earlier calendaring for those cases where the defendant is confined while awaiting trial, but this has the accompanying effect of postponing the cases of free defendants. However, Boston's assistant assignment commissioner maintains that the convenience of the attorneys involved is often considered the most important factor in scheduling.[70] Especially disturbing are those instances where the interest of the accused in a speedy trial runs counter to that of his attorney, who may not wish either to take the time to prepare for trial or to expend the time a trial would consume. Since most defendants unable to raise bail are indigent and unable to pay the fee of a private attorney, counsel is provided either through the court by the appointment of a private attorney or through a legal aid or public defender agency. If the attorney is not particularly interested in the case or in the plight of his client, he is capable of delaying the case almost interminably.

The agonies associated with prolonged pretrial detention are visited upon the families of those detained[71] and eventually will be felt by the entire

---

cellmate. TIME, Jan. 18, 1971, at 49. Institutions become human—or more accurately, inhumane—storage houses. The presence of overcrowding breeds escalating hostility between correction guards and prisoners, who walk in constant fear of each other. As a prison superintendent in Philadelphia has stated, "Our efforts are concentrated on moving people back and forth to court everyday. . . . I'm candid to admit we're running a human warehouse." N. Y. Times, Mar. 8, 1971, at 1, col. 3.

It surely seems self-defeating, for instance, for the criminal law to declare homosexuality between consenting adults to be a crime and then punish those found guilty of this offense by sending them to monosexual jails where (as criminologists have repeatedly observed) homosexuality is rampant—and where, indeed, persons who might otherwise have tried to abstain from homosexuality are likely to be forced against their will to participate in homosexual acts. Schoenfeld, *Psychoanalysis, Criminal Justice Planning and Reform, and the Law,* 7 CRIM. L. BULL. 313 (1971).

69. "Defendants are subjected to the Red Queen's jurisprudence: first the punishment, then the trial. They do time before they are found guilty of the crime." Statement by Mayor John Lindsay, Administrative Board of the Judicial Conference of the State of New York, Oct. 9, 1970.

70. Manning, *supra* note 30.

71. *Cf.* P. MORRIS, PRISONERS AND THEIR FAMILIES (1965). This study indicates that it is good for the father to spend some time in prison

society. Extended pretrial confinement is likely to destroy whatever family unit existed prior to the defendant's arrest.[72] If the defendant was previously employed, it is almost certain that his pay will stop and that he will not have a job to return to. If his family is affected in no other way, they will suffer at least from the loss of income during this period. They are likely to be forced to seek public assistance and to become added statistics on the welfare rolls.[73] The response of moralists that the defendant should have considered the cost to his family before he got himself into trouble is irrelevant to this consideration, because our immediate concern is with those defendants who have yet to be convicted of a crime and are still presumed innocent. Ultimately, the cost is borne by the society. If the detention centers are serving only to turn out better criminals, it is the community and its citizens that will be victimized. But for those who can see the issues of our times only in dollar amounts, the costs of inadequately feeding, housing, and supervising the inmates of the detention centers are exorbitantly high, let alone the dollars which are lost to the community

---

because it will help solve family problems and bring the family unit closer together in hard times. N. Y. Times, July 12, 1969, at 1, col. 6; ABA PROJECT ON MINIMUM STANDARDS FOR CRIMINAL JUSTICE: STANDARDS RELATING TO PRE-TRIAL RELEASE (1968). The consequences of pretrial detention are grave. Defendants presumed innocent are subjected to the psychological and physical deprivations of jail life, usually under more onerous conditions than are imposed on convicted defendants. The jailed defendant loses his job if he has one and is prevented from contributing to the preparation of his defense. Equally important, the burden of his detention frequently falls heavily on the innocent members of his family. K. MENNINGER, THE CRIME OF PUNISHMENT 36; TASK FORCE: THE COURTS, *supra* note 5, at 50.

72. Malchijah Tatum was arrested October 24, 1969, on murder charges. On October 13, 1970, his case was marked ready for trial. Tatum, aged sixty-two, at one point claimed he was ready to die rather than wait any longer to be tried. During this long period of incarceration, he heard from his relatives infrequently. Tatum estimated that he had no visitors, except his lawyer, between May and October of 1970. Interview with Malchijah Tatum in New York City, Oct. 12, 1970.

73. Luis Cintron was indicted on December 14, 1968, for homicide. He was not eligible for bail. He pleaded guilty to second degree manslaughter in September of 1970. Although Cintron was able to obtain employment after previous periods of incarceration, he could never return to an old job. Cintron was the father of an illegitimate child. He had no money to send the child. He seemed to believe that the mother and child were receiving welfare. Interview with Luis Cintron, in New York, Nov. 10, 1970.

through the high incidence of recidivist crime.[74]

On the other hand, a defendant who ransoms his freedom between arrest and trial suffers none of the degradation and indignities associated with a stay in a county jail; moreover, while released, subject to nominal restrictions on his conduct, the bailed defendant is actually free of all restraint because of the lack of supervision. To him a long delay before trial may be desirable. He may even precipitate delay.[75] If he represents a threat to the safety of the community, that danger is not at all alleviated when the defendant is free for an extended period awaiting trial. Estimates of crimes committed in the District of Columbia by persons released on bail during the period between their initial arrest and trial range from 7.5[76] to 70[77]

---

74. In Baltimore, Maryland, a pretrial release program has been in operation since September, 1968. This program investigates the background of an accused to determine whether he should be released on his own recognizance or whether his bail should be reduced. As a result of this work, the program has saved the city of Baltimore over $2,000,000 between September, 1968, and the beginning of June, 1971. This figure is based on the fact that the cost of housing, feeding, and guarding a defendant is $6.15 per day. Only those days between the time of the defendant's release and the final resolution of the case are considered in computing the savings. It can be urged that even though defendants are released the city must still pay the guards' salary. But this cost is considered to be cancelled by the savings to the welfare rolls when a defendant is not in jail awaiting his trial. Telephone conversation with Richard Motsay, Director of the Baltimore Pretrial Release Program, June 11, 1971.

   In 1962, defendants detained pending trial in New York City accounted for 1,775,778 jail days at a cost of $6.25 per day or a total cost of over ten million dollars. *The High Cost of Criminal Laws,* AMERICA, Oct. 24, 1970, at 310–11; *Crime Expense: Now Up to 51 Billion a Year,* U. S. NEWS AND WORLD REPORT, Oct. 26, 1970, at 30–34; Rankin, *The Effect of Pretrial Detention,* 39 N.Y.U.L. REV. 641 (1964).

75. In the QUESTIONNAIRE, *supra* note 12, 49.5 percent of the responses indicated that the accused who is free on bail is the greatest beneficiary of pretrial delay. In comparison, 36 percent of the respondents stated that the defense attorney obtained the most benefit from pretrial delay.

76. Out of 2,776 persons who came before the District Court in the survey period, 207 (7.5 percent) were charged with committing a new crime while released on bail. DISTRICT OF COLUMBIA, *supra* note 20, at 931.

77. Comparison of speech by Deputy Attorney General Richard G. Kleindienst and House District Committee Report on Preventive Detention Provisions of H. R. 16196 *as cited in Preventive Detention Hearings Before the Subcommittee on Constitutional Rights of the*

percent. A case in New York involving thefts of credit cards from hotel rooms of out-of-state businessmen illustrates the point. While free on bail for this offense, the defendant engaged in similar activity. Because of the delay prior to trial the defendant was not only free to continue stealing, but he eventually avoided conviction because the out-of-state witnesses refused or were unable to return to New York to testify.[78] Criminal offenses by defendants free on bail are just another way in which delay affects the entire community.

Although few persons can empathize with the deprivation that an individual suffers during a period of prolonged detention prior to trial, and few citizens ever experience the inconvenience of being a witness in a criminal case, virtually the entire community is concerned about crime, for everyone feels vulnerable as a potential victim. Until the community as a whole becomes aware that at least part of the problem of a high crime rate lies in the delay existing in criminal courts, little will be done. When such awareness is achieved,[79] efforts will be made to correct the situation and make the essential right to a speedy trial meaningful for both the defendant awaiting trial and the community in need of protection.

THE SPEEDY TRIAL RIGHT: WHAT DOES IT MEAN? HOW IS IT ENFORCED?

A problem that arises when one seeks out the meaning of the guarantee of the right to a speedy trial is that the Constitution offers no lead as to what is meant by a speedy trial. Moreover, the individual state statutes dealing with this problem are not at all uniform. Some of the state statutes simply repeat the constitutional language, offering no guidance to the judges and lawyers within those states as to when the right has been violated.[80] Some-

---

Committee on the Judiciary, United States Senate, 91st Cong., 2d Sess. 1031 (1970). In 1968, when 557 persons were indicted for robbery (theft from a person by force) nearly 70 percent of those released prior to trial were rearrested and charged with a subsequent offense.

78. Conference with Murray Diamond, defense attorney, New York City, Nov. 28, 1970.

79. In addition, a large cross section of America is becoming aware of the prison crisis:

> One subsidiary dividend of the social revolution occurring in this country—the Civil Rights movement, war and draft resisters, college rebellions, the drug cult—is that many of the best of the new generation will be ex "cons" with memorable experiences in the country's heretofore remote "joints," as they are called. Goldfarb, *The Horror of the Prisons,* N. Y. Times, Oct. 28, 1970, at 47, col. 4.

80. These provisions usually demand only that "justice be administered speedily" or that "one be entitled to a speedy public trial." *See, e.g.,*

what more guidance is afforded in those states where statutes provide that a defendant must be brought to trial within a certain number of court terms after he has been charged.[81] A term of court offers an imprecise benchmark, however, because the number of terms within a year varies from state to state and may even vary within the courts of a single state. Finally, there is the group of state statutes which provides a specific time limit in which a defendant must be brought to trial.[82] These vary from sixty days to a year.[83] The states have simply reached no consensus as to the meaning of speedy trial.

Moreover, the lack of agreement extends to what the proper remedy shall be and to whom it shall apply when there is a violation of the right to a speedy trial. Some states afford a remedy only to detained defendants, the remedy being immediate bonding or dismissal of the charges, although the

---

ALA. CODE tit. 13, § 330 (1958); LA. CRIM. PRO. CODE ANN. art. 701 (West 1966); MICH. COMP. LAWS § 768.1 (1948); ALAS. R. CRIM. P. 43(b); KY. R. CRIM. P. 902; WYO. R. CRIM. P. 45(b).

81. *See, e.g.,* ARK. STAT. ANN. § 43–1708; COLO. REV. STAT. ANN. § 39–7–12 (1963); DEL. CODE ANN. 10, § 6910; GA. CODE ANN. § 27–1901; IDAHO CODE ANN. § 19–106 (1947); KAN. STAT. ANN. § § 16–1432, 1433; MINN. STAT. ANN. § 611.04 (1963); MISS. CODE ANN. § 2518 (1942); N. Y. CODE CRIM. PROC. § 668; N. C. GEN. STAT. § 15-10; N. D. CENT. CODE tit. 29–18–01; OHIO REV. CODE § 2945.71 (Page 1955); OKLA. STAT. ANN. tit. 22, § § 811–12; S. C. CODE 17, § 509; S. D. CODE § 23–34–2; TENN. CODE ANN. § 40–2102 (1955); TEX. CODE CRIM. PROC. art. 32.01 (1966); UTAH CODE ANN. § 77–51–1 (1953); VA. CODE § 19.1–191; W. VA. CODE ANN. § 62–3–1 (1966); MO. R. CRIM. P. 25.01.

82. CAL. PENAL CODE § § 1381, 1382 (West 1969); HAWAII REV. STAT. 37, § 707–1; ILL. ANN. STAT. ch. 38, § 103–5 (Smith–Hurd 1970); IOWA CODE ANN. § 795 (1950); KAN. STAT. ANN. § § 16–1432, 1433; MASS. GEN. LAWS ANN. ch. 277, § 72 (1959); NEB. REV. STAT. 29–1207 (1971 Supp.); N. M. STAT. tit. 41, § 11–4.1 (1971 Supp.); NEV. REV. STAT. § 178.566; N. H. REV. STAT. 603.1 (Supp. 1970); ORE. REV. STAT. § 134.110; R. I. GEN. LAWS ANN. § 12–13–7 (1956); WASH. REV. CODE tit. 10, § § 37.020, 46.010; WIS. STAT. ANN. § 971.10 (1971); ARIZ. R. CRIM. P. 236; FLA. R. CRIM. P. 1.191; IND. R. CRIM. P. 4; N. J. R. CRIM. P. 3:25.2 (1969); PA. R. CRIM. P. 316(b) (1971).

83. California law states that if a defendant is not brought to trial within sixty days after being charged with a felony, the charge must be dismissed, unless the defendant participated in or consented to the delay. CAL. PENAL CODE § 1382 (West 1969). Under the Indiana Rules of Criminal Procedure a person can be held by recognizance to answer an indictment for up to a year. IND. R. CRIM. P. 4(c) (1970).

charges may be reinstituted by the state, as in Arkansas and Delaware.[84] Another approach protects both the defendants in jail and those on bail and authorizes the trial court to dismiss the charges against the defendant without permitting the state to reinstitute them at a later time.[85] In other words, for failure to bring the defendant to trial within the statutory period, the prosecution is permanently foreclosed from pursuing that case. States like Oregon and Utah make this dismissal mandatory,[86] but other states— New Mexico and Wyoming,[87] for example—place dismissal within the discretion of the trial judge.

---

84. In Arkansas, for example, those not on bail must be tried by the end of the second term after indictment, and those on bail must be tried by the end of the third term after indictment. ARK. STAT. ANN. § 43–1708. But discharge under either of these provisions will be denied if the court is satisfied that material evidence for the state exists and that reasonable efforts have been made to procure it. In such event the case will be continued to the next term. ARK. STAT. ANN. § 43–1709.

   In Delaware a person jailed for a felony and not indicted or tried at the next term of court must be released on bail, unless it appears by affidavit that the witnesses for the state, who must be named, are unavailable. If the person is not then indicted and tried at the second term after his commitment, he must be discharged from prison. DEL. CODE ANN. 10, § 6910. Garner v. State, 145 A.2d 68 (Del. 1958).

85. New Jersey provides that at any time after six months following the return of an indictment or the filing of an accusation, the assignment judge may direct on his or on the defendant's motion that the trial thereof be moved upon a specified day. Upon failure of the prosecuting attorney to do so, the assignment judge may order the indictment or accusation dismissed, which is the equivalent of an acquittal. N. J. R. CRIM. P. 3:25.2 (1969).

86. Oregon provides that after indictment the defendant must be brought to trial within a reasonable period of time or the indictment will be dismissed, providing, however, that the defendant is not responsible for the delay that has occurred. ORE. REV. STAT. § 134.120. In Oregon, the defendant must assert his right to be indicted, but once indicted, the state must afford him a speedy trial and the accused is under no duty to demand it. Bevel v. Gladden, 232 Ore. 578, 376 P.2d 117 (1962); State v. Dodson, 226 Ore. 458, 360 P.2d 782 (1961). In Utah, unless there is good cause to the contrary, charges against the defendant will be dismissed if he is not brought to trial by the next term of the court after his indictment. UTAH CODE ANN. § 77–51–1 (1953). Furthermore, the court must hold at least three terms of the district court per year. UTAH CODE ANN. § 78–3–6 (1953).

87. In Wyoming, the court may dismiss the indictment, information, or

Even in states where there is provision for remedy, however, the remedy may not be available to the defendant who is unaware that he can make such a demand and sits in jail, neglected by his attorney and by the court system as well. Almost universally, legal redress is predicated upon an unmet demand from the defendant or his attorney that he be brought to trial promptly.[88] Secondly, in many states the defendant will not be entitled to the applicable remedy if any part of the delay is attributable to him or to

complaint if there is unnecessary delay in bringing the defendant to trial. WYO. R. CRIM. P. 45(b). However, if the court is convinced that the state has made a reasonable effort to procure evidence and that such evidence will be available at the succeeding term, the case may be continued. WYO. STAT. ANN. § 7–236.

88. This is true whether a trial is guaranteed within a specific time, a term, or a reasonable time. Where a trial is guaranteed within a reasonable time and an unmet demand is a prerequisite to raising the speedy trial issue, see Autrey v. State, 44 Ala. App. 53, 202 So. 2d 88 (1967); State v. Holloway, 147 Conn. 22, 156 A.2d 466 (1959); Loy v. Grayson, 99 So. 2d 555 (Fla. 1957); Barker v. Commonwealth, 385 S. W.2d 671 (Ky. 1965); State v. Banks, 111 La. 22, 35 So. 370 (1904); Couture v. State, 156 Me. 231, 163 A.2d 646 (1960); Greathouse v. State, 5 Md. App. 675, 249 A.2d 207 (1969); People v. Kennedy, 23 Mich. App. 6, 178 N.W.2d 144 (1970); State v. Mahoney (can imply waiver from actions which cause delay), 125 Vt. 488, 207 A.2d 143 (1965).

A demand for a speedy trial must be made in many jurisdictions where one is guaranteed a trial within a specified time. See People v. Worley, 45 Ill. 2d 96, 256 N. E.2d 751 (1970); Randolph v. State, 234 Ind. 57, 122 N. E.2d 860 (1954); State v. Lindhoff, 161 N. W.2d 741 (Iowa 1968); Commonwealth v. Needel, 349 Mass. 580, 211 N. E.2d 335 (1965); State v. Hulsizer, 42 N. J. Super. 224, 126 A.2d 47 (1956); State v. Christensen, 75 Wash. 2d 678, 453 P.2d 644 (1969); R. I. GEN. LAWS ANN. § 12–13–7 (1956); HAWAII R. CRIM. P. 48(b).

Where a demand must be made for one to be guaranteed a trial within a specified term, see Dillard v. State, 65 Ark. 404, 46 S. W. 533 (1898); Adargo v. People (failure to object to trial date considered a waiver), 159 Colo. 321, 411 P.2d 245 (1966); Kominski v. State, 51 Del. 163, 141 A.2d 138 (1958); Malcolm v. State, 225 Ga. 470, 169 S. E.2d 779 (1969); State v. Borough (the defendant must also demonstrate prejudice due to the lapse of time), 178 N. W.2d 897 (Minn. 1970); State v. Hollars, 266 N. C. 45, 145 S. E.2d 309 (1965); State v. Dinger, 51 N. D. 98, 199 N. W. 196 (1924); State v. Doyle, 11 Ohio App. 2d 97, 40 Ohio Op. 2d 251, 228 N. E.2d 863 (1967); Bell v. State, 430 P.2d 841 (Okla. Ct. Crim. App. 1967); State v. Harrison, 83 S. D. 440, 160 N. W.2d 415 (1968); State ex rel. Underwood v. Brown, 193 Tenn. 113, 244 S. W.2d 168 (1951); Hudson v. State, 453

his attorney.[89] Ohio has a rule that requires a defendant to be tried within six months of indictment. If he is not brought to trial within six months, the case is dismissed unless the defendant is at all responsible for the delay.[90] An example is the case of Hazen Solomon. He was arrested for using a stolen credit card and was unable to make bail. His attorney made a motion for a psychiatric examination and it was granted on July 2, 1970. By February 3, 1971, Solomon had still not been examined; and a speedy trial motion, previously made in September, 1970, had been refused, because the judge considered the request for a psychiatrist a continuance, and this divested the defendant of his right to a mandatory speedy trial.[91] The same problem arose in a New York murder case, where a complaint was raised on behalf of a defendant whose case had been pending for twenty-seven months. His plight received publicity because of the sculpture work that he was doing in jail. The complaint alleged that the defendant had been denied a speedy trial because he refused to accede to his attorney's advice to plead

S. W.2d 147 (Tex. Ct. Crim. App. 1970); State v. Bohn, 67 Utah 362, 248 P. 119 (1926); State v. Stoeckle (defendant must take affirmative steps to bring his case to trial), 41 Wis. 2d 378, 164 N. W.2d 303 (1969).

89. This is the case under all three types of provisions: where the defendant must be tried within a reasonable time; where he must be tried within a certain number of terms; and where he must be tried within a specific time.

Where the defendant must be tried within a reasonable time, *see* Glasgow v. State (a tactical decision of the defendant's attorney caused the delay), 469 P.2d 682 (Alas. 1970); State v. Hale, 157 Me. 361, 172 A.2d 631 (1961); Greathouse v. State, 5 Md. App. 675, 249 A.2d 207 (1969); State v. Mahoney, 124 Vt. 488, 207 A.2d 143 (1965).

Where a defendant must be tried within a number of terms of court and delay will be allowed because of his actions, *see* Kominski v. State (court considers activities of both state and defendant on question of delay), 51 Del. 163, 141 A.2d 138 (1958); ARK. STAT. ANN. § 43–1711 (delay upon application of accused); COLO. REV. STAT. ANN. § 39–7–12 (1963).

Where a defendant must be tried within a certain number of days and delay will be allowed because of his actions, *see* McCandless v. District Court of Polk City, 245 Iowa 599, 61 N. W.2d 674 (1954); Commonwealth v. Chase, 348 Mass. 100, 202 N. E.2d 300 (1964); Ramsdell v. Langlois, 100 R. I. 468, 217 A.2d 83 (1966); KAN. STAT. ANN. § 62–1432; NEV. REV. STAT. § 178.556; ORE. REV. STAT. § 134.120; PA. CODE ANN. tit. 19, § 781; WASH. REV. STAT. tit. 10, § 37.020; ARIZ. R. CRIM. P. 236; IND. R. CRIM. P. 4.

90. OHIO REV. CODE § 2945.71 (Page 1955).

91. Cleveland Plain Dealer, Feb. 3, 1971, at 2, col. 1.

guilty.[92] The attorney denied the charge, but whether or not it was true, it is not unusual for a defense attorney to act slowly in a criminal case and be the principal cause of delay. Whether the remedy is lost to the defendant because his attorney is unaware of the need to make the demand, or whether it is lost because the attorney has no desire to speed the process along, the defendant is suffering and losing his right. What is needed is a mechanism that will provide all defendants their day in court within a reasonable time and without dependency upon the attorney to move the case.

In addition to ensuring the defendant's right to a speedy trial, consideration must be given to ensuring that neither the defendant nor his attorney is able to deny the community its day in court. New speedy trial provisions must make sure the defense will not be able to delay a case interminably. A common drawback to existing speedy trial provisions is that they protect only the defendant—and few defendants at that. The Constitution guarantees to each defendant the right to a speedy trial; there is nothing in the Constitution that guarantees to a defendant a corollary right to delay a trial.[93] Yet the American way of defense has become to delay and delay and delay, hoping that the state or its witnesses will eventually lose interest.[94] Any rules to insure the constitutional guarantee of a speedy trial to a defendant need not force the defendant to go to trial in a matter of days after he has been charged. At the same time, however, rules must contain procedures to eliminate the extensive and inexcusable delays that may be occasioned by the defense.

Both good delay and bad delay exist; and although the former is acceptable, the latter must no longer be tolerated.[95] Postponements affect the

---

92. N. Y. Times, Feb. 21, 1971, at 27, col. 1.

93. *Cf.* When a Cleveland attorney was held in contempt because he was absent on the third scheduled trial date for one of his cases, one attorney commented: "The right of speedy trial belongs to the defendant, not to the state. . . . It is the defendant's prerogative if he wants a speedy trial, not anyone else's." Cleveland Plain Dealer, June 8, 1971, § B, at 2, col. 2.

94. QUESTIONNAIRE, *supra* note 12. Accordingly, 68 percent of the attorneys responding felt that delay can be used as a means of frustrating the state's witnesses. When the trial date is finally reached it is hoped that the state's witnesses will not appear. Sixty-four percent indicated that repeated continuances generally increase the possibility that the charges will be dismissed. Moreover, 64 percent believed that repeated continuances improve the defendant's position when entering into plea negotiations.

95. Those delays that promote a fair hearing for both the accused and the prosecutor are good delays. Those delays that are sought as a tactic

entire calendar, not just the immediate case. There may be no way to put to good use time left vacant when a case is postponed, and the postponed case will crowd out another case waiting to be scheduled.[96] If the right to a speedy trial is to be meaningfully enforced, the unchallenged and unquestioned motion by the defense counsel for continuance must end. When a case has been docketed with sufficient notice to all parties, courts should hold defense attorneys and prosecutors to a standard of readiness. Defense attorneys should also be required to notify the court of scheduling conflicts at the time a case is docketed. When an attorney reports a scheduling conflict, the Vera Institute of Justice in New York City would advocate "advance forward practice," which would reschedule the case for a convenient time *prior to* the date of conflict.[97] The indirect effect would be to hasten case disposition and prevent unfounded claims of conflicting schedules.

Instances will arise when continuances are requested for good cause. If counsel is in the middle of trial on another matter, he certainly cannot appear in two courts at the same time. On the other hand, often these conflicts are purposely scheduled by attorneys to forestall the possibility of terminating either case. Philadelphia has made this more difficult by enacting a rule that prohibits a defense attorney from representing more than fifteen defendants against whom indictments have been outstanding for more than twelve months.[98] This lessens the chance that two of his cases will be scheduled at the same time. Even though a conflict may be unintentional, if the attorney has not had the foresight to prevent the conflict when matters were first scheduled, it is not unreasonable to require that he appear in more than one non-time-consuming matter, such as a hearing on a motion or a sentencing procedure, in a single day. Along these lines, the New York City Criminal Justice Coordinating Council suggested a statute that would disallow the adjournment of cases when an attorney

---

in litigation are bad delays. *Continuances in Cook County, supra* note 24.

96. As President Nixon has stated: "A steadily growing backlog of work . . . threatens to make the delays worse tomorrow than they are to-day. . . ." Speech before the National Conference of the Judiciary, in Williamsburg, Virginia, Mar. 11, 1971.

97. Conference with James Lacy, Vera Institute, in New York City, Oct. 13, 1970.

98. Rule 301 promulgated by the Board of Judges of the Philadelphia Court of Common Pleas aims to curtail the backlog of criminal cases in Philadelphia's courts. Moore v. Carroll, 315 F. Supp. 1129 (E. D. Pa. 1970). Such a rule may be enacted in the near future in the state of Ohio, in order to help eliminate the case backlog. Cleveland Press, Mar. 18, 1971, § F, at 5, col. 3.

claims a calendar conflict.[99] Rather than permitting postponements as an act of grace, continuances should be granted where the attorney can show good cause and explain why the postponement is in the interests of justice. The key to clearing up some of the problems associated with delay in our courts is to destroy the myth that courts are run for the convenience of attorneys. Attention can then be turned to revitalizing the justice system in order to reduce delay, while furthering our historic quest for fairness.

DELAY: WHY AND HOW IS IT MANUFACTURED?

The difference between the reality and the constitutional ideal can be accounted for by the persons most directly involved in the management and operation of the criminal courts. Apparently speedy justice is primarily in the interest of the community, and the community is simply not adequately represented in the courts. Between defendants and lawyers—and it must be kept in mind that judges and prosecutors are lawyers too—the procedures are being neatly emasculated to ensure that only their respective interests are protected. At least those defendants who are out on bail seem to benefit from the extended delays and consequent docket clogging. The indigent who is unable to retain his own attorney and secure his pretrial freedom languishes in jail, however, dependent entirely upon the efforts of his appointed or legal aid attorney.[100] One expert even challenges the enthusiasm of the jailed defendant's desire for a speedy trial.[101] According to this contention, the defendant, although unhappy with his pretrial confinement, has little desire to go to trial and face the possible consequences of his act. If this view is correct, then not even those victimized by the delays genuinely want the delay time to be reduced, because no one is ready to pay the piper for his wrongful acts.[102] The jailed defendants ostensibly argue to the con-

---

99. Conference with Mr. Appelton, Criminal Justice Coordinating Council, New York City. Further, they suggest continuance should not be granted when police witnesses are absent.

100. *Justice on Trial,* NEWSWEEK, Mar. 8, 1971, at 18.

101. Harry Subin, Associate Professor of Criminal Law at New York University School of Law, has stated:
    Generally people do not want a speedy trial. Those who are free on bail do not care about a speedy trial—they do not want to come to the day of reckoning, as they are enjoying their freedom. People who are in jail only want to get out of jail—they do not want to take the chance of coming to trial. Interview in New York City, Oct. 11, 1970.

102. Chief Justice Joseph Weintraub of the New Jersey Supreme Court recently commented: "Realistically, most of them [accused defen-

trary. Their common complaint is that the system is too slow and that they are in the meantime relegated to the less than human conditions of county and city jails. In any event, even if the jailed defendants want speedy trials, they have even less influence than the public and are unlikely to have any effect upon how courts are managed. Neither the general public nor the indigent defendant[103] has "a friend in court."

Consistent with the tactic of delay, a mystique has developed among criminal defense attorneys that if a defendant waits out the system long enough, he may never be held accountable for his crimes. And the attorneys have transmitted this mystique to their clients. Though the attorney cannot postpone judgment entirely, if he delays it as long as possible, the prosecutor may be willing to offer a favorable sentence or accept a plea to a lesser charge, just to have the case closed.[104] Part of the logic is impeccable, at least for the bailed defendant. If one is guilty and faces a possible prison term, postpone it as long as possible and enjoy the luxury of freedom on bail. As each month goes by, there is a greater chance that one of the state's crucial witnesses may become unavailable.[105] Of course, the logic fails where the accused has a good defense, for one of his crucial witnesses may lose interest, leave the state, or even die.

Even if the defendant desires a prompt hearing, his success is dependent upon his attorney's willingness to seek promptness and to go to trial.[106] John

---

dants] are guilty and they're in no hurry to go to trial." N. Y. Times, Sept. 17, 1970, at 49, col. 1.

103. *See generally* P. Wald, *Poverty and Criminal Justice* in (Appendix C) TASK FORCE: THE COURTS, *supra* note 5, at 139.

104. QUESTIONNAIRE, *supra* note 12. Better than 60 percent of the respondents indicated the belief that repeated continuances increase the possibility of dismissal and that repeated continuances improve defense counsel's bargaining position in plea negotiations. However, just under 50 percent of the responses indicated that prosecutors will provide a better deal than warranted to a defendant who "waits them out."

105. According to Judge Amos Basel of the New York City Criminal Court, "It's standard procedure for some parole defendants to hang around the halls until they see if the complainant or officer shows up. If he does, they don't appear, but come in later after he has gone and claim they were in the wrong courtroom. So the case gets postponed a number of times perhaps." N. Y. Times, Feb. 11, 1969, at 24, col. 1.

106. Assuming that the defendant and his attorney are willing to go to trial, a courtroom must be available. In many cities, the case may be delayed just waiting for a courtroom. Frequently, however, courtrooms are

T. Corrigan, the Cuyahoga County Prosecutor, has stated: "Any defendant who desired would receive a trial almost immediately"; yet only in a few rare instances have any requests been forthcoming.[107] Generally, lawyers are reluctant to proceed to trial, preferring to delay a case until all sides are worn down. Eventually, they expect the prosecutor to accept a plea that is agreeable to the defendant, or else they expect the defendant, after an extended waiting period in jail, to plead to the charge and end the matter. Close to 90 percent of all felony prosecutions are currently resolved without jury trials, and authorities fear that if a greater percentage required full-scale trials, the system would totally collapse. That result is unlikely, however, because full-scale trials subject the defendant to the threat of a conviction for the maximum charge and the imposition of penalty based upon that charge. Thus, it would not be in the best interests of most defendants to actually go to trial, and few will take the risk.[108] In fact, some prosecutors encourage the rapid release of an offender under the assumption that he will be rearrested for another crime within a short period and willingly plead guilty to one charge if the other is dropped.[109]

Compounding this problem is the inadequacy of fees paid by the court to private lawyers representing indigent defendants. In Cleveland, for example, a court-appointed attorney representing an indigent receives in non-homicide cases $150 for pleading a defendant guilty and $300 for going to

---

available but remain unused for a day or more simply because defense attorneys and prosecutors are unready or unwilling to go to trial.

107. Letter from John T. Corrigan, Cuyahoga County Prosecutor, Cleveland, Ohio, April 12, 1971.

108. [W]e would expect by analogy that when the overall rate of conviction at trial goes down, so would the proportion of guilty pleas. . . . And even if the feedback mechanism were not working efficiently, we would hardly expect the guilty plea rate to go up. Yet that is exactly what happened in Illinois. Even though the rate of guilty findings [at trial] went down sharply from 1963 to 1964 . . . the rate of guilty pleas went up. . . . OAKS & LEHMAN, A CRIMINAL JUSTICE SYSTEM AND THE INDIGENT 57–58 (1968) [hereinafter cited as OAKS & LEHMAN.]

109. The case of Tony Wolmack, charged with possession of narcotics in Hudson County Court, in New Jersey, is instructive. Prior to being arrested and charged with possession of narcotics, Wolmack had been indicted for both possession of a dangerous weapon, and breaking and entering. When the attention of a prosecuting attorney was brought to the fact that the two earlier indictments existed, the prosecutor offered to drop the earlier indictments in exchange for a plea of guilty to the narcotics charge. After a hurried conversation with the defense attorney, the defendant pleaded guilty to possession of narcotics.

trial. If the attorney's motivation is solely a quest for money, then he is less likely to take the case to trial. A trial is time-consuming, and indigency fees are only token reimbursements compared to the fees collectable from a private client and the number of cases an attorney can plead during the time required for one trial. Even if money is not the sole consideration, the inadequacy of the fees must have a bearing on the attorney's willingness to proceed to trial. It is not uncommon for a court-appointed attorney, with a client who insists upon going to trial, to simply request to be relieved of the assignment.[110] Although this is a blatant violation of the canon of ethics supposedly subscribed to by all attorneys,[111] the request to be relieved is all too frequently granted by the trial judge, with little or no inquiry as to the reason for the request. According to one attorney who recently opened his own office, Cleveland attorneys must assure the assignment judge, as a condition of receiving appointments, that they will not seek to be relieved if the case goes to trial.[112]

Delays are not confined to cases involving indigent defendants. The likelihood that a case will be dragged out is even greater for a fee-paying client than for an indigent.[113] For private clients the delay may be engineered not to avoid trial but rather to seek the best deal available from the prosecutor. Although many defense attorneys maintain that the best deal is available after a period of delay, prosecutors like New York City's Steven North contend that prosecutors offer better deals during the earlier stages of the proceedings.[114] The truth is probably somewhere between these two positions. The deal that can be made no doubt depends upon the individual case. In some cases there may be a time when the best deal can be made, but in others there is only one plea possible.

Another common practice that has precipitated delay is the prosecutor's custom of encouraging grand juries to overcharge.[115] When the charge on which the defendant is brought to court is more serious than the facts will

---

110. *Cf.* QUESTIONNAIRE, *supra* note 12, where only 4.5 percent of the respondents indicated that defense attorneys will ask to be relieved of the case if the defendant refuses to plead guilty.
111. Canon of Professional Ethics 4: "A lawyer assigned as counsel for an indigent prisoner ought not to ask to be excused for any trivial reason, and should always exert his best efforts in his [client's] behalf." H. BLACK, BLACK'S LAW DICTIONARY.
112. Interview with Donald Modica, in Cleveland, Ohio, June 4, 1971.
113. *Continuances in Cook County, supra* note 24, at 281.
114. Manuel Zapata, however, a defense attorney who is frequently the adversary of North, contended that he delays cases hoping that the defendant will get a better offer. Interviews with Steven North and Manuel Zapata, in New York City, Oct. 12, 1970.
115. OAKS & LEHMAN, *supra* note 108, at 44–45.

realistically support, overcharging has occurred. This may happen when there is a hunch that the accused has committed a serious offense but the available evidence is not sufficient to convict for the offense charged; it is only enough to convict for a lesser included offense.[116] The evidence may be unavailable for any number of reasons: (1) it does not exist; (2) the police have been unable to come up with it; (3) witnesses refuse to cooperate with the police; (4) evidentiary rules or constitutional provisions prohibit use of the evidence. Even if the evidence is readily available and admissible, the witnesses for the state may not be credible, and there may be little likelihood that they will be believed by a jury. At any rate, rarely are the facts surrounding a crime so clear-cut that the prosecutor does not, in fact, have his choice of what offense to prosecute. Even when there is a violent attack on an individual, the prosecution has its choice of numerous charges ranging from attempted murder to simple assault, and the penalties will vary depending upon the seriousness of the offense. All of these are factors that go into a determination of what is the proper charge.

Overcharging is a common occurrence. Often a defendant is overcharged simply because the prosecutors in the jurisdiction do not adequately screen cases, preferring instead, usually for lack of time and manpower, to rely upon the police version and recommendation. In Philadelphia and Baltimore[117] such a practice is followed: it is not until after the preliminary hearing that the prosecutor has an opportunity to screen the case. Mindful of the problems of this system, the Maryland state's attorney is attempting to initiate a program that involves the screening of cases prior to the

---

116. *See generally* Alschuler, *The Prosecutor's Role in Plea Bargaining,* 36 U. CHI. L. REV. 50 (1968).

117. Interview with James Crawford, First Assistant District Attorney, in Philadelphia, Dec. 1, 1970. In Philadelphia, there is no case screening prior to the preliminary hearing and the hearing is held on the charges framed by the police. After the preliminary hearing, screening of cases is done through a program called pre–indictment probation. If a defendant has no prior record or a very limited prior record, and then he is charged with a nonviolent felony, the defendant appears before Judge Hoffman. In most instances the defendant is placed on probation, and the charges are dropped. If the defendant is in difficulty at another time within the probationary period, he will be charged with two criminal offenses. Approximately sixty cases a week are handled through this program. Interview with Karen Parish, Administrative Assistant to James Crawford, in Philadelphia, April 5, 1971. In Philadelphia, according to Vincent Zaccardi, of the Public Defender's Office, there is need for more thorough case screening prior to the preliminary hearing, because the police arrest too many people. Approximately two-thirds of the defendants represented by the defen-

preliminary hearing.[118] Even though prosecutors recognize the existence of overcharging, they are also aware that the charge will be corrected at a later time. Some prosecutors even consider it a desirable tactic because it leaves room for bargaining with a defense attorney. One Boston prosecutor expressed the belief that defense attorneys consider overcharging beneficial, for once they get the charge reduced, they have something to give their clients to demonstrate they are working in the client's best interest.[119]

Although the maneuvering process required by overcharging may be acceptable to both sides, it takes time. This sows the seeds for delay and clogged dockets. As long as the defendant is free during this time, he is unlikely to complain about the delay. In Los Angeles, extensive screening by the prosecutor's office prior to the filing of formal charges has almost eliminated overcharging and has significantly reduced delay. As a result of this screening process, over half the cases that originate as felonies from police arrests and private complaints are immediately reduced to misdemeanor charges. Consequently they never get into the felony court and

---

der's organization are either acquitted of the charges at trial or the charges against them are dropped. Interview with Vincent Zaccardi, Chief Public Defender, in Philadelphia, Dec. 1, 1970.

In Baltimore, cases are also screened after the preliminary hearing. If the prosecutor does not believe that a case belongs in the felony court even though probable cause has been found, the case will be remanded to the misdemeanor court. Interview with Joseph Koutz, Assistant State's Attorney, in Baltimore, April 7, 1971.

In Boston, Assistant Prosecutor Robert Snider engages in an informal type of screening. In a case where the defendants were charged with receiving a stolen vehicle, the defendants were also in possession of large amounts of drugs. Rather than waste time with the automobile case, the prosecutor was interested in obtaining a conviction for the more serious offense. Interview with Robert Snider in Boston, April 13, 1971.

Additionally, the need for screening is pointed out by Judge Neil Riley, Minneapolis Municipal Judge.

One of the weaknesses of our system of justice is that defendants who never should have been prosecuted have no right to redress. Their lost wages and attorneys fees simply come out of their own pocket. One wonders if the community were to be held liable for these expenses, complaints would be more carefully screened. LEAGUE OF WOMEN VOTERS OF MINNEAPOLIS, HENNEPIN COUNTY MUNICIPAL COURT 28 (1971).

118. Interview with Joseph Koutz, Assistant State's Attorney, in Baltimore, April 7, 1971.

119. Interview with Robert Snider, Assistant Prosecutor, in Boston, April

clog that docket.[120] As a result, Los Angeles is disposing of felony cases within 105 to 120 days after the arrest,[121] significantly less time than that required in most urban centers in this country.

The paucity of lawyers who dominate the criminal courts is another natural reason for the delays in the criminal process.[122] In many courts a small number of attorneys represent a large percentage of the nonindigent

---

12, 1971. According to another prosecutor, overcharging results only when a defendant is connected with organized crime. In such instances it seems justified because the organization guarantees the defendant's bail, pays the attorney fees, and pays the wife of a defendant who must eventually go to jail. Interview with Geoffrey Gaulkin, Hudson County Prosecutor, in Jersey City, New Jersey, Nov. 30, 1970.

However, Thomas Chittenden of the New York State Crime Control Planning Commission has tried to stress to the prosecutors of the cities in upstate New York that overcharging impedes the prosecutor in his job. Rather than pleading guilty, defense attorneys delay a case until witnesses disappear. As a result the prosecutor cannot move his caseload quickly. Interview with Thomas Chittenden, in New York City, Oct. 13, 1970.

120. Interview with George Trammell III, Assistant Prosecutor, in Los Angeles, Nov. 15, 1970. If the defendant does not wish to plead guilty to the reduced charge of a misdemeanor, then the case is referred to the misdemeanor court. The defendant is faced with a meaningful charge and may choose accordingly.

121. Sentencing is not included within the figure of 105 to 120 days. Pursuant to California law, if a defendant demands a speedy trial, his case must come to trial within 85 days. The initial appearance must be within 48 hours of arrest. Within a maximum of 5 days after the initial appearance, a preliminary hearing must be held. If the defendant is bound over for an arraignment, then the information must be filed within 15 days of the preliminary hearing. And the trial must commence no later than 60 days after the preliminary hearing. The difference between the actual and the statutory time is accounted for by waivers by the defendant. Interview with George Trammell III, Assistant Prosecutor, in Los Angeles, Dec. 11, 1970.

In Baltimore, the prosecutor's office and the assignment commissioner are attempting to bring cases to trial within 60 days of the assignment of counsel. In Boston the most important factor in bringing a case to trial remains the attorney's schedule.

122. When there are few attorneys who do criminal work on a retained basis, delay results because defense attorneys will ask for continuances when they are involved in another trial. For example, the assistant assignment commissioner in Boston, Massachusetts, related the schedule of one attorney. During the week of April 12, 1971, the

defendants.[123] In Cleveland, for instance, twelve lawyers are counsel of record in about one-half of the pending felony cases in which a private attorney is retained.[124] What this means to the entire docket is staggering; what it means to the clients who have retained these attorneys is an automatic delay of not less than eleven months. A defendant who retained one of the twelve and was in jail on a nonbailable charge was asked whether he was aware of the delay that awaited his case, simply because of his lawyer's caseload. He responded that he was well aware of the consequences of his choice but felt that the services of the particular attorney were well worth the wait. Such monopolization of the criminal docket, coupled with the archaic methods for scheduling cases, insures that the accompanying delay will affect the entire calendar of docketed cases, not just those in which the twelve attorneys are involved.[125]

Another source of delay, little known to the public, is that many attor-

---

attorney had one case that was to take three days to complete. He was scheduled to go to trial on the fourth day of that week in another Boston case. However, on that same day, he was scheduled to try a murder case in Worcester, Massachusetts. As a result, the case that was to start on Thursday in Boston had to be continued indefinitely. Interview with Leo Manning, Assistant Assignment Commissioner, in Boston, April 13, 1971.

123. Each city has one or more attorneys who handle a disproportionate share of the criminal defense work: in Philadelphia, Cecil Moore and Tom McBride; in Jersey City, Raymond Brown; in Baltimore, Morris Kaplan; and in Cleveland, Charles Fleming, James Willis, Donald Peppers, and Stanley Tolliver. See also Continuances in Cook County, supra 24, at 266.

124. Cleveland Plain Dealer, Mar. 28, 1971, at 11, col. 1; telephone conversation with Thomas S. Andrzejewski, Cleveland Plain Dealer reporter, on July 29, 1971.

125. One attorney has suggested that rather than reducing the number of criminal cases which a defense attorney can handle, which in effect would penalize those defense attorneys who have been successful in the criminal practice, substantial reform is the answer. Presumably, within the ambit of appropriate reform is the need for the development of better means for scheduling cases. Cleveland Plain Dealer, April 12, 1971, § B, at 2, col. 5.

Utilization of computers in scheduling cases on an hour-by-hour basis in courtrooms is desirable. Further, it should be possible to avoid requiring lawyers and witnesses having to spend numerous hours waiting in hallways for a courtroom to become available. See Justice on Trial, NEWSWEEK, Mar. 8, 1971, at 46. An "Appearance Control Project" is being tested in New York City. It places all witnesses on

neys will not permit a case to be resolved until their fees have been completely paid. Our survey of attorneys in eighteen major cities throughout the country found this to be a general practice.[126] It is not unusual for a defendant to appear on the date set for hearing or trial and to be reminded by his attorney of the remaining fee. If the defendant is unable to pay in full at that time, the attorney merely has the case continued to a later date. Similarly, attorneys obtain delays to permit their bailed clients to continue working in order to earn enough money to pay the fee.[127] Certainly, lawyers are entitled to their fees, but they should not be permitted to manipulate a court's calendar and turn the court into a bill-collecting agency. Because collecting fees from a criminal defendant is so difficult, it is understandable why attorneys attempt to use delay as a means of securing the fee.[128] What is difficult to fathom, however, is why judges throughout the country permit them to do so at the expense of efficient court operation.

Mayor John Lindsay of New York has suggested that lay administrators be given full responsibility for court management.[129] President Nixon drove the point home when he stated, "We must make it possible for judges to spend more time judging, by giving them professional help for administrative tasks."[130] Nevertheless, today the control of the day-to-day court man-

---

alert so that they need not spend long periods of time in court unnecessarily.

126. QUESTIONNAIRE, *supra* note 12. Better than 75 percent of the responses indicated that defense attorneys engage in pretrial delay in order to obtain their fees.

127. The attorney usually tells the defendant that he must appear on the date of the court appearance or else a bench warrant will be issued for the arrest of the defendant. The defendant appears, and if he does not have the fee, the case will again be continued. Little does the defendant know that few people are arrested on the issuance of a bench warrant. Interview with James Lacy, Vera Institute, in New York, Oct. 13, 1970.

128. TASK FORCE: THE COURTS, *supra* note 5, at 86; *Continuances in Cook County,* supra note 24, at 265.

129. Statement of John V. Lindsay, Administrative Board of the Judicial Conference of the State of New York, in New York, Oct. 9, 1970.

130. N. Y. Times, Mar. 12, 1971, at 18, col. 1. The Institute for Court Management at the Denver University Law Center offers a twenty-six-week course in court administration. This is the outgrowth of suggestions by Chief Justice Warren E. Burger to introduce modern management techniques into the court system. Ernest C. Friesen, Jr., director of the program, said: "Most courts have merely tried to grind out cases faster rather than trying to evaluate new needs, devise long range plans and reallocate resources." N. Y. Times, Dec. 12, 1970, at 32, col. 2.

agement rests within the discretion of the judges, who determine which practices will be tolerated and which will be penalized. In some multi-judge trial courts there is a statutory hierarchy providing for an administrative judge or a presiding or chief judge who may also serve in an administrative capacity. In any event, regardless of the particular structure of any given court, the management power resides with one or all of the judges of a court. Even with constitutional or statutory requirements that trial must begin within a certain number of days, the corrections for the shoddy practices tolerated by the courts will have to come from the judges themselves. This will mean that attorneys, as they assume a judgeship, will have to change their outlook and direct their efforts towards speedier court procedures.

Even if court management is turned over to a lay administrator, for this personnel change to have any positive impact the administrator must either assure himself that he is assuming control over a workable system or he must redesign it to a point of maximum efficiency. One of the areas requiring considerable attention is the trial scheduling process. In Philadelphia, for example, the defendant must go before a trial commissioner, who asks whether the defendant has an attorney. A defendant without an attorney is granted a three-week continuance to find one, because, according to one assistant trial commissioner, a trial date cannot be set until an attorney enters an appearance. If the defendant returns without an attorney, a further continuance is granted only if he is earning enough money to hire counsel; if not, he is sent to another room where a determination is made as to whether he qualifies for free legal representation.[131] Once the indigency determination is made, the trial commissioner sets a trial date. If, on the other hand, the defendant has retained counsel, the attorney and client appear before a trial commissioner who sets a trial date after the charges have been presented and a plea of not guilty has been entered.[132] Upon the appointed date, the parties must appear and await assignment to an available courtroom. In Baltimore no court appearance is required for scheduling purposes; the attorney, regardless of whether he is retained or appointed, merely receives a notice in the mail of the trial date and assigned courtroom.[133] This type of appearance-free scheduling is a time-saver for both the attorney and the defendant.

---

131. Interview with assistant assignment commissioner, in Philadelphia, April 5, 1971.

132. If a retained defense attorney appears, he can receive the trial date that he requests. He is limited, however, in that trial dates are usually set within four to seven weeks after the arraignment. Interview with John Grigsby, defense attorney, in Philadelphia, April 5, 1971.

133. At a pretrial conference the prosecutor and defense attorney agree on three or four alternative trial dates. The prosecutor goes to the assign-

Computerization of courts, court records, and schedulings may be utilized to assist the court administrator in his role. This will enable courts to keep better tabs on individual cases and on how long a defendant has been awaiting trial.[134] It will also enable courts to schedule cases in a logical way, taking into consideration whether a particular lawyer is already scheduled on another case in another courtroom on a given day.

The introduction of twentieth-century management techniques cannot, however, alleviate all problems. The finest new techniques and devices will not do the job adequately if their introduction is not coupled with a corresponding change of attitude on the part of the judiciary. Simply stated, the public has the right to demand that courts function in the interest of society and not as a private club for lawyers. The practice of permitting cases to linger until such time as the defense attorney and prosecutor agree to dispose of it or let it come to trial, or until such time as they can no longer agree to delay it, is not in the interest of society.[135] Postponements should be granted only upon a showing of good cause, and judges should require

---

ment commissioner's office to set a date; when one of the alternatives is available, the assignment commissioner mails a notice of day and courtroom to the defense attorney. Interview with Arthur Cheslock, Assistant State's Attorney, in Baltimore, April 7, 1971. In New York City one prosecutor has reported the difficulty he has encountered in getting an open trial court when he has a case ready for trial. The prosecutor's office in that city is divided into various divisions. Each division is given certain courtrooms which they are to utilize for that division's cases. For a prosecutor to obtain a courtroom he must go to his bureau chief. If, for example, all trial courts allocated for homicide cases are in use, a prosecutor in the homicide division must go to another bureau chief to see if any other courtrooms are available. Bureau chiefs are reluctant to say that they have an available courtroom. The chief prosecutor does not look favorably upon a bureau chief who cannot keep his trial courts busy with the appropriate cases.

In addition, in New York, a prosecutor with more seniority will get an available courtroom for trial prior to a less experienced prosecutor. This occurs regardless of the comparative age of the cases. Interview with New York City prosecutor, Nov. 20, 1970 (anonymity requested).

134. *E.g.*, a new computer system in Los Angeles will enable judges and law enforcement officials to make decisions more quickly because they will have access to all available information instantaneously. Gross & Rosenthal, *Bringing the Systems Approach to Criminal Justice,* 9:6 NATION'S CITIES 27 (June, 1971).

135. *Burger's Role,* U. S. NEWS AND WORLD REPORT, Jan. 14, 1969, at 14. When asked why a criminal case may take two to four years to complete, Justice Burger answered: "Part of the answer is that the legal

that good cause actually be demonstrated. Moreover, requests for postponements should not even be considered except under extraordinary circumstances,[136] and only when presented to the attention of the court at least
forty-eight hours prior to a scheduled hearing or trial. This would permit
the creation of an efficient "alert" system, so that police officers and other
witnesses who are expected in court could be notified in advance that the
case is being postponed.[137] Sufficient notice would also permit rescheduling
of the judge's time and assure better use of resources.

In present practice attorneys are so confident that their requests for a
continuance will be granted that they often inform their clients in advance
not to appear in court.[138] In some cities, the practice is so refined that a judge
has no role and is not even informed that a case is to be continued. The

---

profession must condemn and I repeat that—must condemn as un-
professional conduct, every tactic, whether by prosecution or defense
counsel, in which delay is used as a tactical weapon for selfish purposes."

136. Adjournments are cherished by defense attorneys. The apocryphal
story of the lawyer lying on his deathbed is apropos. When the priest
came to see the lawyer and asked him if there was anything that could
be done, the lawyer replied: "Yes, see if you can get me a continuance." Cleveland Plain Dealer, Mar. 12, 1971, § A, at 11, col. 1.

137. *Justice on Trial,* NEWSWEEK, Mar. 8, 1971, at 46. An "Appearance
Control Project" is being worked out that places police and other
witnesses on telephone alert, and they agree to show up within an hour
of notification. N.Y.L.J., Feb. 8, 1971, at 1, col. 6. Suggestions have
been made by various groups in New York City for lessening man-
hours for police and complaining witnesses by having the police officer
swear the complaint before a superior officer and then return to patrol.
Complainants and witnesses will just swear out an affidavit that will
release them from the pre–arraignment process. This plan has been
criticized by the Legal Aid Society. The Society contends that the
judge, without witnesses or the police officer present, cannot make a
fair bail determination.

All of this seems rather superficial when the real problem lies not
with the amount of bail or jail at pre-arraignment stage, but whether
the defendant really is charged and screened properly before he is
brought into the process.

138. In some instances the attorney may be so sure that a continuance will
be granted that he will not even appear to ask for the continuance. In
Boston, for example, on April 13, 1971, Ronald Milo appeared before
Judge Rose on charges of assault and battery with a deadly weapon.
When asked if he had an attorney, the defendant replied that his
attorney, Harvey Brawer, had a previous commitment for the same
day. Automatically, the case was continued for one week.

attorney merely calls the trial commissioner and requests that a specific case be removed from the active docket for that term of court. Unless there is active opposition from the prosecutor's office, the attorney need not even explain the reason for his action. Again, the rationale given for permitting the extended time period is to give the two parties a chance to reach an acceptable agreement and avoid trial. However, permitting the defense attorney to pull a case from the active docket means that there will be no action on that case for the remainder of the term and that it is unlikely that the two attorneys will even discuss it before its restoration to the active docket in the succeeding term.

Delay has become such an accepted part of criminal court practice that in the New York City Criminal Court, where the preliminary phases of felony cases are handled, each courtroom has been divided into two parts. In the front part, which is the large and traditional courtroom, a judge reads the docket for the day to determine whether anyone is ready to proceed with his case. In the back, often a converted washroom or robing room, another judge sits and waits to hear any cases which the defense and prosecuting attorneys agree are ready for presentation.[139] Unfortunately, the common complaint of these judges is that few of the scheduled cases are ever ready for trial. Two judges described sitting in the back for an entire morning without ever receiving a case, while in the front the judge was calling hundreds of criminal cases on which no one was prepared to proceed.

TOWARDS A SOLUTION

Judicial acceptance of a management and supervisory role within the courts is the first step in the solution of the problem of delay. A judge's reluctance to deny attorneys all of their postponement requests is understandable, but it is essential that judges begin to realize that these pretrial decisions affect the quality of justice as much as the decisions made from the bench on procedural and evidentiary matters during a trial. In the

---

139. N. Y. Times, Nov. 11, 1969, at 49, col. 6. Former Presiding Justice Bernard Botein commented on the condition of the courts: "Some criminal court judges now are holding their sessions in robing rooms."

More recently, according to Judge Joel Tyler, in New York City, a courtroom is utilized to assure that both sides are ready to proceed to trial or ready to proceed on a motion hearing. The judge who presides in this court can send a case that is ready to proceed to one of four backup courts. Despite the fact that one judge is to assure that cases sent to the backup court are ready, cases are not always ready to proceed. Interview with Judge Joel Tyler, New York City Criminal Court, in New York City, June 1, 1971.

course of a trial, a judge is constantly forced to rule against one or the other attorney. The lawyers may object to and appeal these rulings, but a judge is largely unconcerned with the attorneys' reactions. If this attitude were transferred to getting a case to trial, the first step towards a realization of the constitutional ideal of a speedy trial would be achieved. This first step will be the hardest, because it involves the shedding of the judiciary's traditional role of noninvolvement in the management of his own court. It is far easier to sit back and wait for cases to slowly wind their way to the courtroom. Not only is it more comfortable, but noninvolvement in the mechanics of the justice system supports the aristocratic and intellectual image that judges have of themselves and that the public has come to accept. But more and more judges, led by Chief Justice Warren Burger, have come to realize that a judge's aloofness from the management of his court is helping to strangle the courts.[140] Judges are beginning to play a greater role in their courts. Although greater involvement will lessen the judiciary's popularity with the practicing bar, it will help to reverse the corrosion of the criminal justice system and will make possible the fulfillment of the constitutional ideal.[141]

Succeeding steps may be best taken through legislative enactment of time-line requirements for the disposition of criminal cases. In the absence of legislative action, part of the goal could be achieved through Supreme Court decisions interpreting the speedy trial provisions of the Constitution to mean that a defendant must be brought to trial within a specified number of days. Although such a decision would protect the rights of the defendant, this would resolve only part of the problem. It would have no effect upon the great bulk of cases where the extensive delay has been specifically sought by the defendant or his attorney. Legislatures, on the other hand, as the elected representatives of the people, are in a position to cover the entire

---

140. *What's Wrong with the Courts: The Chief Justice Speaks Out,* U. S. NEWS AND WORLD REPORT, Aug. 24, 1970, at 69. Chief Justice Burger, when asked about the cause of delay in regard to the judge's role, replied, "I hope efficient administration of the courts can be accomplished not simply by adding more judges, but by the more efficient use of judicial manpower and greater productivity. Improved management, and trained administrative personnel are the keys to greater productivity of judges."

141. According to an assistant prosecutor in one northeastern city, the assignment judge's sole concern is moving the backlog of unresolved cases. As a result, the judge has incurred the wrath of the prosecutors and defense attorneys by insisting that the cases proceed according to schedule.

field through the enactment of comprehensive standards and requirements. Instead of seeking ways to avoid the requirements, as local governments tend to do when confronted with Supreme Court decisions, it is more likely that local judges, lawyers, and prosecutors would direct their attention to implementing legislative requirements.

In 1971 United States Senator Sam J. Ervin, Jr., of North Carolina introduced a bill that would require trials in criminal cases within sixty days of the defendant's arrest.[142] The Federal Second Circuit Court of Appeals and some state courts recently adopted new speedy trial requirements emphasizing the rights of defendants who are unable to raise bail or are otherwise ineligible for bail.[143]

---

142. Speedy Trial Act of 1971, S. 895, 91 Cong., 1st Sess., § 3161(b)(1): The trial of a defendant charged with an offense against the United States shall be commenced as follows: "Within sixty days from the date the defendant is arrested or a summons is issued, except that if an information or indictment is filed, then within sixty days from the date of such filing." Senator Henry Jackson announced in December, 1971, that he would seek legislation requiring the states to submit plans which would enable the states to try criminal cases within sixty to ninety days. N. Y. Times, Dec. 8, 1971, at 50, col. 4.

143. The vanden Heuval Commission, which studied the conditions that caused the riots in the New York City jails, has suggested that if the courts do not mandate speedy trials, then the legislature must do so. *Agenda for 100 Days,* THE VILLAGE VOICE, Feb. 18, 1971, at 1, col.1.

The New York legislature in April, 1972, enacted speedy trial requirements just in time to forestall the operation of more stringent requirements which had been set by the New York Judicial Conference. Effective May 1, 1972, the prosecution must be ready for trial within six months. If not, charges will be dismissed. A defendant must be freed on bail or on his own recognizance if he is not brought to trial within three months of arrest. In misdemeanor cases with a possible sentence of more than three months, the prosecution must be ready for trial within ninety days, and on other misdemeanor charges the prosecution must be ready for trial within sixty days, or the charges will be dismissed. The provision does not apply to a defendant charged with homicide or to one who is serving a sentence for another crime.

Delay caused for the following reasons shall not be counted towards the time deadlines: (1) any reasonable delay resulting from proceedings to determine the defendant's competency; (2) the period during which the defendant is incompetent; (3) any delay resulting from an adjournment or continuance granted at the request of the defendant; (4) any reasonable delay resulting from an adjournment or continu-

The Ervin Bill and other measures which have been adopted in some states and federal courts are admirable as far as they go. They concentrate upon the rights of the defendant and protect those defendants who seek speedy justice and are victims of delay. However, these provisions barely dent the overall problem.

What is needed is comprehensive legislation requiring that a case be disposed of or come to trial within a specified period of time, irrespective of whether the defendant desires it or not. In order to emphasize the priority that must be given to jailed defendants, it is our recommendation that

---

ance granted to the prosecutor without the defendant's consent: (a) on a showing by the prosecutor that he needs a continuance to obtain evidence which he has been unable to obtain despite due diligence; (b) because of the absence or unavailability of the defendant; (c) because the defendant is detained in another jurisdiction; (d) because the defendant does not have an attorney and it is not the court's fault; (e) because of the defendant being joined for trial with another defendant, whose time for trial has not elapsed and good cause is shown for not granting a severance, and; (f) any other exceptional circumstances. N.Y.L.J., April 30, 1971, at 1, col. 6. The Second Circuit Court of Appeals on January 5, 1971, published new rules that are to go into effect on May 5, 1971. These rules are generally the same as the New York State Rules. Second Circuit Rules Regarding Prompt Disposition of Criminal Cases promulgated pursuant to 28 U.S.C.A. § 332, January 5, 1971.

Alternate Draft (Alt. 2) of the Proposed Amendments to Rule 45 of the Federal Rules of Criminal Procedure has suggested specific time limits for arraignments. If a defendant is prosecuted on an information, he is to be arraigned within 15 days from the date of the filing of the information if he is being held in custody, or within 30 days if he is not being held. The same time limits are suggested if the defendant is indicted. Trial is to be commenced within 90 days of arraignment, if the defendant is in custody, or 180 days, if the defendant is not in custody. Such time limits may be extended for good cause in the public interest. Committee on Rules of Practice and Procedure, Alternate Drafts of Proposed Amendment to Rule 45 Federal Rules Criminal Procedure (March 1971).

In Ohio, new rules to be effective January 1, 1972, provide that a defendant's case must be finally acted upon by the grand jury within 60 days after the case is bound over to the grand jury. All criminal cases must be tried within six months of indictment. OHIO SUP. R. 8.

In California 75 days after a defendant is held to answer trial is to begin. CAL. PEN. CODE § 1382. Trial is to begin 120 days after arrest in Illinois. ILL. ANN. STAT. ch. 38, § 103–5(a)(1965). In Iowa, a person must be indicted within 30 days after being held to answer; and

legislation be adopted requiring that cases in which the defendant is detained come to trial within 60 days of arrest, and within 120 days if the defendant is out on bail. Such legislation must include appropriate enforcement mechanisms to insure that the time requirements are met. The new standard adopted in New York State excuses the time requirement if the delay is caused by the defendant or his attorney. Permitting the defense the option of choosing a speedy trial or a delayed trial will not help to resolve the problems caused by delay in the justice system. The measures that are adopted must eliminate delay precipitated by the defense, as well as be protective of the defendants' rights.

To effectuate this legislation, the statute must include the imposition of penalties for failure to comply, and the judges must be willing to enforce the statute and its penalty provisions. If it is ascertained that the delay is directly attributable to the defendant himself and there has otherwise been adequate time for preparation, then the defendant can be compelled to go to trial. The Supreme Court has already determined that not every denial of a request for more time violates the constitutional rights of a defendant even if as a result of such denial he fails to offer evidence or is compelled to defend without counsel.[144] State courts have imposed similar requirements: "A defendant who fails and neglects to prepare his case for trial at the appointed time, although sufficient time has been provided for such preparation, cannot complain if the trial is had at the time appointed."[145]

Naturally, the defendant should not be forced to proceed to trial if the delay was not of his own making. If the delay is attributable to the defendant's lawyer, the defendant should not be forced to proceed without his attorney. Where counsel is responsible for a delay exceeding the statutory limitation, the penalties should be imposed on him and not on his client. Tying up the courts through delaying techniques is as much a disruption of the criminal justice process as is actual disruption of a courtroom pro-

---

then, within 60 days of indictment, the defendant must be brought to trial. IOWA CODE ANN. § § 795.1–2 (Supp. 1966). Within six months from imprisonment or bail, one must be brought to trial in Massachusetts. MASS. GEN. LAWS ANN. ch. 277, § 72 (1956). In Nevada, one must be indicted or charged by way of information within 15 days after held to answer for a crime. Within 60 days after indicted or information is filed, trial must begin. NEV. REV. STAT. § 178.556 (1967). In Washington, one must be indicted or information filed within 30 days from date held to answer, and within 60 days from indictment trial must begin. WASH. REV. CODE § § 10.37.020, 10.46.010 (1961).

144. Ungar v. Sarafite, 376 U. S. 575 (1964).
145. Altobella v. Priest, 385 P.2d 585, 586 (Colo. 1963).

ceeding, and should be treated accordingly. The contempt power of the courts should be brought to bear upon those attorneys who, though given adequate time to prepare for a case, seek to delay beyond the period allowed by statute. This was recently done in a Cleveland court when a judge cited a defense attorney for contempt when the attorney could not be reached for notification that his case was to be tried.[146] A fine should be an adequate penalty to deter attorneys from engaging in such dilatory tactics, although when an attorney makes a practice of initiating prohibited delaying techniques in the same case or in many of his cases, then a jail sentence may be appropriate. Without provision for a possible jail sentence, there is the danger that the fine could be looked upon as a cost of doing business, and the attorney could pass the fine on to his client by way of a larger fee. The attorney would then be in a position to defeat the entire statutory scheme.

Where delay is sought because of a missing witness, then a different result should occur. If counsel can show the court that diligence has been exercised in attempting to find the witness, this would create one of the extraordinary situations in which the defense should be permitted more time without penalty. On the other hand, if the witness has been properly subpoenaed and has simply failed to appear, the judge can expedite matters by having the witness brought before the court for contempt and either imposing a penalty or permitting him to purge his contempt by testifying.

Attorneys will surely complain that such procedures would cut down the number of cases in which they are able to serve as counsel, thus seriously diminishing their opportunity to make a living. We are convinced that the proposed legislation would not have such an effect. An attorney acquires clients continuously, but at different times. If he is compelled to dispose of his pending cases within 60 or 120 days, he will probably be able to represent as many clients as he does under the present system. Whatever happens to his income, there is no justification for giving a lawyer an opportunity

---

146. Judge Angellota of Cuyahoga County Common Pleas Court cited Donald Peppers, a defense attorney, for contempt of court because Peppers did not appear at the appropriate time to represent Douglas Powell. Peppers was absent because he was in trial in Akron, but the court was unable to learn of this fact although the clerks and the judge tried several times to reach Peppers' office. The judge commented that an attorney who handled so many cases should have better telephone communication. Further, the judge felt that Peppers was an attorney with very sloppy habits; the judge pointed to the fact that Peppers was ten minutes late to the subsequent contempt proceeding. The judge fined Peppers $100 but said that he would set aside the fine if Peppers would admit his wrongdoing. The case is currently being appealed.

to manipulate the legal process for his own gain, thus denying defendants and community alike a court system that is capable of functioning fairly. There is no reason to believe that speeding up the process creates more trial situations,[147] but even if it does, some increase in the actual trial load can be accommodated by the present number of judges. Once the justice system demonstrates its ability to use its manpower and courtrooms wisely and does provide the opportunity for speedy trials, defendants and their attorneys will realize that it is still not in their interest to go to trial. Accommodation will remain the most beneficial way for most defendants and their attorneys to proceed.

Where the delay has been occasioned by the state and is not attributable to the defense, the charges against the defendant should be dismissed because the prosecution did not adhere to the statutory and constitutional requirements. Individual prosecutors should be subject to the same penalties imposed upon defense attorneys, when the delay is the prosecutor's personal fault. Dismissal should prove to be an effective remedy when the fault lies within the system. Dismissals for failure to comply with the statute will require explanations to the public from judges and prosecutors; if a significant number of dismissals occur, demands for explanations will not be long in coming.

---

147. In response to the New York rule which will require that a case be brought to trial within six months of arrest, one prosecutor, Eliot Golden, Chief Assistant to the Kings County District Attorney, stated that the court rule might impede the speedy dispositions of criminal cases. Defendants will play a "numbers game" and not engage in plea bargaining, hoping that the state will not be able to come to trial within six months of arrest and that as a result the case will be dismissed. N.Y.L.J., April 30, 1971, at 1, col. 1.

3/ THE DECISION TO CHARGE: A PROTRACTED PROCESS

Many Americans believe that if they witness a crime, all they have to do is notify the police and the criminal will be arrested, prosecuted, and convicted. Few are aware of how involved they, as witnesses, will become in the process and how great their inconvenience will be.[1] They soon realize that the mere witnessing of a crime will not automatically result in the conviction and incarceration of the criminal. The police will not arrest for every violation, notwithstanding the existence of statutorily imposed duties to arrest, nor will they even respond to every crime reported.[2] This may come as a shock to most white suburban Americans, but not to the residents of inner-city, black ghettos.[3]

---

1. "Every day the court backlogs leave innocent men in jails and guilty ones on the streets. Witnesses and victims wait hours for cases that are never called. The claims and causes of the injured remain unheard." N. Y. Times, Mar. 8, 1971, at 1, col. 3.
2. "The police must make important judgments about what conduct is in fact criminal; about the allocation of scarce resources; and about the gravity of each individual incident and the proper steps that should be taken." PRESIDENT'S COMMISSION ON LAW ENFORCEMENT AND ADMINISTRATION OF JUSTICE, TASK FORCE REPORT: THE POLICE 14 (1967) [hereinafter cited as THE POLICE].
3. *Cf.* Byrn, *Urban Law Enforcement: A Plea from the Ghetto,* 5 CRIM. L. BULL. 125, 128 (1969). Mayor Lindsay's Criminal Justice Coordinating Council found that the disparity in the amount of crime reported in various sections of the city (e.g., fifty times more reported violent felonies in the North Harlem section than in the Bay Ridge section of Brooklyn) was tremendous. He added, "To create the level of security in North Harlem that exists in Bay Ridge, 98 percent of the crime in North Harlem would have to be eliminated." The report cited a lack of cooperation among the various agencies responsible for

89

Furthermore, not all of those arrested will be charged; not all of those charged, even if guilty, will be convicted; and not all of those convicted will be imprisoned.[4] Figures for New York City indicate than an arrest is made in only one of every four felonies committed and that only one in five of those arrested is ever brought to court on a felony indictment. The charges against many of the one out of twenty criminals who get to court are reduced prior to trial.[5] The criminal system is faced each day with hard choices as to how to allocate and utilize its limited resources to the greatest community advantage. Police departments do not have the manpower to arrest all wrongdoers, nor are there enough judges, prosecutors, or defense attorneys to cope with all those persons guilty of criminal conduct.[6]

The laws of the states and federal governments, moreover, are replete with too many criminal offenses.[7] Each time a new social problem arises that

---

    criminal justice in the city: police, prosecutors, courts, probation and parole agencies, and the jails. N. Y. Times, Mar. 14, 1971, at 1, col. 6.

4. *See, e.g.,* Trammell III, *Control of System Policy and Practice by the Office of District Attorney in Brooklyn and Los Angeles,* 5 THE PROSECUTOR 242, 245 (1969) [hereinafter cited as Trammell].

5. *Logjam in Our Courts,* LIFE, Aug. 7, 1970, at 18, 20.
    See also New York Criminal Justice Coordinating Council Report:
        To back its conclusion that the city's "crime control system poses little threat to the average criminal," the council cited statistics showing that only 18 percent of all reported robberies, 7 percent of all reported burglaries and 6 percent of reported grand larcenies result in arrest. Of all those arrested on felony or misdemeanor charges, the report went on, only 32 percent are found guilty of any charge. N. Y. Times, Mar. 14, 1971, at 1, col. 6.
    The New York detective bureau has been singularly ineffective in solving cases assigned to them: "A study of crimes reported to police during the first six months of 1967 found that only 5.58 percent of the robberies, 1.35 percent of the burglaries and 2.2 percent of the grand larcenies assigned to detectives resulted in arrests by them." N. Y. Times, June 11, 1971, at 39, col. 1.

6. Robert N. C. Nix, Jr., a young black Philadelphia judge, has called for a reevaluation of the police role and arrests. Nix said: "It's ridiculous to think you are going to be able to make an arrest for every crime that's committed. If that was the case, we'd need hundreds and hundreds of more judges and courtrooms and everything else." N. Y. Times, Mar. 8, 1971, at 1, col. 3.

7. "The penal statutes are legion in number. They are an historical collection. They seem to include the panacea for every ill. If there is something wrong, someone will pass a law to correct it, and the law is just as likely to carry a criminal sanction." Breitel, *Controls in*

angers the majority, legislatures are all too willing to enact add...
criminal offenses.[8] Such simplistic treatment of complex human problems
forces the police and particularly the entire judicial process into the center
of the social upheaval, and they become far more accessible targets for
disruption than does the legislature. The decision to label marijuana users
as criminals forced the police and the courts into the center of the genera-
tion gap and provided dissidents with a highly visible target.[9] The lack of
adequate social agencies to handle domestic and neighborhood disputes and
the inability of our society to come to grips with the human problems which
generate these disputes relegate the police and the courts to the role of
arbiter in the highly volatile and oppressed inner-city areas of this country.
Neither the police nor the courts have the training, means, aptitude, or
disposition to deal effectively with these and other social problems, but they

---

Criminal Law Enforcement, 27 U. CHI. L. REV. 427, 431 (1960)
[hereinafter cited as *Criminal Law Enforcement*].

8. Many court reformers have called for legislative action to eliminate
various types of crimes from the criminal court system.

Cases involving drinking account for about one-third of the arrests
made; these, according to former Judge Bernard Botein, should be
handled as a medical rather than as a judicial problem. Other
categories of cases that could be taken from the criminal courts,
according to Judge Botein, are those involving prostitution, narcotics, traffic (this has been done in New York City), homosexuals and
housing violations. N. Y. Times, Aug. 23, 1970, § 4, at 10, col. 1.
President Nixon echoed the same sentiments at a national judiciary
conference on March 11, 1971, saying, "Minor traffic offenses, loiter-
ing, drunkenness and other 'victimless' crimes should be taken out of
the courts and handled by other agencies." N. Y. Times, Mar. 12,
1971, at 1, col. 1. *See generally* THE SAN FRANCISCO COMMITTEE ON
CRIME, A REPORT ON NON-VICTIM CRIME IN SAN FRANCISCO 13,
§ 11–15 (1971).

9. In recent years the wisdom of imposing severe penalties for marijuana
use has been increasingly questioned.

Marijuana use is a "crime without a victim." There is therefore no
complainant. Hence police must find new ways of apprehending
these offenders since no citizen will be complaining of the pro-
scribed conduct. This has forced police to use such tactics as agents
provocateurs, harassment, and entrapment. Some of the uses of
these techniques are contrary to our sense of justice. To allow a
policeman to entice a citizen into crime is not only unjust but also
signifies the illegitimate use of power. . . . These police practices can
only increase disrespect for the law while in no way effectively
controlling the use of marijuana. Cavalluzzo, *Marijuana, The Law
and the Courts,* 8 OSGOODE HALL L. J. 215, 231 (1970).

all too often are the only agencies available.[10]

Coupled with the fact that there are too few police and legal personnel to cope with the existing high crime rate, the additional role of social arbiter makes decisions about allocating the available resources even more difficult. The decisions that are made often lack wisdom and reason and have led to the chaos that exists in the criminal justice process.

THE CHARGING PROCESS

The charging process—a reasonably uncomplicated procedure of common law that involved at most two steps, a court and a grand jury—has been refined by our society into a highly complicated and time-consuming process. While the charging process was developed in England before the existence of police departments and state's attorneys, called prosecutors, its modern counterpart has simply incorporated the police and prosecutor into the decision to charge and made it a four-step process. As a result, the charging of a felony suspect has become painfully complicated and consumes a great deal of time from when the police become aware of a criminal act and of who the criminal is, until the formally charged defendant must enter a plea of guilty or not guilty before a judge with authority to dispose of the case.[11]

The initial decision to charge a person with a crime is made by the police and the prosecutor. This decision is subsequently reviewed by a court and finally, in most states, by a grand jury. Although the decision of each of these agencies is predicated upon different concerns and interests, essentially they duplicate one another's work. When all have completed their responsibilities for charging, the criminal justice process is just then ready to begin the long and arduous task of determining whether the defendant is innocent or guilty.

THE ROLE OF THE POLICE

Important decisions affecting the entire criminal justice process are made by the commanding officials within the police department. Policy decisions

---

10. The domestic dispute has placed an overwhelming burden on the large metropolitan police force. In one urban area, during the period from October 13, 1966, to November 9, 1966, one out of every three calls for police assistance was to quell a disturbance. Domestic disputes are considered a form of disturbance. Parnas, *The Police Response to the Domestic Disturbance,* 1967 WIS. L. REV. 914.

11. As of October, 1970, over half of the prisoners in the New York City jails had been there at least three months waiting for disposition of

such as deployment of forces and responses to citizen calls will, in large part, set the tone for the selection of crimes to be prosecuted.[12] Police departments, faced with rising crime rates and too few men because of money shortages, must make hard decisions regarding the best way to use the limited number of men and still maintain order within the community.[13] Cities often make a conscious choice to commit a high percentage of men to those areas where the greatest number of crimes are reported. By saturating an area with policemen, it is hoped that the display of force and the extensive visibility of the police will deter persons from committing crimes. But at the same time that more violators in the area are apprehended, a certain amount of crime in other parts of the city goes undetected. Even though the decision to deploy in this manner is logical and necessary, it means that perpetrators of identical crimes committed in different parts of the city will not be treated alike.[14]

The policy with respect to responding to citizen complaints and calls for

their cases, and more than 40 percent of the prisoners had been incarcerated for over twelve months without a trial. N. Y. Times, March 8, 1971, at 1, col. 5.

12. Because of the large number of penal statutes, all crime cannot be prosecuted. As a result, police forces are strategically deployed, and deployment changes are made from time to time to meet the prevailing conditions. The manner in which forces are deployed partially decides what crimes, and which criminals, will be prosecuted. *Criminal Law Enforcement, supra* note 7, at 431. In New York, the police deploy 30 men to the Auto Squad. Their job is to solve and prevent auto thefts. Last year, in New York, there were 95,000 auto thefts. Chicago's Auto Squad has 150 men, who were faced with 37,000 thefts last year. Hellman, *Stealing Cars Is a Growth Industry,* N. Y. Times, June 20, 1971 (Magazine), at 42. By utilizing manpower in this manner, the officers are diverted from enforcing other statutes.

13. Those who decide upon the deployment of police forces make the decision by trying to maximize the use of limited men, equipment, and resources. Kadish, *Legal Norm and Discretion in the Police and Sentencing Processes,* 75 HARV. L. REV. 904, 908 (1962).

14. At least in one large city with a sizeable Negro population the Negro press commonly exploits the charge that the police are harder on Negroes than on whites, a charge that finds apparent support in the far greater percentage of Negroes arrested. The facts, however, suggest a subtler kind of discrimination. . . . Rather than overly strict enforcement against Negroes, what commonly is involved is a calculated nonenforcement of certain laws against the Negro population, justified on the ground that a lesser standard of morality prevails. . . . This, of course, constitutes a form of discrimination

help will similarly shape the number of crimes that are detected and the criminals who are prosecuted. In Milwaukee, motivated by a belief that answering calls promotes citizen participation in law enforcement that far outweighs any resulting inefficiency, police policy dictates that all citizen complaints and calls for assistance be answered. The response is the dispatch of a squad car to investigate the complaint.[15] Naturally, some of the calls are without merit and divert the police officers from other more essential tasks. However, it does create a feeling of security that the police are, in fact, available if needed, and this in turn is believed to create among the people a willingness to cooperate with the police and to assist in law enforcement.

Detroit police, on the other hand, facing urban problems of greater intensity than those in Milwaukee, do not respond to all citizen calls. The police dispatcher, after gleaning the information from a caller, will order a squad car to investigate a complaint only if the dispatcher believes that an emergency situation exists which warrants immediate police action,[16] such as a report of violence or the commission of a serious felony. If the dispatcher does not believe that the caller requires immediate police intervention, he will instruct the caller to come to the police station and fill out a complaint. Consequently, there will be no response if the information provided by the caller is insufficient to determine whether a crime has been or is about to be committed.[17] Similarly, where it is apparent that the caller as well as the person he is complaining about are in the wrong, and there is no report of violence or threat of violence, the police will decline to respond.[18]

As violent crimes that require an immediate police response increase, police departments throughout the country are developing policies that free them from matters which are ancillary to their main purpose of preserving peace while preventing and detecting crime. The amount of police manpower in every city that is diverted from keeping the peace and is occupied in providing other services is astounding.[19] Consequently, more and more

---

no less significant than the commonly charged overzealous arrest of Negroes. *Id.* at 913–14.

15. AMERICAN BAR FOUNDATION, THE ADMINISTRATION OF CRIMINAL JUSTICE IN THE UNITED STATES, PILOT PROJECT REPORT: Vol. 5, MILWAUKEE COUNTY, WISCONSIN 1–11.

16. AMERICAN BAR FOUNDATION, THE ADMINISTRATION OF CRIMINAL JUSTICE IN THE UNITED STATES, PILOT PROJECT REPORT: Vol. 2, DETROIT, MICHIGAN 50.

17. *Id.* at 52–54.

18. *Id.*

19. Livermore, *Policing,* 55 MINN. L. REV. 649, 683–710 (1971) [hereinafter cited as *Policing*].

callers are being directed to contact appropriate social agencies in lieu of police intervention. Formerly, for instance, it was not unusual for the police to receive and respond to calls concerning stray animals. Today, in many cities, the caller is advised to notify the animal protective agency. Similarly, where the normal response of the past would have been to dispatch a police car to investigate all traffic accidents, the Cleveland police today respond only if there is a report that someone has been injured or that traffic is being blocked.[20]

Aside from deployment and dispatching policies, the role of the police hierarchy in the apprehension and charging of criminals is concentrated on how to choose men for the force, how to train them, and what attitudes towards the job of policing to exhibit for the men on the beat.

THE POLICE OFFICER ON THE BEAT

The difficult decisions that initiate the criminal process are made by the officer on the beat. Theoretically guided by department policies, he is, in fact, the single person who can start or abort the entire process at this inchoate stage by his determination of whether or not to enforce a particular law by arresting the perpetrator of the act.[21]

A police officer may arrest any person who commits a crime in his presence.[22] Even though the officer has not witnessed the crime, if the crime is a felony he is permitted to arrest if there is probable cause to believe that a crime has been committed and that the suspect is the guilty party.[23] Although most departments have regulations requiring an officer to arrest all suspects when these requirements are fulfilled, it simply is not done. Not only does the officer bring to his job the requirements of the department and

---

20. A similar policy is being utilized in Minneapolis. *Id.* at 653.

21. One study has revealed at least three broad areas where the police know that a crime has been committed and oftentimes know the offender, but fail to make the arrest for "reasons which seem to reflect the police officer's conception of his job." These areas of nonenforcement include: narcotics law violators who inform against other "more serious" violators, felonious assailants whose victims do not sign a complaint, and numbers racketeers. Goldstein, *Police Discretion Not to Invoke the Criminal Process: Low Visibility Decisions in the Administration of Justice,* 69 YALE L. J. 543 (1960) [hereinafter cited as *Low Visibility*].

22. For a comparison of arrest standards in the absence of a warrant, *see* D. KARLEN, ANGLO-AMERICAN CRIMINAL JUSTICE 111–12 (1967) [hereinafter cited as KARLEN].

23. *Id.* at 111–12.

the training that he has received, such as that may be, but like any other citizen he is also guided by his own attitudes, prejudices, and inclinations, which are likely to play a greater role in determining how he acts than does department policy.[24] Since the immediate decision to arrest can only be made on the spot by the officer, society can only hope that he will be guided by its rules, regulations, and policies.

Even though the primary obligation of the beat officer ends after the arrest is made and he is relegated to the role of witness while the other components of the criminal justice machinery take over, the police officer usually believes that he has a continued stake in the case. Arresting a suspect, especially after viewing the crime itself or the damage left in the wake of a crime, is a highly personal matter. As far as the policeman is concerned, the only way to vindicate his decision to arrest is through conviction of the offender.[25]

Conviction will be achieved on the basis of evidence that is admissible in a court of law. Although the admissibility of evidence is a technical legal question to be decided by judges, the police officer must be cognizant at all times of evidentiary considerations.[26] Nothing is more frustrating to the police, and incomprehensible to the general public, than when seemingly reliable evidence is excluded from a trial, thereby precluding the conviction of an obviously guilty person.

The exclusion of evidence is based upon the Bill of Rights guarantee that

---

24. *See generally* LaFave, Arrest: The Decision to Take a Suspect into Custody (1965) [hereinafter cited as Arrest].

25. One study revealed that:

   Distortion of the facts becomes the most persuasive and the most significant of abuses. The police ethic justifies any action which is intended to maintain order or to convict any wrongdoer (i.e., anyone actually or potentially guilty of crime). In studying search and seizure, for example, we found that the police tend to justify a search made "in good faith"—really looking for a crime—regardless of whether it is a lawful search or not. Once again, the facts are distorted so as to justify the search in the eyes of the courts. . . .
   P. Chevigny, Police Power—Police Abuses in New York City 277–78 (1969) [hereinafter cited as Police Power].

26. In a report to Mayor Lindsay, Manhattan District Attorney Frank S. Hogan made recommendations to cut delays in the criminal process. Included was the suggestion that police concentrate on those crimes where there is a greater chance for conviction. "Implying that the Police Department had a quota system for arrests, Mr. Hogan suggested a reduction in 'poor arrests' that produce 'unprosecutable or tenuous cases,' and called for a halt to mass arrests of suspected drug addicts and prostitutes." N. Y. Times, Feb. 22, 1971, at 33, col. 6.

all persons shall be secure from unreasonable searches and seizures.[27] Without this guarantee, all of us would be devoid of every shred of privacy. Our homes and our persons would be subject to continuous intrusions by government officials, and our ability to live as free men would be nonexistent.[28] In order to make the guarantee a real and meaningful protection, the courts have devised specific rules that define the ways in which the evidence to be used in a criminal case may be legitimately acquired. For these rules to exist and protect the innocent, they must be applied to all members of the community, and that includes the guilty. Supreme Court Justice William O. Douglas summed up the dilemma and the frustration over a decade ago when he said, "A rule protective of law-abiding citizens is not apt to flourish where its advocates are usually criminals." [29]

If the officer arrests a suspect and the arrest does not measure up to minimal constitutional standards, any evidence obtained from a search incidental to that arrest will not be admissible in court.[30] Thus, one purpose of the exclusionary rules is to insure that the police themselves obey the law while enforcing it. Whether the exclusionary rule is effective in this respect has been a point of great debate. There are those who contend that the rules are disregarded by the police and that in deciding whether to arrest, the sole criterion used by the officer is whether the arrest serves the interest of the police department, as he perceives it.[31] Undoubtedly the legality of the evidence is a factor that the police officer considers in deciding whether to take a suspect into custody. But how crucial he considers that factor to be is the focus of the debate.

---

27. U. S. CONST. amend. IV. In 1961, the Supreme Court held that evidence taken in the course of an illegal search could not be used in a state criminal prosecution. Mapp v. Ohio, 367 U. S. 643 (1961).

28. The *Mapp* Court said:

The ignoble shortcut to conviction left open to the state tends to destroy the entire system of constitutional restraints on which the liberties of the people rest. Having once recognized that the right to privacy embodied in the Fourth Amendment is enforceable against the states, and that the right to be secure against rude invasions of privacy by state officers is, therefore, constitutional in origin, we can no longer permit that right to become an empty promise. . . . [W]e can no longer permit it to be revocable at the whim of any police officer who, in the name of law enforcement itself, chooses to suspend its enjoyment. *Id.* at 660.

29. Draper v. United States, 358 U. S. 307, 314 (1958) (dissenting opinion).

30. Wong Son v. United States, 371 U. S. 471 (1963).

31. POLICE POWER, *supra* note 25, at 278.

In certain situations the officer on the beat may feel that an arrest would be futile because it would not lead to conviction. But even under these circumstances the officer may take the suspect into custody to fulfill other goals.[32] He may be motivated by the belief that the arrest and detention, no matter how short, represent a form of punishment, even if the courts take no action. In this instance, the officer is substituting his judgment for that of the court and is determining that punishment of some sort should be imposed.[33] He may even arrest in hopes that the trial judge will ignore the Supreme Court's rulings and permit the evidence to be used at trial. In some situations the officer will arrest solely because people expect full enforcement, and the failure to arrest would subject the officer and the department to criticism. But no discussion of evidentiary considerations would be complete without mention that at times an arrest is a means of rebellion. Notwithstanding the officer's awareness of the inadequacy and inadmissibility of the evidence, he may be so antipathetic to the Supreme Court and its rulings that he will refuse to follow them.[34] If the suspect is later freed because of a lack of evidence, the police can place the blame on the courts for freeing criminals.

If the beat officer chooses to use his discretion in favor of the wrongdoer, that person is generally home free. Although the beat officer is but one component of the charging process, he has the power to short-circuit it in the beginning. How he exercises this power will largely determine how well the community he serves respects not only the police department but the entire criminal justice apparatus. The decisions regarding whom to arrest, when to arrest, and especially how many to arrest have tremendous impact upon the entire criminal justice process.[35]

The officer may choose not to arrest because he knows the courts are clogged and is aware of how many times he will have to appear in court before a particular case is resolved.[36] Although a decision to limit the case

---

32. In Minneapolis, as a result of a racial incident which led to a bar brawl, one white man was arrested when he tried to go after a black despite the police warnings. A black was booked, based on a citizen's arrest for assault. The citizen's arrest was honored, not because the black man was believed to be guilty, but because by arresting a black and a white it was hoped that the crowd would think the police were being fair. It was thought that this action would restore peace. *Policing, supra* note 19, at 681 n. 25.

33. ARREST, *supra* note 24, at 200.

34. "[Norms] located within the police organization are more powerful than court decisions in shaping police behavior. . . ." SKOLNICK, JUSTICE WITHOUT TRIAL 219–20 (1966) [hereinafter cited as SKOLNICK].

35. *Policing, supra* note 19, at 726–27.

36. A policeman will frequently choose not to make an arrest when he

flow is not one for the beat officer but is more properly one for the police leadership, in conjunction with the prosecutor and the courts,[37] the officer may nevertheless set himself up as the decision-maker. The laws to be enforced are then determined from his narrow perspective. He becomes the first judge in the process and decides from his narrow perspective what laws are to be enforced. In so doing, he is thwarting the will of the legislature, which enacts the laws. Moreover, society runs the risk that the officer, in choosing not to enforce a particular law, may decide to administer a dose of summary justice on the street. Although a tongue-lashing administered by a police officer may be more effective in correcting the ways of a minor offender than a lecture from a judge, there are several potential dangers to the community from such action. In addition to the officer's becoming prosecutor, judge, and jury, the threat exists that he may administer more than just verbal punishment.[38] Even if the officer refrains from violence, the on-the-street brand of summary justice could easily provoke community problems. No matter how flagrant the illegality of the wrongdoer, a confrontation between a member of the community and a police officer may be misunderstood by passersby and lead to violence. In such an instance, the officer is hardly fulfilling his major responsibility of preserving the peace,[39] but rather he is provoking disorder.

considers the number of off-duty hours that he will have to spend in court. Defense attorneys, in order to take advantage of the policeman's desire to avoid courtroom appearances, will obtain several continuances in a case and, when the exasperated policeman fails to appear, move for a dismissal. *Id.* at 716 n. 61.

37. The Criminal Justice Bureau of the New York City Police Department will monitor the work of the prosecutors and the courts. The Bureau hopes to determine what effect arrests have on the crime rate and, if convictions are not resulting, whether the police, courts, or prosecutors are responsible. N. Y. Times, July 9, 1971, at 1, col. 2-3. *See generally* SKOLNICK, *supra* note 34, at 233–34.

38. [After] witnessing some gratuitous punching after a foot chase, I was taken aside by a rookie and told that it was department policy (although of course it is not) to work over those who flee so that they would not again be so rash. Part of the explanation for this vigilante justice lies in the fact that here offenses are committed directly against the police. Another part is that the police believe that no penalty will be given by the courts. *Policing, supra* note 19, at 713.

39. Many people envision the police as having three basic tasks: the maintenance of law and order, the detection of crime, and the administration of various public welfare regulations such as licensing of firearms. KARLEN, *supra* note 22, at 1–3.

Situations occur daily where police officers are compelled to decide whether an arrest is of value to the criminal justice system and to the society as a whole. When responding to a call for help arising out of a family dispute, the officer must determine what is necessary to restore order. Since often no other social agency is available to intervene when these disputes occur, the beat officer bears the burden of decision.[40] If he arrests the belligerent family member, the officer knows that invariably the next day cooler heads will prevail and the family will elect not to pursue the matter. The wheels of the justice system will have been set in motion, but they will then be halted by the victim who no longer wishes his problem to be subject to criminal jurisdiction. However, should he make the decision not to separate the combatants by arresting one, later that night he may find that he has made the wrong decision—that the family dispute has escalated into homicide. Consequently, if he elects not to arrest, he must assure himself that neither participant is armed and that they no longer have a propensity to resume their warfare. In his role as peace-keeper and marriage counselor,[41] he must constantly keep in mind that many homicides are committed among people who have known each other, and often within a family. According to 1970 figures compiled by the Cleveland Police Department, of 286 homicides in the city, 133 were done by a friend or a relative.[42]

A similar instance of police misuse occurs when their services are sought primarily as a debt-collection agency. Passing a check with insufficient funds and failing to pay for goods or services may be crimes, but the officer will not arrest unless he can be assured that the complainant desires to prosecute and is not only interested in receiving his money.[43]

The exercise of discretion in domestic disputes and debt collection may be sound, but unfortunately the discretion in many other instances is motivated by nothing more than the individual police officer's prejudices. That blacks and young people, especially those with long hair, will be arrested in situations where the discretion of the police officer would prompt him not to arrest another member of the community is a simple fact in this country.[44] Marginal offenses that would not warrant the arrest of a suburban-

---

40. *Low Visibility, supra* note 21.
41. Policemen think they primarily fight crime; however, most of their work is done as social workers. *Policing, supra* note 19, at 714.
42. Cleveland Plain Dealer, June 6, 1971, § A, at 12, col. 3.
43. If the officer is convinced that the complainant will not drop the charges if he is paid, the officer can convince the prosecuting attorney to initiate prosecution. Brezner, *How the Prosecuting Attorney's Office Processes Complaints,* 27 THE DETROIT LAWYER 3, 4 (1960).
44. Related to this dilemma is the problem of "underarresting" in situa-

ite will bring forth the full fury of the law in the ghetto. It would seem on the basis of arrests made that gambling flourishes in the inner city but is almost nonexistent in the suburbs. However, the neighborhood poker games that the police wink at in the affluent sections of a city may result in arrest and prosecution elsewhere.[45]

On the street, confrontations between police officers and citizens are at best touchy situations and at worst the precursor of disorder and violence.[46] How the officer on the beat confronts people will have a substantial effect on the outcome of the encounter. If the officer treats the people in the community he is patrolling as an invader treats the citizens of an occupied country, then he will meet the hostility normally accorded an occupying force. When police stop initiating street encounters solely because a person is black or unconventionally dressed, and when the encounters that do occur are handled by the police in the same manner and with the same courtesy as they are when the person stopped is a middle-class suburbanite, the tension in the streets and hostility towards the police will be markedly reduced. In 1971, in Queens, New York, Albert Legister, a black, was trying to prevent traffic from going through a flooded area of his street because each car would force water into his basement. When the police interceded to prevent Legister from holding up traffic, a heated argument led to an altercation involving police, Legister, and his wife, and prompted charges

---

tions which involve black perpetrators and black victims. One commentator said: "The police have an informal policy of discouraging Negro assault victims from filing complaints, and it was reported that officers newly assigned to primarily black districts quickly adopt this practice regardless of the attitudes and policies they brought with them from primarily white districts." D. NEWMAN, CONVICTION: THE DETERMINATION OF GUILT OR INNOCENCE WITHOUT TRIAL 157 (1966) [hereinafter cited as CONVICTION].

45. *See* Comment, *Prosecutorial Discretion in the Initiation of Criminal Complaints,* 42 SO. CAL. L. REV. 519, 528 (1969) [hereinafter cited as *Prosecutorial Discretion*].

46. Police conduct giving rise to disputes with the public lies in an area where there are differing views on the proper scope of police activity and evolving doctrines as to the scope of police power. Many of the disputes have arisen in connection with political and civil rights demonstrations where a normally law-abiding section of the population is involved with the police in ways which are not subject to wholly clear rules. . . . The citizen, without admitting it, may think he should be able to get away with a certain amount of illegality. The policeman, without admitting it, may think he should have a certain amount of discretion to exceed his strict powers when con-

against the police of excessive force.[47] Even though the community disowns the police when they react imprudently, the attitudes and actions of the police reflect, on the whole, how the majority in the community wants blacks and young people treated.

This same discretionary power is also used in reverse to deny full police protection in the inner-city areas. Conduct that would warrant police action elsewhere may be ignored or dismissed by the police officer. An assault between ghetto blacks, even where there is knifing involved, may be dismissed by the beat officer as a normal part of the subculture of the black ghetto.[48] Within our memory is hearing a policeman say that there is no such thing as rape in the ghetto. Such notions offer little comfort to the victims of assault or rape.

The pattern which emerges shows that on-the-street exercises of police discretion often result in the prosecution of blacks for crimes which would be overlooked if committed by a white person. At the same time, because the police may dismiss certain conduct as normal and natural to the ghetto, victims of crime are being denied police protection.[49]

The exercise of police discretion is viewed by some as the humanizing agent in the criminal justice system, and the officer's decision of whether or not to arrest as the factor which brings the professed norms of society, as delineated by the legislature, into line with society's actual norms. However, the reconciliation of norms that does take place on the street is in need of scrutiny. Few would doubt the value of police discretion, which tends to unburden the criminal process of a part of its unmanageable caseload, if it always reflected the wisdom of community consensus. Unfortunately, it tends to represent the attitudes of only a part of the community, and its repercussions are felt by a distinctly different segment of the community.

In order to make the law more meaningful to the existing society, the wisdom of the legislature should be directed towards reviewing all offenses and repealing many now outmoded laws. It is the existence of unenforceable laws and of laws that no longer possess the concurrence of the governed that creates much of the potential for unequal enforcement and on-the-street harassment. Since the beat officer is clothed with the authority of a

---

vinced he is dealing with a law-breaker. KARLEN, *supra* note 22, at 15–16.

47. N. Y. Times, June 15, 1971, at 39, col. 1.

48. *See* CONVICTION, *supra* note 44.

49. Not only are some laws selectively enforced against certain minority groups, but other laws are not enforced and thus deny protection to certain minority groups. *Prosecutorial Discretion, supra* note 45, at 528.

judge and there is little effective recourse from his rulings, overcriminalization should be avoided to minimize the potential for abuse at that juncture of the criminal justice process.[50]

In the absence of legislative reconsideration, controls on police discretion can only come from within the criminal justice apparatus. Extensive training of police officers is a necessary first step,[51] although the repugnance of many police officers for training in community relations has been well documented. Further, the prosecutor who must carry the arrest through to a conviction should be a part of the policy-making apparatus, so that police action is closely attuned to his concepts and awareness of the community's needs.[52]

The role of the police in screening felony cases does not end with the arrest and taking into custody of the defendant. Although the arresting officer takes a back seat at this point, decision-making power is vested in the specialized (e.g., homicide, robbery, narcotics, etc.) or detective units.[53] Until recently New York City detectives took any case that occurred during their tours of duty. However, they have initiated a program of reorganization into specialized units with the hope that the detectives will have more success solving crimes if they develop an expertise in a particular field.[54]

The detective at this stage owns the case and has almost total discretion as to whether to proceed with the prosecution. He can simply release the suspect if he does not believe that the evidence warrants prosecution, or he can initiate formal proceedings. When the detective decides that the accused should be prosecuted, then the suspect is formally booked.[55] The booking procedure provides the first formalization of the charge.[56] At this stage of the prosecution, the power of the police to determine the course of a particular case theoretically ends.

---

50. *See* note 7 *supra.*

51. In the United States many "large cities have some sort of police school, but these often present no more than unrelieved lectures, to which there is no obligation to pay attention." Also, though "the educational level of policemen is somewhat above the national average, . . . it falls short of what might reasonably be expected of a professional group." KARLEN, *supra* note 22, at 13.

52. Trammell, *supra* note 4, at 245.

53. *See generally* THE POLICE, *supra* note 2, at 53.

54. N. Y. Times, June 11, 1971, at 39, col. 1.

55. WESTLEY, VIOLENCE AND THE POLICE 36–40 (1970) [hereinafter cited as WESTLEY].

56. If the police decide to charge a suspect, whom they have interrogated, the arrest and the charges are noted on police records. The defendant's

Each felony case is directed to the prosecutor's office by the detective in charge. Although the detective will work in concert with the prosecutor who reviews the case, and although he and the other police on the case may have great influence on the prosecutor, the power to determine whether to prosecute and whether to treat the matter as a felony is the prerogative of the prosecutor.[57]

In most cities a fine relationship exists between the police and the prosecutor's office. Since both are working towards the same general goals, each is dependent upon the other's labors to facilitate its own work. As a result, prosecutors are fully aware that they cannot often refuse a police request to prosecute, and the police are aware that they cannot pressure for prosecution in too many questionable cases, for it is the prosecutor who ultimately must justify that decision in court. For the most part, a mutuality of interests and limitations upon each agency's prerogatives tend to maintain cooperation that is based upon a healthy respect.

The balance of interests breaks down somewhat in those jurisdictions where the prosecutor's function is divided between a city prosecutor, whose responsibility for felony cases extends only to the preliminary proceedings in the municipal court, and a county prosecutor, who has final jurisdiction over felony cases once they get beyond the preliminary stages. When the police are disgruntled with a city prosecutor's decision not to proceed against a particular suspect or are dissatisfied with his decision to proceed on a misdemeanor rather than on a felony charge, they can bypass this decision and request that the county prosecutor take the case directly to the grand jury and seek a felony indictment.[58] Even here, however, police latitude is circumscribed because they must work daily with the city prosecutor on all other felony and misdemeanor charges; if they bypass his office too often, they will be courting animosity. In those jurisdictions where one prosecutor's office spans the duration of the case, one line of authority and one set of policies will prevail.

THE ROLE OF THE PROSECUTOR IN THE CHARGING PROCESS

The prosecutor is perhaps best able to reconcile all divergent interests in the charging process and to determine how to proceed in each individual

---

name and some identifying information are also noted in summary form. Amsterdam, Segal, & Miller, *Entrance into the Criminal Case— Representing the Client Shortly After Arrest,* 14:1 PRAC. LAW. 20, 24 (1968) [hereinafter cited as *Representing the Client*].

57. *See generally Prosecutorial Discretion, supra* note 45, at 519.

58. Similarly it has been reported in Cleveland that police often will go

case.[59] Since he has daily contact with the police, he is aware of the law enforcement needs and the pressures on the street, and knows which crimes require visible and immediate judicial action in order, hopefully, to act as a deterrent against that crime.

Since he is invested with the responsibility of representing the state in all criminal actions, the prosecutor is also fully aware of the dilemma facing the criminal courts. Because the courts are at present unable to handle their caseloads, the burden rests upon the prosecutor to decide which cases are of such critical importance that they should be introduced into the judicial maelstrom. Balancing these competing interests becomes the focal point of the screening process at this stage of a criminal case. His job is further complicated by the interest of the police in proceeding against a suspect who has been arrested and detained, an interest reinforced by the public expectation that persons committing criminal acts will be prosecuted.

The prosecutor who institutes felony charges against all defendants arrested by the police fails to make the necessary choices at this stage of the proceedings. Although he may be mollifying the public and the police, he is not adequately doing his job. He is shifting attention away from his office and focusing it on the inability of the courts to cope with their responsibility. At the same time, a prosecutor's failure to screen at this level introduces some cases which are not important enough to merit full prosecution.[60] By clogging the courts with marginal cases, he is unfortunately ensuring that the more serious crimes, those which merit the full attention of the criminal system, will not get the scrutiny they deserve.

Consequently, the screening procedure in a prosecutor's office becomes a critical stage in the criminal process. The absence of any screening precipi-

---

to the prosecutor who presents cases to the grand jury in order to get an indictment even when probable cause is found not to exist at the preliminary hearing. Interview with Richard McMonagle, defense attorney, in Cleveland, Ohio, May 23, 1971.

59. But the concomitant idea that

a prosecuting attorney should be permitted to use his discretion concerning the laws which he will enforce and those which he will disregard appears to the ordinary citizen to border on anarchy. The fact that prosecuting attorneys are compelled to do this very thing is generally ignored. . . . Arnold, *Law Enforcement—an Attempt at Social Dissection,* 42 YALE L. J. 1, 7 (1932) [hereinafter cited as *Social Dissection*].

60. "In Philadelphia, cases that once get into the system tend to stay there. . . . Prosecutors ordinarily assigned to the preliminary stages are the least experienced, it is reported, and lack either the confidence or the authority to knock out the weakest cases early on." N. Y. Times, Mar. 8, 1971, at 1, col. 3.

tates a flood of cases into the courts. Conversely, careful and fair screening preserves scarce court time.[61] The quality of justice available to any defendant or victim may consequently be predetermined by how well the cases are screened before they get to court.

Like the power of the police during the period in which the determination to arrest is made, the prosecutor's authority over the case is total. Unlike the police, however, the prosecutor has many more options. He can accept the police recommendation and issue a complaint charging the defendant with a felony. He can go beyond the police recommendation and expand the charge to include more than one felony count, if that is even remotely justified by the facts.[62] For example, a person who is apprehended by the police as he comes out of a robbery victim's home is subject to being charged with—in addition to robbery—burglary, larceny, and carrying a concealed weapon if he is armed. This practice, known as "bedsheeting," involves charging the defendant with every applicable crime, in the expectation that the prosecutor can exact a better deal in exchange for a promise to dismiss some of the charges. Conversely, the prosecutor may dismiss the charges outright or disagree with the police assessment of the crime and, instead, institute misdemeanor charges against the accused.[63] Assistant Prosecutor Robert Snider of Boston faced such a problem with the case of a defendant named Bartholomew. Bartholomew had been charged with larceny, but a review of the case by the prosecutor indicated that the proper charge was "receiving a stolen automobile," and as a result the case had to be returned to the grand jury for a second indictment.[64]

A misdemeanor charge at this stage of the proceedings is the easiest way of disposing of a case while still letting the offender know that the law has taken note of his conduct. Compared to a felony proceeding, a misdemeanor generally involves little time on the part of the courts and prosecutors. Perhaps the procedure surrounding misdemeanors is subject to criticism

---

61. "The ultimate resolution of criminal cases resulting from prosecutor screening is necessary for the maintenance of the criminal justice system. There are not enough prosecutors, defense attorneys, judges and jails to handle the massive felony docket." McIntyre and Lippman, *Prosecutors and Early Disposition of Felony Cases,* 56 A.B.A.J. 1154 (1970) [hereinafter cited as *Early Disposition*].

62. For a discussion of multiple punishment and consecutive sentences, *see* Johnson, *Multiple Punishment and Consecutive Sentences: Reflections on the "Neal" Doctrine,* 58 CALIF. L. REV. 357 (1970).

63. *Prosecutorial Discretion, supra* note 45, at 524–25.

64. Bartholomew and a co-defendant were also in possession of a large amount of narcotics when arrested. The prosecutor was primarily

because it is too summary in nature.[65] Nevertheless, the advantage of referring the defendant's case for prosecution as a misdemeanor is that it relieves the felony process and permits the more serious offenses to receive greater attention.

Most misdemeanors, at least outside New York City, are handled with great dispatch. New York has managed to complicate misdemeanor cases to the point that the procedure is almost as cumbersome and time-consuming as in felony cases. Because of the lesser penalties attached to misdemeanors, many defendants plead guilty at their initial court appearance in order to end the entire proceeding. The case can then be disposed of in the court where the defendant initially appears; and unless he has a criminal record, the likelihood of his being sentenced to jail is remote. A defendant who is fully aware that sufficient evidence exists to charge him as a felon is quite likely to accept the expedited procedure and be free of any charge hanging over his head.

Municipal courts, in which misdemeanors are prosecuted and the preliminary stages of felony cases take place, may be the worst courts in this nation. The summary treatment given persons in the municipal courts may highlight the sham that our system for the administration of justice has become. Establishing guilt is of no concern, and often persons who have committed questionable misdemeanors, or are in fact not guilty, simply plead guilty in order to go home.[66] A plea of not guilty, on the other hand, results in a trial date being set. Unless the defendant is able to raise bail or is eligible for release without bail, he will have to wait in jail until his trial.

For the defendant held by the police on a felony charge, disposition of the charge within the misdemeanor process enables him to resume his life with minimal disruption.[67] The argument raised against this resolution is that if the police have charged the person with a felony, then he should be prosecuted as a felon. In an ideal legal system this would be a justifiable argument, but in one struggling to survive, the argument is naive. The prosecutor's reasons for washing out a case or reducing a charge at this

---

concerned with the drug charges. If the automobile theft case was to be tried, however, Snider wanted to be sure that Bartholomew was charged with "receiving a stolen automobile." Interview with Assistant Prosecutor Robert Snider, in Boston, April 12, 1971.

65. Katz, *Municipal Courts—Another Urban Ill,* 20 CASE W. RES. L. REV. 87, 90 (1969) [hereinafter cited as Katz].

66. *Id.* at 87–95. The New York City Criminal Court disposed of 75 percent of all felony cases by dismissing the charge before the trial or by accepting guilty pleas to reduced misdemeanor charges. N. Y. Times, Jan. 31, 1971, at 67, col. 5.

67. CONVICTION, *supra* note 44, at 106.

stage are many, not the least being that the facts may make a felony conviction questionable. Moreover, numerous cases originally prosecuted as felonies are eventually settled as misdemeanors; if they are to be resolved in this manner ultimately, the best time to do so is before the case is treated as a felony by the courts.

Court diversion programs offer another alternative to the prosecutor. The programs provide a means of informal probation and are generally available to persons accused of felonies. If the defendant agrees, the programs permit the prosecutor to defer charging the defendant and to refer him to the appropriate court diversion program. If the accused successfully completes the program, the prosecutor agrees never to institute the charge, provided that the accused stays out of trouble for a given period of time. In Philadelphia, a pre-indictment probation program is available to a first offender accused of a minor felony. However, if the defendant is arrested again, he will be charged with both offenses.[68] New York now offers a counseling and treatment program for drug addicts accused of crimes.[69]

The advantages of such programs to both the accused and the criminal justice system are manifold. The accused is given his freedom. He is often exposed to programs which provide employment training, job placement, and, occasionally, as in New York, the opportunity for medical treatment. Above all, he comes out of the program without a criminal record and its accompanying social stigma. The benefits to society are equally significant. Without exposing the case to the overcrowded courts, the accused has been in a program that probably offers greater opportunity for rehabilitation than jail or prison confinement. Moreover, there is a chance that the justice system is contributing a reformed, useful individual to the community,

---

68.   It involves first offenders or people with "minimal" police re-
       cords. . . . If the prosecutor and the court agree that the defendant
       in such instances poses no risk to the community, they are taken
       out of the machinery and placed in a probationary status for six
       months or more. . . . Those who stay out of trouble during this time
       have the charges against them dropped. N. Y. Times, Mar. 8, 1971,
       at 1, col. 3; at 26, col. 2.
       According to an administrative assistant to Philadelphia's First As-
       sistant Prosecutor James Crawford, approximately sixty cases per
       week are handled in the pre-indictment probation program. Interview
       with Karen Parish, in Philadelphia, April 5, 1971.
69.   New York has instituted a program designed to handle the problem
       of narcotics addicts. The new program offers counseling, often by
       former drug addicts, and the opportunity to obtain proper treatment
       in one of the thirteen drug treatment centers participating with the city
       in the program. If the suspect completes the rehabilitation program,

without the expense to the community of imprisonment.[70]

With these opportunities to limit the flow of felony cases into the courts, effective screening at this stage can be a vital link in the determination of which cases merit prosecution. Whether it is an effective tool to limit court congestion depends upon the seriousness with which it is approached in each jurisdiction and the willingness of the prosecutor to commit his limited manpower to this task. If it is not approached with the determination required to sift out cases that should not be prosecuted as felonies, the prosecutor's exercise of the screening power is meaningless, little more than a show of official beneficence that is subject to great abuse.[71]

The effectiveness of screening at this stage is also reduced in cities where the prosecutor who initiates the felony charge does not have continued responsibility for the entire case. Cleveland employs this bifurcated prosecutorial structure: the city prosecutor who initiates the case knows he is subject to the second-guessing of the county prosecutor. As a result, screening at this stage becomes ineffective. The city prosecutor, rather than pruning out cases, tends to file the complaint on the recommendation of the police, thereby introducing the case into the felony process. Meaningful screening is thus deferred, and the best opportunity to avoid unmerited

---

the charges against him are dropped. Unfortunately, money is the greatest obstacle to the effectiveness of the program, and this prevents the courts from treating addicts in a meaningful way. N. Y. Times, May 31, 1971, at 17, col. 5. This is especially critical in New York City, where it is estimated that 50 to 60 percent of the crimes there are committed by drug addicts. N. Y. Times, Dec. 6, 1970, § 1A, at 1, col. 1.

The basic problem with all such programs designed at rehabilitation of the prisoner is finding the funds to carry them out. In August, 1970, it was reported that ninety-five District of Columbia convicts were in jail even though they had been officially assigned to halfway houses. There were no halfway houses to take them to and no supervision available. Otten, *Crime: The Neglected Battlegrounds,* Wall Street Journal, Aug. 20, 1970, at 10, col. 3.

In Cleveland, a new court employment program has been developed, with the assistance of federal funds, that offers a second chance to those first offenders who are arrested on misdemeanor charges. If such an individual is unemployed or underemployed, the individual is given counseling, job training, and employment. If the participant completes the program successfully, the charges are dropped. Cleveland Plain Dealer, Mar. 28, 1971, at 11, col. 1.

70. *Id.*
71. Although prosecutor screening is taken seriously in Los Angeles, De-

felony prosecutions is lost.

In Detroit, on the other hand, there is provision for a more thorough review after arrest and prior to the initiation of formal charges to reduce the number of cases.[72] When a detective presents a felony arrest to the prosecutor, he is immediately assigned to an assistant district attorney, who ultimately determines whether to institute charges. The assignment of the case not only vests the responsibility for the decision but also prevents the police from carrying a case from one assistant to another until they find one willing to prosecute.[73]

The assistant district attorney reviews the police report, questions the detective about the case, and requests any additional investigation that he may need. For some felonies, and often in rape cases, the assistant prosecutor interviews witnesses and victims. If the suspect is represented by counsel, the assigned prosecutor will discuss the case at the defense attorney's request, prior to filing a formal complaint. Only after this brief review is completed will the assistant district attorney decide how to proceed. Reports indicate that 30 percent of the felony cases in Detroit are screened out of the process at this point, and the felony docket becomes less crowded and more manageable.[74]

In New York City there is virtually no prosecutorial screening prior to the introduction of formal proceedings. Observation of the complaint room of the Manhattan branch of the New York City Criminal Court indicated that detectives from all over the county were filing formal charges, and the single prosecutor present was incapable of reviewing the cases. In the event that the police officer or detective had technical difficulties with the charging papers, the prosecutor assisted. One New York assistant prosecutor stated that he cannot screen cases but can only dismiss a charge in open

---

troit, and Houston, the procedure is not utilized very extensively in New York or Chicago. *Early Disposition, supra* note 61, at 1156.

72. Interview with Arthur Koscinski, Assistant Prosecutor–Chief of Warrant Division, in Detroit, Aug. 3, 1971.

73. Defense attorneys know which prosecutors are overly sympathetic to defendants charged with certain crimes. SUBIN, CRIMINAL JUSTICE IN A METROPOLITAN COURT: THE PROCESSING OF SERIOUS CRIMINAL CASES IN THE DISTRICT OF COLUMBIA COURT OF GENERAL SESSIONS 43 (1966). Similarly, the prosecutor's overly sympathetic reaction will be known by police. As a result, police will try to steer cases to other prosecutors.

74. *Early Disposition, supra* note 61, at 1156. The assistant prosecutor in charge of screening estimated that 20 percent of all cases are eliminated at this point. Interview with Arthur Koscinski, Assistant Prosecutor–Chief of Warrant Division, in Detroit, Aug. 3, 1971.

court.[75] Under these conditions, the screening is consigned to the judges and prosecutors, once the case is formally in court. Because of the extensive burden on prosecutors and judges in that court, the effectiveness of their screening is suspect. If screening is to be effective, it must be done early and in an atmosphere where the prosecutor can review the case and talk to the participants informally. Only in that manner can the merits of not prosecuting a particular case become clear, and a well-reasoned decision be made.

The availability to defendants in Los Angeles County, California, of a speedy trial is partly attributable to the early and extensive screening by the prosecutor's office. Los Angeles County is the largest county in the country, with more than seven million inhabitants and a correspondingly high crime rate. In 1967 there were 67,175 felony arrests in the county.[76] To have prosecuted all or nearly all the felons would have crippled the courts. The prosecutor's office operates from the assumption that the courts cannot handle all antisocial behavior but must be reserved for the serious offenses. Consequently, the office eliminates as many cases as possible prior to filing formal charges and handles these less serious problems by other means.[77] The use of policy directives from the main office to the seven branch offices located in the courthouse insures that the decision not to prosecute is uniform throughout the county.

Just as in the other cities, the decision to prosecute rests with the prosecutor, but in Los Angeles the decision is based upon an understanding that there is a need for screening. Unlike the situation in most cities, the Los Angeles detective who has prepared the case will not get a complaint from the prosecutor as a matter of routine. The assistant prosecutor will review the police report, the accused's prior criminal record, and the statements given to the police by the witnesses. The prosecutor may turn the matter back to the police for further investigation, or he may call in the district attorney's own investigators in order to secure more information.[78]

The Los Angeles screening process strives to reduce as many cases as possible to misdemeanors, or to refer the suspects to social agencies. Crimes arising out of marital situations, except for the most serious felonies, are directed to the domestic relations commissioner of the court to determine

---

75. Interview with an assistant district attorney, in New York City, Nov. 29, 1970 (anonymity requested).

76. Trammell, *supra* note 4, at 245.

77. Criminal charges arising out of domestic situations, for example, are referred to a commissioner who handles these cases for the courts. Interview with George Trammell III, Long Beach District Attorney, in Long Beach, California, Dec. 11, 1970.

78. *Id.*

whether the case can be resolved without criminal sanctions. If the suspect has a lawyer, the complaint will be held in abeyance until the lawyer has had an opportunity to confer with the assistant prosecutor. The screening process in Los Angeles reduced the more than 64,000 felony arrests in 1967 to only 24,505 felony prosecutions. More than 60 percent of the felony arrests were resolved by misdemeanor prosecutions, dismissals, or referral to nonjudicial proceedings or social agencies.[79] Further, when the prosecutor declines to charge a person arrested by the police, he states in writing why the police complaint was rejected. In this way, the police become familiar with the charging practice, and the prosecutor's office and police agencies can work together more effectively.

The effectiveness of both the Los Angeles and Detroit efforts in reducing the case flow of felonies is due to the willingness of both cities to commit resources to the screening stage early in the procedure. In Baltimore, on the other hand, the state attorney's office does not screen cases before charges are filed. Screening occurs after the preliminary hearing and prior to the presentation of the case to the grand jury. According to the assistant state's attorney, between March and October of 1970, 1,500 cases were eventually remanded to the municipal courts because they were inappropriate for felony prosecutions. Although the municipal court had originally found probable cause that a felony had occurred, the judge on remand never imposed the maximum misdemeanor sentence available. If screening had been initiated prior to the preliminary hearing, certainly many of these cases would never have been even considered for felony prosecution.[80]

The decision to prosecute is universally based upon the same factors, and frequently those factors are similar to the ones that originally motivated the police officer to arrest and hold a suspect.[81] Aside from the importance of

79. Trammell, *supra* note 4, at 245. Interview with George Trammell III, Long Beach District Attorney, in Long Beach, California, Dec. 11, 1970.

80. Interview with Joseph Koutz, Assistant State's Attorney, in Baltimore, April 8, 1971. As a result of the success with the pre-grand jury screening, the program will be expanded so that screening will occur prior to the filing of charges.

81.   [T]he prosecutor must be allowed to consider whether "a prosecution will promote the ends of justice, instill a respect for law, and advance the cause of ordered liberty," and to take into account "the degree of criminality, the weight of the evidence, the credibility of witnesses, precedent, policy, the climate of public opinion, timing, and the relative gravity of the offense." LaFave, *The Prosecutor in the United States,* 18 AM. J. COMP. L. 532, 536 & n. 25 (1970).

the alleged crime, the most significant criterion is whether the case provides enough admissible evidence to secure a conviction. It is a waste of time for the court, prosecutor, police, and witnesses to involve themselves in a case where the evidence will not support a conviction of the charge. Notwithstanding the small percentage of felony cases that go to trial,[82] the decision at this stage must still be based upon the convictability of a defendant in the event of trial.[83] Although the police consider this criterion when they arrest, the prosecutor's office has the legal training and experience to make a more educated decision.[84]

Even though the police have already determined that the defendant has committed a felony, the prosecutor must decide for himself whether the facts of the case satisfy the essential elements of the crime, as codified by the legislature. In determining the defendant's innocence or guilt, the prosecutor will consider all available information, including illegally seized or hearsay evidence, which he could not introduce at trial.[85]

If the prosecutor concludes that the accused is guilty, he must then determine whether to file formal charges. This decision is based upon his assessment of the quality of admissible evidence and his judgment of whether it is sufficient to convince a judge or jury to convict the defendant.[86] Even if the prosecutor believes his chances for a conviction at trial are negligible, he may prosecute based upon the realization that few trials occur and that it is likely the accused will plead guilty as charged or to a lesser offense, without ever testing the evidence.[87] However, these marginal cases tend to

---

82. Trammell, *supra* note 4, at 245.

83. Kaplan, *The Prosecutorial Discretion,* 60 Nw. U. L. Rev. 174, 180 (1965–1966) [hereinafter cited as Kaplan].

84. As a general proposition, a detailed consideration of the available evidence itself would be more likely to result in an accurate evaluation of its adequacy than would reliance on a police officer's oral or written summary of it. Perhaps in the interest of time preservation, a detailed consideration is not customary in any of the jurisdictions studied. In each of them, the source of information most often relied on is the police officer and his report or summary of the case that he brings with him when he requests a warrant. Occasionally witnesses or the suspect of the victim are also interviewed, but there is no readily discernible pattern. F. MILLER, PROSECUTION: THE DECISION TO CHARGE A SUSPECT WITH A CRIME 16 (1969) [hereinafter cited as DECISION TO CHARGE].

85. Kaplan, *supra* note 83, at 178.

86. *Prosecutorial Discretion, supra* note 45, at 526–28.

87. *See* Note, *Guilty Plea Bargaining: Compromises by Prosecutors to Secure Guilty Pleas,* 112 U. PA. L. REV. 865 (1964).

clog the courts and to last interminably, until an accommodation is reached between the prosecutor and the defense attorney. If a deal cannot be arranged and a trial becomes inevitable, the prosecutor is free to dismiss the charges prior to the trial. This practice is an abuse of the courts and may force an innocent person to plead guilty to a lesser offense rather than face the possibility of conviction for a more serious crime.

An additional factor that may shape the prosecutor's decision to charge is the attitude of the community towards a particular criminal statute.[88] For example, with more and more young people from affluent suburbs using marijuana, public attitudes are changing to the point that many prosecutors ignore possession charges and only go after dealers and large suppliers.[89]

Sympathy or hostility for either the defendant or the victim may also be a factor in the prosecutor's decision.[90] Having a victim who is unwilling to cooperate,[91] or one who is likely to generate hostility from the jury, will militate against prosecution because a conviction is unlikely. Moreover, if the accused is a first offender, the likelihood of his going to prison, except for the most serious felonies, is remote. As a result, the prosecutor may decide not to introduce the case into the felony process but rather to deal with the case as a misdemeanor or through referral to an administrative program.[92]

Energetic screening is a means of refining the charging process into an effective and realistic method of determining which persons and which crimes will be prosecuted. The power that this society has vested in the police and prosecutor creates a pattern of selective law enforcement. Although the laws impose a duty upon the police to arrest all violators and a corresponding duty upon the prosecutor to institute charges for all violations, this provides an impossible and probably undesirable goal.[93] Notwith-

---

88. One example of this would be the gambling laws, where there will be at best selective prosecution; the police will apprehend and prosecutors will charge numbers racketeers, but will not proceed against the casual suburban card player. *See* note 21 *supra; Prosecutorial Discretion, supra* note 45, at 528.

89. Interview with Geoffrey Gaulkin, Hudson County Prosecutor, in Jersey City, New Jersey, Nov. 30, 1970.

90. One writer has noted that charges such as rape and robbery filed by suspected prostitutes seldom result in a prosecution. *Prosecutorial Discretion, supra* note 45, at 530.

91. In assault cases between family members the complainant may hesitate to cooperate with the prosecutor. DECISION TO CHARGE, *supra* note 84, at 173–78.

92. *Prosecutorial Discretion, supra* note 45, at 529.

93. DECISION TO CHARGE, *supra* note 84, at 151–52.

standing the duty imposed by law, a citizen cannot compel a prosecutor to file charges. Abuse of a prosecutor's discretion to charge is subject to court action, but review of his decision is a rarity. The only real limitation upon selective law enforcement is that the decision to prosecute cannot be based upon race, religion, or other constitutionally protected criteria.[94] However, the burden of proving that the prosecution is based upon an illegal reason rests with the defendant. Since such an allegation is virtually impossible to establish, there is no effective check on the possibility that the discretionary power will be abused through arrests based upon race, age, and life style.

Society thus faces a paradox: selective enforcement, within constitutional bounds, is necessary to permit the courts to function, but in this discretionary power lie the seeds for great injustice. Although provision for more extensive screening is a valuable addition to any criminal court system, regulation must accompany the screening process to assure its appropriate use.

FORMAL SCREENING PROCESS

Only after the suspect is charged with a felony does the formal screening process involving courts and the grand jury begin. Although federal and most state courts require that a defendant be brought before a court for charging[95] without undue delay, the time period varies. Federal courts generally charge within a matter of hours,[96] but some police claim the authority to hold a suspect for several days without charging.[97]

---

94. It has been held:
    [T]he conscious exercise of some selectivity in enforcement is not in itself a federal constitutional violation. Even though the statistics in this case might imply a policy of selective enforcement, it was not stated that the selection was deliberately based upon an unjustifiable standard such as race, religion, or other arbitrary classification. Oyler v. Boles, 368 U. S. 448, 456 (1962).

95. It is at this time that the defendant is notified of his charges, of his right to a preliminary examination, of his right to be represented by counsel or his right to obtain assigned counsel, of his right to remain silent, and of his possible release on bail. F. REMINGTON, D. NEWMAN, E. KIMBALL, M. MELLI & H. GOLDSTEIN, CRIMINAL JUSTICE ADMINISTRATION 479–88 (1969) [hereinafter cited as REMINGTON & NEWMAN].

96. In the federal system, any confession made during an improper delay between the arrest and first court appearance is inadmissible as evidence. Mallory v. United States, 354 U. S. 449 (1957).

97. For a thorough discussion of the relevant state statutes, see LaFave,

The first court appearance is variously called an arraignment or a preliminary appearance. With a magistrate, justice of the peace, municipal court judge, or police court judge presiding, the accused is informed of the charges against him and of his constitutional rights.[98] Because first appearances for felonies and misdemeanors are often held in the same arraignment room, the atmosphere in the court is frequently tumultuous.[99] Except in those cities where counsel is required at every court proceeding, few felony defendants are represented by counsel at the preliminary appearance. Even those who can afford an attorney will rarely have had time to retain one. Since the court is one of inferior jurisdiction, the presiding judge at the preliminary appearance. With a magistrate, justice of the peace, municipal Even if the defendant wishes to plead guilty to the felony, the judge cannot accept the plea but must transfer the case to a court of general jurisdiction. Thus, a plea of not guilty must be entered, and other than establishing what the next procedure is to be and where and when it is to take place, only a bail determination is made.[100]

PRELIMINARY HEARING

The next step, if the defendant desires it, is the preliminary hearing. This is another step in the screening process and provides an independent evaluation of the decision to arrest and charge. At this hearing the magistrate, unlike a jury, is not interested in learning whether the defendant is guilty beyond a reasonable doubt, but only whether the prosecution presents enough evidence to establish probable cause; namely, the likelihood that the defendant has committed the crime.[101] If the preliminary hearing is held promptly after an arrest, it can also lessen inconvenience to the defendant, in the event that the charges are found to have been unwarranted.

Since the Constitution does not guarantee the right to a preliminary hearing, the mechanics of the hearing are governed by state law. Most states require that the hearing be held within a reasonable time, some specifying that the hearing be held within ten days or two weeks of the preliminary

---

Detention for Investigation by the Police: An Analysis of Current Practices, 1962 WASH. U. L. Q. 331, 332–33.

98. *Representing the Client, supra* note 56, at 57–60.

99. REMINGTON & NEWMAN, *supra* note 95, at 480–81.

100. *Representing the Client, supra* note 56.

101. The preliminary hearing "is a preliminary examination of the confrontation of society and the accused during which the magistrate must determine whether or not the criminal process should continue. Simply stated, the magistrate decides whether to send the accused home or bind him over for the grand jury." *Preliminary Hearings in Pennsylvania: A Closer Look,* 30 U. PITT. L. REV. 481 (1969).

court appearance, which directly follows the arrest.[102] Despite these statutory requirements, the hearings are usually delayed by the defense attorney, acting out of either his own or his client's interest.[103]

Most often the cause of delay at this point is the attorney's stalling to collect his fee or a part of it. Although few judges will acknowledge the reality of the situation, they are aware of what is happening and know from the record how long the preliminary hearing has been delayed. One candid municipal court judge remarked that he would not force a lawyer to proceed unless his fee was paid, because he knew "what it's like to have to make a living on these cases."

The case may never get beyond this stage. One Cleveland attorney described appearing twice with his client for a scheduled preliminary hearing. Each time the prosecuting witnesses were present, and each time the defense attorney asked for and received a continuance, without challenge or explanation. On the third occasion, he noticed that the witnesses were not present. When the case was called, the defense attorney replied that he was ready and demanded that the hearing proceed. The prosecutor was unable to account for his missing witnesses and the judge dismissed the charges. The county prosecutor could have taken the case to the grand jury, regardless of the dismissal in municipal court, but the case was relatively unimportant and was never revived.

Prior to June of 1970, there was no constitutional right to legal assistance at the preliminary hearing.[104] Some cities provided counsel at this stage of the proceedings, but many did not.[105] Where no legal assistance was made available, the defendant either represented himself or, in most cases, waived the hearing. Given the financial plight of the cities and the new constitutional requirement to provide counsel at the preliminary hearing, many cities now provide legal aid attorneys to represent the indigent at the preliminary hearing and then appoint a private attorney for the later stages of the case. Such has been the Baltimore solution.[106] There an attorney from the public

---

102. Pennsylvania requires that the hearing must be held no sooner than three nor more than ten days after the preliminary arraignment. PA. R. CRIM. P. 119(f)(1). The initial arraignment occurs within a short period after arrest.

103. *Representing the Client, supra* note 56.

104. Coleman v. Alabama, 399 U. S. 1 (1970). This case is discussed in 56 A.B.A.J. 1094 (1970); 3 CONN. L. REV. 366 (1971); and 39 U. CIN. L. REV. 792 (1970).

105. Cleveland, for example, does not provide an attorney until after indictment. Cleveland Press, Nov. 23, 1970, at 9, col. 1.

106. Interview with Arthur Cheslock, Assistant State's Attorney, in Baltimore, April 7, 1971.

defender's office represents the indigent defendant at the preliminary hearing; if the case reaches the trial court, however, a private attorney is assigned. This lack of continuity of representation tends to diminish the quality of the earlier legal assistance. Because the public attorney is not responsible for the case throughout, his interest in the case is diminished, and he is unlikely to be concerned with terminating the case at the preliminary hearing.

Similar criticism has been raised in Cincinnati, where the Legal Aid Society provides the preliminary hearing representation for indigent defendants. After a defendant is indicted in Cincinnati and a private attorney is appointed, the private attorney rarely communicates with the legal aid lawyer, for he believes little can be learned from the legal aid attorney's experience with the case.[107] In New York City the Legal Aid Society represents an indigent defendant throughout the entire criminal case, but this does not solve the problem, because different legal aid attorneys appear on the defendant's behalf in the separate proceedings.[108] In New York, unlike Cincinnati, the legal aid attorneys prepare a case file which is relied upon by each attorney who later deals with the case.[109] Since each has only limited responsibility, however, no one attorney ever becomes fully familiar with a case, and early resolution is unlikely.

That prosecutors are unconcerned whether there is a preliminary hearing is not surprising. The benefits of the hearing largely accrue to the defendant. The purpose of the hearing is to test the sufficiency of the charge, and evidence must be brought forth by the prosecutor to establish probable cause. This enables the defense to discover part of the state's case. For example, the defense attorney becomes aware of the identity of some of the prosecutor's witnesses. By cross-examining these witnesses at the preliminary hearing, the defense attorney may discover the strengths and weaknesses of the state's case.[110] To prevent the preliminary hearing from becoming a "fishing expedition," one New York City Criminal Court judge confines the defense attorney's cross-examination of the state's witnesses to questions concerned solely with probable cause.[111] Constitutional flaws in

---

107. Katz, *Gideon's Trumpet: Mournful and Muffled,* 55 IOWA L. REV. 523, 543 (1970).

108. *Logjam in Our Courts,* LIFE, Aug. 7, 1970, at 24.

109. Mills, *I Have Nothing to Do with Justice,* LIFE, Mar. 12, 1971, at 59.

110. Note, *Preliminary Hearing in the District of Columbia—an Emerging Discovery Device,* 56 GEO. L. J. 191, 193 (1967) [hereinafter cited as *Discovery Device*].

111. Interview with Judge Joel Tyler, New York City Criminal Court, in New York City, June 1, 1971.

the methods used to arrest, search, and interrogate may be uncovered, and the defense attorney can also establish a basis for a motion to suppress and therefore bar crucial evidence from a subsequent trial.

The prosecution derives little benefit from the preliminary hearing, and then only in narrowly circumscribed and technical situations.[112] When the preliminary hearing is delayed, the prosecutor can avoid it entirely by going directly to the grand jury and seeking an indictment.[113] To avoid disclosing any evidence, prosecutors will occasionally go to great lengths to delay a preliminary hearing and take the case directly to the grand jury. This is the practice for homicide cases in New York City. There, according to an assistant prosecuting attorney, preliminary hearings are never held in homicide cases. The district attorney's office takes all homicide cases immediately before the grand jury to avoid disclosing any of its case.[114] Similarly, in Cleveland the preliminary hearing is often postponed and then either waived by the defendant or the matter is taken to the grand jury by the prosecutor before the rescheduled hearing is held.[115] Our study of the Cleveland courts showed that preliminary hearings were held in only one out of every six cases.[116]

In some cities, the preliminary hearing has become the termination point for a substantial number of cases. An American Bar Foundation study estimated that the clearance rate for felonies at this stage of the process was 80 percent in Chicago and 65 percent in Brooklyn, New York.[117] These are cities where there is virtually no opportunity for prosecutor screening prior to the introduction of charges into the lower courts by the police. These courts do not have final jurisdiction over felonies, and the cases are either dismissed or reduced to misdemeanors after the review at the preliminary hearing. Those reduced to misdemeanors are disposed of when the defendant pleads guilty to the reduced charge, for which he is usually promised probation or a very nominal punishment.

---

112. One benefit the prosecution derives from the preliminary hearing is that testimony of witnesses may be admissible at the subsequent trial, if the witness changes his testimony at trial. California v. Green, 399 U. S. 149 (1970).

113. *Discovery Device, supra* note 110, at 192–93.

114. Interview with Steven North, Assistant District Attorney, in New York City, Nov. 18, 1970.

115. The reasons for the high number of waivers in Kansas, Michigan, and Wisconsin are surveyed in Dawson & Miller, *Non-Use of the Preliminary Examination: A Study of Current Practices,* 1964 WIS. L. REV. 252.

116. *See* Appendix A.

117. *Early Disposition, supra* note 61, at 1156.

A device used in the New York courts to clear cases is called the Conditional Discharge, whereby a defendant is permitted to plead guilty in a case where the charge has been reduced to a misdemeanor. As an additional inducement, if the defendant has never been in trouble before and the prosecutor is willing, as he will be because of the clogged court, the plea of guilty is accepted but the defendant is not convicted. He is discharged by the judge on the condition that he not be arrested again for a full year. Should he be arrested again, the original charge will be revived, and he will be sentenced on his plea of guilty. The benefits of such a device are manifold. A case is disposed of and the defendant, while hopefully benefiting from the shock of seeing the criminal process in operation, escapes without a criminal record. The problem with the Conditional Discharge, as disclosed by a judge of the New York City Criminal Court sitting in Manhattan, is that even if the defendant should get into trouble again within the year, the original charge will not be resurrected: "There are simply too many cases handled in this court to keep track of them all."[118]

The quality of the screening done at the preliminary hearing is totally dependent upon the judge. To ensure that the defendant is being charged on adequate grounds, the judge is required to find that probable cause exists, but too often very little screening takes place. In light of the number of defendants who cannot make bail and the great delays that develop at the trial level, a thorough screening is necessary. If the judge at the preliminary hearing does not adequately fulfill this function, then the task of screening is consigned to the trial court. An attorney in the public defender's office in Philadelphia reported that almost half the felony cases that reach the trial court in that city end in dismissals or acquittals.[119] Many of these cases never would have contributed to the backlog if adequate screening had been performed at the preliminary hearing.

THE GRAND JURY INDICTMENT

Even though the police have screened and decided to charge,[120] the

---

118. Interview with Judge Joel Tyler, New York City Criminal Court, in New York City, Dec. 1, 1970.
119. Interview with Vincent Zaccardi, in Philadelphia, Dec. 1, 1970.
120. The decision whether or not to arrest is a form of police screening. "The arrest is legal if it is made upon 'probable cause'—information which would have moved a reasonable man, under the circumstances, to believe that the crime in question had occurred and that it was committed by the accused." Goldstein, *The State and the Accused: Balance of Advantage in Criminal Procedure,* 69 YALE L. J. 1149, 1163–64 & nn. 38–41 (1960).

prosecutor has screened and filed charges, and the municipal court judge has screened and found probable cause,[121] another opportunity for screening exists. The laws of many states still require that prior to a defendant's being formally charged with the commission of a felony, he must be indicted by a grand jury.[122] The grand jury provides the fourth stage of the screening process and offers the least potential for effective screening.

An indictment will not be returned by the grand jury unless probable cause, the same standard used at the preliminary hearing, exists. However, the differences between the grand jury and the preliminary hearing are great. While the preliminary hearing is a full-scale adversary proceeding, the grand jury operates behind closed doors, proceedings are secret, and the accused has no right to be present.[123]

Like that of the preliminary hearing, the purpose of the grand jury is to protect the accused from unfounded charges.[124] Regrettably, it has become a rubber stamp for the prosecutor.[125] A prosecutor in Jersey City best described the control exercised over the grand jury when he pointed out that if the prosecutor wishes to proceed with the prosecution of a particular case, the grand jury returns an indictment on his recommendation. If the prosecutor wishes to dispose of a case, on his recommendation the grand jury returns a no bill, which terminates the case.[126]

---

121. This screening is satisfied by a "skeletal outline of evidence admissible in court to support each element of the offense—a skeletal quality . . . virtually assured by certain grim facts." *Id.* at 1166.

122. *Id.* at 1169–70.

123. *See generally* ORFIELD, CRIMINAL PROCEDURE FROM ARREST TO APPEAL 135 (1947).

124. It performs this "protective function when it determines whether there is sufficient evidence against a specific individual charged with a specified crime to justify a trial." Note, *The Grand Jury as an Investigatory Body,* 74 HARV. L. REV. 590 (1961) [hereinafter cited as *Investigatory Body*].

125. In practice,

> the district attorney, because of his access to information, prestige as an important government official, and familiarity with grand jury procedure, tends to direct the grand jury's operations. Normally the district attorney determines the subject matter of the investigation, and also has considerable control over its conduct. Although he can be excluded from the proceedings, he customarily conducts the primary examination of the witnesses and decides which witnesses will be called. *Id.* at 596 & nn. 43–47.

126. According to the Hudson County Prosecutor, his office has been able to educate the grand jury. In various cases, the prosecutor who pre-

By serving as a rubber stamp for the prosecutor, the grand jury is failing in its historic purpose of protecting the accused from arbitrary government action and failing as well in its screening role. Nevertheless, many prosecutors remain adamant in their desire to preserve the grand jury. The institution enables the prosecutor to conduct an investigation with the power to subpoena witnesses,[127] examine them under oath, preserve their testimony on record, and question a potential defendant without his attorney being present.[128] Moreover, the grand jury enables the prosecutor to engage in wide-ranging investigations seeking a wrong, rather than beginning with the commission of a crime and investigating from that point.

Mindful that each step in the judicial process consumes some time, whether it is worthwhile or not depends upon how much is accomplished at that stage.[129] The grand jury proceeding, which accomplishes nothing and merely duplicates previous steps, certainly causes unwarranted delay.[130] Our study of the Cuyahoga County Court of Common Pleas showed a considerable expenditure of time between the preliminary hearing or the waiver of the hearing and the return of an indictment by the grand jury. Seventy-five

---

sents the case to the grand jury will tell the grand jury that he recommends that an indictment be returned or that a no bill be returned. Usually the prosecutor makes this suggestion to the grand jury without requiring witnesses to testify. If, however, the grand jury wishes to hear the testimony of any witness before deciding whether or not to indict, the witnesses will be called. Interview with Geoffrey Gaulkin, Hudson County Prosecutor, in Jersey City, New Jersey, Nov. 30, 1970.

127. *Investigatory Body, supra* note 124, at 593.

128. The secrecy issue is also discussed Kuh, *The Grand Jury Presentment: Foul Blow or Fair Play?,* 55 COLUM. L. REV. 1103, 1115 (1955).

129. The report of Manhattan District Attorney Frank S. Hogan noted that the procedures of the grand jury "now consume up to six weeks. . . ." In the interest of a speedy trial the report recommended an amendment to the state constitution "to allow defendants to waive grand jury hearings and indictments in felony cases. . . ." N. Y. Times, Feb. 22, 1971, at 33, col. 6.

130. Delay is not in the interest of the public, as can be seen in the case of James McDonald, who was to be tried on robbery charges. The charges against the defendant were dismissed by the court because the defendant was not given a copy of the indictment until after fourteen months had elapsed, even though the state knew where to find the defendant. Such delay, whatever its cause, is inexcusable. Cleveland Plain Dealer, June 17, 1971, at 2, col. 1.

percent of the cases in which there were preliminary hearings required more than twenty-five days after the hearing before the grand jury acted, and 20 percent of the cases took more than fifty days for the grand jury to act.[131]

Getting witnesses to appear, a concern at each stage of the prosecution, presents another problem. To ensure the availability of witnesses and reduce the inconvenience caused to witnesses by multiple appearances, the prosecutors in Chicago try to take cases to the grand jury immediately after the defendants have been bound over at preliminary hearings. If they succeed in this goal, the preliminary hearing and the grand jury proceeding can be completed within one day. This is especially attractive since the two proceedings essentially duplicate each other in function. This approach requires that the grand jury sit at all times that the court is in session and requires more than one jury sitting at a time. Because so little is accomplished by the grand jury towards the equitable resolution of criminal cases, the corresponding expenditures of time and money are hardly commensurate with the value received, except that one period of nonaction between two stages has been eliminated. But the essential problem, duplication, persists.

Only six states continue to require prosecution by indictment in all felony cases.[132] Other states, such as Illinois, Maryland, Ohio, and Pennsylvania, permit the defendant to waive grand jury action and avoid the delay.[133] However, waiver remains a rarity both because it is sometimes complicated and because it is not suggested to the accused unless he is in a hurry to plead guilty. Consequently, almost all felony cases in Chicago, Baltimore, Cleveland, and Philadelphia are processed through the grand jury. Twenty-one states permit the prosecutor to choose between proceeding on an affidavit that he may file or taking the case to the grand jury.[134] Many of the states

---

131. *See* Appendix A.

132. DEL. CONST. art. 1, § 8; N. Y. CONST. art. 1, § 6; S. C. CONST. art. 1, § 17; TENN. CONST. art. 1, § 14; TEX. CONST. art. 1, § 10; W. VA. CODE ANN. § 62–2–1 (1966).

133. ALA. CODE tit. 15, § 260 (Supp. 1969) (grand jury indictment can only be waived by a plea of guilty); GA. CODE ANN. § 27–704; MASS. GEN. LAWS ANN. ch. 276, § § 41, 42 (1959); N. H. REV. STAT. ANN. § 601.2 (1955); N. C. GEN. STAT. § 15–140.1 (Supp. 1969); OHIO REV. CODE 2941.021 (Page Supp. 1970); ORE. CONST. art. VII, § 5; VA. CODE § 19.1–162; ALAS. R. CRIM. P. 7(a)–(b); ILL. CT. R. 401(b); ME. R. CRIM. P. 7(a)–(b); MD. R. P. 708–9; N. J. R. CRIM. P. 3:7–2 (1971); PA. R. CRIM. P. 215(a).

134. State v. Roy, 40 N. M. 397, 60 P.2d 646 (1936); ARK. CONST. amend. 21, § 1; CAL. CONST. art. 1, § 8; CONN. GEN. STAT. ANN. § 54–46;

in this group limit the prerogative to noncapital cases.[135] The practice in the West is to do away with the grand jury requirement, but it persists in the East. In Los Angeles, where California law permits the prosecutor to choose between utilizing the grand jury or proceeding on his own charge, few cases are referred to the grand jury.[136] In Indiana, a grand jury indictment is not required, and in many small counties the prosecutor files affidavits in the superior court, which has ultimate jurisdiction over felony cases. Thereby both the preliminary hearing and grand jury are avoided. In Indianapolis, however, where delay is a problem, prosecutors follow traditional charging practices and use the grand jury in many cases.

Although waiver of indictment is infrequently utilized, even where permitted by law, Judge Robert Kreindler of the New York City Criminal Court has urged its adoption in New York, where indictment is mandatory. Relying upon the experience in federal courts, Judge Kreindler argues that the right to waive an indictment would help to relieve the congestion in the New York courts. Experience in the federal courts would indicate that a defendant waives his right to an indictment when he decides to plead guilty shortly after arrest or preliminary hearing. Once the United States Attorney is notified of the decision, he prepares an information and has the case placed on the court's calendar within a week or ten days, in order to receive the plea of guilty.[137]

In order for Judge Kreindler's proposal to have any effect upon the backlog in New York City, the defendant must be willing to plead guilty to a felony charge at an early stage in the case. The pressures to plead guilty early may be great enough upon those defendants who are unable to secure

---

HAWAII REV. STAT. 37, § 711–8; IDAHO CONST. art. 1, § 8; IND. ANN. STAT. § 9–908 (1956); IOWA CODE ANN. § 769.1 (1950); KAN. STAT. ANN. § 62–801; LA. CRIM. PRO. CODE ANN. art. 382; MICH. COMP. LAWS § § 767.1, 767.2 (1948); MINN. STAT. ANN. § 628.29 (1945); NEB. REV. STAT. § 219–1601 (1964); NEV. REV. STAT. § 173.025; VT. STAT. ANN. tit. 13, § 5652; WASH. REV. CODE tit. 10, § 37.026 (1962); ARIZ. R. CRIM. P. 78; COLO. R. CRIM. P. 7(a)–(b); FLA. R. CRIM. P. 1.140(a) (2); KY. R. CRIM. P. 6.02; WYO. R. CRIM. P. 9.

135. See, e.g., CONN. GEN. STAT. ANN. § 54–42; HAWAII CONST. art. 1, § 8; VT. STAT. ANN. tit. 13, § 5651 (Supp. 1968); FLA. R. CRIM. P. (a)(1).

136. Interview with George Trammell III, Long Beach District Attorney, in Long Beach, California, Dec. 11, 1970.

137. Kreindler, *A Proposal to Streamline the Administration of Criminal Justice,* N.Y.L.J., Mar. 29, 1971, at 1, col. 4.

their release on bail, but financial inequities should play no part in a system that seeks equal justice. For an appreciable number of defendants to agree to such a waiver would probably require considerable compromise from the prosecutor in order to secure the plea. Rather than adopting a proposal that permits a defendant to set his own terms or operates more harshly upon those who are unable to raise bail, a screening process which directs cases out of the process prior to this point becomes a necessity. Judge Kreindler's proposal would probably have little impact upon the overall problem of delay in New York, however, because it skirts the major problem. Defendants are in no hurry because delay works to their benefit.[138] Waiver of grand jury indictment, in states where the defendant is given the prerogative, has not substantially lessened the problem, because few defendants are interested in time-saving devices.

The problem of the duplication in function of the preliminary hearing and the grand jury indictment is a grave one. For a system that is choking to death because there are too many required stages in each case—both formal and informal—the cost in delay for two probable cause hearings is too great. Four states have circumvented this part of the problem by providing for prosecution by information only if a preliminary hearing or probable cause determination has taken place, or if the defendant has waived the preliminary hearing.[139] In those states, at least, the time involved in two probable cause determinations has been avoided.

---

138. A case in point is that of Curtis Armstrong, arrested on March 21 and charged in Brooklyn Criminal Court with grand larceny in the third degree. Unable to meet the bail set at $1,000, he was held in jail. Armstrong exercised his right to demand a preliminary hearing to determine probable cause. The arresting policeman failed to appear at the first hearing but did appear at the second on April 28. The next month Armstrong was indicted. On June 16, he was offered a chance to plead guilty to a misdemeanor, attempted grand larceny, but opted to go to trial, even though he was still in jail. Further administrative delays plagued the case through the summer; and in September, the prosecutor renewed his offer to allow Armstrong to plead to the lesser charge. Again, Armstrong declined. At the trial on October 29, the judge offered him a chance to plead guilty. This time Armstrong agreed to plead guilty to the original charge, because the judge indicated he would try to give him a one-year prison sentence. If he had been convicted at trial he could have received four years in prison. N. Y. Times, Dec. 6, 1970, § 1A, at 1, col. 1.

139. Mo. R. Crim. P. 23.02; Mont. Rev. Code 95–1301 (1947); S. D. Comp. Laws 23–20–2 (1967); Wis. Stat. Ann. 971.02 (West 1971).

TOWARDS A REVAMPING OF THE SCREENING AND CHARGING PROCESS

The discussion of the four-part screening process involving decisions on the part of the police, prosecutor, judges, and grand jury shows the magnitude of the formal criminal process. The design of the screening system shows the seriousness of the decisions that must be made and illustrates the care intended to be taken before a person is forced to defend his freedom and protect his good name. It is a design, however, that is no longer followed: the protection is virtually nonexistent, and the decisions are preordained and made by rote. Until the preliminary process is completed there can be no meaningful plea of guilty or not guilty to a felony charge. Only after the preliminary processes are completed can the decision to go to trial in a felony case be made.

A process that plants the seeds of delay at the inception of prosecution, while offering no real protection to the persons for whom it was intended, should not be defended merely because it is the traditional way. The existing screening and charging process, which frequently requires over two months, does charge in a cumbersome and extended manner, but rarely screens. At present the procedure frequently enables the guilty defendant to obtain a favorable disposition regardless of the merits of a case, because the system cannot handle all of its cases. At the same time, the innocent are penalized, for they are denied speedy justice and are exposed to cursory screening.

The goals of the screening and charging process are admirable but require transformation into workable procedures. In addition to simply charging a suspect with a crime, the process seeks to ensure, through a determination of probable cause, that the charges are well founded. Simultaneously, assurance is sought that the accused is aware of his rights and understands the charges against him. Society's interests bear heavily at this point because the screening process is also intended to determine that prosecution of a particular defendant is not a waste of the criminal justice system's limited time and resources.

The key to reversing the trend of greater and greater delays in the criminal justice system lies in its preliminary stages. If the proposed time line for disposition of criminal cases is to become a reality, the process must be reconstructed at its earliest stage. The number of preliminary steps must be cut, and those that are retained must be redeveloped so that the goals of charging and screening are fulfilled within the concepts of equitable and speedy justice. Each step of the procedure must become a meaningful judicial exercise, not just a formalistic, court-clogging requirement.

EXPANDED BOOKING PROCEDURE

From the suspect's arrest through his first appearance in court, everything that is accomplished with respect to the suspect fits nicely within the police station booking procedure. The preliminary appearance has become nothing more than an extension of the booking procedure and formal registration of the initial complaint. Even the determination of bail at the first appearance is based upon established formulas rather than individual determinations. Moreover, the first appearance is conducted in a tumultuous municipal court and generally lacks any semblance of dignity or justice.

When an individual is arrested on a felony charge, he is booked at the police station and then detained until a first court appearance. Rather than requiring this separate court appearance, the substantive aspects of it can be engrafted onto the booking procedure and handled by the police as soon as the suspect is taken into custody.[140] The desk sergeant or an equivalent person, while obtaining the usual booking information, can notify the de-

---

140. Among other recommendations to cut delays in the criminal justice field, Manhattan District Attorney Frank S. Hogan suggested placing more authority for screening at the booking procedure. He urged the expansion of two Vera Institute of Justice programs: "[P]rearraignment verification of criminal complaints so policemen do not have to spend long hours in court, and the year old project under which prosecution witnesses are excused from misdemeanor hearings until they are absolutely needed." N. Y. Times, Feb. 22, 1971, at 33, col. 6.

An experimental pre-arraignment procedure that was used in the Bronx and Queens criminal courts in 1970 was recently extended on a larger scale to the Brooklyn courts. Under this plan the police officer and the complainant will be able to give the facts in the case immediately following the booking procedure at the precinct. In addition to freeing policemen to return to work and saving witnesses and injured parties the inconvenience of waiting out delays in the process, the city expects a substantial savings in police hourly wages. The collateral benefits of the plan include a more efficient arrest process that will allow the policeman to spend more time at his job of protecting the community and that will foster better cooperation by complainants and witnesses. N.Y.L.J., Feb. 5, 1971, at 1, col. 4.

While the focus of such a program is on the saving of time and money and not on the elimination of duplicate procedures that tend to clog the system at the arraignment stage, a complete report of the case at the time of the complaint will provide a more effective screening process and will enable the judge at the arraignment

fendant of his rights, inform him of the charges on which he was arrested, and make a preliminary determination of bail. Persons accused of misdemeanors can be permitted to post a bond and secure their release at this stage without first appearing in court, and there is no fundamental reason why station-house bail cannot also be made available to felony suspects.

Preliminary determinations of bail by magistrates at the first court appearance are rote assessments anyway, ascertained by statutory formulas based upon the preliminary charges filed against a defendant. Rarely is the defendant represented by counsel at this preliminary stage, and little consideration is given to the accused's position and ability to raise the bail. Unfortunately, the mechanical bail setting that is performed at the preliminary appearance sticks with the defendant throughout the proceeding regardless of his inability to raise the money.[141] Our proposal would require a thorough review of the station-house bail determination within forty-eight hours, if the defendant has been unable to secure his freedom. Moreover, our bail recommendation, which is explained in the next chapter, is directed at the release of defendants without money guarantees, wherever reasonable.

At this stage, the principal function of the booking officer is to arrange with court officials the time and place of the preliminary hearing. If the defendant is freed on bail by the booking officer, the preliminary hearing, a probable cause determination, should be scheduled within seven days of the defendant's arrest. If the defendant is not eligible for release by the booking officer because of the nature of the charges or because of his inability to raise money bail, then the preliminary hearing should be scheduled within forty-eight hours of the defendant's arrest. If the forty-eight-hour deadline cannot be met, and the fault lies with the state, then the defendant should be released without a money bail requirement and the preliminary hearing rescheduled for a time within the original seven days.

---

proceedings to make a more realistic determination of bail. However, the New York Legal Aid Society objected to the program because the judge is often prevented from providing a proper bail determination, and many defendants are consequently detained unnecessarily. N.Y.L.J., Feb. 8, 1971, at 1, col. 6.

Precinct pre-arraignments have been discontinued in favor of night arraignment courts.

141. An expanded booking procedure could provide an opportunity for more realistic bail setting, since more information could be made available. Judges often maintain that if they had known all the facts about a defendant they would have set lower bail. N. Y. Times, Oct. 11, 1970, at 80, col. 2.

If the fault for the delay lies with the accused, then he should not be released.

The purpose of the rigid formula is twofold. Not only does it provide protection against arbitrary disregard of individual rights by the booking officer, but it also enables the criminal justice system to eliminate the formalistic and nonproductive preliminary appearance. The judge at the preliminary appearance is thereby freed for more productive tasks.[142] By eliminating the first appearance and requiring the preliminary hearing to be held within a fixed number of days, the number of opportunities for delaying the ultimate resolution of the case are reduced. Moreover, prosecutors will be forced to deal with a case immediately so that a probable cause determination can be made shortly after arrest, when the facts are freshest.

THE RIGHT TO COUNSEL AT THIS STAGE

To assure that no defendant is unnecessarily detained, the booking officer should be authorized and required to appoint counsel for indigent defendants and any other defendant who is being held. The appointments would come from a list of attorneys provided by the court. The booking officer should be responsible for notifying the appointed attorney and the court immediately after the appointment takes place. Notification to the court will signify that the attorney has been contacted by the booking officer and that the attorney has accepted the responsibility. Spurious claims of indigency can be handled at a later time by the court.

When counsel is appointed and notified, a time should be set by the attorney and the booking officer for an appointment between the indigent defendant and his attorney. Concurrently, a time should be set for a conference between the appointed attorney and the prosecutor who will be assigned to the case. For a defendant who is held in custody, the attorney's appointment with the defendant and his subsequent conference with the prosecutor should be held within twenty-four hours of the arrest and book-

---

142. Another method of freeing judges for more significant tasks, suggested by State Senator John H. Hughes, Chairman of the New York State Joint Legislative Committee on Crime, would be to appoint "parajudicial personnel" to handle pretrial hearings. N. Y. Times, Oct. 11, 1970, at 80, col. 6. The same suggestion was put forth by Herman B. Glaser, Chairman for the New York Council for Civic Affairs, saying that of the 30,000 lawyers practicing in New York "there are hundreds of highly qualified attorneys who would gladly volunteer to act as night court judges during the emergency as a service to the community."

ing. The appointment and conference for a defendant who is not held in custody should occur within five days of the arrest and booking. Defendants who are not indigent and who retain their own attorneys should be held to the same time schedules, to preserve the interests of the individual and the justice system. If a defense attorney requests a continuance, it should be granted only upon a showing of necessity and only if the defendant is not in custody. No continuance should be for more than forty-eight hours.

This proposed revamping of the charging process is being purposefully and rigidly cast. Primarily, it will ensure that a detained suspect has legal assistance at the earliest possible moment. Secondarily, it will provide enough formality to prevent the charging procedures from stretching out unreasonably. The flexibility of the existing court procedures is one of the causes of delay. Attorneys are free to postpone as they wish, deferring hearings and the resolution of cases to suit their own convenience.

ATTORNEY-PROSECUTOR CONFERENCE

The effectiveness of the attorney-prosecutor charging conference is predicated upon the understanding that more than 90 percent of all felony cases end in nontrial dispositions. Unfortunately, little is done by the attorneys in a case until they are under an absolute deadline to resolve the case or go to trial. Consequently, felony cases linger on criminal court dockets, slowly threading their way through the early formal stages and clogging the courts. Neither the prosecutor nor the defense attorney feels compelled to discuss the case until all of the potential delay is exhausted. As a result, these cases must be scheduled by the courts even though they will eventually result in guilty pleas to the charge, with a recommendation for reduced punishment, or to a lesser charge. This prevents the courts from giving priority scheduling to those cases that must be tried, since each case looks alike to those making the schedule, and the judges do not know which cases will be settled without trial.

The purpose of the charging conference is to move negotiations between the prosecutor and the defense attorney to the earliest possible stage.[143] This

---

143. George Trammell III, Los Angeles District Attorney, has illustrated the significance of the conference:

> After indictment, there is still a large caseload to dispose of. To handle the court's caseload, the District Attorney's office in Brooklyn has again shown leadership in managing a very workable procedure to reduce felony trial calendar congestion. To reduce the number of cases which actually go to full trial, a system has been instituted whereby one week after the defendant is arraigned on the

will force the prosecutor to screen out those cases that normally result in dismissal at a later time. In addition, the prosecutor will be compelled to spend time on the case prior to the preliminary procedures and be forced to revise what is often an unrealistic police charge. By getting the prosecutor and defense attorney together at the beginning of the process, the projected result is a realistic charge based upon the prosecutor's review of the case—his assessment of the convictability of the defendant and the admissibility of the evidence. Correspondingly, the defense attorney faced with a realistic charge and within the context of a strict time-line requirement will either have to go to trial at an early date or be prepared to plead his client guilty on the knowledge that he will be convicted as charged.

The success of the conference will be dependent upon the attitudes of the attorneys. Attorneys must enter into the conference openly and with the intent of seeking a resolution for the case. With this approach, they will find that it is relatively easy to dispose of a great percentage of their cases in a simple, less time-consuming manner than is used at present. They will also discover that the results obtained at this juncture are comparable to the pleas that currently are obtained after months and years of waiting. As the attorneys discuss the case, they will be able to point out the weaknesses in each other's position. Eventually, each attorney will recognize that his initial impression must be reevaluated and that the truth lies somewhere in between the versions offered by the police, the witnesses, and the defendant. The charging conference, then, will result in the emergence of convictable charges rather than in the existing reducible charge.

Prosecutors and defense attorneys with whom we have discussed this proposal have reservations about it, but we believe that those reservations stem from a mental set created by the traditional patterns of the justice system. One prosecutor felt that a truly realistic and convictable charge would leave the prosecutor devoid of any reduction that he could offer to induce a plea. If such were the case, he continued, no defendant would have anything to lose by waiting and going to trial. The defense attorney's objection was similar, though emanating from an entirely different perspec-

---

indictment, his case is set down for a pretrial conference in a special court known as "Conference and Discussion," where an attempt is made to work out an early disposition of the case. The Assistant District Attorney, the defense attorney, and the judge all participate in the "negotiation" in open court. The case is evaluated from the standpoint of the facts pointing to guilt, the defendant's prior record, and mitigating or extenuating circumstances. Over 60% of the court cases are disposed of by a plea as a result of this pretrial conference. Trammell, *supra* note 4, at 246.

tive. He contended that a defendant must be offered something in order to get him to plead. By prolonging criminal cases, the prosecutor is forced to come forward with an offer that will appear attractive to the defendant, even if that offer is the most the prosecutor could have eventually gotten out of the case. Both positions are the products of a system that is geared to delay, and neither considers the increasing unworkability of that system.

A realistic charging process would eliminate many cases from the felony stream. Whether these cases are proper subjects for court diversion programs, prosecution as misdemeanors, or outright dismissal, their elimination at the outset would free court dockets. Once the prosecutor shows at the inception of this reform that his office is prepared to try cases within the speedy trial requirement, guilty pleas will flow as they do now because the charges will be realistic. Defendants will be as ready to plead then as they ultimately are now, once the opportunity to wait out the prosecutor no longer exists and the prosecutor makes it clear that he is trying cases and convicting defendants. The significant difference would be that a case will require less time to come to trial. Even if fewer pleas result, the judges and courtrooms freed by an effective screening process could handle some additional trials.

If the case is resolved at the charging conference, any reason to hold the preliminary hearing disappears. The defendant should agree in writing that he is ready to appear and plead guilty in lieu of the preliminary hearing. His statement should also include the charge to which he has agreed to plead and any arrangement that has been made regarding punishment. The appearance to plead guilty should take place at the time when the preliminary hearing was originally scheduled. Since the plea is entered without any prior judicial review of the charge, some evidence should be presented to the judge at the time the plea is taken to support the defendant's guilt. In Boston, before a guilty plea is accepted, the arresting officer must testify as to the defendant's guilt, and the defendant must agree that what the officer states is an accurate representation of the facts. The testimony of the arresting officer and the concurrence of the defendant would be sufficient evidence to satisfy this suggested requirement.

THE PRELIMINARY HEARING COURT

Under existing court structure in most states, preliminary hearings take place in municipal courts, which also have complete jurisdiction over misdemeanors. If the defendant, as a result of the charging conference, were prepared to plead guilty to the felony charge, that plea could not be accepted by the municipal court judge. The case would have to be referred to the trial court. The existence of a two-tiered court system for felony cases would cause delay under the proposal discussed here, just as it does under the existing structure when a remorseful defendant wishes to plead guilty at his preliminary appearance.

To eliminate the delays inherent in the two-tiered court structure, the Wayne County Recorder's Court in Detroit offers a simple solution that could be adopted in other cities. This court possesses complete jurisdiction in all felony cases, extending from the preliminary hearing through the trial. As a result of the single court system, a judge can dispose of a felony case at any stage of the proceedings, once the defense and prosecution have reached agreement.

In addition to their inability to dispose of felony cases, municipal courts often lack the decorum and atmosphere in which to consider serious crimes. In some cities, the preliminaries for felony cases take place in courtrooms that are packed with persons charged with minor offenses. The judges in these courtrooms are pressed to conclude their daily calendars, and persons facing lengthy imprisonment for serious crimes are often treated in the same haphazard manner as persons charged with minor offenses. If there were one court charged with the responsibility for felony cases and another for lesser offenses, the charge that results from the conference between the defense attorney and the prosecutor could simply be referred and docketed in the appropriate court.[144] The proposed charging process, however, is not dependent upon an end to the two-tier felony court system. A felony charge to which the defendant agrees to plead guilty, after the conference between his attorney and the prosecutor, could be directed to the trial court; if no agreement was reached, the preliminary hearing could still take place as scheduled in the municipal court.

In addition to consigning felony cases to the jurisdiction of one court, we believe that the interests of speedy justice would be further advanced by assigning each case to one judge, from its preliminary stages through resolution. Today, in most jurisdictions, the only person who remains the same throughout a criminal case is the defendant and possibly his retained attorney. Some prosecutors deal only with preliminary hearings, and then different prosecutors will handle the later stages. In some cities, even the various preliminary stages will be handled by different prosecutors. The same situation exists where the defendant is represented by a public defender organi-

---

144. Among the suggestions made by Mayor Lindsay in his statement to the Administrative Board of the Judicial Conference was the controversial proposal to abolish the city's Criminal Court and merge its functions into the state court system. N. Y. Times, Oct. 11, 1970, at 80, col. 2.

zation: each stage finds the defendant represented by a different attorney, unfamiliar with the case. The problem is compounded when the judge who presides at the various stages is unfamiliar with what has gone before.[145]

All interests would benefit if the same officials were responsible for a case from beginning to end. Society's interest in ensuring that its courts dispense justice and that justice be provided speedily would be particularly enhanced if one judge had the personal responsibility for a case. Several federal district courts, including those sitting in Cleveland and New York, have adopted personal docket systems, whereby a judge is assigned a case after the completion of the preliminaries.[146] The personal docket system guarantees that the judge is thoroughly familiar with the case, ends the practice whereby lawyers delay a case until the matter is scheduled before a favorable judge, and vests in a single judge the responsibility for the completion of a case

---

145. "Some of the sequences in processing of a case—the path from arraignment to final disposition—involve as many as six changes in the judge, the district attorney and, for indigent defendants, the Legal Aid Society attorney according to the report." N. Y. Times, Jan. 31, 1971, at 67, col. 5. The confusion is well illustrated in the case of Haywood Boose, arraigned in Brooklyn Criminal Court on March 18, 1970, for burglary. Legal Aid was assigned the case and a hearing was set for March 24 with Boose held in jail because he could not raise the $1,500 bail.

>   March 24. Back in court. But a different courtroom, a "hearing part," with a different judge, a different prosecutor, a different Legal Aid lawyer. Boose decided he would find his own lawyer, one who would stay with him all the way through. The judge adjourned the case to give him time. Legal Aid relieved. N. Y. Times, Dec. 6, 1970, § 1A, at 1, col. 1.

>   Although Boose was an indigent, no one questioned his ability to get a private attorney. At the rescheduled hearing on April 8, Boose had not found a lawyer and the case was adjourned, again without questioning his chances of finding counsel. At the next date, the judge assigned Boose a lawyer, the same one originally appointed at the arraignment. At the trial on August 31, Legal Aid asked to be relieved of the case because of a conflict of interest, as they were defending Boose's co-defendant. The court appointed a private attorney on September 21, and on November 4, Boose pleaded guilty to a lesser charge. *Id.*

146. Cleveland Plain Dealer, Mar. 13, 1971, § A, at 12, col. 2; N. Y. Times, Mar. 15, 1971, at 28, col. 1.

>   According to a recent study of personalized docket systems throughout the country, more personnel are needed in order to make the system work. As a result, the costs of the personalized docket are great. Cleveland Plain Dealer, July 12, 1971, at 1, col. 2.

within the proposed time-line requirements. Even the federal district court system would be improved if the personal docket approach were extended to include the preliminary hearing and bring the entire case within the jurisdiction of one judge.

PROBABLE CAUSE DETERMINATION

When a case is not screened out of the felony process at the charging conference or resolved by an early plea of guilty, the preliminary hearing should proceed as scheduled. The state must first produce sufficient evidence to establish that probable cause exists to justify charging the defendant with the crime. After probable cause has been ruled upon by the judge and found to have been proved, then the prosecutor would have the burden of showing the court why a detained accused has not been released on bail and does not meet the standards for bail that will be set forth in the following chapter. Preliminary hearings should not be waivable by the defendant or avoided by the prosecutor, unless the case has already been resolved.

Once the preliminary hearing has established the existence of probable cause, there is no reason for a second probable cause determination. The grand jury hearing is a duplication which only enables the prosecutor to obtain prospective witnesses' testimony on record. If the prosecutor feels the need to call the state's witnesses prior to trial, their appearance should be at the preliminary hearing, where the defendant's attorney has an opportunity to hear their testimony and cross-examine the witnesses. We do not propose the elimination of the grand jury system in its entirety, but only where the defendant has been taken into custody and where the mandatory preliminary hearing is held. The grand jury could continue to function, albeit on a much smaller scale, investigating criminal activity where there has been no arrest and overseeing public officials as a check against official misconduct.

This proposal for the restructuring of the screening and charging process, while reducing the number of steps in felony prosecutions, would require substantial commitment of resources at the earliest steps in the process. The burden would fall upon the prosecutor's office, which, instead of assigning one man to assist in the charging process, would have to involve a significant number of its staff at this stage of a felony case. Prosecutors are already hard put to fulfill all of their responsibilities, but the recommendation is offered in the belief that the only way to reduce the crippling backlog within the criminal justice system is to dispose of cases at their inception, and that early disposition can become a reality if the preliminary stages are restructured and taken more seriously.

4 / BAIL: FREEDOM BEFORE TRIAL

Since early colonial days, America has had a tradition of holding accused persons in jail for extended pretrial periods. John Peter Zenger, sometimes known in America as the father of freedom of the press, spent ten months in jail while awaiting trial for criminal libel against the English governor.[1] Consistent with the English law operating in the colonies, Zenger was accorded his right to have bail set. The magistrate, who was responsible to the governor, set bail at 400 pounds, notwithstanding Zenger's adequate evidentiary presentation that this exceeded his net worth ten times, and that it was impossible for him to acquire the sum.[2] Today, the practice of denying the accused freedom by the intentional or unintentional setting of bail in an amount the defendant cannot afford persists, although it is subjected to increasing attack. These frontal assaults on the bail system have necessitated a focusing upon the protections which the Constitution and statutes give to the accused prior to trial.

RIGHT TO BAIL

The Eighth Amendment of the Bill of Rights is unclear regarding the actual protection it affords the accused. Adopted in 1791, it states: "Exces-

---

1. A. SCHLESINGER, BIRTH OF A NATION 163 (1968).
2. J. ALEXANDER, A BRIEF NARRATIVE OF THE CASE AND TRIAL OF JOHN PETER ZENGER 48 (1963).

137

sive bail shall not be required. . . ."[3] Whether or not this language creates an affirmative right to bail has been vigorously argued over the years, particularly during the extensive congressional debates surrounding the consideration of the District of Columbia's preventive detention provision. The Constitution makes no other reference to bail, and since the Supreme Court has never squarely faced the issue of a right to bail, it remains a subject of conjecture and dispute among constitutional authorities.[4]

The failure of the Supreme Court to reach the issue of a right to bail is explained partly by the difference between the language of the Judiciary Act of 1789[5] and that of the Eighth Amendment, which was enacted two years later. The Judiciary Act provided that "upon all arrests in criminal cases, bail shall be admitted, except where the punishment may be death. . . ."[6] The language of the Judiciary Act indicates an intent to provide for bail as a matter of right in all but capital cases. Whether the framers of the Bill of Rights assumed that the Judiciary Act established an absolute right to bail and that the only need was to protect the individual from excessive bail or whether their intent was to cut back on the grant of a right in the Judiciary Act and the tradition stemming from the Magna Carta is unknown. The result of this dispute as to intent has been the creation of two separate theories under which the problems involving bail have been resolved. When the controversy involved excessive bail, the Court could apply the language of the Eighth Amendment; and where a right to bail was at issue, the Court could decide under the Judiciary Act. Reliance on the convenient Judiciary Act has avoided the necessity of deciding whether a right to bail exists under the Constitution. The Judiciary Act is not applicable to prosecutions in state courts, so whether the Eighth Amendment guarantees a federal right to bail remains a crucial question.

The closest the Supreme Court has ever come to interpreting whether the Eighth Amendment guarantees a right to bail was in *Stack v. Boyle,* a case primarily concerned with the setting of excessive bail. There the Supreme Court ruled that "[b]ail set at a figure higher than an amount reasonably calculated to fulfill this purpose [to secure assurance that the defendant will

---

3. U. S. CONST. amend. VIII.
4. *See, e.g.,* Mitchell, *Bail Reform and the Constitutionality of Pretrial Detention,* 55 VA. L. REV. 1223 (1969) [hereinafter cited as *Constitutionality of Pretrial Detention*]. Professor Tribe of Harvard offered a response to Attorney General Mitchell. Tribe, *An Ounce of Detention: Preventive Justice in the World of John Mitchell,* 56 VA. L. REV. 371 (1970) [hereinafter cited as *An Ounce of Detention*].
5. 1 Stat. 73.
6. 1 Stat. 73 at 91.

stand trial] is excessive under the Eighth Amendment."[7] The Supreme Court was saying, in effect, that the Constitution prohibited the courts from denying the right to bail by the indirect, though common, practice of requiring unreasonably inflated bail. If bail cannot be denied indirectly, then it would seem unlikely that it could be denied directly in noncapital cases. The implication of the Court's decision is that the Constitution guarantees a right to bail, but it is at present a right supported only by logically persuasive arguments and not by conclusive court decision.

If a right to bail were found in the Eighth Amendment, it would not be an absolute right, as no constitutional rights are absolute. All are subject to curtailment when the government shows a compelling need for infringement and limitation.[8] Both state and federal governments deny bail when the defendant is charged with an offense which could carry the death penalty.[9] The rationale for this denial of bail is fairly obvious: no amount of money will ensure the defendant's appearance at trial if, upon conviction, he risks loss of his life.[10] Bail is also denied in noncapital cases to persons who have a history of flight to avoid prosecution.[11]

Clearly, the denial of bail to one charged with a capital offense, and to one who has demonstrated his unwillingness to stand trial, is substantially different from the concept of preventive detention, which authorizes the

7. 342 U. S. 1, 5 (1951).
8. Cantwell v. Connecticut, 310 U. S. 296 (1939); Feiner v. New York, 340 U. S. 315 (1951).
9. This is specified by rule in the federal system and by statute in states. Note, *Bail in the United States: A System in Need of Reform,* 20 HASTINGS L. J. 380, 382 & nn. 19, 20 (1969) [hereinafter cited as *System in Need of Reform*]. Rule 46(c) provides:
   AMOUNT. If the defendant is admitted to bail, the amount thereof shall be such as in the judgment of the commissioner or court or judge or justice will insure the presence of the defendant, having regard to the nature and circumstances of the offense charged, the weight of the evidence against him, the financial ability of the defendant to give bail and the character of the defendant. FED. R. CRIM. P. 46(c).
10. It is also reasonable to conclude that in capital cases bail should be denied because of the potential danger the accused presents to the community. *See also* Mitchell, *Bail Reform and the Constitutionality of Pretrial Detention,* 55 VA. L. REV. 1223 (1969), *as quoted in, Preventive Detention, Hearings Before the Subcommittee on Constitutional Rights of the Committee on the Judiciary, United States Senate,* 91st Cong., 2d Sess. 1128, 1129 (1970) [hereinafter cited as *Preventive Detention, Hearings*].
11. *In re* Lamar, 294 F. 688 (D. N. J. 1924).

retention of a defendant who has demonstrated a propensity to commit another crime if released. In the former instances, the reasons for the denial of bail go directly to the accepted rationale for requiring bail, that of assuring the defendant's presence at trial. The rationale for preventive detention, however, is not the traditional one, but is based upon the likelihood of further criminal conduct by the accused if he is released.[12] Determining correctly which defendants should be preventively detained is dependent upon the ability of the judicial officer to predict the likelihood of future criminal behavior.

Preventive detention is a use of bail not contemplated by the framers of the Judiciary Act or the Bill of Rights,[13] but the lack of precedent for this use of bail is not adequate reason to dismiss the concept as unconstitutional. The Bill of Rights should be capable of responding to new and serious threats to community safety just as it must meet new threats to personal freedom from government.[14]

The constitutional history of the United States is a history of crises through which the strength of the Constitution has been enhanced by a broad and flexible reading of what the Constitution allows. In the past, the great issues were concerned with economics and government involvement in the economy. The Great Depression, the experimentation of the New Deal, and the pressure on the Supreme Court to assist in the nation's economic revival settled the issue of whether the federal government was constitutionally empowered to regulate the economy.[15] If the Constitution were inflexible and rigidly interpreted, it would have gone the way of other

---

12. *Constitutionality of Pretrial Detention, supra* note 4, at 1232–35.

13. *Cf. Stack v. Boyle,* 342 U. S. 1, 8 (1951), where the Court stated: "Admission to bail always involves a risk that the accused will take flight. That is a calculated risk which the law takes as the price of our system of justice." *But see* the Judiciary Act of 1789, which established the distinction between capital and noncapital offenses, and authorized release for capital crimes only at the discretion of the higher court justices. Judiciary Act of 1789, 1 Stat. 73 at 91 (1789).

14. The dual vitality of the Bill of Rights is illustrated by two cases in the First Amendment area. In *Yates v. United States,* 354 U. S. 298 (1957), the Supreme Court reaffirmed the doctrine that abstract advocacy is protected by the First Amendment, while in *Adderly v. Florida,* 385 U. S. 39 (1966), the Court held that the state's power to control the use of public property included the ability to remove demonstrators from jail property.

15. Schecter Poultry Corp. v. United States, 295 U. S. 495 (1935); *contra* NLRB v. Jones & Laughlin Steel Corp., 301 U. S. 1 (1937); Steward Machine Co. v. Davis, 301 U. S. 548 (1937).

noble experiments in self-government and been replaced countless times rather than withstanding the test of almost two hundred years.

It has been an innovative two centuries for the Constitution and the nation for which it provides the fundamental law. The Constitution has been tested and at times strained by the tremendous changes that have taken place. As efforts to solve contemporary problems continue, the Constitution will be tested again and again to determine what limits it places on the government's power to solve these problems. Whether the Constitution will allow a preventive detention program as one acceptable answer to some of the nation's crime problems will not be known until the Supreme Court confronts the issue.

PREVENTIVE DETENTION IN THE DISTRICT OF COLUMBIA

In 1970 Congress adopted a program of limited preventive detention in the District of Columbia Court Reform and Criminal Procedure Act. The constitutionality of preventive detention is an issue to be determined by the Supreme Court, but the reasonableness of the federal experiment and its potential for solving any of the problems are to be determined by applying other standards.

Contrary to the statements of both proponents and opponents, preventive detention is not a new and unique measure but merely a codification[16] of what is a reality of life to all persons jailed before trial: confinement without a determination of guilt.[17] The program was adopted in an attempt

---

16. Pub. L. No. 91–358, § § 23–1321–32 (July 29, 1970) [hereinafter cited as *Criminal Procedure Act*].

17. As commentators have stated:

Many judges have tried to deal with the problem by practicing a "sub rosa" form of preventive detention in bail determinations, but the practice has met with little success in separating likely offenders from safe risks. Given the present state of the predictive art, codification of this practice would probably not measurably enhance the safety of the community. *An Ounce of Detention, supra* note 4, at 372–73 & nn. 5–6.

Until 1966, judges in the Federal courts and in the Federally administered District of Columbia had developed a rough-hewn method of keeping many such defendants locked up while awaiting trial. A 179-year-old Federal law (Judiciary Act of 1789)—still in effect— requires that every defendant in a Federal court be allowed freedom on bail, unless the crime he's accused of is murder or some other act serious enough to warrant the death penalty. But if the judge sets bail too high for the defendant to raise, the jail door stays shut.

to reduce the allegedly large recidivist crime rate among persons free on bail who are awaiting trial.[18] Unfortunately, it will have hardly any effect upon the incidence of crime, for it does not and could not constitutionally authorize unlimited pretrial detention of any defendant.

The Act permits a defendant to be held up to sixty days and requires that his case be listed on an expedited calendar.[19] If, at the end of sixty days, his case has not come to trial, the defendant is to be treated like any other person accused of crime and is to be subject to the same release conditions. Regrettably, it is virtually impossible to bring someone to trial in the District of Columbia within sixty days.[20] Since the defendant is eligible to

---

Thus over the years Federal judges had been able to detain people they deemed dangerous by setting high bail, often by a scale rising according to the seriousness of the offense. Large, *Quest for a Fair, Effective Bail System,* Wall Street Journal, July 17, 1968, at 14, col. 4 [hereinafter cited as Large].

18. In fact, however, "[o]nly 5.9% of all persons indicted in the United States District Court for the District of Columbia in 1968 allegedly committed an offense while on bail awaiting another charge." *An Ounce of Detention, supra* note 4, at n. 3.

The figures from a recent Washington crime study indicate that 426 out of 712 defendants received some form of pretrial release. Of these, 11 percent were rearrested, but only 3 percent on some felony charge. Those originally arrested for some crime of violence (106) demonstrated some predilection for repeating criminal acts, as 17 percent were rearrested. However, of these arrests only 5 percent were charged with a violent criminal act. N. Y. Times, June 15, 1970, at 35, col. 2.

Another Washington survey, the District of Columbia Crime Commission Survey, studied 2,776 cases in the district court. A total of 207 (7.5 percent) were charged with committing a crime while out on bail, but only 124 (4.5 percent) were charged with a crime of actual or potential violence. D.C. CRIME COMMISSION REPORT 931 (1966).

Testimony given to Senator Ervin's subcommittee at the time that preventive detention was being considered painted a considerably grimmer picture: of 130 persons released, it was found that 45 of them (34 percent) were later indicted for at least one additional felony. This is illustrated by the case of Tyrone Parker, arrested early in 1967 for armed robbery. In the next two years, he was charged with assault with a gun, armed robbery, robbery and assault, burglary, assault with a board and a gun, bank robbery, and bank robbery again. In each case, he was released and has never been convicted. N. Y. Times, Jan. 30, 1969, at 1, col. 6.

19. *Criminal Procedure Act, supra* note 16, at § 23–1322(d)(1).

20. *See* Wald Memorandum in *Preventive Detention, Hearings, supra* note 10.

be free after the sixty-day period, he obviously represents the same threat to the physical well-being of his fellow citizens as he did when he was originally arrested. If the defendant is as predictably vicious and violent as the government claims when it seeks to have him detained, then the only real remedy is to bring him to trial quickly and, if he is convicted, to incarcerate him for the full term allowed by law. Sixty days, compared to the amount of time presently consumed in the District between arrest and trial, will pass very quickly, and the detainee will again be on the streets for the remainder of the delay. If, however, preventive detention results in the realization of a real sixty-day calendar, and defendants begin coming to trial within that period, then the program will have made a substantial contribution to society. The contribution will, however, be in the creation of an expedited calendar rather than in preventive detention.

The sixty-day limitation is not the only problem with preventive detention. Rather than fostering the completion of criminal cases within sixty days, preventive detention will probably increase the congestion in the criminal courts, thereby creating greater delays.[21] Rightfully, the decision to detain a defendant cannot be made unilaterally by the prosecutor. Detention can occur only after a full hearing before a judicial officer, whose ruling is subject to appeal.[22] Instead of eliminating steps in the criminal procedure, preventive detention creates new and additional steps. This is the exact opposite of what is needed. A wide range of time-consuming judicial proceedings is likely, thereby diverting from other cases the attention and time of judicial officers and prosecutors. If preventive detention is used frequently, the net effect may well be to increase the time between arrest and case disposition for all criminal cases. If this occurs, then the detained defendant ultimately will be on the streets as long as he would have been before the advent of preventive detention, notwithstanding his incarceration for sixty days.

---

21. Statement of Sam Ervin, Oct. 27, 1969, in *Preventive Detention, Hearings, supra* note 10, at 1183.

22. Criminal Procedure Act, *supra* note 16, at § 23–1324. This appeal right is available to the person who is detained and to the person who is required to return to custody after specified hours. The appellate stages, from the original application to the judicial officer, are to the court of original jurisdiction and, following an unfavorable disposition, to the appellate court. *Id.* at § 23–1324 (a & b). The United States Attorney also has the right to appeal a judicial officer's decision to release a person, with or without release conditions, or to appeal the judicial officer's denial of the prosecutor's request for detention. *Id.* at § 23–1324(c & d).

Although the concept itself may not be unconstitutional, the application of preventive detention to specific defendants may well be.[23] To determine whether a decision to detain is constitutional, as applied to each accused, may well require the full scale of appeals available in the federal court system. This is not likely to alleviate the problems of congestion and delay. At the request of defense counsel, the hearings to determine whether a defendant is to be detained have on occasion been conducted behind closed doors.[24] These closed-door hearings have been justified on the theory that they avoid pretrial publicity and alleviate the problem of searching out jurors who have not been influenced by the advance publicity. If closed-door hearings become the practice, whether requested by the defense or not, then serious questions will be raised regarding the Sixth Amendment right to a public trial.[25]

The categories of persons subject to preventive detention are sloppily drafted and too open-ended, bringing too many defendants within their scope. In addition to applying to persons charged with crimes of violence who have been previously convicted of such crimes, the Act also authorizes that persons charged with "dangerous crimes,"[26] though not previously convicted, may be detained "if the Government certifies by motion that based on such person's *pattern of behavior* consisting of his past and present conduct, . . . there is no condition or combination of conditions which will reasonably assure the safety of the community."[27] Although the judicial officer must find that there is a substantial probability that the defendant is guilty of the offense charged, before he is subject to detention,[28] this requirement is much less stringent than the constitutional standard of requiring proof beyond a reasonable doubt. Even more disconcerting is the breadth of behavior that may be used to create the pattern of conduct

---

23. The ABA Pretrial Release Report indicated:

   It seems more probable that the constitutional defects in preventive detention, if they in fact exist, lie in due process limitations on predicting future criminal conduct. At the heart of the problem is the inherent difficulty in making such predictions with sufficient accuracy. Where the consequences of a mistaken prediction is unwarranted detention, due process of law may be violated. ABA PROJECT ON MINIMUM STANDARDS FOR CRIMINAL JUSTICE: STANDARDS RELATING TO PRETRIAL RELEASE 70 (1968) [hereinafter cited as PRETRIAL RELEASE].

24. Letter from Thomas A. Flannery, United States Attorney, to Maryland Congressman Lawrence Hogan, April 2, 1971.

25. The Washington Post, Mar. 27, 1971, § A, at 1.

26. *Criminal Procedure Act, supra* note 16, at § 23–1331 (3).

27. *Id.* at § 23–1322(a)(1).

28. *Id.* at § 23–1332(b)(2).

justifying detention. The possible kinds of conduct that may be presented in court to show the defendant's propensity towards commission of additional acts of violent crime are unlimited. Unless restricted to past convictions (and the Act may be so construed), this provision is too prone to abuse by a judicial officer who is overly eager to detain.

Preventive detention has also been attacked as a racist proposal because most of those affected will be black. Unquestionably most of the persons who are arrested and convicted of crime in the District of Columbia are black,[29] but what is too often overlooked is that most of the victims are also black.[30] Black criminals prey upon black people, and the victims of the inner city of the District of Columbia are desperately in need of protection from the crime that threatens to engulf that city.[31] Furthermore, if the bail program of the District of Columbia were adopted in the states and if, rather than the existing money bail standard, the sole criteria for release were (1) the likelihood that the defendant will show up for trial, and (2) the likelihood the defendant will refrain from committing a violent crime during the interval, far fewer black defendants would be held prior to trial than are presently incarcerated. Abusive bail practices exist in the states, and little has been done in most states to correct the problem.

Finally, the effectiveness of preventive detention is based solely upon the ability to predict which defendants are likely to commit violent criminal

---

29. REPORT OF THE PRESIDENT'S COMMISSION ON CRIME IN THE DISTRICT OF COLUMBIA 21 (1966):

As reflected by arrest statistics, the perpetrators of serious crime in the District are most often young male Negroes. In the 1950–1965 period 80 percent of all persons arrested for serious offenses were Negro and 31 percent were juveniles (persons under 18). In 1965, 36 percent of those arrested for housebreaking, and 27 percent each in the cases of robbery and auto theft, were 15 years of age or younger. However, most murders and aggravated assaults are committed by persons 30 or older.

30. The REPORT stated:

Negroes also are the primary victims of serious crimes, with the exceptions of robbery and commercial housebreaking. Victims of homicides, rapes and aggravated assaults are likely to have been related to or acquainted with their assailants. A significant number of these crimes occur indoors, which makes prevention and control by the police difficult. *Id.*

31. Although "crime is generally increasing throughout the United States, Washington's increase in recent years has been greater than that in cities of comparable size." *Id.* at 20. *See also Crime Expense: Now Up to 51 Billions a Year,* U. S. NEWS AND WORLD REPORT, Oct. 26, 1970, at 30–34.

acts between the time of arrest and final disposition of the case. None of the studies, including one completed by the government's National Bureau of Testing and Standards, would indicate that such predictions are valid.[32] Few would deny that some persons who are awaiting trial are committing additional crimes during this period, but picking the person likely to commit another crime seems nearly impossible. If the judicial officers who make the determination of pretrial detention hold the government to the strict standards of the Act, the prosecutor may have difficulty satisfying the burden levied upon him of showing in a particular case that no release conditions, such as placing the defendant in the custody of a third party, will reasonably assure community safety.

Contained within the bail-jail maelstrom are self-fulfilling prophecies. Whenever a person free on bail commits a crime, it indicates the need for preventive detention, but we will never have any data on persons who are detained but would not have committed a crime.[33] To limit a man's freedom is, at any time, a dangerous game.[34] To do so when there has been no

---

32. For a discussion of this study, see Ervin, Foreword to *Preventive Detention: A Step Backward for Criminal Justice,* 6 HARV. CIV. RIGHTS—CIV. LIB. L. REV. 291, 294(1971) [hereinafter cited as *A Step Backward*].

33. 　　But systematic experimentation designed to determine whether predictions of violence are accurate has never been carried out—and for understandable reasons. When an expert predicts that a given individual will engage in violence if allowed to remain free, the natural community response is to confine him and take no chances. But if he is confined, it will be impossible to determine whether the prediction was correct: whether he would, in fact, have engaged in the predicted conduct had he remained at liberty. Dershowitz, *When in Doubt, Don't Let Them Out,* N. Y. Times, April 25, 1971, § 4, at 8, col. 1 [hereinafter cited as Dershowitz].

34. One commentator noted: "Under the concept the presumption of innocence is rendered meaningless and ineffective. How can an accused be presumed innocent when his liberty has been restrained on the basis of chances?" Miller, *Preventive Detention—a Guide to the Eradication of Individual Rights,* 16 How. L. J. 1, 15 (1970). Attorney General Mitchell has stated that the presumption issue is not relevant to the constitutionality of pretrial detention. Mitchell wrote:
The presumption of innocence is not a presumption in the strict sense of the term. It is simply a rule of evidence which allows the defendant to stand mute at trial and places the burden upon the government to prove the charges against him beyond a reasonable doubt. Apart from the Supreme Court's dictum in *Stack v. Boyle,* there is no basis for thinking that the presumption of innocence has

conviction requires the utmost care. Whether sufficient care has been incorporated into the District of Columbia crime bill depends entirely upon how zealously the judicial officers are willing to protect every individual's freedom.

Perhaps the two most valid criticisms of preventive detention are, first, that it does not get at the real problem of delay, which is what permits defendants to be free for such extended periods prior to trial; and, second, that future conduct is simply not susceptible to sufficiently accurate prediction to justify incarcerating a person prior to a finding of guilt.[35] This second problem is not adequately answerable. Although some of those detained would have committed crimes, it is obvious that some will be needlessly detained. Propensity is not the same as likelihood, and freedom may be too fragile a commodity to permit tinkering. Experience with preventive detention will not answer the problem either, because past decisions by judicial officers cannot be qualitatively analyzed so that past mistakes will not be repeated.

Recent concern with malfunctions in the criminal justice process has resulted in interim measures to ease the corrosion and debilitation of the system, without making substantial overhaul. From this perspective, preventive detention may well be nothing more than another placebo offering little hope of dramatic reversal of the decay and providing even less promise of tackling the basic issue of delay.

BAIL AS A DELAYING TECHNIQUE

Delay in trial is directly tied to the bail system. Defendants who are free on bail are under no pressure whatever to agree to a plea of guilty.[36] This

---

any application to proceedings prior to trial. *Constitutionality of Pretrial Detention, supra* note 4, at 1231 & nn. 37–38.

35.   There is growing evidence [based upon follow-up studies of escaped and judicially released inmates] that psychiatric and judicial predictions of violence are extremely inaccurate—that the vast majority of persons confined on the basis of these predictions would not, in fact, engage in violence if released. This evidence is not conclusive; nor could it be until society is prepared to incur the risks of releasing at least some detainees under controlled conditions. Dershowitz, *supra* note 33, § 4, at 8, col. 1.

36.   People out on bail almost "never" have to go to trial. If you can get your client out on bail, he won't be tried for at least three years, if at all. The case will go from one DA's back drawer to another's until it either dissolves into dust or the DA agrees to a plea of time

is true no matter how favorable the terms of an offered plea might appear to one not involved. The paroled accused feels capable of "holding up" the state for a better deal. If a defendant does not care about a felony record (and few realize the future implications of such a record),[37] his sole desire is to avoid spending time in prison, so he will hold out until the prosecutor finally agrees to recommend probation. More and more defendants are becoming aware that the state cannot try them. The prosecutor is faced with the difficult choice of deciding which defendants seem so dangerous or which crimes are so important to the community's interests that they must go to trial. On the remainder of cases, he must be willing to deal. Dealing is the essence of the criminal process, and at every step of the proceedings it is the defendant who is in command.[38] If he is faced with a hostile judge or prosecutor, he can drag the case out in hopes that at a later time a different judge or prosecutor will be more pressured by the backlog and be willing to offer a favorable deal.[39] The larger the city, the greater the incidence of crime, and thus the more unvarying this rule.

The individual who is denied bail does not have the same leverage with which to play the game. Each day spent in the lockup is punishment, and if the defendant has been in jail for a considerable time prior to pleading guilty, the judge and prosecutor may be willing to let him go free on the

---

served. Mills, *I Have Nothing to Do with Justice*, LIFE, Mar. 12, 1971, at 66 [hereinafter cited as Mills].

"But, even for those who do secure their release pending trial, the delay means that a criminal charge hangs like a cloud over a man for two years without any judicial determination of guilt or innocence." Address by Chief Justice Earl Warren, Yale University, in N. Y. Times, April 28, 1968, at 48, col. 1.

37. Possessing such a record may very well curtail some civil rights, such as voting. *See* Parker v. Ellis, 362 U. S. 574 (1959).

38. The judicial quagmire has been analyzed to be in the following state: Trials are obsolete. In New York City only one arrest in thousands ends in trial. The government no longer has time and money to afford the luxury of presuming innocence, nor the belief that the truest way of determining guilt is by jury trial. Today, in effect, the government says to each defendant, "If you will abandon your unsupportable claim of innocence, we will compensate you with a light sentence." Mills, *supra* note 36, at 59.

Furthermore, one prosecutor in Boston remarked that in the past year he had spent only fifty-six days in trial. Interview with Robert Snider, Assistant District Attorney, in Boston, April 12, 1971.

39. This tactic will be eliminated if the individual docket system is adopted and if defense attorneys and prosecutors are responsible for a case from beginning to end.

day he enters his plea.[40] Lacking the tools, however, makes waiting out the prosecutor much more difficult. The defendant may be willing to go for a less favorable plea because he is being punished by incarceration. The jailed defendant has his employment and personal relationships at least temporarily terminated. He is caged; and even though there has not been a determination of guilt, the condition of his caging is the same as for many persons who have been convicted. His life as a free person and his right to privacy automatically cease, and naturally his family suffers proportionately to the contribution, economic and emotional, that he was making to the family unit before his arrest.[41]

The case of Thomas Goins, reported in the *New Yorker*,[42] pinpoints one of the most serious disadvantages suffered by a jailed defendant. Goins was the victim of careless and imprecise police work which came terribly near to tragedy. One night on a New York City street he found six hundred glassine envelopes containing heroin. He notified the police, only to find himself shortly thereafter arrested and charged with possession of narcotics. His employer met his bail requirements and also provided him with competent legal assistance. Goins was freed within twenty-four hours of his arrest. Then, under the direction of his attorney, he sought out those people who were witnesses to what had happened the previous night. The charges against him were subsequently dismissed when the prosecutor was presented with the defense's evidence. Had Goins been unable to secure his freedom, he would have been unable to return to the scene as quickly as he did and secure the assistance of those persons who saw him pick up the envelopes in the street and enter a tavern to call the police. Had Goins been in jail from the time of his arrest, the trial might well have been resolved

---

40. Mills, *supra* note 36, at 59.
41. In its report to Mayor Lindsay, the New York Criminal Justice Coordinating Council took a dim view of the present bail practice:
    In discussing the question of fairness, the council report said that, "the bail system, which treats pre-trial release as a privilege to be bought or earned, and which incarcerates persons in crowded large institutions for long periods before adjudication of guilt or innocence, is perhaps the most nefarious element in the entire criminal justice system." N. Y. Times, Mar. 14, 1971, at 1, col. 6.
    One attorney noted:
    The inadequacy of the bond procedure in state courts [results] in great prejudice to the defendant in that bonds are set by uninformed and uneducated justices of the peace, . . . and are ridiculously high. This results in many people staying in jail that ought not to; and a great disrespect for the legal process by the defendants going through it. QUESTIONNAIRE, Chapter 2, n. 12.
42. E. Kahn, *Annals of Law,* NEW YORKER, Feb. 6, 1971, at 76.

solely on the basis of the judge's or jury's opinion of who was telling the truth: the arresting officer responding to Goins' call, who thoroughly confused the matter, or the defendant himself, without the corroborating testimony of witnesses. Granted, not many felony charges are based on a total misunderstanding, as in the Goins case. We will never know, however, how many misunderstandings have resulted in convictions because the defendants, unlike Goins, had to remain in jail and were unable to assist in the preparation of their case.

An accused in jail is of little value to his attorney during the preparation of his defense.[43] Unlike Goins, he cannot look for witnesses or personally contact anyone who might be able to assist in his trial defense, and his attorney must consequently assume complete investigatory responsibility. In many ways the jailed defendant is an absolute liability to his defense counsel, since the attorney must go to the jail every time he wants to see his client or consult with him on a particular fact.[44]

Frequently, the defendant in jail is virtually forgotten by his attorney; rather than consult with his client every time a question comes up, the attorney may defer looking into the matter until it is convenient to visit the jail. The jails are filled with defendants who have been waiting for trial for several months and who complain bitterly that in all that time they have seen their attorneys only once or twice.[45] Lest one be too quick to condemn these seldom-seen attorneys, it must be accepted that an attorney with a heavy caseload cannot make frequent visits to the jail if he is doing his job for his other clients.

The jailed defendant is also subject to constant pressures to plead guilty.

---

43. PRETRIAL RELEASE, *supra* note 23, at 23.
44. According to one Cleveland defense attorney, if you go to see a defendant in the Warrensville workhouse, half the day is consumed. If the attorney requests that the defendant be brought to the downtown jail so that the two may confer, two weeks may elapse before the attorney sees him. Interview with defense attorney, in Cleveland, May 23, 1971 (anonymity requested).
45. This lack of legal advice is cited as one of the major reasons for the October riots at the Tombs in New York. To alleviate this problem the Legal Aid Society has begun training paraprofessionals to act as ombudsmen within the city's prisons. This will provide more continuous legal advice to prisoners and take some of the burden off the legal aid lawyers. N. Y. Times, June 1, 1971, at 27, col. 1.

In the Bergen County, New Jersey, jail, Peter DelVecchio is the ombudsman. The ombudsman may ask a judge to reduce bail or release a defendant on his own recognizance. In most cases, however, the inmates ask DelVecchio to call relatives to arrange bail. N. Y. Times, July 11, 1971, § 1, at 36, col. 3.

He is aware that the time spent in jail awaiting trial is "dead time" and is not necessarily applied to his sentence if he is convicted.[46] Unlike his bailed counterpart, the jailed defendant cannot afford to follow the advice of virtually all defense attorneys to "wait out the prosecutor." There is nothing to wait out; punishment is in progress.[47] A guilty plea to a lesser offense could result in a short jail term or even probation. Most importantly, it moves the defendant closer to his much sought freedom.

Our statistical survey did not discover a substantial difference in the percentages of defendants pleading guilty, based upon a bailed or jailed condition.[48] The study did clearly indicate, however, that there is better than a two-to-one chance that the convicted defendant who was unable to make bail will be sentenced to the penitentiary or reformatory than the defendant who was out on bail.[49] Only 24.9 percent of the bailed defendants who were convicted received prison sentences, but 59.9 percent of the defendants who were denied bail or were unable to make bail went to prison. Of the bailed

46. *Cf.* the practice in New York, where "dead time" will be credited against the resulting sentence. Thus, if the defendant is in jail awaiting trial for twelve months, and the sentence resulting from a plea agreement is sixteen months, the defendant must spend only four additional months in jail. Interview with Manuel Zapata, defense attorney, in New York City, Oct. 11, 1970.

47. However, the jailed defendant may wait out the prosecutor, hoping that the state's case will evaporate and that he then will be able to plead guilty to a lesser charge. Luis Cintron was charged with homicide; he waited out the prosecutor and eventually pleaded guilty to second degree manslaughter. By postponing the decision to plead guilty for several months, although in jail, the defendant was sentenced to five to seven years, rather than facing a possible life sentence. Interview with Manuel Zapata, defense attorney, in New York City, Nov. 29, 1970.

48. *See* Appendix A.

49. Judicial reformers have put together a damning list of evils arising from the use of high bail as a device for jailing the accused. An American Bar Association advisory committee has cited studies showing that if a defendant has been free he stands a better chance of being acquitted at his trial, or being placed on probation if convicted, than the man who has been awaiting trial in jail. . . . The ABA advisory committee also declared: "The consequences of pretrial detention are grave. Defendants presumed innocent are subjected to the psychological and physical deprivations of jail life, usually under more onerous conditions than are imposed on convicted defendants. The jailed defendant loses his job if he has one and is prevented from contributing to the preparation of his defense." Large, *supra* note 17, at 14, col. 4.

defendants 55.1 percent had their sentences suspended, but that treatment was accorded to only 23.4 percent of the convicted defendants who had been in jail from the time of their arrest.[50]

There is good explanation for these great discrepancies. While the bailed defendant is "waiting out the prosecutor," he is able to build a new record. If necessary, he can change his associates, develop a commendable work record, and reestablish his family ties. If the case is delayed for a year or more, by the time the defendant is sentenced his attorney will be able to present to the court a good argument based upon the defendant's exemplary conduct while the case was pending, and explain away the criminal act by saying that there were mitigating circumstances involved in the crime and that the defendant should not now be sentenced to prison.[51] The defendant in jail, on the other hand, has no opportunity to build a new record; thus it is less likely that his attorney will be able to present any mitigating circumstances.

Admittedly, there is a certain amount of distortion in these statistics. Not all of the defendants who have been denied pretrial freedom are in jail solely because they were unable to raise bail. Included within the group would also be those defendants who have been charged with first degree murder, against whom the evidence of guilt is great, and who are (by law in Ohio, as in almost all states) ineligible for bail.[52] Furthermore, a defendant who pleads guilty to any degree of homicide is less likely to have his sentence suspended than if he were pleading guilty to a felony not involving death. Notwithstanding the effect that the homicide cases would necessarily have

---

50. *See* Appendix A.
51. For example, the final resolution of the "Harlem Five" case, which produced an angry blast at the judiciary system by New York Police Commissioner Patrick Murphy, illustrates the advantages of delay to the bailed defendant. Originally charged three years earlier with conspiracy to murder policemen, the defendants were convicted of the lesser offenses of illegal possession of guns and homemade bombs. Justice Fraiman of the New York State Supreme Court granted five years' probation to two of the defendants, citing their demonstrated "excellence," "leadership potential," and "outstanding intelligence." The justice apparently took note of the defendants' behavior during the three years that the charges were pending and their active involvement in community affairs in Harlem. N. Y. Times, June 11, 1971, at 1, col. 7.
52. OHIO CONST. art. 1, § 9. One New Jersey court offered the justification for this:
    The underlying motive for denying bail in the prescribed type of capital offenses is to assure the accused's presence at trial. In a choice between hazarding his life before a jury and forfeiting his or

on the statistics, they only partly explain the discrepancies between the final outcome of cases of defendants who are free on bail and those who are not.

Another valid consideration is that in addition to those guilty of capital crimes, there are others in jail for whom bail has been set but who have been unable to meet the conditions. The bondsman is a big factor in the continued retention of defendants. The bondsman knows the community of criminals with whom he deals; if he is unwilling to write a bond, even if the defendant can pay the premium, then the chances are good that the bondsman is aware of additional factors which will result in imprisonment upon conviction. Further, those crimes for which unattainable bail is set are frequently ones that involve the more serious felonies[53] and for which one can naturally expect jail sentences.

For defendants who are in jail because they are unable to satisfy the bail conditions, New York City has considered instituting in-jail bail hearings on a regular basis. By requiring judges to hold such bail reduction hearings periodically, bailable inmates would be given individualized attention and have a better opportunity for pretrial release.[54] Besides providing for a realistic review of an individual's bail status, this approach would help to satisfy prisoner complaints.[55]

his sureties' property, the framers of the Constitution obviously reacted to man's undoubted urge to prefer the latter. State v. Konigsberg, 33 N. J. 367, 373, 164 A.2d 740, 743 (1960).

Thirty-eight other states have provisions regarding bail and capital offenses, similar to those of Ohio. *See* Murphy, *State Control of the Operation of Professional Bail Bondsmen,* 36 U. Cin. L. Rev. 375, 378 n. 14 (1967) [hereinafter cited as *Operation of Professional Bail Bondsmen*].

53. In many situations, the question of bail is academic; no matter how small the bail, the defendant will not be able to afford the bond. Consequently, some experts advocate that a defendant should be placed on pretrial probation when a prosecutor knows that even if a defendant is found guilty he will not spend any time in jail. Interview with Michael Meltsner, Columbia Law School, in New York City, Oct. 18, 1970. Interview with James Crawford, First Assistant Prosecutor, in Philadelphia, Dec. 1, 1970.

54. The defendant feels as though he is receiving individualized attention because he is having direct contact with the judge. Ordinarily, out-of-jail bail reduction hearings are held without the defendant present. The opportunity for pretrial release may result because the defendant's bail may be more reasonable without the arresting officer or the prosecutor present to urge an excessive bond. Interview with Michael Dontzen, Mayor Lindsay's Liaison with Department of Corrections, in New York City, Nov. 18, 1970.

55. In-jail bail proceedings will reduce prisoners' complaints if there are

The bail structure in the context of the criminal justice morass is like *Alice in Wonderland*. Tragedy surely stalks a system where a defendant who has been detained for a period of several months for failure to make bond may go free the day he acknowledges his guilt and pleads guilty, while the defendant who maintains his assertion of innocence must continue to be detained until his case can be docketed for trial.[56] Although most defendants are guilty, some are innocent, and the pressure works equally upon them and to their disadvantage. Criminal courts were established to protect the innocent and the community, and to punish the guilty. Yet it is the guilty, and especially the guilty who are free on bail, who define the terms on which the system operates. The criminal justice system is almost reduced to accepting whatever plea the defendant is finally willing to make, as to both the nature of the offense and, especially, the nature of the punishment.

---

a significant number of bail reductions. Bail reduction hearings were previously conducted in the New York jails but were abandoned because bail was rarely reduced. Interview with George McGrath, Commissioner of Corrections, in New York City, Nov. 17, 1970.

56. Mills, *supra* note 36, at 62. The following discourse illustrates this dilemma:

"I'm not guilty." He says it fast, nodding, sure of that. . . .

. . . "I'm innocent. I didn't do nothing. But I got to get out of here. I got to—"

"Well, if you 'did' do anything and you are a little guilty, they'll give you time served and you'll walk."

. . . "Today? I walk today?"

"If you're guilty of something and you take the plea."

"I'll take the plea. But I didn't do nothing."

"You can't take the plea unless you're guilty of something."

"I want the year. I'm innocent, but I'll take the year. I walk today if I take the year?"

. . . "You walk if you take the plea, but no one's going to let you take the plea if you aren't guilty."

"But I didn't *do* nothing."

"Then you'll have to stay in and go to trial."

"When will that be?"

"In a couple of months. Maybe longer."

Santiago has a grip on the bars. "You mean if I'm guilty I get out today?"

"Yes." . . .

"But if I'm innocent, I got to stay in?"

"That's right." . . .

It's too much for Santiago. He lets go of the bars, takes a step back, shakes his head, turns around and comes quickly back to the bars. "But, 'man'—." *Id.*

THE MECHANICS OF THE BAIL SYSTEM

Though money bail is central to most state and city bail systems, it is rare that the amount which the defendant and his family can truly afford is taken into consideration. The concern in non-murder cases is reduced to the question of what amount of money will ensure the defendant's presence at trial. Lately, however, the community threat which the defendant poses has had a significant influence. The standards frequently subscribed to in the determination of bail are those of the Federal Rules of Criminal Procedure,[57] which were approved by the Supreme Court when it dealt with the excessive bail provision of the Eighth Amendment.[58] These rules provide that in determining the amount of bail necessary to ensure the defendant's presence, the judge should consider "the nature and circumstances of the offense charged, the weight of the evidence against him, the financial ability of the defendant to give bail and the character of the defendant."[59] Elaboration upon these standards generally centers around the character of the defendant and the quality of his ties to the community. Are his ties sufficiently binding to keep him in town, or are they so weak that they fail to provide any reason why he should stay around for trial? Family ties and employment record are frequently determinative. If the defendant lives with and has helped to support his family, then there is greater likelihood that he will remain in the vicinity and maintain those ties. In such a situation, low bail or release without money bail would be perfectly justified, because the defendant is a good risk. The transient defendant, having no reason to remain in the community, is generally considered a bad risk for release.[60]

The initial bail decision is made at the defendant's first court appearance.[61] In state courts in urban areas, the decision is made by a municipal court judge. On a given morning he may be faced with a noisy, crowded courtroom where over a hundred persons charged with felonies and misdemeanors will be making initial court appearances.[62] In the busiest

---

57. FED. R. CRIM. P. 46.
58. *See* Stack v. Boyle, 342 U. S. 1 (1951).
59. *System in Need of Reform, supra* note 9, at 387–88 & nn. 58–68. FED. R. CRIM. P. 46 (c).
60. *See, e.g.,* CAL. PENAL CODE § 1275 (West 1969); HAWAII CONST. art. 1, § 9; ILL. ANN. STAT. ch. 38, § 110–2 (Smith–Hurd 1970); IOWA CODE ANN. § 763.16 (1950).
61. LaFave, *Alternatives to the Present Bail System,* 1965 U. ILL. L. F. 8, 9.
62. The crowded conditions and the lack of decorum in the court where the preliminary hearing is held make the job of screening defendants for a realistic and individualized determination of bail nearly impossible. For example, the judge presiding over the arraignment of Julio

cities, the courts are divided: one judge will preside at the first appearances for felonies and another judge in a separate courtroom will hear the misdemeanors. Under either system, however, the judge is not likely to engage in any judicious screening for purposes of determining bail.[63]

Like his colleagues who conduct the trial portions, the municipal court judge is obsessed with clearing his docket for the day.[64] If he spent a significant amount of time on each case at this very first appearance, he could do an adequate job but at the same time he would not clear his docket, and most of the defendants who were to have appeared before him on that day would be returned to the lockup without a court appearance and without having had an opportunity to be considered for bail. The next day these defendants would be brought forth once more, but now they would be joined by all of the persons arrested in the intervening twenty-four hours. How long could the system withstand the pressures of such a situation? It would certainly take days, and more likely weeks, before any defendant had an initial appearance before a judge for the purposes of being formally notified of the charges against him, being apprised of his rights, and being given an opportunity to have bail set. Judges react to this potential situation

---

Roldan, the Tombs prisoner who committed suicide out of frustration, was found to have only 1.7 minutes or 102 seconds to dispose of each case on the day of Roldan's arraignment.

Judge Solniker was asked by the Board of Correction interviewers what factors he considered when setting bail. He cited the kind of crime—"if burglary is in a residential apartment, I tighten up because of the narcotics probability and the tendency of violence to innocent people." He stated he also considers the "yellow sheet" of the defendant, a police record that reflects prior arrests and convictions. If the defendant is represented by Legal Aid, an ROR (Release on Recognizance) report is prepared which indicates whether the defendant is married, employed, etc., and gives information which the judge can consider in determining the likelihood of the defendant jumping bail and leaving the jurisdiction. N. Y. Times, Nov. 18, 1970, at 52, col. 1.

63. *Cf.* On April 2, 1971, in the Hudson County Court of New Jersey Judge Benedict Beronio, a defendant charged with loan sharking and possession of instruments used for gambling was placed on $2,500 bail at the preliminary hearing. The prosecutor sought to raise the bail to $10,000 because the defendant had attempted to influence a witness. The defense attorney argued that the defendant was an employed family man and that the bail should be continued at $2,500. The judge, with the concurrence of both attorneys, compromised and reset bail at $7,500, enabling the defendant to secure his pretrial freedom.

64. Katz, *Municipal Courts: Another Urban Ill,* 20 CASE W. RES. L. REV. 87, 95–98 (1968–1969).

by disposing of cases in a manner that enables the process to continue functioning. If the results produced are inequitable and shabby, most people are somewhat placated by the fact that a proceeding is in progress or is at least giving off a semblance of motion.

A judge will rarely inquire into the defendant's character in determining bail.[65] Since there is no time to check family ties and employment records, the decision comes down to the objective material of the charge, which can be referred to superficially and rapidly. At this stage, the charge is most often the product of a police decision with, at best, cursory approval from a member of the prosecutor's staff. The police decision as to the charge has been made without considering the strength of the case, reliability of witnesses, constitutional questions relating to evidence, or importance to the community of prosecuting the charge to its full extent. The police opinion as to culpability is devoid of the realities of convictability, and thus the charge which they select is often an overcharge. If the defendant is to plead guilty, as most eventually will, it is likely that the plea will be to a lesser charge, yet the bail determination is made at this point on the initial, inflated charge. In some cities, the judge will also have the past conviction record of the accused to help him make the decision as to bail. The pressures of the docket make it difficult for the judge to find out anything more about the accused. His decision concerning bail will be made, therefore, on the basis of the initial charge and the man's record, despite the fact that neither constitutes an adequate foundation on which to base a credible or valid decision as to how much money will ensure the defendant's presence at trial.[66]

Rather than making individualized bail determinations, judges have set ideas for bail, based upon categories of offenses.[67] Some courts follow a practice similar to that in Los Angeles and set bail in accordance with an approved bail schedule adopted by the judges.[68] We are not far removed

---

65. R. GOLDFARB, RANSOM: A CRITIQUE OF THE AMERICAN BAIL SYSTEM 13–15 (1965) [hereinafter cited as RANSOM].

66. A study by New York City's Criminal Justice Coordinating Council has shown that bail is determined according to the charge and the defendant's prior record. However, there is little or no relationship between the charge and previous criminal record, and the likelihood of a defendant appearing for trial. Interview with Mr. Appelton, New York City's Criminal Justice Coordinating Council, in New York City, Nov. 30, 1970.

67. According to one attorney, there is a great need to control judges in the setting of bail, and specific standards for the setting of bail should be enacted. Interview with Michael Meltsner, Columbia Law School, in New York City, Oct. 18, 1970.

68. Superior Court bail schedule, approved and adopted by the Superior

from a time when it was a not uncommon court policy to automatically increase the bail requirement for black defendants.[69] Such decision-making amounts to legalized ransom, and it certainly bears no relationship to determining an amount that, while enabling the accused to be free on bail, would be significant enough to assure his return to the courthouse for trial.

The power to determine bail is the authority to set bail at an amount of money which denies freedom to a defendant. While subject to appellate review, the amount is within the discretion of the judge, and his decision is rarely overturned.[70] The attitude of the judge determines whether or not a defendant's bail will be set at an amount that he and his family can raise. If the judge favors pretrial release, then the bail will be reasonable; if not, he can set it beyond the means of the defendant. The judge who sets an unusually high bail can simply avoid setting out the rationale for the amount determined, and an appellate court will not reverse his decision unless there is clear evidence of abuse of discretion.

On occasion a judge will clearly enunciate the reason for high bail. A judge in New York City set bail at $5,000 for two prostitutes with records of nine and twenty-two arrests, respectively. The judge stated that high bail was warranted because prostitutes are a hindrance to people on the street and contribute to the spread of venereal disease. Accepting that preventive detention is not available in New York City, the judge remarked, "There is authority for police action when the welfare of the public is in serious jeopardy."[71]

Without calling it preventive detention, the money bail system is thus subject to frequent use as a weapon of punishment and pretrial detention.[72] During the height of the civil rights demonstrations, for example, an arrest-

---

Court judges presiding in Criminal Departments, at their monthly meeting on July 18, 1969, is an example.

69. *System in Need of Reform, supra* note 9, at 391.
70. RANSOM, *supra* note 65, at 139. The author further states:
    [I]t is very difficult for a defendant who has been abused by being incarcerated for preventive detention, or who wants to dispute whether he should have been imprisoned with or without good reason, to ever be able to prove this and seek redress. A clever judge will not articulate for the record why he has set bail at a certain unattainable amount or even why he has denied bail. Since his judgment is discretionary, the appellate courts will not upset his decision by reversing him unless the abuse is clear, far-reaching, and beyond reasonable allowance. *Id.*
71. N. Y. Times, July 7, 1971, at 1, col. 2.
72. RANSOM, *supra* note 65, at 46.
    On the other hand, some judges feel that bail is more often than not

ed individual would be charged with the violation of several criminal statutes.[73] To prevent the defendant's release on bail, all the judicial officer had to do was exact a separate bail for each charge, thereby ensuring that it was beyond the reach of most defendants. Some judges subscribe to the philosophy that a "taste of jail" will do the accused some good and set bail high enough to make sure the defendent stays in jail.[74] The casual way in which bail is determined also permits the judge to set it so high that the defendant will be in jail and be subject to the pressures to plead guilty quickly and with few demands.

THE BAIL BONDSMAN

Once bail is set, the defendant, his family, friends, employer, or even a stranger may come forth, deposit the stipulated amount, and secure the defendant's freedom. Few people have sufficient readily available cash, easily convertible securities, or mortgage-free real estate, and thus the scene is set for the person who truly determines bail or jail for most defendants: the professional bondsman.[75]

Bondsmen in most large cities are responsible for over 75 percent of all bail bonds.[76] Most bondsmen are backed by insurance companies, but in

---

set too low, and as a result, "the number of fugitives on the street exceeds the number of defendants in jail." N. Y. Times, May 7, 1971, at 25, col. 1.

73. Besides multiplying the number of violations, judges dealing with civil rights demonstrators were also known to exact separate bonds at each step of the proceedings, costing the defendants separate premiums for each bond. RANSOM, *supra* note 65, at 67.

74. Even more alarming is the magistrate who sets bail extremely high even when acquittal is a certainty. Schwartzwald, *Our Bail System— Instrument of Injustice?,* 35 MANITOBA B. NEWS 209 (1965).

75. The bondsman "is a businessman who, for a price, enables an accused otherwise suited for release on bail to satisfy the financial condition of his freedom." FINAL REPORT OF THE D. C. BAIL PROJECT, BAIL REFORM IN THE NATION'S CAPITAL II (1966) [hereinafter cited as BAIL REFORM IN THE NATION'S CAPITAL].

[B]ondsmen hold the keys to the jail in their pockets. They determine for whom they will act as surety—who in their judgment is a good risk. The bad risks, in the bondsmen's judgment, and the ones who are unable to pay the bondsmen's fees remain in jail. The court and the commissioners are relegated to the relatively unimportant chore of fixing the amount of bail. Pannell v. United States, 320 F.2d 698, 699 (D. C. Cir. 1963).

76. *Operation of Professional Bail Bondsmen, supra* note 52, at 401.

rare instances they operate on their own assets. Their fees depend upon the individual defendant and the amount of collateral pledged by the defendant and his family. In those states that regulate the bondsman, the statutory maximum for his services has normally been set at 10 percent,[77] although some states use a 5 percent maximum.[78] Bondsmen themselves will often lower their fee to 5 percent, if offered cash collateral.[79] When cash collateral is submitted, it is usually put in a savings account. When the bond is subsequently discharged, the person who put up the collateral receives the original amount plus the interest. Where bondsmen are not subject to state regulation, the ceiling is provided by the market.

The individual who secures his own release without the help of a bondsman will have the money returned to him by the court at the time the case is concluded. On the other hand, the defendant whose freedom has been secured by a bondsman at the cost of 10 percent of the face value of the bond has made an irretrievable expenditure for his freedom. Nonetheless, few would argue that it has not been money well spent, for it provides the defendant with a chance to prepare for his trial, whether it is helping a lawyer investigate, earning money for his attorney's fee, or setting a pattern of behavior which results in a lighter sentence.[80]

The burden of the bail system falls upon the poor.[81] The affluent criminal

---

77. *Id.* at 375 & n. 3.
78. In New York City, the authorized rates are 5 percent on the first $1,000, 4 percent on the second $1,000, and 3 percent on all amounts above that sum. In Worcester, Massachusetts, and in St. Louis, Missouri, the rate is 10 percent; in some other areas, the rate will be whatever unrestricted amount the bondsman can persuade the defendant to pay. Botein, *The Manhattan Bail Project: Its Impact on Criminology and the Criminal Law Processes,* 43 TEX. L. REV. 323 (1964–1965).
79. Interview with bail bondsman, May 4, 1971 (anonymity requested). If bail is set at $5,000 or more, in addition to his fee the bondsman frequently requires collateral to minimize his risk if the bond is forfeited.
80. PRETRIAL RELEASE, *supra* note 23, at 60–65.
81. Professor Caleb Foote has remarked:
    [I]t has been established that pretrial imprisonment of the poor solely as a result of their poverty, under harsher conditions than those applied to convicted prisoners, so pervades our system that for a majority of defendants accused of anything more serious than petty crimes, the bail system operates effectively to deny rather than to facilitate liberty pending trial. Foote, *The Coming Constitutional Crisis in Bail: I,* 113 U. PA. L. REV. 959, 960 & n. 3 (1965) [hereinafter cited as *Crisis in Bail].*

can raise the cash and know that he will get it back; the middle-class citizen can probably raise the bondsman's fee and must pay the premium to obtain his freedom. The poor, however, are unable to raise any bond money, so they languish in jail. None of these economic factors has a significant value in determining whether the defendant is a good risk for bail. The money orientation of our society has evolved a procedure for selecting those who will be free on bail that has nothing to do with the purpose of bail.

Considering bondsmen's responsibility for approximately 75 percent of the bail bonds in the country,[82] their power in the criminal justice system is devastating. Like the defendants and the lawyers, they possess the power to cripple the system. During the bondsmen's strike in New York City in the early 1960s,[83] bondsmen refused to write bonds except where 100 percent collateral in real estate or bankbooks existed. As a result, the jails were crowded to the bursting point.[84] Short of a strike, many bondsmen will simply refuse to write a bond unless the collateral offered is in excess of the face value of the release bond, or unless there is a guarantor for the bond with assets equal to or greater than the amount of bail.[85] The bondsman operates within the framework of free enterprise. If, for any reason, he chooses not to write a bond for a particular accused, there is no recourse from his decision. The decision to "go or not to go bond" for an accused may be totally arbitrary.

The successful bondsman operates a profitable business that is beneficial to many. Conversations with a bondsman who was assured anonymity did nothing to refute the theory that, above all, it is a business enterprise. He indicated that it takes him only "thirty seconds on the telephone to size up a guy" for whom he is considering writing a bond. If he decides to "go bond" for him, this bondsman will travel to the jail and ask the accused the same questions again, and if his answers vary from the responses during the telephone conversation, he knows the man lied and will not bail him out. The bondsman's decision is not always his own, since he must write bonds

---

82. *Operation of Professional Bail Bondsmen, supra* note 52, at 401.
83. On December 21 and 22, 1961, the bondsmen moved to vacate bond forfeitures; when the Kings County District Attorney opposed the motions, the bondsmen went on strike. *Bail or Jail,* 19 THE RECORD OF THE ASSOCIATION OF THE BAR OF THE CITY OF NEW YORK 11, 13 (1964).
84. *Operation of Professional Bail Bondsmen, supra* note 52, at 401.
85. Of the eight bondsmen interviewed in a New York study, all indicated that they wrote bonds only where a guarantor existed with assets equal to or greater than the amount of bail determined. *See* Note, *A Study of the Administration of Bail in New York City,* 106 U. PA. L. REV. 693, 704 (1958).

for some defendants to preserve a valuable relationship with a particular lawyer: "I take my share of dogs because you have to. As long as the lawyers realize that you're helping them out, they'll send you your share of the good cases as well." The bondsman is not completely at the mercy of lawyers. Lawyers need the bondsmen to bail their clients, and a lack of honesty on the part of the lawyer in dealing with the bondsman can be extremely costly:

> One lawyer had a kid walk in off the street, hand him a $50 retainer, and tell him he's in trouble. They turned the kid in, and the lawyer called me to write a bond for him. I asked the lawyer to tell me something about the kid. He claimed he's known the kid's parents for twenty years. I wrote the bond and the kid jumped. When I called the lawyer to get to the parents, he'd never seen them nor knew who they were. The guy's blacklisted. My agency will never write another bond for him.[86]

In principle, one may have little sympathy for the accused felon who jumps bail and seeks to avoid trial, but few people are aware of what he faces if caught by the professional bondsman, who must either produce the defendant or pay up on the bond. In order to protect the bond, bondsmen have been known to kidnap, drug, and beat persons who have jumped bail and then return them to the state court with jurisdiction, notwithstanding the existence of legal processes providing for extradition.[87] One lawyer swore to us that he knew a bondsman who had been responsible for the death of an uncooperative defendant. Whether that claim is true or not, it represents the fear one attorney has of bondsmen; while the claim is extreme, the fear is not unusual.

Many bondsmen will use the local police to assist them in rearresting a bail jumper.[88] The bondsman must have complete confidence in his ability to recapture missing defendants, for the bondsman who cannot maintain close to a 100 percent appearance rate is soon out of business. To an extent, the police welcome this role of the bondsman. The police prefer not to go

---

86. Interview with bail bondsman, May 4, 1971.
87. Occasionally the bondsman's efforts to deliver a defendant to the court lead to violence. A bondsman's assistant was killed with the defendant he was trying to take into custody in Cincinnati, Ohio. The defendant had been convicted of resisting arrest, disorderly conduct, and malicious destruction of property. Cleveland Plain Dealer, May 13, 1971, § A, at 7, col. 3.
88. Besides being assisted by local police in the asylum state, it is not uncommon for the bondsman to be "accompanied by 'off-duty' policemen from the demanding jurisdiction." See Note, *Bailbondsmen and the Fugitive Accused—the Need for Formal Removal Procedures,* 73 YALE L. J. 1098, 1101–3 & n. 28 (1964).

into the ghetto to recapture a defendant; frequently, when they are assigned such duty, they just report that the person could not be located and never go. The bondsman, using his own contacts and techniques, can operate with substantial freedom and security in the ghetto. The tales the bondsman can relate involving forays into the ghetto are remarkable:

> One night I was in bed at 10 P.M. when I got a call. The indemnifiers claimed that a defendant was about to skip and the judge wanted him brought in. I found out where he was (how I found out is unimportant). I called the sheriff's office and two deputies went with me. I knocked softly on the door—the deputies stayed outside. The door was opened and the defendant was sitting in a chair twenty feet away from the door. There was a machete next to him; upstairs two guys were cutting heroin. I softly told him that he was coming with me, and he did. The deputies never knew—or cared to know—what was going on in the house.[89]

To ensure that the accused will not jump bail out of ignorance or as a result of false pressure from his attorney, the good bondsman will inform the defendant exactly what his rights are and what his subsequent obligations will be regarding his court appearances.

> Once I had a kid out on bail who jumped and had gone to Canada. Now I'm in trouble! I talked to the parents and they told me that his attorney had told him to have $2,500 for the attorney's legal fees when he appeared in court for the arraignment or he'd go up for twenty years. I called the kid and promised him that if he'd come back, I'd get the judge to reinstate the bond and appoint counsel for him, since he didn't have any money. I did. You have to keep your promises in this business or you're out of business.[90]

The most tragic cases of people left in jail to await trial are those who just cannot pay the bondsman's premium. They are punished for their poverty. The bondsman denies his Midas touch to others as well: those who he "knows" will jump. This group includes those who have been arrested for a crime for which there are traditionally poor "show rates," such as prostitution, or those who have a lengthy criminal record, no roots in the community, and little reason to remain in the local jurisdiction.[91]

The problems of some of the detained poor could be solved if, rather than relying upon an arbitrary set sum for certain offenses, judges would tailor the bond to the particular defendant. This would mean lowering the re-

---

89. Interview with bail bondsman, May 4, 1971.
90. *Id.*
91. *Id.*

quirement when a defendant had no record and had lived in the area for many years, but raising it for the person for whom the contrary was true. At the arraignment, the judge should carefully question the defendant who has not previously made bail. If it is clear that no bondsman will write the bond and no one will raise it for him, then the judge should take it upon himself to set an early trial date. Such a change would not equalize the position of the indigent who is denied liberty prior to trial strictly because of his inability to meet the means test, but it would soften the consequences of his indigency.

ELIMINATION OF MONEY BAIL OR MINIMIZATION OF THE PROFESSIONAL BONDSMAN'S ROLE

The bail system need not be based upon money. Money bail has not been the only means of obtaining release in recent years. In 1961, concerned about the detained but unconvicted accused persons who were languishing in the New York City jails because they were unable to meet the requirements of money bail, Louis Schweitzer donated the money which gave rise to the Vera Institute of Justice.[92] The initial goal of this group was to make the use of release on recognizance programs an acceptable procedure in the local New York City criminal courts, and to create a program that had nationwide adaptability.

In cooperation with the New York University Law School, the Institute launched the Manhattan Bail Project in 1961. A group of interested law students interviewed detainees to determine their "parole risk."[93] The questioning focused upon the individual's residential stability, employment history, family contacts in the area, and prior criminal record.[94] After his meeting with the accused, the interviewer verified through phone calls and record checks the information he had obtained. The accused was awarded points for positive information, such as a solid employment history or a long-time community residency. His point total was reduced when he was identified as a past offender. If the person scored above a set minimum of points, the interviewer could recommend to the judge some form of release on recognizance. The early results were rewarding: with the verified information, judges tended to release four times as many accused, and 98.4 percent of those released met their court appearance requirements.[95]

---

92. Institute on the Operation of Pretrial Release Projects, BAIL AND SUMMONS: 1965 viii (1965) [hereinafter cited as BAIL AND SUMMONS].
93. Ralls, *Bail in the United States,* 48 MICH. S. B. J. 28, 29 (1969).
94. *Id.*
95. Davis, *Bail—an Examination of Release on Recognizance,* 39 MISS. L. J. 303, 311 (1967–1968).

To place these figures in perspective, it must be kept in mind that this initial program of recognizance release excluded homicides, narcotics offenses, sex crimes, and police assaults.[96] Persons charged with such crimes were excluded not so much from the belief that these people were not releasable, but from the belief of the program planners that a better public image would be fostered if a "hands off" approach were followed in the early stages. Since the Manhattan Bail Project, other similar programs have operated without this exclusionary policy, and project administrators have reported no adverse results in expanding release procedures to include those persons formerly considered "untouchable."[97]

New York City instituted its formal release on recognizance program (ROR) in March, 1964, under the Office of Probation of the New York City Criminal Courts.[98] Investigation of ROR eligibility is made on all defendants who appear for arraignment, except in the following instances: (1) when the defendant has been charged with homicide; (2) when the defendant has been charged with the infliction of a possibly fatal injury upon another, while that person remains in critical condition; (3) when a bench warrant is outstanding for the accused or he is being held for extradition; or (4) when the person is financially able to post bail and engage a private attorney. The investigators place their major emphasis on verifying information obtained from interviews with those detained.[99] They seek an accurate determination of the defendant's stability in the community and the probability of his appearing for trial, if released. An assessment of his release potential is obtained by sifting through factors concerning his length of residence in New York, his association, if any, with a family group, his

96. NATIONAL CONFERENCE ON BAIL AND CRIMINAL JUSTICE PROCEEDINGS of May 27–29, 1964, at 78, 84.
97. One study revealed the following:
> In the case of this defendant charged with murder in the second degree, I made the recommendation. . . . He had no previous record, lived in the community and had a job. The Judge accepted the recommendation. There was a little screaming from the relatives of the deceased, but the Judge stood by his guns. A notice was sent to the defendant after he was indicted. He showed up. He was ordered to come to pretrial and to trial. He was tried, was found guilty of manslaughter, and was sentenced to the Ohio State Reformatory, where he is at the present time. BAIL AND SUMMONS, *supra* note 92, at 74.
98. RANSOM, *supra* note 65, at 166; *Workshop: Establishing Bail Projects,* 1965 U. ILL. L. F. 42 (1965) [hereinafter cited as *Workshop*].
99. Letter from Jack L. Highsmith, Branch Chief of Release on Recognizance of the Office of Probation for the Courts of New York City, Mar. 25, 1971.

support of dependents, his overall employment record, and his prior criminal record. Based upon the report of the person who investigated the
accused, the presiding judge makes his determination of whether to release
or not.

Using the year 1969 as a sample, New York City figures indicate that
28,460 defendants were released, half with an ROR rating and half without.
Those released without a rating were cases where the judge determined on
the basis of his analysis of the facts that the defendant was a favorable risk
for release, despite the lack of a positive rating from the reviewers. Each
release is a significant tax saving to the public, which would otherwise have
to pay $11.97 a day to maintain each defendant in jail.[100] Despite the
confidence displayed in those released, bench warrants had to be issued for
9.8 percent of those for whom there was a rating made, a figure which has
shown a steady rise since 1964. For those who did not qualify for a release
rating but were released anyway by a judge, 10.3 percent did not appear,
and bench warrants were subsequently issued.[101] The latter percentage is the
lowest since 1964. These figures include those persons whose nonappear-
ance was an unintentional violation, the result of an oversight. There is no
question that a significant percentage are intentional violators; the screening
system has been unable to separate the violators from those who have every
intention of honoring their promise to return. It was estimated in a study
by the Vera Institute of Justice that there were 177,000 unexecuted bench
warrants amassed over the 1960–1970 decade in New York City.[102] This
figure included anything that was a nontraffic offense. Although a warrant
squad is detailed to enforce these bench warrants, if preliminary checks fail
to locate the person there is rarely any effort made to run a follow-up, as
the time demands are too great.[103]

Indianapolis initiated a recognizance release program in December,
1969. The program permitted access to the defendant at the earliest time
after arrest, authority to release qualified misdemeanants, the power to
recommend bond based upon what the defendant could afford, and liberty

---

100. *Id.*

101. *Id.*

102. N. Y. Times, June 19, 1970, at 1, col. 1. "Hundreds of defendants
escape prosecution each week, their cases relegated to a permanent
'pending' status, because the Police Department warrant squads fail
to execute many court-ordered arrest warrants." Sgt. John McClosky of the Manhattan South warrant squad said: "We don't keep
records because we have no use for that information, and anyway it
might depress us."

103. "[T]here is the feeling in the courts, expressed bitterly by many judges
and assistant district attorneys who are confronted with lost-defendant

to use any police records on the defendant. In 1970, the Indianapolis Bail Project released over 2,000 persons. Forty-three percent were released on their own recognizance, and only 60 persons (2.9 percent) missed a scheduled court appearance. Besides the tremendous savings in bond costs to those accused and in detention costs to the taxpayers, 692 of the 2,027 defendants released (34 percent) were found not guilty of all charges and were spared the hardship of unwarranted detention.[104]

If a city has adopted an ROR program, circumstances may arise in which a person is eligible for release but the judge is somewhat reluctant to give him complete personal freedom. Several restrictions have been designed to provide freedom with varying degrees of restraint. A person may be placed under the supervision of an outside party or organization, and travel, association, or residence restrictions may be designated as conditions of release.[105] The most restrictive provision allows release by day and return to a detention facility for the evening.[106] This obviously is a limitation on the freedom of the accused, but it does make it possible for him to continue working to support a family and to raise legal fees.

In any determination of what release conditions to recommend or use, a variety of conflicting pressures push and pull at the judicial officer making the decision. He must first consider the preferred right of the individual to be free while awaiting trial, but he must also analyze the threat, if any, that the person represents to the community and the likelihood of his appearing for subsequent judicial proceedings once released. With an increasing awareness of the effect of the jails as a breeding ground for criminals, the public and local judicial administrators must question whether the potential threat is greater in releasing the accused or in giving him an opportunity to obtain an education in crime through exposure to the inmates of the local jail.[107]

Ever since the application of the constitutional concept of equal protection to the indigent, the cries have been long and loud that somehow the

---

cases each day, that almost the only time a lost defendant is found is when he is arrested on another offense." Sgt. McClosky agrees this is what happens "in most cases." *Id.* at 31, col. 2.

104. Letter from Professor James Droege, Indiana University, Indianapolis School of Law, May 26, 1971.

105. RANSOM, *supra* note 65, at 153, 154.

106. *Criminal Procedure Act, supra* note 16, at § 23–1321 (July 29, 1970): "Impose any other condition, including a condition requiring that the person return to custody after specified hours of release for employment or other limited purposes."

107. *Justice on Trial,* NEWSWEEK, Mar. 8, 1971, at 16, 18–19: "When I first went," said Charles McGregor, 48, an ex-con and

poor accused should have an opportunity to meet bail requirements. The complete removal of money from the bail system and a program of release determinations based solely on personal qualities offer the most satisfactory answer.[108] Systems have been proposed and instituted, however, that retain monetary bail but keep its discriminatory effects to a minimum.

One such program is the 10 percent bail deposit provision that has been adopted and administered in Illinois.[109] Essentially, the program requires the person for whom bail has been set to execute a bail bond and deposit with the clerk of the court an amount equal to 10 percent of the bail, but in no case less than $25. When the conditions of the bail bond are fulfilled, 90 percent of the deposited sum is returned to the defendant and thus only 1 percent of the original total bail is retained by the court to cover the administrative expenses of the program.[110] The defendant may, if he has the available cash or real estate, deposit the entire amount of the bond and receive it all back when he appears for trial.[111]

The Illinois procedure has several desirable effects. Guaranteed the return of all but 10 percent of the deposit fee if he complies with the provisions of his release, the person is more likely to be able to borrow the required sum from friends or relatives at considerably reduced expense.[112] The argument posed by the bondsmen, in opposition to the plan, that the result would be increased expense to the state in administrative costs and in recovering those persons who jump bail has not been supported. The courts were previously handling the paper work for the bail bonds without a fee, and under the new procedure the courts recover their administrative costs.

past president of the reformist Fortune Society in New York, "I was a 17-year-old sneak thief. When I came out, I knew how to cut narcotics, how to wear a mask for burglaries, how to embezzle . . . that was my school of crime."

108. RANSOM, *supra* note 65, at 185; *System in Need of Reform,* *supra* note 9, at 403. Foote, *The Coming Constitutional Crisis in Bail: II,* 113 U. PA. L. REV. 1125, 1128 (1965).

From the analysis of equal protection I conclude that extension of the Griffin rule to bail is particularly appropriate, and that pretrial detention of an accused who would go free but for differences in financial circumstances is a violation of the equal protection clause. . . . The words excessive bail in the amendment must be given an interpretation consistent with the Griffin rule as forbidding any financial discrimination against the accused. *Id.* at 1180.

109. ILL. ANN. STAT. ch. 38, § 110–7 (Smith–Hurd 1970).
110. *System in Need of Reform, supra* note 9, at 401.
111. ILL. ANN. STAT. ch. 38, § 110–8 (Smith–Hurd 1970).
112. Bowman, *The Illinois Ten Per Cent Bail Deposit Provision,* 1965 U. ILL. L. F. 35, 38, 41 [hereinafter cited as *Bail Deposit Provision*].

Also, the expenses for extradition (i.e., where the bondsman uses the formal legal process to return the accused) are predominantly borne by the state and their respective law enforcement organizations.[113] In addition, the records through 1966 indicate that the 10 percent bond shows a forfeiture rate only slightly exceeding that of its predecessor, the professional surety bond, although the 10 percent bonds are being used in a volume which exceeds that of the former professional bond.[114] The thrust of the new statute is the levying of separate criminal penalties for jumping bail, rather than monetary fines.

The effect on the some 300 bondsmen who operated in Chicago prior to the adoption of the system has been widespread unemployment.[115] The concept is presently being considered for adoption in such other cities as Philadelphia, Pittsburgh, Los Angeles, and San Francisco.[116] Bondsmen in these and other cities patently oppose such a program, as for most it would mean seeking another livelihood.

The bondsman with whom we spoke expressed his disapproval of the program. He maintained that it was pushed through the Illinois legislature by the attorneys in the state because everyone who had anything to do with the bail system was getting paid off, and that in order to increase the fee available for the payoff, bail was being set at exorbitant rates.[117] After paying

---

113. *Id.* at 39–40.
114. One study revealed the following:

> In the Municipal Court of Chicago in 1962, 51,161 professional bail bonds were written and 5,487 forfeited, a forfeiture rate of ten percent. Figures for Municipal District One show that in 1964, 27,956 ten percent bonds were written and 2,154 forfeited, a seven percent forfeiture rate. In 1965, 46,418 ten percent bonds were written and 4,910 forfeited, a ten percent forfeiture rate, and in 1966, 68,355 ten percent bonds were written and 8,106 forfeited for an eleven percent rate. Boyle, *Bail Under the Judicial Article,* 17 DePaul L. Rev. 267, 274–75 (1968) [hereinafter cited as *Judicial Article*].

> The bondsman interviewed said that despite the fact that more figures are not available on Chicago's "no-show" rate, he has reason to believe that it has increased dramatically. His statement, while somewhat self-serving, deserves consideration until some data is available to refute it.

115. Interview with bail bondsman, May 4, 1971.
116. *Id.*
117. Similar bail reform legislation was introduced in the Indiana General Assembly but was blocked by the lobbying efforts of the bondsmen. Letter from Professor James B. Droege, Indiana University, Indianapolis School of Law, May 26, 1971.

an inflated fee to the bondsman, the defendant would be left without money to pay his attorney. The bondsmen were not bringing the defendants in after they failed to show up, and since everyone was involved in the "honest graft," the bonds were not forfeited. The attorneys suffering from this cozy relationship sought the 10 percent system from the state legislature to save their clients' money and to give themselves some assurance of payment. Conveniently, the Illinois statute permits a defendant to sign over to his attorney 90 percent of the sum returned to the defendant when he appears for trial.[118] The bondsman argues that the program has been misused and is ineffective. He maintains that many defendants released under the program never appear for trial. Although bench warrants are issued, no one ever makes a serious effort to find these people, and the only ones ever returned are those rearrested for a subsequent offense. No one is personally responsible for forfeiting a bond under the 10 percent plan, and the only loser is the system which has failed to bring someone to trial on a charge.[119]

Chicago has combined the 10 percent bail program with a release on recognizance program.[120] An interviewing staff for the release program sees all the detainees who have not been able to make bond and informs them of the 10 percent program, which enables some to obtain release. Of the 7,700 persons interviewed in 1970, 887 were released on recognizance. There were 204 forfeitures, 10 to 15 percent of which were unintentional.[121] It was evident, however, that those persons who did not appear were generally not relocated unless they were rearrested for a subsequent offense.[122] These figures tend to bear out the opposition to the program expressed by the bondsman with whom we spoke. His arguments, while self-serving, have some support.

---

118. ILL. ANN. STAT. ch. 38, § 110–7 (f) (Smith–Hurd 1970).
119. Interview with bail bondsman, May 4, 1971.
120. *Workshop, supra* note 98, at 42.
121. Memorandum from Marshall J. Pidgeon to Chief Judge John S. Boyle of the Circuit Court of Cook County, Illinois, Feb. 26, 1971.
122. The Baltimore pretrial release staff makes a bail recommendation to the court; in most instances the court will follow that suggestion. In approximately one–third of all the cases handled in the Baltimore program, the defendant was released on his own recognizance. Of those who were released on their own recognizance, only eighteen have failed to appear for trial at the appointed time; and all but two of those eighteen have been rearrested. Interview with Richard Motsay, Director of Baltimore Pretrial Release Program, in Baltimore, April 8, 1971.

On May 30, 1971, Philadelphia began a release on recognizance program. From May 30, 1971, to July 31, 1971, release on recogni-

The Bail Reform Act of 1966[123] and the superseding sections of the District of Columbia Court Reform and Criminal Procedure Act of 1970[124] adopted similar 10 percent bail provisions as one of the alternative forms of release. Essential, however, is the recognition within the act that some form of personal recognizance is preferable to money. The movement today, and rightfully so, is in the direction of a bail system that places the emphasis on the person, not on his ability to pay.

A REASONABLE RESPONSE

The concept of monetary bail is not satisfactory.[125] It seems to work because it is the most convenient method available, but it does not truly meet the goals of providing maximum pretrial freedom to the accused and of protecting the community, goals which we, as a nation, have embodied in the concept. On its face, bail discriminates against the poor, and so it denies freedom to countless defendants who would otherwise be good bail risks.[126] Moreover, money is hardly the most binding tie in this society. For

---

zance has been recommended to the court in 35 percent of the cases (2248/6397). The courts have followed the recommendations in 1357 cases. In addition, the courts have, on their own, granted release on recognizance to another 731 defendants. Of all those defendants released on their own recognizance, only 79 failed to appear at the appropriate time. Thirty-six out of the 79 were cases in which the ROR program had suggested their release. As of July 31, 1971, fifty-two of those who failed to appear had been apprehended. Memorandum to President Judge D. Donald Jamieson from David Lester, Director, ROR Program, Philadelphia, Aug. 6, 1971.

123. 18 U. S. C. §§3146–48 (Supp. IV 1965–1969).
124. *Criminal Procedure Act, supra* note 16.
125. A report by the State Senate Committee on Crime and Correction on the August riot at the Tombs made several recommendations to reduce delay in the system, as well as recommending a move away from the strictly monetary bail practice.

A section, "Reforming the Criminal Justice System," urged a change in the bail system, noting that "when a judge imposes bail on a defendant who is obviously indigent, he is, in effect, mandating that the defendant will remain in a cell until he is brought to trial." ... The committee recommended, to avoid holding men in prison too long, that Probation Department personnel be increased to speed release on recognizance procedures and that courts review arrests to determine if men were being unnecessarily held. N. Y. Times, Oct. 6, 1970, at 1, col. 2.

126. *Crisis in Bail, supra* note 81, at 960.

many persons, family and other personal relationships, as well as professional and employment commitments, mean much more than a sum of money.[127] When the sum of money has little relationship to the person's actual income but is determined principally on the basis of the charge, this is particularly true. The abuses of professional bondsmen also contribute greatly to the intolerable conditions imposed by the existing money bail system.

When the person charged with a crime is a transient, without binding ties or a history in the community in which he is alleged to have committed the crime, money bail is justified. If, however, money bail is a great hardship, and if the ties that bind the defendant to persons in his home jurisdiction are strong and he would normally be released in his own community, then release into the custody of those persons willing to assume the burden is justified. Even in those instances where money bail is deemed the only reliable surety (and that should be only as a last resort), an adjustment must be made in the way the amount is set and the system is administered.

Even if money bail were universally retained as the bail standard, large-scale improvements could be made. The constitutional standard to which we pay lip service should be enforced in each of the states. This would require that the amount of bail be determined by the defendant's ability to pay, and the amount required should be just enough so that it is a significant sum to the defendant, but not so great as to deny him freedom.[128] In other words, if a millionaire and a pauper are charged with the same offense, there is no justification for requiring the same amount of bail for each. Bail should be set in such amounts that render the professional bondsman unnecessary to the criminal justice system. If 10 percent of the bond, the amount of money the accused generally pays as a fee to the bondsman, is in actuality all that the defendant must post to secure his freedom, then bail should typically be just 10 percent of the amount that courts have regularly de-

---

127. Some states recognize this and authorize that bail be set with these factors as criteria. *See, e.g.,* IOWA CODE ANN. § 763.16 (1950); ME. R. CRIM. P. 46(a), (c).

128. In effect, whenever the defendant cannot meet bail (and inability to produce bail is by no means equated to excessiveness), he had been effectively denied the right to pretrial freedom. *See* Bandy v. United States, 81 S. Ct. 197 (Douglas, Circuit Justice, 1960); United States v. Rumrich, 180 F.2d 575 (6th Cir. 1950). In *Bandy,* Justice Douglas commented that it would be unconstitutional to make bail so excessive as to make sure that a defendant could not obtain his freedom. Yet he grasped the dilemma when he pointed out that when the defendant is indigent, even a modest bail may have the practical effect of keeping the defendant in jail.

manded. The Illinois 10 percent deposit plan, followed in the federal district courts when money bail is required, seems to have worked satisfactorily and is suitable for use in other states.[129] Breaking the power of the bondsman is a significant step and should have high priority in the process of setting the house of criminal justice in order.[130]

The expanded booking procedure, developed in the previous chapter, will expedite the setting of bail. The booking officer will make the initial bail determination. If this determination results in a denial of release to the suspect, either because of the threat he poses to the community or the inability of assuring his presence for trial, then a thorough judicial review of the station-house bail determination shall be held within forty-eight hours of the defendant's arrest.

For nontransients, the policy of pretrial freedom should be pursued to its limits. The underlying policy of the Constitution is to favor pretrial freedom, and this is a national principle that can be put to work. The personal release programs existing in varying degrees throughout the country have proved to be more successful and reliable than money bail. Admittedly, the personal recognizance programs have been more successful because they have frequently been limited to a very carefully screened group of defendants. But the community cost in terms of dollars spent in the maintenance of crime-breeding jails and the human cost of confining persons in those institutions militate for this change. Release of the defendant on personal recognizance or to the custody of persons or organizations, with the further imposition of a periodic check-in requirement, may, in the long run, have lasting benefits. If employment training and job supervision were included during this pretrial period, the society would begin using the delay to its advantage. It is time to face squarely the disillusioning fact of life that confinement in a county jail rehabilitates no one and inflicts lasting punishment upon the innocent defendants who are so confined.

A broadened release program must be coupled with the enforcement of the community's speedy trial rights.[131] If speedy trial requirements are not incorporated as a part of an expanded release program, we could witness the total crippling of the system. If many defendants are released under the existing patterns, whereby defendants and their attorneys are able to stretch

---

129. *Judicial Article, supra* note 114.
130. The Illinois 10 percent law caused the abrupt disappearance of the bail bondsman in that state. *Id.* at 272. As it stands now, "[t]he jurisdictions of the United States are virtually alone in according to the professional bondsman a critical role in the administration of the criminal process." BAIL REFORM IN THE NATION'S CAPITAL, *supra* note 75, at 11.
131. According to Chief Justice Burger: "The need for preventive detention

the proceedings indefinitely, then the defendant who has nothing to lose because he is free on bail will seek postponement of his judgment day as long as possible. Equal justice must not mean an equal opportunity to evade the demands of justice but must reflect a system that treats all defendants equally and fairly. Fairness does not require that the defendant be in a position to break the system. All defendants must be required to answer the charges brought against them, and the community has the right and obligation to itself to insist that the defendant be required to answer within a reasonable time. The key to the elimination of delay lies not in keeping defendants in jail prior to conviction, for that is an unnecessary, debilitating, and costly negation of our most fundamental principles. Instead, the only reasonable response is to enforce sensible rules that penalize dilatory tactics which prevent disposition of criminal cases. The defendant who is free on bail and personally responsible for delaying justice may be withdrawn from bail and incarcerated, even under this proposal, just as the person who jumps bail need not be freed again when he is returned to the jurisdiction for trial.

There are certain persons who have demonstrated by their past conduct that they pose such a great threat of physical violence to their fellow citizens that a wise and constitutional system of bail need not require that they be freed pending adjudication.[132] If preventive detention is wisely administered and limited to those few cases where the government is able to demonstrate on the basis of past convictions for violent crimes that the individual does, in fact, represent a predictable threat, a bail system that does favor freedom for the overwhelming majority of defendants need not be ashamed that it denies that freedom to a few, as long as those detained are brought to trial quickly. Preventive detention, not disguised as high bail, promises far fewer cases of injustice than the bail system that exists in the vast majority of cities and towns of the United States. The District of Columbia experiment in preventive detention has had initial success. The fact that the United States Attorney moved to detain only seven persons between February and July of 1971 indicates that proper care and judgment can be shown in this matter.[133] Limited preventive detention may have a collateral benefit far greater than the actual results of detaining a few hapless defendants. It may

---

might be eliminated if statutes or court rules were adopted to require that defendants be brought to trial within a set period of days." N. Y. Times, July 4, 1971, § 1, at 1, col. 5.
132. Hruska, *Preventive Detention: The Constitution and the Congress,* 3 CREIGHTON L. REV. 36, 39 (1969).
133. "Of the seven, one defendant was found to have been on parole and a parole hearing was held; two entered pleas of guilty; charges were

help to lessen the oppressive fear of crime that hangs so heavily over the American society and is inhibiting the life of American cities.

dropped on one case; one detainee escaped and two persons eventually were ordered held under a less harsh work-release program." Cleveland Plain Dealer, July 5, 1971, § A, at 20, col. 2.

5 / INDICTMENT
TO TRIAL:
NONPRODUCTIVE
TIME

DELAY AND ITS ABUSE

Delay in the administration of the criminal system is caused in substantial part by the lack of progress towards disposition of cases after indictment by the grand jury. Though excessive and generally nonproductive time is consumed by the formal charging of a defendant, it is in the post-indictment period that months of delay become years of delay. The time after indictment could and should be utilized to limit and elucidate the issues of actual dispute so that the prosecution and the defense can negotiate as informed equals on a plea of guilty or prepare to try the case in an efficient and speedy manner.

The case of Ralph Johnson, discussed in Chapter 1, is illustrative of both tremendously wasteful delay and the risks attendant on a failure to use the time for valid purposes. Initially indicted for first degree murder, a capital offense, Johnson was ineligible for bail. After nearly a year in jail and just days before the trial was scheduled to begin, the indictment was amended to second degree murder, a bailable offense carrying a penalty of life imprisonment[1] with parole available after ten years.[2] At the same time, a prosecutor was offering, and the defense attorneys were urging Johnson to accept, a plea of guilty to the charge of manslaughter, which carries a penalty of one to twenty years[3] with parole available after ten months.[4]

---

1. OHIO REV. CODE § 2901.05 (1955).
2. OHIO REV. CODE § 2967.13 (Page Supp. 1970).
3. OHIO REV. CODE § 2901.06 (1955).
4. OHIO REV. CODE § 2967.19(A) (Page Supp. 1970).

177

Johnson was repeatedly asked by his attorneys to plead guilty. The last time he was asked was just before the trial was to begin, and he then came very close to acquiescing. His lawyers continued pressuring him, and finally he agreed.

> I had become so disgusted. Everybody was saying that you don't have a chance, you don't have a chance and this and that and the other. I said maybe I don't have a chance after being in jail almost a year.

Johnson's lawyers informed the judge that their client was ready to change his plea to guilty. Johnson stood before the judge, flanked by his attorneys and a short distance away from the prosecutor.

> The judge had gotten to the point where he said, "Are you pleading guilty to this crime?" All of a sudden it hit me, why should you plead guilty? This was what was running through my mind, now why should you plead guilty to something you didn't do? All of a sudden I said, "No, I don't want to plead guilty. Continue with these proceedings." The judge got up from his bench and stood in the door with his hands on his hips and looked at me. He didn't know what to think.

A jury was quickly selected, and the trial took three days. At the end of the trial, the jury required only forty-five minutes to find Ralph Johnson not guilty. After nearly a year in jail Johnson was a free man.

Most of the year that Johnson spent in jail occurred after an indictment had been returned by the grand jury. The principal justification for allowing time between the action taken by the grand jury and the time set for the beginning of the trial is to permit the prosecutor and defense attorney to marshall witnesses and evidence in preparation for trial.

What the Johnson case illustrates is that both the prosecution and the defense fail to use the post-indictment period for realistic evaluation of the relative strength of their case and that of the opposition. Numerous factors exist which make such an evaluation under the present system difficult if not impossible; the disturbing conclusion is that Johnson's lawyers wanted him to plead guilty to a charge for which his fellow citizens found little difficulty acquitting him, and the state wasted its limited resources on a prosecution of highly questionable merit.

Johnson was doubly abused by the post-indictment delay: first, he languished in jail for ten months awaiting trial, and second, the time was not used to inquire into the charge to determine whether he should be tried. He was burdened with delay and received none of its theoretical benefits.

The crushing trial loads of prosecutors in urban areas make it foolish to imagine that much of the post-indictment interval can possibly be spent in active preparation of a case for trial. It is a rare felony case that gets prepared more than a day or two before trial. That, however, is somewhat better than in trials of misdemeanors, where the prosecutor frequently sees the file for the first time immediately before trial. Defense attorneys face caseloads similar to those of their counterparts, the prosecutors, and simply do not have the time for extensive pretrial preparation. In other words, while delay is the norm of the system, it does not exist nor is it used to prepare cases for trial. Delay exists for other reasons, and its continuance is supported by other interests.

What little movement there is in a criminal case during this period is towards a compromise disposition of the case. Prosecutors are compelled to deal in order to avoid taking every case to trial, a situation which neither the prosecutor nor the court structure could handle. Defendants, on the other hand, are aware of the extreme gravity of the punishment if they should be convicted as originally charged. Neither the defendant nor his attorney relishes the prospect of risking that punishment. Furthermore, if the defendant is guilty—and most reaching this stage are guilty of at least some offense included within the one charged[5]—the defendant's interests focus on the best deal he can get.

If conducted in an informed manner, negotiation to obtain a plea of guilty to a lesser charge or in return for a recommendation of reduction or suspension of sentence is a valid and efficient way to use limited judicial resources. The abuses occur because of the lack of information on both sides as to the content and strength of the opposition's case, and thus an ignorance of the real facts of the case. The post-indictment period should be a period of active, mutual, two-way discovery, so that the plea of guilty, which will in all likelihood result, will be an informed plea, and so that both the public and the defendant will receive justice from the criminal courts.

MOTIONS PRACTICE AND DELAY

From the arraignment on the indictment until the date scheduled for trial, there are no formal procedures scheduled in most courts. The little in-court activity that does take place during this time is confined to the motions practice.

The purpose of the motions practice is manifold. Through motions the defense attorney is able to challenge the sufficiency of the charging instrument, test the validity of preceding stages of the prosecution, and challenge the legality of evidence to be used by the state. Both prosecution and defense

5. Snepp, *A Procedure for Negotiated Pleas,* 9 TRIAL JUDGES' JOURNAL
   80 (1970).

may use this period to attempt to learn some of the substance of the opposition's case. When properly used, motions practice provides an opportunity to narrow, sharpen, and clarify some of the issues in the case and to determine whether a trial is necessary and justified as serving the interests of either the state or the defendant.

Although these procedures may facilitate speedy disposition of cases, they also loom as delaying devices for either attorney. Each motion, unless uncontested, requires an answer, and either side may request an opportunity to argue in court on the validity of the motion. Motions going to the legality of the methods used by law enforcement agencies in securing evidence usually require an evidentiary hearing to determine whether that evidence may be used at trial. The motions practice can be used as a device to delay the case, tie up opposing counsel, require the presence of witnesses again and again before trial, and occupy judges with considering and ruling on the motions.

Delay may be occasioned when motions are handled singly. Few states require attorneys to submit at one time all the motions that they intend to use. The lawyer who seeks to delay a case may simply keep submitting motions on various matters as the preceding one is ruled upon.[6] Even the most ingenious lawyer eventually runs out of motions, but if delay was a partial goal of this maneuvering, then he has succeeded in gaining several months.

An attempt to block this avenue of delay and to promote greater efficiency in the post-arraignment procedure was made in the United States District Court for the Southern District of California. The Omnibus Hearing, which has subsequently been adopted in some other federal districts, was developed there in order to consolidate the motions practice. The hearing is scheduled two or three weeks after the arraignment. Each of the attorneys is supplied in advance with an extensive checklist relating to discovery, suppression of evidence, special defenses, and stipulations. The checklist also provides an opportunity to inquire into the reasonableness of the bail set and the sufficiency of the charge. By forcing the attorneys to raise all these matters at one time and by disposing of them all together, no benefit is to be gained by interposing meaningless and improper issues. In addition, the attorney who continues to raise unnecessary questions runs the risk of detracting from the meritorious motions that he is making at the hearing. The use of the checklist provides some assurance that crucial defenses will not be overlooked, even if the defendant is represented by an attorney who

---

6. It has been reported that the practice of defense attorneys in Washington, D. C., is to delay a case by making motions, rather than by seeking a continuance. Interview with former Washington, D. C., defense attorney, June 1, 1971, in Cleveland, Ohio (anonymity requested).

is unfamiliar with criminal procedure. The multiple goals served by the Omnibus Hearing, reduction in the opportunities for dilatory practices and enhancement of the guarantee of effective counsel, commend it for consideration in the states.[7]

In addition to the use of the motions practice as a delaying tactic by attorneys, the time that a judge may take to rule on a motion also contributes to delay. Some judges are notorious for the amount of time that they allow to elapse between the filing of a motion and the time of their ruling on the issue. In the case of Ralph Johnson, three months elapsed before the judge ruled on the defense motion to examine hospital and medical records. The issue presented in the motion was not an easy one nor is the law on the subject clearly defined, but the length of time between the filing and the ruling was inexcusable. Johnson was in jail until his acquittal, including the three-month period while the judge's ruling was awaited.

DISCOVERY: BASIC PROBLEMS

A substantial portion of the maneuvering through the motions practice is aimed at learning as much as possible about the opponent's case. In both civil and criminal cases pretrial discovery is an extension of the pleading process, for it is a means of serving notice on the opposing party of the facts and theories to which he will have to respond in the course of trial. The historical obstacles to discovery in civil cases have been sufficiently removed so that expansive discovery rights are now available. The great change in civil practice wrought by the advent of discovery has not, however, resulted in a comparable development in criminal practice. In most states, discovery in criminal cases remains negligible.[8]

Discovery was expanded in civil litigation to reduce the risk of surprise, limit the issues in a case, assure presentation of all relevant evidence, narrow

---

7. Miller, *The Omnibus Hearing—an Experiment in Federal Criminal Discovery,* 5 SAN DIEGO L. REV. 293 (1968). *See also* ABA PROJECT ON MINIMUM STANDARDS FOR CRIMINAL JUSTICE: DISCOVERY AND PROCEDURE BEFORE TRIAL 135 (1969) (tentative draft).

8. The right of discovery has apparently "been limited for four basic reasons: First, to minimize opportunities for perjury; second, to prevent fear and intimidation of witnesses; third, to avoid a lack of reciprocity of rights; fourth, to protect the balance of interests." Comment, *Criminal Discovery,* 10 ST. LOUIS L. J. 518 (1965–1966).

United States Supreme Court Justice Brennan, while on the New Jersey Supreme Court, bitterly disagreed with at least part of the justification for denying discovery:

That old hobgoblin perjury, invariably raised with every suggested change in procedure to make easier the discovery of truth, is again

the differences between the parties, and encourage settlement.[9] The expansion of discovery was not an end in itself but was based upon the assumption that full disclosure would maximize the opportunity to arrive at judgments consistent with the evidence available in the controversy.

When each of the parties is alerted in advance to all the issues in a case, the trier of fact, whether a judge or a jury, is aided in arriving at a verdict because all the relevant evidence on a subject is likely to be presented and fully cross-examined. Since discovery sifts out those issues not actually in controversy, the trier of fact is not distracted by extraneous matters.[10] Full discovery also tends to encourage pretrial settlement of disputes because it enables each attorney to make a realistic evaluation of the strength of his own case relative to that of the opposition.

One of the basic reasons that criminal practice does not follow the model of civil practice is that a criminal case is not, even in theory, a two-sided search for truth with each party equally bound to further that search.[11] No demand is made upon the adversaries to join together in a search for truth. In a civil suit, however, despite unequal allocation of the burden of proof, there is such a demand and expectation of the adversaries.

The defense attorney's sole duty and obligation in a criminal case is to his client. This obligation is fulfilled by obtaining a fair trial for his client or, if no trial is held, by securing for his client the best deal possible by pleading him guilty to a reduced charge.[12] Prosecutors argue that only they, as the representatives of the state, are committed to a search for the truth.[13]

---

disinterred from the grave where I thought it was forever buried under the overwhelming weight of the complete rebuttal supplied by our experience in civil causes where liberal discovery has been allowed. State v. Tune, 13 N. J. at 209, 98 A.2d at 894 (1953) (dissenting opinion).

9. *See, e.g.,* Comment, *Developments in the Law—Discovery,* 74 HARV. L. REV. 940, 946–51 (1961) [hereinafter cited as *Developments*].

10. G. RAGLAND, DISCOVERY BEFORE TRIAL 260 (1932).

11. "Frequently the partisanship of the opposing lawyers blocks the uncovering of vital evidence or leads to a presentation of vital testimony in a way that distorts it. . . . [T]he lawyer aims at victory, at winning the fight, not at aiding the court to discover the facts." Bunce & Youngquist, *Discovery and Disclosure: Dual Aspects of the Prosecutor's Role in Criminal Procedure,* 34 GEO. WASH. L. REV. 92, 105 n. 107 (1965–1966) [hereinafter cited as Bunce].

12. Mills, *I Have Nothing to Do with Justice,* LIFE, Mar. 12, 1971, at 57–68 [hereinafter cited as Mills].

13. Flannery, *Prosecutor's Position on Discovery in Federal Criminal Cases,* 33 F. R. D. 47, 78–79 (1963).

The one-sidedness of this search is perhaps the most frequently heard and oldest objection to the broadening of criminal discovery. Judge Learned Hand summed up this position when he said that "the accused has every advantage" and should not "in advance have the whole evidence against him to pick over at his leisure, and make his defense, fairly or foully."[14]

The logic of Judge Hand's objection to discovery is persuasive only if the assumption upon which it is based is valid. It is premised upon the assumption that defendants in criminal cases have trials, an assumption that is no longer true. The very survival of the criminal justice system requires that the overwhelming majority of defendants do not have trials. The basic orientation for formulating criminal procedures must shift to the reality that in some jurisdictions more than 90 percent of the convictions result from guilty pleas.[15] Because there are so few trials, it is invalid to assert that the difference in commitment to the revelation of truth at trial is a bar to the expansion of discovery.

To justify the retardation of the expansion of discovery in criminal procedure, the argument has also been advanced that a defendant in a criminal case has much more at stake than his counterpart in a civil suit. Consequently, the temptation to bribe or frighten witnesses prior to trial or the desire to secure perjured testimony is much greater than it is in civil litigation.[16] However, this argument also is based upon the assumption that criminal charges result in trial. The likelihood that any witness will give testimony, whether perjured or true, is very slim because of the paucity of trials.

Even though the old assumptions about criminal procedure are no longer valid, the road is not yet cleared for an extensive expansion of discovery in criminal cases. The underlying basis for the expansion of discovery in civil litigation was the mutual obligation to disclose evidence that could be fairly demanded of both the plaintiff and the defendant. The criminal defendant, however, is invested with special historical and constitutional protections. These protections may severely restrict the obligations which can be im-

---

14. United States v. Garsson, 291 F. 646, 649 (2d Cir. 1923). In addition to *Garsson,* there were other cases handed down by the distinguished Second Circuit in this period that took the harsh "prosecutorial" view of discovery. *See, e.g.,* United States v. Muraskin, 99 F.2d 815 (2d. Cir. 1938); United States v. Dilliard, 101 F.2d 829 (2d Cir. 1938).

15. THE PRESIDENT'S COMMISSION ON LAW ENFORCEMENT AND ADMINISTRATION OF JUSTICE, TASK FORCE REPORT: THE COURTS 9 (1967) [hereinafter cited as THE COURTS].

16. State v. Tune, 13 N. J. 203, 98 A.2d 881 (1953); People v. DiCarlo, 161 Misc. 484, 485, 292 N. Y. S. 252, 254 (1936).

posed upon him to disclose his case to the government while he obtains discovery of the state's case. Foremost is the Fifth Amendment privilege against self-incrimination. Since a defendant cannot be compelled to be a witness against himself,[17] the state's ability to gain discovery of the defendant and his case may be severely restricted.

DISCOVERY: PRESENT STATUS FOR THE DEFENDANT

The development of discovery in criminal cases has been slow[18] and, until recently, confined to the demands of the Constitution. Although no right to discovery is contained within the Constitution, its corollary, a duty to disclose certain matters in the possession of the prosecution, may be imposed upon the state.[19] This duty to disclose encompasses all evidence in the possession of the prosecution that is favorable to the accused.[20] A prosecutor cannot withhold from the defense evidence that would tend to exculpate the accused or mitigate his sentence. It was argued in a separate concurring Supreme Court opinion that the state's duty to disclose "requires something more than that the state did not lie. It implies that the prosecution has been fair and honest and that the state has disclosed all information known to it which may have a crucial or important effect on the outcome."[21] Despite

---

17. U. S. CONST. amend. V.
18. Everett, *Discovery in Criminal Cases—in Search of a Standard,* 1964 DUKE L. J. 477 & n. 1 [hereinafter cited as Everett].
19. This distinction between "discovery" and "disclosure" is a technical, but persistent, one. The Constitution does not compel discovery, but it does compel disclosure when nondisclosure would violate the requirements of due process. The distinction has never been clearly articulated; however, its existence is notable in the line of cases commencing with *Mooney v. Holohan,* 294 U. S. 103 (1934) and culminating with the concurring opinion of Justice Fortas in *Giles v. Maryland,* 386 U. S. 66, 98–99 (1967).
20. Brady v. Maryland, 373 U. S. 83 (1963). The *Brady* rule has some very old antecedents. The Supreme Court of Michigan, for example, held in 1888 that a prosecutor in propounding his questions to an expert witness had an obligation to give the expert all material facts on the case and not just those facts which tended to support the prosecution's theory of the case. People v. Vanderhoof, 71 Mich. 158, 39 N. W. 28 (1888). The duty to disclose favorable evidence is also recognized by the Canons of Professional Ethics. Canon 5 states in part: "The suppression of facts or the secreting of witnesses capable of establishing the innocence of the accused is highly reprehensible." *See also* Note, *The Duty of the Prosecutor to Disclose Exculpatory Evidence,* 60 COLUM. L. REV. 858 (1960).
21. Giles v. Maryland, 386 U. S. 66, 101 (1967) (concurring opinion).

the broad pronouncements of the Supreme Court, it is not clear how broadly this duty to disclose is followed in practice.[22]

Although due process is the standard against which the constitutional validity of prosecutions is to be measured, it does not generate all of the procedures that are desirable for a fair, effective, and efficient criminal system. The purpose of the Constitution in the criminal area is to define only the minimal standards of fairness, and thus the development of discovery is only minimally attributable to constitutional mandate. Likewise, in the future, the Constitution cannot be expected to be the moving force behind the further development of criminal discovery.

If any discovery is available to the defendant, it would seem that his own confession or statements should be discoverable by him.[23] Without knowledge of the contents of his confession, it is impossible for the defendant to make an informed plea. If there is a trial in the case, then the trial may be little more than an appeal from the confession. The Supreme Court has indicated that allowing inspection may be the "better practice," but it has not held that inspection is required by the Constitution.[24] In most jurisdictions the power resides, therefore, within the discretion of the trial judge to determine whether inspection is appropriate in a particular case. Some of the states, particularly Louisiana and New Jersey, permit the defendant to examine his statements unless the prosecution can show that such an inspection would result in a disservice to the public interest.[25]

Historically, resolution of evidentiary questions has centered upon the concern for protecting the defendant's rights in property.[26] Strangely, his own statements have never been considered as belonging to him in any

---

22. For a summary of these questions and an analysis of some of the post-*Brady* problems, *see* Cannon, *Prosecutor's Duty to Disclose,* 52 MARQ. L. REV. 516 (1969).

23. These statements "may be relevant in determining what plea to offer and whether to move for suppression or exclusion of certain evidence, either before or at trial. . . ." Everett, *supra* note 18, at 479.

24. Cicenia v. Lagay, 357 U. S. 504 (1958).

25. The Supreme Court of Louisiana has held that denying a defendant pretrial inspection of his confession is "tantamount to depriving such accused of a fair trial and is in violation of his constitutional rights." State v. Dorsey, 207 La. 928, 22 So. 2d 273, 285 (1945); *see also* State v. Johnson, 28 N. J. 133, 145 A.2d 313 (1958).

26. The federal cases in this area and, eventually, Rule 16 of the Federal Rules of Criminal Procedure reflect the protections afforded by the Fourth Amendment to the Constitution, which primarily stresses protection of one's property. Weeks v. United States, 232 U. S. 383 (1913); Alderman v. United States, 394 U. S. 165 (1969).

proprietary sense.[27] The argument was developed that a confession did not constitute an appropriation of a right of possession. Having lost nothing to which he was entitled, neither he nor his attorney could compel its return to assist in preparation of a defense.[28]

Reasons for allowing the defendant to inspect his own confession go beyond the arbitrariness of this property distinction. The state cannot argue, for example, that such discovery discriminates against it in being one-sided, because the state has already been the beneficiary of one-sided discovery in having the right to obtain statements from the defendant while he was in custody. The fear that the defendant will construct an alibi through perjured testimony, if he knows the exact contents of his confession, should not argue against permitting discovery of a confession: a confession is the single most effective item of evidence in any criminal trial, and its impeachment power is so great as to make a subsequently created alibi worthless.

For the state to secure a conviction at trial, it is going to have to rely on witnesses. The defense, therefore, has a great interest in knowing the identity of potential witnesses and in having some idea of what they are likely to say should the case proceed to trial. Many states require by statute that the defense be furnished with a list of witnesses known to the prosecutor or those he intends to call at trial.[29] The federal rule is much more limited: it requires producing such a list only in capital cases and is diluted even further by its provision that the list need not be produced until three days before trial.[30] The value of a witness list as a discovery device is directly related to whether it is provided sufficiently in advance of a scheduled trial to give the defense time to investigate witnesses and to prepare to impeach their testimony.

In addition to the names of witnesses, the defense would obviously like to know what they have said previously about the matters in dispute. The

---

27. Shores v. United States, 174 F.2d 838 (8th Cir. 1949). The court in *Shores* concluded its property analysis of confessions by saying: "It is not the physical object but merely the contents which the defendant has supplied." *Id.* at 844. It is significant that the court in *Shores* determined the status of confessions in terms of what it interpreted to be the intent of the drafters of Rule 16 and quoted from one of the drafters in support of its property analysis.

28. "The federal courts have generally denied a defendant's motion for production of a copy of his oral confession or statement on the ground that Rule 16 requires that the defendant have a proprietary interest in the document." *Developments, supra* note 9, at 1053.

29. 6 J. WIGMORE, EVIDENCE §§ 1851–55 (1940).

30. 18 U. S. C. § 3432 (1969).

general rule has been that testimony before a grand jury is secret and not subject to inspection by the defendant,[31] but the sacrosanct nature of grand jury testimony is beginning to give way.[32] Although the federal courts tend to require that the defendant show a "particularized" need for the disclosure, the trend is towards disclosure.[33] California and four other states now grant the defendant an absolute right to inspect the grand jury minutes prior to the commencement of trial.[34] Furthermore, in parts of California, at the time of the arraignment the defendant is given a transcript of the minutes of the grand jury proceeding. At its 1970 meeting, the American Bar Association approved the recommendation of its special committee on minimum standards for criminal justice that the prosecuting attorney shall disclose to defense counsel "those portions of grand jury minutes containing testimony of the accused and relevant testimony of persons whom the prosecuting attorney intends to call as witnesses."[35]

The grand jury is a mechanism that has been refined into an ex parte discovery proceeding for the exclusive benefit of the state. The statements of witnesses are entered and preserved on the record for the state without cross-examination.[36] The grand jury no longer serves its traditional function as a protector of the accused. Instead, it serves only to permit the prosecution to discover evidence and prepare its case; nothing comparable is available to the defendant.

Another class of materials important to the preparation of a defense is statements voluntarily given by prospective witnesses to government agents, prosecutors, and investigators.[37] A bar to discovery of these materials is the

---

31. 46 VA. L. REV. 1002 (1960).

32. *Id.* at 1004–6.

33. *See, e.g.,* Dennis v. United States, 384 U. S. 855 (1966); FED. R. CRIM. P. 6(e).

34. ABA PROJECT ON MINIMUM STANDARDS FOR CRIMINAL JUSTICE: STANDARDS RELATING TO DISCOVERY AND PROCEDURE BEFORE TRIAL 65 (1969) (tentative draft).

35. *Id.* at 13.

36. The lack of cross–examination of witnesses before the grand jury means that even if a transcript is obtainable by the defense its worth is questionable. Goldstein, *The State and the Accused: Balance of Advantage in Criminal Procedure,* 69 YALE L. J. 1149, 1181 (1960).

37. [D]efense counsel [will] wish to see any statements of a probable Government witness, both as a basis for deciding what plea to enter and for possible impeachment of the witness by prior inconsistent statements if his testimony at the trial varies materially from the pretrial statements. Even the statements of persons whom the Government does not plan to call as witnesses may be valuable to the

notion of the attorney's "work product."[38] The rationale for not allowing discovery of materials classified as "work product" is that such materials constitute internal working papers of the prosecution and that the opposition has no right to go through the notes and memoranda accumulated by the state's agents in preparation of its case. As applied in criminal law, "work product" includes statements given by prospective witnesses to police officers as well as notes prepared by the state's attorneys and investigators.[39]

DISCOVERY: PRESENT STATUS FOR THE PROSECUTION

Notwithstanding the fact that the prosecution starts with the immense advantage of having as its resource the investigative powers and prowess of all local law enforcement agencies,[40] the opposition to expanded discovery has been led by prosecutors. The argument against expanded discovery is based on the premise that such expansion, because of the constitutional guarantees against self-incrimination, would have to be one-directional, from the state to the accused, with the state receiving nothing in return. It is clear that if the opposition is to be blunted, the drive to broaden discovery requires that it not be all one way. In fact, recent developments have seen the creation and expansion of rights of discovery in favor of the state.

The state has as valid an interest in knowing what witnesses the defense intends to call as the defense has in knowing in advance the names of the state's witnesses. Statutes requiring the disclosure of names of witnesses have been enacted in a few states and have been held not to violate the defendant's protection against self-incrimination.[41]

As discussed above in relation to bail, constitutional rights are not absolutes but are subject to qualification and limitation. There are numerous examples of legislative action that qualify and limit the privilege against self-incrimination. Statutes that require a driver of an automobile to stop and identify himself after an accident, for example, have been upheld as valid exercises of state police power despite the fact that such disclosure

---

defense in suggesting the availability of evidence which might aid its theory of the case. Everett, *supra* note 18, at 479–80.

38. Hickman v. Taylor, 329 U. S. 495 (1947).

39. *See, e.g.,* Colebrook v. State, 205 So. 2d 675 (Fla. 1968); Jones v. Florida, 394 U. S. 720 (1969). *See* Annot., 35 A. L. R. 3d 412, 464–65. *See also* The Jencks Act, 18 U. S. C. § 3500 (1969).

40. Bunce, *supra* note 11, at 105.

41. *See, e.g.,* People v. Schade, 161 Misc. 212, 229 N. Y. S. 612 (Queens Cty. Ct. 1936), cited in *Developments, supra* note 9, at 1055 n. 853.

may subject the individual to criminal prosecution.[42] Similarly, individuals engaged in certain businesses are required to keep records for inspection by government agencies.[43] In criminal law, there are two long-recognized exceptions to the absoluteness of the privilege against self-incrimination. The first of these is the practice followed in many states which requires a defendant to plead a defense of insanity prior to trial or be barred the use of that defense.[44] The second exception is the requirement in sixteen states that a defendant plead an alibi in advance of trial or forfeit that defense.[45]

The issue of the constitutionality of the notice-of-alibi statutes was settled by the Supreme Court in 1970.[46] A Florida statute that requires the defense to notify the court and the prosecutor of its intent to prove an alibi and to disclose the identity of proposed alibi witnesses, and authorizes the state to take depositions of those witnesses, was held not to violate the Fifth Amendment privilege. The Florida statute is arguably at odds with the basic Anglo-American legal principle that the burden of proof in a criminal case rests exclusively with the state. According to this principle, the defendant need not produce anything unless the prosecution first demonstrates at trial that its case is sufficient to go to the jury. Statutes such as the one in Florida require that the defendant produce information without a prior test of the sufficiency of the prosecution's case. The decision represents a major breakthrough in compelling disclosure by the defense and paves the way for substantial mandatory two-way discovery.

Discovery in the federal courts is predicated upon mutuality.[47] For the defense to learn of the prosecution's case, it must be willing to allow discovery by the government. The government may obtain books, papers, medical reports, and other tangible objects which the defense intends to produce at trial if the defense has sought similar materials from the government. The decision upholding the Florida statute does not, however, rest upon a request by the defendant and his attorney to avail themselves of discovery.

The extent to which discovery of the defendant may be ordered is far from settled. A California decision greatly expanded the power of that state's courts to order a defendant to disclose information to the prosecu-

---

42. California v. Byers, 402 U. S. 424 (1971).
43. Louisell, *Criminal Discovery and Self–Incrimination: Roger Traynor Confronts the Dilemma,* 53 CALIF. L. REV. 89, 94 (1965).
44. *See* Comment, *The Self–Incrimination Privilege: Barrier to Criminal Discovery?,* 51 CALIF. L. REV. 135, 137 & n. 23 (1963).
45. 22 CASE W. RES. L. REV. 119, 120 & n. 9 (1971).
46. Williams v. Florida, 399 U. S. 78 (1970).
47. FED. R. CRIM. P. 16(e).

tor.[48] This expansion was justified on the ground that the development of discovery on behalf of the defendant had taken place "to promote the orderly ascertainment of truth" and could be made to work both ways.[49] One proponent of two-way discovery advocated the extension of the rationale of notice-of-alibi statutes to require that the defense notify the prosecution in advance of trial of any defense it intended to use.[50] This departure from the historical protection afforded the defendant is also justified on the theory that the right to a fair trial applies to the state as well as to the defendant and that the state's interest in securing this right is furthered by its being notified of defenses which it will have to counter.

The decisions authorizing discovery by the prosecution do not emasculate the Fifth Amendment privilege against self-incrimination. No decision has authorized pretrial disclosure of any information that the defendant was not intending to disclose at trial. All that the decisions have taken away from him is the right to choose when to disclose it.[51]

DISCOVERY AND THE AVOIDANCE OF TRIALS

The court decisions and textual material written on the subject of pretrial discovery are virtually always concerned with those rare cases that result in trials. The greatest need is not in the further refinement of the trial process, but in the rapid and equitable clearing of the 90 percent of the cases that are settled without trials. It is a great waste of intellectual energy and scarce judicial resources to resolve the questions surrounding the expansion of mutual rights of discovery in a manner that is only applicable to the 10 percent of criminal cases that go to trial.

---

48. Jones v. Superior Court, 58 Cal. 2d 56, 372 P.2d 919, 22 Cal. Rptr. 879 (1962).
49. *Id.* at 58, 372 P.2d at 921, 22 Cal. Rptr. at 880.
50. Interview with Judge Edward Gaulkin (retired), New Jersey Superior Court, Appellate Division, in Newark, Nov. 30, 1970.
51. In analyzing the *Williams* case, it has been said:
    > The notice-of-alibi rule merely requires pretrial disclosure of what the defendant intends to reveal during trial. The Court found nothing in the Constitution which gives a defendant the right to conceal his defense until the conclusion of the State's case. Moreover, a continuance would be available to the State if it could show surprise because of the introduction of an alibi during the trial. Florida's notice-of- alibi rule only permits the state to achieve before trial what it could accomplish by a continuance during trial, thus avoiding the delay and inconvenience that accompany the latter. 22 CASE W. RES. L. REV. 119, 120 (1971).

The system demands for its preservation that all but a small fraction of cases result in pleas of guilty or in dismissal. It has a compelling interest in reducing this fraction still further and in ensuring that processes for disposing of cases without trial are equitable.

If the defendant and his counsel are apprised of the relative strength of the state's case, it is logical for the defendant to plead guilty either to a reduced charge or in return for a definite or reduced sentence rather than risk the perils of a trial and the potential imposition of the maximum sentence. If, on the other hand, the defense is left in the dark until trial but has reason to suspect that there are crucial weaknesses in the state's case, the inclination to gamble and put the state to the burden of a trial is much greater. The same lack of information plagues the prosecution. Overworked prosecutors are forced to rely upon a case file prepared solely by the police. The prosecutors are thus also working in the dark, since the case has not been prepared with a sensitivity to the ramifications of latent legal issues, which may transcend the facts. A consequence of this lack of information is pleas to charges that are neither equitable to the defendant nor in the best interest of the community.

The best type of discovery is informal.[52] Two attorneys who have a healthy professional respect for each other should sit down together and try to delineate the dimensions of a pending case. Together, they are able to ascertain what the relevant facts are and determine where their respective strengths and weaknesses lie. A result of such trading of information is that the parties are often able to avoid a trial. When available, informal discovery procedures are effective and serve worthwhile ends. It is the arbitrariness of the availability of discovery that creates the problem. Availability of informal discovery is a function of the personal respect and relationship that exist between the prosecutor and defense lawyer. Discovery is, therefore, likely to be available in one case but not in another. Indigent defendants often suffer from such informality because they tend to be represented by younger, less experienced attorneys who have had little opportunity to establish a relationship with the prosecutor or a reputation in the legal community which the prosecutor will feel compelled to respect.

To equalize the availability of discovery, formal requirements must be established to insure that discovery exists for all defendants. Availability must be equalized and generalized without creating formal, lockstep proce-

---

52. Assistant Prosecutor Robert Snider of Boston and Assistant State's Attorney Arthur Cheslock of Baltimore maintain that they will open a file to the defense attorney so the defense attorney will know the strength of the state's case. Interview with Mr. Snider, in Boston, April 13, 1971, and interview with Mr. Cheslock, in Baltimore, April 8, 1971.

dures to be used in all cases. Any rules designed to promote discovery should encourage the fullest use of informal methods and provide for formal court-imposed discovery only as a last resort.

The proposals developed and put forth above concerning the earliest stages of a felony prosecution contain the seeds for early discovery proceedings. The mandatory conference between prosecutor and defense attorney, which is recommended to follow shortly after the booking procedure and before the mandatory preliminary hearing, provides an opportunity for extensive, albeit informal, early discovery. If discovery takes place within the context of a strict time line, it can be a means towards the achievement of speedy and just disposition of controversies. Counsel for the state and the defense will exchange information at the very beginning of a controversy and again after formal charging.

This exchange of information will not add additional delay to the process. Instead the exchange will allow the attorneys to make an informed decision as to whether the case should be settled, through dismissal or a plea of guilty, or whether it is one of those few cases that should be funneled into the trial process. At present, this crucial decision is made by default, with each side waging a war of attrition to see which one will be successful in waiting out the other.

WHAT SHOULD BE DISCOVERABLE?

What should be discoverable must be delineated within a framework of mutuality. That framework is bound on the one hand by the defendant's special constitutional guarantees and on the other by the greater obligation that the Constitution vests in the prosecutor to insure that justice, not just conviction, is the result of his efforts.

Statements made by the defendant to the police should be automatically available to the defense attorney.[53] Expediency, as well as fairness, will be well served by such a practice. If the statements are admissible into evidence and amount to a confession, it is unlikely that the case will go to trial. Both sides should be compelled to exchange, as early as possible, lists of witnesses who would be called to testify if the controversy were to go to trial. Since the defendant would not be offering any information that would not eventually come to the prosecution at trial, he is not being forced to surrender anything. These witnesses should be made available for questioning by the opposing attorney.[54] As the deposition procedure is a time-consuming and

---

53. *See* note 23 *supra.*

54. The current practice, however, does not provide for this:

Law enforcement personnel sometimes appear exceedingly reluc-

costly one, it would make a great deal of sense for the attorneys to exchange the statements that they have taken from the witnesses. Since this exchange, however, would involve entry into the attorney's "work product," as presently construed, the exchange would have to be voluntary and mutual. In any event, both attorneys would know the names of the opposition's prospective witnesses and could seek to interview them and take their depositions. The defendant would not be subject to a pretrial interview with the prosecuting attorney unless he and his attorney chose to waive the defendant's right to be free from self-incrimination. Documents and scientific and medical reports that the prosecutor and the defense attorney intend to produce at trial should be made available as early as possible.

Society's dependence upon the criminal justice system, whether that dependence is for the purpose of protecting individual rights or of protecting community rights, is too great to proceed with the illusion that truth emerges through the combat of equally equipped adversaries at a trial where neither has divulged anything beforehand. If there is equality at present, it is the equality of ignorance. Furthermore, it is time to acknowledge that the illusion of truth emerging or justice being done under existing methods for dealing in pleas is as remote as the probability of a given case ever reaching trial. The critical need is for information, so that the decisions which are made truly reflect the facts of a particular case and respect the interests which must be served. Finally, the system requires not only that the decisions be informed but that they be made as early in the process as possible.

PLEA BARGAINING

During the period following the arraignment, the prosecutor and defense attorney consume a considerable amount of time merely jockeying for position.[55] Our study of felony cases conducted in Cuyahoga County dis-

---

tant to converse with a defense attorney, and they may even be prevented from doing so by the policy or directives of their agency. It is not unknown for a prosecuting attorney to suggest to his prospective witnesses that they not talk with anyone about the subject of their prospective testimony and, whether designedly or otherwise, this suggestion frequently discourages communication with a defendant's attorney. Everett, *supra* note 18, at 491.

55. According to a Fort Worth lawyer, some attorneys will wait and have their clients withhold their guilty plea until the day of trial, "when it becomes apparent that the state will not make a better offer." One attorney from Pittsburgh remarked, "The day of trial is really the only opportunity to plea bargain." QUESTIONNAIRE, *supra* note 12, Chapter 2.

closed that in nearly half the cases three to twelve months elapsed between the arraignment and either the beginning of trial, the defendant's plea of guilty, or the dismissal of the case by the prosecutor.[56] Throughout the country, the amount of time elapsing at this juncture remains high or is increasing and the result is an ever increasing backlog of unresolved cases.[57]

To dispose of cases and to keep the system moving, the prosecutor is often ready to make some concession to the defendant. At the same time, the defense attorney and the defendant are interested in the lightest penalty available and are willing to plead guilty if the punishment offered is less severe than might be decreed by a trial court. The etiquette of plea bargaining differs from city to city.[58] It may occupy several months, if the practice of the attorneys is to become involved in a series of offers and counteroffers. Or it may be a one-time effort by the prosecutor to reduce the charge or recommend a lenient sentence, in return for a plea of guilty, or a single offer by the defense attorney to plead his client guilty, in return for reduction. In some situations, it may be done prior to the scheduled trial date; in others, it may normally occur on the first date set for trial.[59] Occasionally it happens before the defendant in the courtroom, but more often the lawyers negotiate out of the defendant's presence.[60] Although the absence

---

56. *See* Appendix A.

57. In Philadelphia in December, 1970, sixty days elapsed, in an average case, between the arraignment and the time a case was ready to proceed to trial. In April, 1970, eighty-one days elapsed between the araignment and the time a case was ready to proceed to trial. Willmann & Polansky, *supra* note 10, Chapter 2.

According to the circuit court administrator in Kansas City, Missouri, most cases are set for trial approximately four weeks from the date of the arraignment. Letter from Austin Van Buskirk, Court Administrator, Kansas City, Missouri, April 5, 1971.

In Baltimore, arraignments, as a separate court appearance, are held in only a small percentage of the cases. The assignment clerk is trying to set cases for trial within sixty days after there is an attorney of record. Interview with Arthur Cheslock, Assistant State's Attorney, in Baltimore, April 7, 1971. An attorney of record may not be present until after the preliminary hearing or grand jury proceedings.

58. The plea negotiating processes in Philadelphia and New York are compared and contrasted in White, *A Proposal for Reform of the Plea Bargaining Process,* 119 U. PA. L. REV. 439, 441–42 (1971) [hereinafter cited as White].

59. THE PRESIDENT'S COMMISSION ON LAW ENFORCEMENT AND ADMINISTRATION OF JUSTICE: THE CHALLENGE OF CRIME IN A FREE SOCIETY 134 (1967) [hereinafter cited as CHALLENGE OF CRIME].

60. ABA PROJECT ON STANDARDS FOR CRIMINAL JUSTICE: STANDARDS

of the judge during the negotiations avoids undue pressures upon the attorneys, often the judge is present and serves as an outside factor forcing attorneys to come to terms.[61]

Pleas of guilty are responsible for the disposition of the vast majority of felony cases. Our Cuyahoga County court study indicated that 76 percent of the felony cases which went beyond the grand jury proceeding ended in pleas of guilty to the indictment or to a lesser offense. Of the remainder, the prosecutor went to trial on 9 percent of the cases and dismissed the charges on 14 percent.[62] The 1970 statistics from Philadelphia, including misdemeanors, show that 79 percent of the cases involved plea bargaining, 20 percent resulted in dismissals, and a little more than 1 percent were resolved by jury trials.[63] The Philadelphia plea bargaining figure includes both guilty pleas and those cases in which the defendant waived a jury trial in preference to a trial before a judge. To persuade a defendant to waive his right to a jury trial and have a trial before a judge instead, the prosecutor lets him know that his waiver will be a factor in mitigating his sentence if the judge finds him guilty.[64]

The purpose of plea bargaining today has changed somewhat from its earlier emphasis of providing a means to avoid the harshness of the death penalty. During the seventeenth and eighteenth centuries, when most felonies were punishable as capital offenses, public demands for less harsh punishment prompted English barristers representing the Crown to waive the felony charge if the defendant would plead guilty to a noncapital offense.[65] Today the emphasis is on moving the backlog of unresolved cases and now,[66] as then, the attorneys manipulate the facts to reduce the charge and arrive at an agreement.[67]

RELATING TO THE PROSECUTION FUNCTION AND THE DEFENSE FUNCTION 250 (1970).

61. ABA PROJECT ON MINIMUM STANDARDS FOR CRIMINAL JUSTICE: STANDARDS RELATING TO PLEAS OF GUILTY § 72 (1971).

62. *See* Appendix A.

63. Data received from John Willmann, Deputy Court Administrator, Philadelphia, April 5, 1971.

64. White, *supra* note 58, at 441. Fifty-six percent of all dispositions in 1970 in Philadelphia were by judge trials. Data received from John Willmann, Deputy Court Administrator, Philadelphia, April 5, 1971.

65. Dash, *Cracks in the Foundation of Criminal Justice*, 46 ILL. L. REV. 385, 396 (1952) [hereinafter cited as Dash].

66. "The widely held view that prosecutors never bargain is a myth. As a practical matter they must in order to stay in business." Polstein, *How to "Settle" a Criminal Case,* 8 PRAC. LAW., 35, 37 (1962).

67. Dash, *supra* note 65, at 396.

In England the suggested plea agreement was made in open court before the public, the judge, and the jury, if one had been sworn.[68] Today, plea arrangements are made privately to avoid any public or jury prejudice to the defendant if an agreement is not reached. In New York City, these discussions between the prosecutor and defense attorney are overheard by the judge and occur in court because of the inability of the participants to get together elsewhere.[69] Dealing usually takes place out of the accused's presence so that the attorneys can dicker if necessary.

The forum for conducting plea negotiations, as well as the number, length, and formality of such meetings, varies from jurisdiction to jurisdiction. To encourage plea bargaining, Cleveland, Detroit, and Baltimore have developed a semiformal procedure:[70] a pretrial conference. This conference brings the prosecutor and defense attorney together with the hope of settling the case. Flexibility in the bargaining process is the rule in all jurisdictions, because of the belief that flexibility will aid in reaching an agreement. No statute delineates how the negotiations are to proceed, what may be negotiated, or how long the negotiations may continue before the case must come to trial.[71] The attorneys enjoy unbridled freedom to make their own arrangements and proceed at their own convenience and pace.[72]

Tragically, the absolute deference paid to the convenience of lawyers[73] creates the appearance, if it does not establish the fact, that the interests of the client, if he is awaiting the outcome in jail, and of the community, if the defendant is charged with a violent crime and is free on bail, are

---

68. HALL, THEFT, LAW, AND SOCIETY 100 (1935), quoting the remarks of M. Cottu made in the early nineteenth century.
69. White, *supra* note 58, at 448.
70. In other cities, the procedure is very informal. Plea negotiating may be done in a hurried conversation in the halls of a courthouse. CHALLENGE OF CRIME, *supra* note 59, at 134.
71. In Baltimore, however, if the case is not resolved at the pretrial conference, the prosecutor and defense attorney will try to agree on two or three alternative trial dates. When the trial date is set, all parties are notified. Interview with Arthur Cheslock, Assistant State's Attorney, in Baltimore, April 7, 1971.
72. Lois Luipage, for example, is accused of a murder which took place on September 8, 1968. On February 11, 1970, the case was set for a pretrial conference on June 15, 1970. San Francisco Chronicle, April 4, 1970, at 2, col. 1.
73. In Boston, once the arraignment is completed, the trial date is set when it is convenient for the attorney. A defense attorney's schedule and his desire to bring a case to trial are of prime concern in establishing a trial date. Interview with Leo Manning, Assistant Assignment Commissioner, in Boston, April 13, 1971.

forgotten. The prosecutor has too many other cases to be concerned about how long the negotiations in a particular case drag on. He will simply direct his attention and efforts to cases that are riper for disposition. This arrangement is satisfactory to defense attorneys, who generally operate from the mental set that cases, like wine, improve with age. As one Dallas defense lawyer remarked, a defense attorney can beat any case if he has enough time.[74] The judge is not going to pressure the attorneys to determine whether a given case can be settled now or must be tried, if there is some chance that the case may be settled at a later time.

The pressures of too many cases and too little time cause the emphasis of plea negotiations to be upon settlement regardless of whether there is a relationship between the settlement and the facts of the case. One Cleveland prosecutor, for example, who is heralded for his ability to move cases,[75] regularly reduces charges at the pretrial conference after only the most cursory examination of the facts. It is common for this prosecutor to reduce a charge of burglary for a first offender, which carries a statutory sentence of life or five to thirty years,[76] to malicious entry, with a sentence of one to two years.[77] Since the need is to move cases, there is little evaluation of the factual basis supporting the original charge and little concern demonstrated for whether the defendant will be involved again in criminal activity. It is the same in all cities; the deal is usually made irrespective of the facts of the case[78] or of the theoretical goals of the criminal law.

The paradox is absolute: the system provides for an extensive, formal, time-consuming, and finicky charging process. Then, irrespective of the charge, a case is disposed of. There is no time to consider consequences, let alone goals.

The highly negotiable commodity in which everyone deals is time.[79] A reduction in the charge guarantees to the defendant a reduction in the

---

74. *Logjam in Our Courts,* LIFE, Aug. 7, 1970, at 19 [hereinafter cited as *Logjam*].

75. Cleveland Plain Dealer, April 1, 1971, § D, at 2, col. 3.

76. OHIO REV. CODE § 2907.09 (Page Supp. 1970).

77. OHIO REV. CODE § 2907.13 (Page Supp. 1970).

78. In a case still pending, the defendant was charged with larceny and burglary of a record store. The defense attorney has stated that there is no doubt that the defendant committed such acts. Nevertheless, because the defendant had no record, the prosecutor offered to reduce the charge to malicious entry, if the defendant were to plead guilty. Also, the prosecutor suggested that the likelihood was great that the defendant would be given probation. Interview with Cleveland defense attorney, May 17, 1971 (anonymity requested).

79. The state says to the defendant:
    "If you will abandon your unsupportable claim of innocence, we

maximum amount of time he can be forced to serve, since most criminal statutes are framed in terms of statutorily set minimums and maximums that depend upon the charge.[80] Furthermore, many states follow the practice of determining eligibility for parole by the minimum sentence imposed by the judge.[81] As the charge is reduced so will be the minimum sentence, thus making the defendant eligible for an earlier parole. Where a judge intends to impose a specific sentence, the defendant can influence its length by withholding his willingness to plead until he is satisfied with the terms offered. Probation, especially for first offenders, is also a possibility which is frequently demanded in return for the plea that the prosecutor wants and the system requires.[82] To justify a recommendation of probation, prosecutors will often consider the time already spent in jail while awaiting disposition of the case.

Although the negotiation is based upon the charge, the actual currency is always the time that will be served. Even in cities where prosecutors have established a policy of not reducing charges, trials are still avoided and cases settled because the critical factor, time, remains negotiable. In Boston, for example, where a policy of not reducing charges is in effect, the assistant prosecutors offer a specific recommendation for reduction in sentence in return for a plea of guilty to the original charge.[83] Similarly, in Chicago the practice is for the prosecutor to make acceptable sentence recommendations to the judge in return for the defendant's promise to plead guilty.[84] Care is taken to insure that the judge is amenable to the sentence agreed upon by the defendant. The bargain is obviously meaningless unless all are assured that the judge will follow the prosecution's suggestion.[85] To gain such

---

will compensate you with a light sentence." The defendant says, "How light?"—and the DA, defense lawyer and judge are drawn together at the bench. . . . The conference . . . proceeds as the playing of a game, with moves and countermoves, protocol, rules and ritual. Mills, *supra* note 12, at 59.

80. Enker, *Perspectives on Plea Bargaining,* in THE COURTS, *supra* note 15, at 108–9.

81. *E.g.,* OHIO REV. CODE § 2967.19 (Page Supp. 1970).

82. *See* Note, *Guilty Plea Bargaining: Compromises by Prosecutors to Secure Guilty Pleas,* 112 U. PA. L. REV. 865, 866 n. 7 (1964) [hereinafter cited as *Compromises*].

83. Interview with Assistant Prosecutor Robert Snider, in Boston, April 12, 1971.

84. *Justice on Trial,* NEWSWEEK, Mar. 8, 1971, at 22, 29 [hereinafter cited as *Justice*].

85. When there is a judicial practice of following recommendations, the promise of a recommended sentence can be tantamount to a promise of a definite term. But each defendant who pleads guilty in

compliance, the case might be moved to the docket of a different judge[86] or, in jurisdictions where that is not possible, delayed still further until a different judge is assigned to take pleas.[87]

When the defendant's criminal conduct has violated several statutes and the prosecutor has produced a multiple offense charge, settlement is frequently achieved by the prosecutor's promise to dismiss all but one of the charges in return for a plea of guilty to the remaining one. Such agreements may be illusory, because multiple convictions generally result in concurrent sentences,[88] but the defendant feels that he has benefited from the agreement, for the potential consequences, serving a series of consecutive sentences, are ominous. Of course, there is always the possibility that if the defendant is convicted on all counts the judge may defy the usual practice and impose consecutive, rather than concurrent, sentences.

One means frequently used to produce a multiple charge indictment is to add the crime of conspiracy to the substantive crime. Whenever two or more persons are charged with the same criminal act, it is probable that they were engaged in a criminal conspiracy. As a result, in Philadelphia, according to Assistant District Attorney James Crawford, a charge of conspiracy is added to most indictments involving two or more defendants.[89] Adding the conspiracy charge increases the chance of getting a plea of guilty to the substantive charge, and then the conspiracy charge is dropped.

For the prosecutor who is concerned with a won-lost record, a motivation that all publicly deny, the multi-count indictment enables the prosecutor to boast an impressive number of convictions based upon one of the original charges. In Dayton, Ohio, a former assistant prosecutor said that the goal within the prosecutor's office was to have guilty pleas to the original

reliance on a prosecutor's promise to recommend a specific sentence takes the risk that in his particular case the judge will not follow the suggestion. . . . In addition, many defendants may enter into agreements with prosecutors to avoid imposition of the maximum sentence, but, unless they are informed of actual sentencing patterns, may needlessly bargain away their right to trial since sentences often fall considerably below the maximum provided by the legislature. *Compromises, supra* note 82, at 866.

86. THE COURTS, *supra* note 15, at 11.
87. In Boston, for example, if the judge responsible for accepting guilty pleas is known as a harsh sentencer, few guilty pleas will be forthcoming. When a different judge is vested with responsibility for accepting guilty pleas, defendants will again be willing to plead guilty. Interview with Assistant Prosecutor Robert Snider, in Boston, April 13, 1971.
88. *Compromises, supra* note 82, at 868.
89. Interview with James Crawford, First Assistant Prosecutor, in Philadelphia, Dec. 1, 1970.

charges of the indictment in close to 65 percent of the cases. In a multi-count indictment, if an assistant prosecutor secured a guilty plea to one of the counts, although agreeing to dismiss the remaining counts, such a plea was considered entered against the original indictment and would go towards satisfaction of the quota.[90]

Overcharging and the subsequent reduction of the inflated charge have become the prosecutor's means of preserving the system.[91] If the prosecutor does not appear willing to offer concessions in return for a plea of guilty, the result will be an increase in the number of cases for which there must be a trial. Prosecutors are fully cognizant of the inability of their staffs to handle a greater number of trials,[92] and they are aware that a reduction in the percentage of guilty pleas would increase the time required to dispose of all cases.

As the need to move cases dominates other considerations, offers of reduction of the charge or the sentence are often made automatically without evaluation of the case. A prosecutor in the Bronx, New York, reported:

> When I get a case, I try to look at it objectively, to figure out what the eventual disposition would be considering all delays. . . . If I get a burglary . . . that I think will be disposed of as a misdemeanor after

90. Interview with John Kessler, Pilot City Project, in Dayton, Ohio, Jan. 28, 1971.

91.   Before a prosecutor can reduce the charge against a defendant in exchange for a plea of guilty, he—or someone else—must have formulated the initial charge. . . .

   Defense attorneys in almost every jurisdiction claim that prosecutors "overcharge." Houston's Clyde W. Woody observes, "It is like horse trading anywhere. Of course both sides start out asking for more than they expect to get."

   . . . Prosecutors are quick to condemn overcharging, but they define overcharging as a crude form of blackmail—accusing the defendant of a crime of which he is clearly innocent in an effort to induce him to plead guilty to the "proper" crime. Alschuler, *The Prosecutor's Role in Plea Bargaining,* 36 U. Chi. L. Rev. 50, 85 (1969) [hereinafter cited as Alschuler].

   Defense attorneys, when critical of overcharging, make reference to two forms of overcharging: first, the unreasonable multiplication of the number of accusations against a single defendant; second, charging a single offense at a higher level than warranted by the facts. *Id.* at 85.

92. During 1970, in Boston, one assistant prosecutor spent fifty-six days actually trying cases. Seventy-four days was the maximum time spent in trial by any one prosecutor. The Boston courts are open eleven months during the year. Interview with Assistant Prosecutor Robert Snider, in Boston, April 13, 1971.

a string of adjournments, I figure it's better to get it out of the way at the first or second appearance than have it kicked from one judge to another for maybe a year.[93]

The factors considered by this prosecutor are relevant to the problems of getting the case through the process, but they are of no relevance to the issues of the particular case. Unlike the prosecutor quoted, however, few prosecutors feel that they can engage in the luxury of an early evaluation of the cases they receive. The offer of reduction comes when the case must finally be settled or be scheduled for trial. The opportunity to dispose of it early in the process, and probably with similar results, has already been lost. Automatic reductions, unaccompanied by any meaningful evaluation of the facts of a given case, often result in "giveaways,"[94] with the defendant, in some instances, literally getting away with murder.

When knowledge of a giveaway becomes public, the effect is to further erode public confidence in the ability of the courts and the justice system to protect the community. Two such giveaways resulted from the congestion in the courts of New York City. Stanley Poler, a New York resident, sounded the public alarm in one such case. Poler aided the police in the capture of two burglary suspects. Both of the suspects were recidivists and had engaged in a great many burglaries. Despite their history, both defendants were permitted to plead guilty to the charge of trespassing, a relatively minor offense. But the community's safety from the two burglars was short-lived, as one was sentenced to two months in jail and the other to nine months. Stanley Poler was justified in commenting that our prisons have revolving doors.[95]

When police officers charged with illegal acts are the recipients of giveaways, the public's confidence can never be wholly regained. Joseph DeVito, a former member of the New York City Police Department, was

---

93. *Logjam, supra* note 74, at 23.

94. Kuh, *Plea Copping,* 24 N. Y. COUNTY BAR BULL. 160 (1966–1967).

95. N. Y. Times, Feb. 9, 1971, at 38, col. 3. Another beneficiary of a "giveaway" plea was Albert Jones. He admitted that he strangled Beverly Ribet, June 5, 1970, after forcing his way into her car. Although Jones was originally charged with murder, murder while committing a robbery, and murder while committing rape, the defendant was permitted to plead guilty to the reduced charge of manslaughter. N. Y. Times, Feb. 2, 1971, at 46, col. 8.

In Gary, Indiana, a defendant was charged with assault and battery with intent to kill after he had shot his girlfriend in the chest and right thigh, and then shot her daughter twice in the leg. The prosecutor accepted a plea of guilty to the charge of carrying a pistol without a permit. Cause No. 37763, Criminal Court, Lake County, Indiana.

arrested and charged with conspiring to sell large amounts of heroin,[96] the drug which is responsible for more than half the serious crimes in New York City, since addicts must commit crimes to get the money to support their habit.[97] DeVito was permitted to plead guilty to the greatly reduced charge of official misconduct. Disclosure of the DeVito case generated significant press and public criticism. In an attempt to restore public confidence, two agencies set about to investigate the case, with no results, as yet. DeVito's case is a classic example of either a giveaway or overcharging. If the original charge was justified by the facts, the disposition of the case shows an appalling lack of concern for the community's need for protection from traffickers in illegal drugs.[98] If, on the other hand, the reduced charge was all that the facts of the case would justify,[99] then DeVito was terribly wronged by the initial charge and will suffer that stigma for the rest of his life. In either event, valid interests have been ignored.

Plea bargaining is necessary to the operation of the system,[100] but as these two extreme, although not uncommon, examples indicate, it can produce wretchedly inequitable results. Prosecutors must make offers that will induce pleas and avoid trials, but community interests and fears must be considered.

THE DEFENSE AND PLEA BARGAINING

So few cases are tried[101] that defense attorneys prepare cases only if trial cannot be avoided. The defense attorney's principal function is to delay a

---

96. N. Y. Times, Feb. 4, 1971, at 1, col. 3.
97. N. Y. Times, Dec. 6, 1970, at 24, col. 6.
98. Melvin Fischler, DeVito's co-defendant, was also charged with conspiring to sell heroin. Since Fischler had testified before the grand jury and the State Commission of Investigation about his dealings with DeVito, he was permitted to plead guilty to possession of heroin, a lesser included offense. Robert Nahman, Assistant Queens District Attorney, promised to recommend leniency in the sentencing of Fischler. N. Y. Times, July 3, 1971, at 5, col. 1.

    Thus, leniency is recommended for one defendant who turns state's evidence against a co-defendant. The co-defendant, however, is then permitted to plead guilty to a lesser offense, rather than face a trial on the original charge.

99. Thomas Mackell, Queens District Attorney, thought the plea and the defendant's resignation from the police force was a "good accomplishment." N. Y. Times, Feb. 4, 1971, at 1, col. 3.

100. *See* note 66 *supra.*

101. One study indicated "that guilty pleas account for 90 percent of all

case until the prosecutor makes an offer that he deems acceptable and that he can sell to his client.[102] If the professional duty of defense attorneys is limited to representing the best interests of their clients, then it cannot be said that the tactic of waiting out the prosecution is a violation of this duty, because few defendants are willing to leave the determination of their fate to a trial.[103]

Defense attorneys know their adversary and are able to tell when a prosecutor is "puffing" and not making a fair offer.[104] When a fair offer, or one deemed to be final, is made, the defense attorney will take it to his client to persuade him to plead guilty. Ordinarily the defendant will follow his attorney's advice, because usually the prosecutor's offer will mean little or no time in jail.[105] Immediate freedom is the all-consuming and understandable interest of the defendant. Few are concerned with the long-term effects of a felony conviction,[106] such as how it will influence future prosecutions should they be in trouble again.[107] Only in those instances where the negotiated settlement would require the defendant to be incarcerated for a long period of time might he refuse to follow his attorney's advice. Even in such instances refusal by the defendant is rare, because he is able to compare the prosecutor's offer with the possible maximum sentence should he be convicted as charged.

convictions; and perhaps as high as 95 percent of misdemeanors." THE COURTS, *supra* note 15, at 9.

102. Delay to the person out on bail may mean never having a trial at all. Mills, *supra* note 12, at 66. One must also remember, however, that defense attorneys do not always act in their client's best interests.
   Defense attorneys also often face formidable caseloads. Because plea bargaining can be fairly quick and at the same time obtain a benefit for the defendant, they are hardly averse to seeking accommodation with the prosecutor. However, the value of such accommodations to defense counsel occasionally may lead them to enter pleas which are not in their defendants' best interests. Note, *The Unconstitutionality of Plea Bargaining*, 83 HARV. L. REV. 1387, 1390 (1970) [hereinafter cited as *Plea Bargaining*].

103. "The pressures to plead are sometimes cruel, the risks of going to trial high and well-advertised. There is, for waverers, the cautionary tale of one man who turned down one to three years on a deal—and got 40 to 80 as an object lesson when a jury convicted him." *Justice, supra* note 84, at 32.

104. Alschuler, *supra* note 91, at 79–80.

105. Mills, *supra* note 12, at 62.

106. *See* Note, *The Legal Status of Convicts During and After Incarceration,* 37 VA. L. REV. 105 (1951).

107. White, *supra* note 58, at 47.

Notwithstanding the influence that attorneys have on their clients, the ultimate decision rests with the defendant. The power of criminal defendants in the courts is tremendous. If defendants in any one city decided to stop pleading guilty and, instead, demanded their constitutional right to a trial by jury, the entire structure would stand still for a brief moment and then collapse.[108] The prosecutor and the defense attorney arrange the props and set the stage for the principal player, the defendant, to plead guilty.[109]

Delaying tactics used by the defense attorney are in the best interests of the defendant, especially if he is free on bail, but rarely is he consulted on the matter. If the defendant is in jail awaiting disposition of his case, the length of time he spends in jail will have an effect upon the prosecutor's willingness to deal and his inclination to sweeten the offer. The painfulness of pretrial incarceration[110] makes it difficult to explain to one who has suffered it that the ultimate resolution of his case benefited from his detention. The defendant who is free on bail, however, is the one who truly holds all the trump cards.[111] He can delay the process without suffering any of the detriments of life in jail. As data from the analysis of the Cuyahoga County Court of Common Pleas indicates,[112] being in jail after arrest puts a defendant at a disadvantage compared to those who are released on bail after arrest: 74.4 percent of the defendants who were in jail from the time of arrest were sentenced to additional incarceration upon conviction, but only 41 percent of those who were free on bail went to prison or the workhouse after conviction. Defendants hold the keys to the workability of the criminal justice system, but the defendant who is incarcerated pending the outcome of his case pays dearly for those keys. The defendant who is incarcerated

---

108. *Justice, supra* note 84, at 32.

109. Mills, *supra* note 12, at 59–63.

110. *Justice, supra* note 84, at 28.

111.   The prosecutor's bargaining position is weaker if the defendant is free on bail and he must make substantially greater concessions to induce a guilty plea. Bailed defendants will naturally be reluctant to enter a plea which will result in loss of freedom. Unlike the defendant in prison, the bailed defendant can only profit by postponement of his case. Over time, evidence may disappear, memories may fade, and the defendant may be able to build a record of good behavior to help him at sentencing. Furthermore, a bailed defendant is likely to be represented by a private attorney who deals infrequently with the prosecutor. The private attorney will thus have little incentive to develop a good working relationship with the assistant prosecutor and can concentrate on obtaining the best possible result for his client. White, *supra* note 58, at 444–45.

112. *See* Appendix A.

is more likely to agree to an initial offer from the prosecutor, even though it involves additional imprisonment, than is the defendant who is free on bail and can take the chance that a more acceptable offer will be forthcoming.

Defendants are becoming aware of their power to determine whether the system continues to function. Quite often a defendant will indicate, especially in the most crowded and backlog-beset courts, what it will take to induce his plea of guilty. More likely than not, in the courts with the worst backlogs, the prosecutors will eventually feel compelled to accommodate the defendant.[113]

An example of this kind of accommodation was reported in *Newsweek*. Donald Payne was charged with the serious crime of armed robbery, which carries a statutory penalty of one to twenty years. In an effort to clear the case the prosecutor offered to recommend to the court imprisonment for a period of three to eight years, thereby reducing the maximum time Payne might serve by more than 50 percent. When the defendant held out for one to five, the prosecutor eventually agreed.[114]

A New York lawyer related an incident in which the prosecutor offered to recommend a five-year sentence for a defendant charged with a very serious crime. The attorney, cognizant of the near certainty of conviction if the case went to trial and of the sentence that awaited the defendant if convicted, believed the offer to be eminently fair and tried to persuade his client to accept it. The defendant declined the offer and announced his intention to hold out for a one-year sentence. When the prosecutor came back and offered to recommend four years, the defendant persisted in his refusal. Eventually, the prosecutor capitulated, the defendant pleaded guilty, and the prosecutor recommended a one-year sentence.[115]

The essential ingredient in maintaining the justice market is the defendant's willingness to sell his guilty plea, and the prosecutor's willingness to buy it. Under existing conditions, it is purely a seller's market, except in those rare instances where the glare of publicity has focused upon the defendant. The failure of defendants to act collectively and withhold guilty pleas is all that permits courts such as those in New York City to face each succeeding day.

---

113. Mills, *supra* note 12, at 59.
114. *Justice, supra* note 84, at 20.
115. Interview with Gilbert Rosenthal, defense attorney, in New York City, Oct. 10, 1970. On the other hand, some prosecutors contend that the earlier the defendant will plead, the better deal he can get. Interview with Steven North, Assistant Prosecutor, in New York City, Nov. 18, 1970.

Inherent in the plea bargaining process is a great danger that the innocent defendant who is forced to choose between the uncertainties of a trial and the apparent benefits of a guilty plea to a reduced charge will sacrifice the principle of innocence and enter a guilty plea.[116] It is not easy for the individual who has already been deprived of his freedom to see the benefits of continued insistence on his innocence when such insistence means additional months awaiting trial and the possibility of conviction at trial.[117] Before there can be a trial, a courtroom and a judge must be available,[118] and the defendant's attorney must clear his calendar to try the case. The defendant waits and waits before his assertion of innocence will be tested. Immediate freedom, even at the price of a felony record, is abundantly more attractive under such conditions.[119] The criminal justice system has developed complex procedures to ensure that an innocent person is not convicted, yet it is the innocent defendant who is now the victim of the complexity.

The regular clientele of criminal courts and jails are aware that sentences pronounced upon defendants who plead guilty are far more lenient than those imposed if the same defendant demands his right to trial and is found guilty by a jury.[120] This practice is patently unconstitutional because of its "chilling effect" upon the exercise of the fundamental right to trial,[121] but the practice persists. The rationale for the distinction in sentences is that the defendant who pleads guilty has saved the system the tremendous costs and time of a trial and, furthermore, has admitted his guilt, a first step towards rehabilitation.[122] In a few cases this rationale is justified, but in most instances the confession of guilt is the result of nothing more than sophis-

---

116. *See generally* Gentile, *Fair Bargains and Accurate Pleas,* 49 B. U. L. REV. 514 (1969).

117. Mills, *supra* note 12, at 62.

118. In Boston, on April 13, 1971, when the calendar was first called, two trial courts were open and available—Judge Dwyer's and Judge Lindscott's courts. If an attorney wishes to go to trial in Boston, courtrooms can be found.

119. In the District of Columbia, several defendants awaiting trial stated that they would prefer being in prison than sitting in the D. C. jail. They also felt that they would have to "cop a plea" to get out of limbo. Letter from Senator Sam Ervin, Jr., of North Carolina, July 29, 1971.

120. *See* Comment, *The Influence of the Defendant's Plea on Judicial Determination of Sentence,* 66 YALE L. J. 204, 206, 209 (1957) [hereinafter cited as *Influence*]. *See also* D. OAKS & W. LEHMAN, A CRIMINAL JUSTICE SYSTEM AND THE INDIGENT 194 & n. 429 (1968).

121. Scott v. United States, 419 F.2d 264 (D. C. Cir. 1969).

122. *Influence, supra* note 120, at 210.

ticated maneuvering on the part of the defendant to obtain a favorable deal, thus making the terms of the deal the motivation for his admission of guilt.[123]

The statistics gathered from the Cuyahoga County courts illustrate how markedly the sentences differ depending upon whether a defendant pleaded guilty or was convicted after a trial. Of the few trials held, there were only 85 convictions after trial, with or without a jury. Of those 85, 74.1 percent, or 63 defendants, received prison sentences, with only 1 out of the 63 sentenced to the county workhouse while the others were imprisoned in state institutions for a year or more. On the other hand, slightly under half (49.5 percent) of the more than 1,100 defendants who pleaded guilty as charged or to lesser offenses received prison sentences. A full third of those who were convicted on their own pleas (179 out of 566, as compared to 1 out of 62 who were convicted after trial) and were incarcerated were sent to the county workhouse, and the remaining two-thirds were sent to state institutions. Half of the defendants who pleaded guilty were given suspended prison sentences or fines alone, but those who could not reach an accommodation with the prosecutor or protested their innocence all the way to trial received suspended sentences or fines in less than 1 out of 4 cases.[124]

The risk is great that the defendant who holds out for a trial will do considerably worse at the hands of the judge and jury than he would have done had his attorney been able to arrange a deal with the prosecutor. The defendant who does no better at trial than he would have if he had accepted the prosecutor's offer has lost, because the added time that he spent awaiting trial, even if he was in jail, is not necessarily applied towards his prison sentence. Concerted action among defendants would cripple the system, but since such concert is impossible, each individual defendant relies upon his own chances.

Raymond McLaughlin, a three-time loser who was charged with assault with intent to rape in Jersey City, New Jersey, illustrates the considerations that a defendant must make in determining his plea. McLaughlin calculated his chances of success if the case went to trial and he reasoned, quite soundly, that his chances rested upon a plea of guilty. He told one of the researchers for this project that this time he was innocent of the charge but knew enough not to tell that to the judge. He said, "I know the system, the man cannot take the plea if you say you didn't do it." McLaughlin understood that if he went to trial and took the witness stand to deny the woman's claim, he would be questioned about his three prior convictions and the jury simply would not believe him. Upon conviction by a jury, he was convinced

---

123. *Plea Bargaining, supra* note 102, at 1389.
124. *See* Appendix A.

that he would receive the maximum sentence,[125] twelve years.[126] He expected to be rewarded for his plea of guilty and hoped for a one- or two-year sentence, but realistically anticipated getting three to five years. In any event, five years in prison looked much better to McLaughlin than twelve years of potential confinement.[127]

THE ROLE OF JUDGES IN PLEA BARGAINING

The person with the power to consummate the agreement between the defense and prosecuting attorneys is the judge. Through his authority he can accept the plea and then pronounce sentence upon the defendant.[128] In the vast majority of cases, the judge will abide by the prosecutor's recommendation because he has a direct interest in shoring up the prosecutor's credibility in his negotiations with defense attorneys.[129] The prosecutor's ability to obtain pleas and dispose of cases without going to trial is as great a benefit to the judge as it is to the prosecutor, since the judge has the responsibility to insure that the criminal justice system appears capable of functioning.[130] The judge is satisfied that the state's interests are protected when the prosecutor is satisfied with the outcome of a particular case. The prosecutor's, and hence the state's, satisfaction may not, however, always be consistent with the community's need for protection from a particular defendant. Thus the judge's compliance in the bargain and assurance that the community's interest has been respected may not be justified.

A problem that judges have in determining whether or not to accept a defendant's plea and the prosecutor's recommendation which is tied to that plea is that the community interest which they as judges are to protect is not susceptible to general definition. In any given case, there is little reason to believe, for example, that imprisonment for ten years rather than three years will increase the likelihood of the defendant's rehabilitation; in some cases, it might well be true that the likelihood of rehabilitation decreases

---

125. Interview with Raymond McLaughlin, in Jersey City, April 29, 1971.

126. N.J.S.A. 2A: 90–2 (1969).

127. Telephone conversation with Dennis McGill, Public Defender, Jersey City, N. J., Aug. 10, 1971.

128. Not only is the judge empowered to accept a plea, but he also operates from a position where he can force one. N. Y. Times, July 30, 1971, at 37, col. 2.

129. Additionally, the judge usually is unable to attack the plea. *See* note 132 *infra.*

130. "Guilty pleas help keep crowded criminal dockets current and enable other defendants pleading not guilty to obtain speedy trials." *Influence, supra* note 120, at 219.

with the length of the sentence served.[131] Judges must also weigh the social costs of trials against the delay they cause in the ultimate disposition of other disputes. Furthermore, if there is a trial, police officers will have to be freed of their beat assignments while they are tied up in court, and that is a use of manpower which most police forces can ill afford.

The judge who pays scant attention to the facts of particular cases and relies upon the prosecutor's judgment undoubtedly approves some give-aways, but he enables the system over which theoretically he is the master to survive.[132] Quantity, not quality, is the key to that survival;[133] the trial judge, like all the other participants, simply goes through the required judicial motions in an attempt to make the system look just.

To introduce at least a minimal level of quality into the resolution of cases, judges are now required to ascertain that there is some evidence of guilt in the record, in addition to the plea of guilty by the defendant.[134] In Boston, for example, evidence of guilt is being added to the record by having the arresting officer testify at the hearing at which the defendant pleads guilty; and in Philadelphia, the prosecuting attorney reads that part of the police report into the record which concerns the incident to which the defendant has chosen to plead guilty. The protection that these measures seek to provide the innocent defendant who is pleading guilty out of fear or convenience is not airtight, and the evidence that supplements the plea can be fabricated. If there is evidence in the record, however, the defendant will not be heard later to claim that his plea was not fair and that he is innocent of the charge.[135]

---

131. *Justice, supra* note 84, at 34.
132. One must also keep in mind the following:

> The judge . . . generally lacks the resources and knowledge to make an effective attack on a plea which a counseled defendant wishes to sustain. Overcoming a prosecutorial case without the defendant's aid would require investigatory resources to develop the defendant's side of the case. The inevitable duplication of defense counsel's efforts, while resisted by a defendant trying to obtain the benefits of his bargain, seems rather absurd. But the more limited the judicial investigation and the greater the dependence of an accuracy hearing on courtroom examination of the defendant, the less the results will differ from the decisions made by defense counsel. Without a much greater commitment of judicial resources to investigation, a hearing is not likely to uncover inaccuracy in the counseled defendant's plea. *Plea Bargaining, supra* note 102, at 1394.

133. *Id.* at 1388.
134. Boykin v. Alabama, 395 U. S. 238 (1970).
135. North Carolina v. Alford, 400 U. S. 25 (1970).

In addition to the evidence of guilt placed in the record, the judge will engage the defendant in an on-the-record interview to ascertain whether the defendant is entering the plea of his own free will and has not been coerced, threatened, or promised reward or penalty in return for the agreement to plead.[136] This questioning has been refined in most cities so that it is clear that the defendant has agreed to enter the plea upon the promise of the prosecutor to recommend a lenient sentence. The defendant is also told that the judge is not bound by the prosecutor's suggestion.[137] In some cities, however, the old practice still obtains whereby the judge and the defendant engage in a charade with the defendant asserting that no representations have been made to him and that he simply and spontaneously has decided to plead guilty. All the participants are aware of the dishonesty of the game they are playing, but at one time the game was thought necessary to a valid waiver of the constitutional right to trial.[138]

The ceremony surrounding the entry of the plea of guilty is designed to create the illusion that the parties have reconciled their differences and have brought the matter before a neutral judge who, having played no prior role in the settlement, is in a position to act out of great wisdom and either approve or disapprove the settlement. In most instances, he is prepared to accept any settlement, so long as the case can be terminated. If it is necessary to encourage a settlement, the judge will pressure one or the other attorney if he feels that the attorney is hanging back and not dealing. In some jurisdictions, the judge, rather than being detached, may play an active role, alternately cajoling and pressuring one side and then the other, until the attorneys reach agreement.[139] If the judge has not been directly involved, the lawyers, upon reaching their agreement, will find out in advance from the judge if the agreed-upon solution is acceptable to him. It makes no sense to convince the defendant to accept the agreement that requires his plea of guilty to be fulfilled, if the judge will not abide by the terms.[140] Since in most cities the judge is too burdened with work to make

---

136. In Boston, before a defendant's guilty plea to the crime is accepted, he is asked if he understands the rights he is waiving by pleading guilty. The defendant is also asked whether he has made a full disclosure of all the facts of the case to his attorney, whether he was satisfied with the advice and judgment he received from his attorney, and whether he felt the attorney acted in the defendant's best interest. Then the plea is accepted. However, the defendant knows the appropriate responses.
137. This warning is given in Philadelphia and Boston.
138. This is the practice in New York. Mills, *supra* note 12, at 59–63.
139. N. Y. Times, July 30, 1971, at 37, col. 2.
140. *Justice, supra* note 84, at 32–34.

an independent determination of the fairness of the agreement, the way it is worked out by the attorneys is the way that the case is invariably terminated.

REFORM OF PLEA BARGAINING

The alternative to plea bargaining, trials in all cases, is simply not feasible and probably not necessary. To advocate an end to plea bargaining would be similarly unrealistic, because it would mean an end to pleas of guilty in most cases. Likewise, to propose that sentences conferred upon a plea of guilty and those determined after a finding of guilt by a jury should be identical would also eliminate pleas of guilty. There are not enough judges, prosecutors, defense lawyers, courtrooms, and prospective jurors in the United States to require trials in all criminal cases. What must be done is to refine and reform the plea bargaining system to eliminate its major abuses.

The ability of a defendant to wait out the state and then virtually set his own penalty, and the fear that the innocent person will find it in his interest to plead guilty rather than wait in jail for a trial, are abuses that must be eliminated. These abuses are possible because of the delays inherent in the criminal justice system. If the system were redesigned so that a defendant and his attorney could not drag out the process, the defendant would within a reasonable amount of time either have to plead guilty or face a trial. At the same time, if the prosecutor's charges were realistic and not inflated, there would be less need and incentive for the defense to delay the resolution of the case. Moreover, the innocent defendant, if assured that his right to a speedy trial was a meaningful reality, would not find the advantages of pleading guilty so disproportionately outweighing the advantages of waiting for a trial. He would, of course, still face the hazards of a jury trial and the possibility of conviction. Trial procedures are sufficiently developed, however, so that it is unlikely that an innocent man will be convicted.

Time has been the breeding ground for the growth of the criminal justice system's ills, and thus the time element must be reversed if those ills are to be eliminated. The primary step, outlined above in the material on delay and the charging process, is the development of the time-line approach under a formula which guarantees the right to a speedy trial to both the accused and the community. One time line is not sufficient, for within that structure there must be time limitations imposed upon each phase of a criminal prosecution.

The time-line proposal is that a defendant must be brought to trial, or his case disposed of, within 60 days if he is in jail, or 120 days if he is out on bail. The proposal further asserts that the limitation must be binding upon both sides and that the defendant and his attorney should no more be able to delay resolution of a case than the prosecutor. During the charging period, a mandatory conference will take place between the prosecutor and defense attorney to determine whether the matter can be resolved at once without introducing it into the formal felony process. By opening the negotiations at this early stage, it is anticipated that many cases will be terminated, especially if the premium now placed upon delay in the post-charging stages can be eliminated.

Control of delay during the post-charging phases of a criminal case is an attainable goal. Attainment, however, is dependent upon strict observance of the time during which a defendant must come to trial, coupled with comparable strictness in the creation and enforcement of time limitations for the motions practice, discovery procedures, and plea bargaining.

Once the charging process is completed, the period before trial is perfectly susceptible to division into segments for the purpose of raising motions, discovering the opponent's case, and conducting serious plea bargaining. To prevent the use of these steps as a delaying tactic, it is a simple matter to set a time by which they must be completed. The period immediately following the completion of the charging process, whether that is at the conclusion of the preliminary hearing or, as at present, after the grand jury indictment, should be set aside and designated specifically for raising motions and engaging in discovery. In actuality, this period will serve as a prelude to serious plea negotiation because, at its conclusion, the attorneys will know what evidence in their possession and in that of the opposition is admissible and will be better informed as to the strength of the opposition's case. A twenty-day period following the charging process should be ample for this purpose. This requires that judges, as well as the attorneys, change their habits and rule on the motions by the end of the twenty-day period.

Within one week of the preliminary hearing, the prosecutor should submit to defense counsel a bill of particulars specifying the nature of the conduct which the accused has allegedly committed and which the state would be prepared to prove at a trial. Immediately after the one-week period, the attorneys could exchange information, which they would be required to do under the proposed expanded discovery laws. The direction of these laws should be towards requiring openness between the attorneys. As communication between the attorneys will have begun in the period immediately following arrest, it is hoped that an informal give-and-take relationship will have been established which would facilitate exchanges of information without compulsion from the court. Lists of witnesses, copies of documents, statements of experts, notification of specific defenses, medical reports, and the like, can only facilitate a better understanding of the case and promote its early termination.

Concurrently, motions challenging the sufficiency of the charge, the propriety of the early proceedings, and the admissibility of evidence should be filed with the court. At the end of the twenty-day period, the attorneys should meet with the judge in an on-the-record hearing, comparable to the Omnibus Hearing utilized in some federal district courts. The purpose of the hearing would be to permit argument on the motions, if argument is appropriate, and to permit the judge to rule on matters of discovery that one of the parties has sought and which have not been voluntarily forthcoming from the other. The hearing would also provide an opportunity to examine the methods used by the police in securing the evidence that the prosecutor intends to use at trial, if a question has been raised about their constitutionality. At the conclusion of the hearing, the judge would go through each of the items raised and indicate his rulings on each motion and issue. At this point, the attorneys will be fully aware of the issues in the case and can make an informed determination of whether it is in the best interests of their client, be that the state or the defendant, to proceed to trial.

When the judge has concluded ruling on all issues at the hearing, a trial date should be selected within the time restrictions, depending upon whether the defendant is in jail or free on bail. For the incarcerated person, the trial must be set within the remaining thirty-eight days of the sixty-day period; if the defendant is free, any time within the next ninety-three days would meet the requirement. In either event, the attorneys have ample time to prepare for trial. A second, and earlier, date should be designated by the judge for the filing of a form by the two attorneys indicating whether the parties have attempted to negotiate a settlement in the case. That second date should be within two weeks of the motion hearing. The purpose of the form is to indicate to the court either that a settlement has been reached or that the defendant has refused the prosecutor's offer of a reduced charge or penalty in return for a plea of guilty.

The introduction of greater prosecutorial supervision in the earliest charging process, plus the introduction of a pre-charge conference, will result in the early disposition of many cases. It is conceivable that most of the cases remaining after the motion and discovery hearing will be destined for trial. Nonetheless, the formal plea bargaining period is considered necessary for two reasons. Initially, it will serve to educate the public that this is an accepted and controlled practice within the criminal justice system. Secondly, it will place time parameters around the process and alert the attorneys that they either agree at this point or the case goes to trial. If the defendant and the prosecutor agree to a resolution of the case, the judge should simply indicate his approval or disapproval of the agreement. If he approves of the settlement, a court appearance should be scheduled where the plea of guilty would be taken by the judge and the necessary supplemental testimony required to substantiate the plea would be placed in the record.

Where the defendant, with the advice of counsel, has been unable to agree upon a settlement with the prosecutor, the period for plea bargaining should be terminated at the end of the two-week period. Rather than permitting the prosecutor and defense attorney to wait each other out, they will each quickly realize that they must either bargain honestly and in good faith well before trial or go to trial. An added inducement to both sides to take the plea bargaining period seriously would be to require that after the termination of the designated period the case can be resolved in only one of three manners: (1) the defendant pleads guilty as charged, (2) the prosecutor dismisses the case outright, or (3) the case is tried as originally scheduled. This further limitation would help to eliminate overcharging and encourage both sides to resolve the case at the earliest possible time.

One additional requirement would serve to protect the community interest and insure that defendants within each community are treated the same as others who are charged with similar crimes and possess identical records. Courts should impose restrictions upon how far a particular class of crimes may be reduced. No two cases are ever identical; the facts and the quality of evidence are always different, but some essential ingredients remain the same. For example, the person who is charged with a violent crime and has a history of violent crimes should face definite incarceration if convicted and not have his fate determined solely by the whim of the prosecutor assigned the case. Similarly, depending on the crime, first felony charges should not be reduced to the misdemeanor level, once the felony process has been initiated. Such standards would place judicially supervised limitations upon plea bargaining that would be far more substantial than the existing cursory examination which takes place in each case. Standardization would have the dual effect of eliminating the giveaway deal and ensuring prosecutorial integrity in the charging process.

The purpose of this proposal is to speed up the criminal process in an effort to reintroduce into the system the notion of justice for the community and the defendant. Plea bargaining is consciously elevated from its bastard status in an effort to control it and make it the subject of public scrutiny.

The dimensions of the present crisis in the criminal system have prompted this analysis of the system's problems to emphasize the need for eliminating delay as the system's most definitive trait. That emphasis is a rightful one, but it is essential not to lose sight of the fact that speed in the disposition of criminal cases is not the goal but rather the necessary condition for the realization of the goal of justice. Speed is a prerequisite to fair dispositions, but it must never be elevated to the point of being an alternative to justice. As the absence of speedy disposition makes the goal of justice unattainable, devices such as plea bargaining which bring the goal closer to realization are satisfactory as long as there is protection for the innocent defendant from being lost in the shuffle or railroaded into entering a plea of guilty.

The post-charging process set forth in this chapter is rigid. Its adoption would require a wholesale change in the work habits and attitudes of judges, prosecutors, and defense lawyers. It is understood that such a dramatic change in habits may be unattainable. Nevertheless, the flexibility of the past has amounted to running the courts for the convenience of some defendants and those who manage the courts. The results of past flexibility are the shambles that may be found in almost every urban American criminal justice system. If the defendant is to have justice, and if justice is to be guaranteed to the community, a wholesale reformation of the system is essential. Eric Sevareid, at the conclusion of an excellent Columbia Broadcasting System series on justice and the courts, stated that Americans have become terribly afraid of crime and the inability of their courts to control it. His final sentence was: "An America that lives scared won't live free."[141] The stakes involved in whether this nation reforms its court system and makes it capable of functioning are that great.

---

141. CBS News Correspondent Eric Sevareid and CBS Reports, "Justice in America, Part III: Crime and the Courts" (June 15, 1971).

CONCLUSION

While in jail awaiting trial, Ralph Johnson and nineteen other inmates sent a letter of protest to those outside the walls. They protested the fact that they had been in jail from nine to sixteen months, living in barbaric conditions, while they waited to answer the criminal accusations against them. Their protest went beyond the condition of the cells in which they were forced to live and included what imprisonment had really cost them: loss of jobs, removal from their homes, and the fear of permanent alienation from their families. Their letter ended: "It is of little or no consequence to be found innocent after losing everything, due to these injustices."

A civilized society must answer for the injustices that are perpetrated in its name. The thousands of Ralph Johnsons throughout the country are the victims of a system which promises "innocence until proven guilty" as its standard. But persons sitting in jail are not considered sufficiently "worthy" of concern for their complaints to generate change. The popular and "worthy" victims are those in the community who fall prey to the burglar, robber, rapist, mugger, or murderer. Nevertheless, the system has been as unable to protect the legitimate interests of the community as it has been to protect those charged with crime. Attempts at change have resulted in the patching together of procedures which are not capable of bearing the weight and burden that the twentieth century imposes and that the twenty-first promises. Procedures are not ends in themselves but were designed to serve goals, and it is the goals that must be preserved.

What is not appreciated is that the fabric of American society is inextricably bound to the fate of the criminal justice system. The inability of the system to protect the rights of men, whether victim or accused, is the precursor to the destruction of the rights that have contributed greatly to that which is good in America.

Every aspect of our national life is interwoven with the criminal justice system. The ability of men to function freely is secure only in the knowledge that the law and its institutions stand ready to ensure the privacy, safety, and security of each person. When rights are infringed, free men must be able to rely upon the law to restrain such infringement. Without belief in the law as the means of social control, each man would become a judge and

217

jury of one to protect himself and to enforce his own private vision of what the law should be and how it should be applied.

The deterioration of the justice system has already scarred the lives of people living in urban areas. Mass migrations from cities to suburbs have left behind and abandoned those people who are unable to escape. Urban dwellers restrict their movements in order to be inside during the hours of darkness and install multiple locks on all doors and windows. Even if the fear of danger exceeds the reality, it is no less stultifying and oppressive, because it is what people believe to be true that determines how they live and act.

The failings of the criminal justice system are but one aspect of this society's deterioration, but they are highly visible. The system's inability to cope with its task is demoralizing and breeds fear, producing serious repercussions throughout the society. In addition to the problems caused the entire society by the failures of the criminal system, it has become moribund, unable to distinguish between the innocent and the guilty, and unable to ensure either the defendant or the community a speedy trial in order to vindicate the innocent and punish the guilty.

Judges and lawyers, the managers of the courts, are now trapped in the maelstrom of deterioration of which they are at least a partial cause. The prosecutor, charged with funneling cases through the system, is expected to protect the innocent and secure punishment for the guilty. If he attended to each case as he should, fully concentrating upon each procedural step, there would be cases which could not be processed at all because there would be neither the time nor the personnel. The attorney charged with the responsibility of defending persons accused of crime must be similarly perplexed by the role that has developed for him. The role of the defense attorney is to hold the hand of his client and delay the system until such time as the case can be most favorably disposed of. If he feels guilty about using ethically questionable techniques to secure the necessary delay, he need only tell himself that he is serving the best interests of his client by using all the devices that the law tolerates and that are being employed by other attorneys.

The pinnacle of self-doubt must be reserved for urban criminal court trial judges. Occupying a special position of community trust and esteem, the reflective judge must realize he is unable to fulfill that trust and is, instead, presiding over the disintegration of the American criminal justice system. These self-doubts and anxieties were well expressed by a criminal court trial judge in a letter to one of the authors:

> I remain terribly frustrated and increasingly annoyed with this court. We are being pressured constantly to "produce," which means forcing

> pleas to lesser charges just to dispose of cases. I feel like a fool and a clerk in a bargain basement, and part of the terrible system, helping in the denigration of our brilliant judicial heritage. I don't know how much longer I can take this. . . .

A substantial part of the debasement of "our brilliant judicial heritage" may be attributed to lawyers. As the courts have become overburdened, lawyers, both prosecuting and defense attorneys, have acted as though those courts were their private preserves. The legal fraternity has acted as a catalyst to the deterioration of the criminal justice system by engaging in gross overcharging and exorbitant threats of punishment, on the one hand, or by using dishonest techniques of delaying cases and jamming court calendars, on the other. Some in the bar would dismiss this indictment as only applicable to the few denizens of the criminal courts, who are generally held in disrepute by their brethren who practice in the corporate and estate areas. Those who are a part of the great business and corporate law firms shun the less lucrative and less respectable work of the criminal courts, thus assuring that the criminal courts will be the exclusive preserve of those they scorn. A universal reassessment on the part of judges of their duty to govern and control the activities of the lawyers who practice in their courts would not be sufficient to reverse the trend of deterioration. A change of judicial attitude is demanded, but additional tools are needed to reconstruct the criminal justice system.

The procedures presently used from arrest until trial were designed for a society where the courts had the time and manpower to try cases judiciously and to consider the merits of each controversy. The eighteenth-century nation whose way of life these procedures reflect has been replaced by a society where people are crowded into urban areas and where the courts are no longer capable of reflection upon each matter brought within their jurisdiction. The procedural steps that have been piled upon the system so preoccupy the participants that the means dominate the ends which the means are to serve. Successive screening procedures, for example, are supposed to sift out cases so that those remaining are the ones that should be tried, but little actual sifting occurs, and too many cases flow into the trial process, making trials a virtual impossibility. Felony trial courts are reduced to auctions where successive bids are made until one is finally accepted. The auction process invariably compromises and often totally disregards both the defendant whose freedom is at stake and the community whose security is in jeopardy.

Because the procedural steps established for criminal prosecutions have enjoyed a venerable history and represent a link to the founding of this nation, proposals to change them will meet with strong resistance. The goals the system was designed to facilitate remain valid, despite two hundred years of extensive changes within the society. The reformation must be not of the goals but of the way in which the goals are achieved.

The Constitution promises to each defendant a speedy trial. The proposals made above are intended specifically to make that promise a reality. There are too many cases lodged in the courts with felony jurisdiction. Cases are prosecuted as felonies, even though a substantial number will eventually be disposed of as misdemeanors. If the cases reduced to misdemeanors in the end never made their way to the felony docket, felony courts would not be so overburdened. A crucial point in the process is the initial determination of the quality of a criminal act and the decision of how to prosecute the person who has committed the act. If this determination is inaccurately made, the entire criminal justice system suffers in the long run. Present practices provide for several levels of screening through multiple formal procedures that fail to screen. Instead, they succeed only in proceduring to death the system and the ideals upon which it is founded.

Our recommendations in this area are simple and decidedly moderate. We propose that the prosecutor should formulate the initial charge and that the police be relegated to a supportive role. The system intends the prosecutor to be the formulator of the charges and to bear responsibility for the case immediately after an arrest has been made. In practice, however, prosecutors have abdicated this responsibility to the police and provide solely technical assistance rather than real charge evaluation. Prosecutor involvement immediately after arrest portends the elimination of many cases then, rather than later, and will contribute to making court caseloads manageable. Introduction of the defense attorney at this earliest stage will improve the quality of defense work and provide a competent adversary with whom the prosecutor can deal. The only magic attached to the plea bargaining, which now typically takes place months or even years after an arrest, is that by the time it occurs all concerned are tired of the case and ready to have it terminated by any means. If the adversaries are brought together when the facts are fresh, and if their actions are circumscribed by strict speedy trial requirements, legitimate agreements should be more readily forthcoming than they are after months or years have elapsed.

Our screening proposal retains the preliminary hearing, the one formal step that serves useful and legitimate ends. The preliminary hearing still affords the accused the opportunity for an in-court examination of the case to assure that he is not arbitrarily charged or harassed. We would make this stage mandatory for all cases not concluded in the immediate post-arrest period and require that it be held shortly after arrest. Both requirements, if effectively and scrupulously enforced, will serve the ends of justice by eliminating opportunities for the prosecutor to deny a preliminary hearing and for defense attorneys to set the stage at this point for delay.

The key to revitalizing the criminal justice system and its ability to deliver a speedy trial must be standards that make a speedy trial mandatory and that would deny to defendants and defense attorneys the opportunity to choose delay as a tactic. The case that lingers for a year affects all other cases as well. Each postponement requires rescheduling and denies the time originally allotted to the case and subsequently allotted to other cases. Delay has become the ultimate technique of the defense lawyer in criminal cases, and it is not only tolerated but encouraged. Attorneys delay to secure a better deal, to provide sufficient time to collect their fees, or to persuade their clients that they are working on their behalf. The Constitution does not make these practices respectable, nor is there any reason for courts to continue countenancing a technique that makes it impossible for them to function.

Strict overall time requirements, demanding disposition or trial within 60 days if the defendant is in jail or 120 days if he is free on bail, must be enacted to cover the entire case and each separate stage of a case. Within this time line, we have recommended stringent specifications for each pretrial stage. There is no justification for continuing to allow the motions practice to be used as a delaying technique, interminably postponing the disposition of a case. Towards the same end, our recommendations contain severe limitations upon the amount of time the attorneys may spend in plea negotiation after a preliminary hearing is held.

We have also proposed, in addition to the time restrictions, a limit upon the substance of the agreement which the prosecutor and defense attorney may reach. If the prosecutor knows that there are limitations upon how much he may reduce a charge, it is likely that the original charge will more realistically reflect the convictability of the defendant. Restrictions upon the extent of possible reduction will also benefit the community by eliminating the possibility of a giveaway deal, which often amounts to nothing more than a symbolic slap on the wrist for the commission of a serious offense. Substantive limitations will also serve notice on the defense of just how much plea bargaining can produce and, coupled with the time limitation, should lead to realistic assessments of positions. An agreement will have to be reached, or the case will be scheduled for trial. Under present practice, if agreement is not reached, the attorneys can agree to do nothing and confer again some months later.

The proposals presented in this report are not viewed as a panacea for all the present ills of the criminal justice system. They are intended to correct some of its most glaring faults, so that the system is able to regain public confidence by fulfilling its traditional goals and by living up to its original values. A system that does not and cannot protect the rights of the innocent and punish the guilty is not deserving of public confidence or respect. In a free society, institutions must justify their existence; if they fail, they deserve to be discarded. In our opinion, the American criminal justice system remains the most brilliantly devised method for administering justice in a free society. In the course of two centuries, as a result of conditions that the system could neither control nor influence, it has been overwhelmed by the problems of urbanization, overpopulation, and the depersonalization of society. Nevertheless, the goals remain valid, and alternative systems for administering justice pale by comparison.

If the goals and values on which the American criminal justice system was founded are to continue into the twenty-first century, then the system must be mended. There are signs that the nation is ready to make the necessary commitment, no matter how fleeting and weak those signs appear. The promise of the American criminal justice system demands that the effort be made.

APPENDIXES

Appendix A
COURT STATISTICS

The material in this appendix was gathered from the records of the Cuyahoga County (Ohio) Court of Common Pleas. The sample chosen was equal to approximately one-half the total felony cases considered in that court in 1968.

Docket records and case files within the Court of Common Pleas served as the chief source of information. Where the Common Pleas records were incomplete, material concerning preliminary stages was gathered from the records of the municipal court in which the felony case originated.

In compiling the data the following information was gathered:

1. Date of arrest
2. Bail history—whether bail was set, made, or forfeited
3. Charge
4. Date of preliminary hearing, if any
5. Date the accused was bound over to the grand jury
6. Date of indictment
7. Date of arraignment
8. Type of counsel
9. Motions
10. Continuances—on whose motion a continuance was made, by defense, prosecutor, or by agreement
11. Plea entered in the case
12. Form of disposition—jury trial, court trial, plea of guilty, dismissal
13. Date plea of guilty was entered, trial began, or case was dismissed
14. Date of sentence
15. Sentence

225

TABLE 1. TOTAL NUMBER OF DAYS BETWEEN ARREST AND DISPOSITION IN FELONY CASES

NUMBER OF DAYS	NUMBER OF CASES	PERCENTAGE
1–30	47	2.9%
31–60	126	7.8%
61–90	126	7.8%
91–180	394	24.4%
181–210	114	7.1%
211–270	168	10.4%
271–300	82	5.1%
301–365	162	10.0%
366–400	108	6.7%
401–500	185	11.4%
501–600	60	3.7%
601–730	28	1.7%
Over 730	15	.9%
Unavailable	1	.1%
Total	1616	100.0%

TABLE 2. NUMBER OF DEFENDANTS RELEASED ON BAIL, DETAINED IN JAIL, OR ON PERSONAL RECOGNIZANCE

	NUMBER OF CASES	PERCENTAGE
Bail	958	59.3%
Jail	331	20.7%
Personal recognizance	83	5.1%
Released on bail, then returned to jail	22	1.1%
Detained in jail, then released on bail	220	13.6%
Unavailable	2	.1%
Total	1616	100.0%

TABLE 3. NUMBER OF PRELIMINARY HEARINGS

	NUMBER OF CASES	PERCENTAGE
Preliminary hearing	256	15.9%
Waiver	900	55.6%
Original indictment	460	28.5%
Total	1616	100.0%

TABLE 4. DAYS BETWEEN ARREST AND PRELIMINARY HEARING

NUMBER OF DAYS	NUMBER OF CASES	PERCENTAGE
1–10	84	32.8%
11–25	87	34.0%
26–50	39	15.2%
Over 50	11	4.3%
1–10 (1) with one formal continuance	2	.8%
11–25 (1) with one formal continuance	7	2.7%
26–50 (1) with one formal continuance	6	2.3%
Over 50 (1) with one formal continuance	2	.8%
1–10 (2-3) with two or three formal continuances	3	1.2%
11–25 (2-3) with two or three formal continuances	4	1.6%
26–50 (2-3) with two or three formal continuances	8	3.1%
Over 50 (2-3.) with two or three formal continuances	3	1.2%
Total	256	100.0%

TABLE 5. DAYS BETWEEN PRELIMINARY HEARING AND
INDICTMENT OR NO BILL

NUMBER OF DAYS	NUMBER OF CASES	PERCENTAGE
1–10	10	3.9%
11–25	46	18.0%
26–50	146	57.0%
51–100	51	19.9%
Over 100	3	1.2%
Total	256	100.0%

TABLE 6. DAYS BETWEEN ARREST AND INDICTMENT WHEN
A PRELIMINARY HEARING WAS HELD

NUMBER OF DAYS	NUMBER OF CASES	PERCENTAGE
1–10	2	.7%
11–25	14	5.0%
26–50	105	42.1%
51–75	90	35.1%
76–100	32	12.5%
101–120	8	3.1%
Over 120	5	1.5%
Total	256	100.0%

TABLE 7. DAYS BETWEEN ARREST AND INDICTMENT OR NO BILL WHEN PRELIMINARY HEARING WAS RECORDED AS WAIVED

NUMBER OF DAYS	NUMBER OF CASES	PERCENTAGE
1–10	15	1.7%
11–25	51	5.7%
26–50	560	62.1%
51–100	261	29.1%
Over 100	13	1.4%
Total	900	100.0%

TABLE 8. NUMBER OF INDICTMENTS, INFORMATIONS, AND NO BILLS

	NUMBER OF CASES	PERCENTAGE
Indictment	1521	94.2%
Information	15	.9%
No bill	79	4.9%
Unavailable	1	.1%
Total	1616	100.0%

TABLE 9. DAYS BETWEEN ARRAIGNMENT AND PLEA OF GUILTY, DISMISSAL, OR BEGINNING OF TRIAL

NUMBER OF DAYS	NUMBER OF CASES	PERCENTAGE
1–3	128	7.9%
4–15	204	12.6%
16–30	174	10.8%
31–60	127	7.9%
61–90	77	4.8%
91–180	230	14.2%
181–270	252	15.6%
271–365	216	13.4%
366–485	90	5.6%
486–605	27	1.7%
606–730	12	.7%
Over 730	2	.1%
Unavailable	77	4.8%
Total	1616	100.0%

TABLE 10. FINAL DISPOSITION

	NUMBER OF CASES	PERCENTAGE
Pleads guilty as charged	310	19.2%
Pleads guilty to a lesser charge	846	52.4%
Trial by jury, defendant found guilty as charged	36	2.2%
Trial by jury, defendant found not guilty	32	2.0%
Trial by jury, hung jury	7	.4%
Trial by jury, defendant found guilty of a lesser charge	15	.9%
Trial by judge, defendant found guilty as charged	34	2.1%
Trial by judge, defendant found not guilty	22	1.4%
Trial by judge, defendant found guilty of a lesser charge	4	.2%
Nolle (dismissal by prosecutor)	215	13.3%
Case abated by death	11	.7%
Referred to medical care	3	.2%
No bill by grand jury	79	4.9%
Unavailable	2	.1%
Total	1616	100.0%

TABLE 11. SENTENCE

	NUMBER OF CASES	PERCENTAGE
Ohio Penitentiary	221	13.7%
Ohio Reformatory	228	14.1%
Lima State Hospital	6	.4%
Suspended	483	29.9%
Restitution and costs	11	.7%
Workhouse or county jail	180	11.1%
Workhouse or county jail suspended	71	4.4%
Fine alone	26	1.6%
Psychiatric treatment	5	.3%
Dismissed or acquitted	379	23.5%
Unavailable	6	.3%
Total	1616	100.0%

TABLE 12. TYPE OF COUNSEL

	NUMBER OF CASES	PERCENTAGE
Appointed	730	45.2%
Retained	788	48.8%
No counsel	20	1.2%
Unavailable	78	4.8%
Total	1616	100.0%

TABLE 13. COMPARISON OF TOTAL NUMBER OF DAYS DEPENDENT UPON TYPE OF COUNSEL

NUMBER OF DAYS	APPOINTED NUMBER OF CASES	RETAINED NUMBER OF CASES	NO COUNSEL NUMBER OF CASES	ROW TOTAL NUMBER OF CASES
1–30	17(1.1%)	18(1.2%)	1(.1%)	36(2.4%)
31–60	54(3.6%)	24(1.6%)	1(.1%)	79(5.2%)
61–90	72(4.8%)	38(2.5%)	2(.1%)	112(7.4%)
91–180	219(14.5%)	156(10.3%)	5(.3%)	380(25.1%)
181–210	55(3.6%)	56(3.7%)	3(.2%)	114(7.5%)
211–270	75(5.0%)	86(5.7%)	1(.1%)	162(10.7%)
271–300	42(2.8%)	38(2.5%)	1(.1%)	81(5.4%)
301–365	59(3.9%)	100(6.6%)	0(.0%)	159(10.5%)
366–400	42(2.8%)	63(4.2%)	2(.1%)	107(7.1%)
401–500	52(3.4%)	124(8.2%)	4(.3%)	180(11.9%)
501–600	25(1.7%)	34(2.2%)	0(.0%)	59(3.9%)
601–730	4(.3%)	24(1.6%)	0(.0%)	28(1.9%)
Over 730	2(.1%)	13(.9%)	0(.0%)	15(1.0%)
Column total	718(47.5%)	774(51.2%)	20(1.3%)	1512(100.0%)

TABLE 14. COMPARISON OF BAIL STATUS DEPENDENT UPON TYPE OF COUNSEL

	APPOINTED NUMBER OF CASES	RETAINED NUMBER OF CASES	NO COUNSEL NUMBER OF CASES	ROW TOTAL NUMBER OF CASES
Jail	234(15.5%)	69(4.6%)	3(.2%)	306(20.2%)
Bail	279(18.5%)	592(39.2%)	11(.7%)	882(58.3%)
Personal recognizance	29(1.9%)	52(3.4%)	1(.1%)	82(5.4%)
Released on bail, then returned to jail	17(1.1%)	4(.3%)	1(.1%)	22(1.5%)
Detained in jail, then released on bail	159(10.5%)	57(3.8%)	4(.3%)	220(14.6%)
Column total	718(47.5%)	774(51.2%)	20(1.3%)	1512(100.0%)

TABLE 15. TOTAL NUMBER OF DAYS FOR CASE DISPOSITION DEPENDING
UPON WHETHER DEFENDANT IS RELEASED ON BAIL OR DETAINED
IN JAIL WHEN ATTORNEY APPOINTED BY COURT

NUMBER OF DAYS	JAIL NUMBER OF CASES	BAIL NUMBER OF CASES	PERSONAL RECOGNIZANCE NUMBER OF CASES	ON BAIL, THEN RETURNED TO JAIL NUMBER OF CASES	IN JAIL, THEN RELEASED ON BAIL NUMBER OF CASES	ROW TOTAL NUMBER OF CASES
1–30	7(1.0%)	0(.0%)	1(.1%)	0(.0%)	9(1.3%)	17(2.4%)
31–60	18(2.5%)	9(1.3%)	2(.3%)	0(.0%)	25(3.5%)	54(7.5%)
61–90	32(4.5%)	17(2.4%)	4(.6%)	0(.0%)	19(2.6%)	72(10.0%)
91–180	88(12.3%)	82(11.4%)	7(1.0%)	2(.3%)	40(5.6%)	219(30.5%)
181–210	17(2.4%)	24(3.3%)	3(.4%)	3(.4%)	8(1.1%)	55(7.7%)
211–270	27(3.8%)	25(3.5%)	2(.3%)	0(.0%)	21(2.9%)	75(10.4%)
271–300	13(1.8%)	14(1.9%)	2(.3%)	3(.4%)	10(1.4%)	42(5.8%)
301–365	20(2.8%)	29(4.0%)	1(.1%)	4(.6%)	5(.7%)	59(8.2%)
366–400	6(.8%)	24(3.3%)	3(.4%)	1(.1%)	8(1.1%)	42(5.8%)
401–500	4(.6%)	31(4.3%)	4(.6%)	3(.4%)	10(1.4%)	52(7.2%)
501–600	1(.1%)	21(2.9%)	0(.0%)	0(.0%)	3(.4%)	25(3.5%)
601–730	1(.1%)	2(.3%)	0(.0%)	0(.0%)	1(.1%)	4(.6%)
Over 730	0(.0%)	1(.1%)	0(.0%)	1(.1%)	0(.0%)	2(.3%)
Column total	234(32.6%)	279(38.9%)	29(4.0%)	17(2.4%)	159(22.1%)	718(100.0%)

TABLE 16. TOTAL NUMBER OF DAYS FOR CASE DISPOSITION DEPENDING UPON WHETHER DEFENDANT IS RELEASED ON BAIL OR DETAINED IN JAIL WHEN ATTORNEY RETAINED BY DEFENDANT

NUMBER OF DAYS	JAIL NUMBER OF CASES	BAIL NUMBER OF CASES	PERSONAL RECOGNIZANCE NUMBER OF CASES	ON BAIL, THEN RETURNED TO JAIL NUMBER OF CASES	IN JAIL, THEN RELEASED ON BAIL NUMBER OF CASES	ROW TOTAL NUMBER OF CASES
1–30	7(.9%)	6(.8%)	1(.1%)	0(.0%)	4(.5%)	18(2.3%)
31–60	10(1.3%)	7(.9%)	0(.0%)	0(.0%)	7(.9%)	24(3.1%)
61–90	6(.8%)	16(2.1%)	3(.4%)	0(.0%)	13(1.7%)	38(4.9%)
91–180	20(2.6%)	111(14.3%)	15(1.9%)	0(.0%)	10(1.3%)	156(20.2%)
181–210	3(.4%)	44(5.7%)	4(.5%)	2(.3%)	3(.4%)	56(7.2%)
211–270	8(1.0%)	67(8.7%)	2(.3%)	2(.3%)	7(.9%)	86(11.1%)
271–300	4(.5%)	29(3.7%)	4(.5%)	0(.0%)	1(.1%)	38(4.9%)
301–365	5(.6%)	80(10.3%)	10(1.3%)	0(.0%)	5(.6%)	100(12.9%)
366–400	1(.1%)	57(7.4%)	5(.6%)	0(.0%)	0(.0%)	63(8.1%)
401–500	3(.4%)	110(14.2%)	6(.8%)	0(.0%)	5(.6%)	124(16.0%)
501–600	1(.1%)	32(4.1%)	1(.1%)	0(.0%)	0(.0%)	34(4.4%)
601–730	0(.0%)	23(3.0%)	1(.1%)	0(.0%)	0(.0%)	24(3.1%)
Over 730	1(.1%)	10(1.3%)	0(.0%)	0(.0%)	2(.3%)	13(1.7%)
Column total	69(8.9%)	592(76.5%)	52(6.7%)	4(.5%)	57(7.4%)	774(100.0%)

TABLE 17. COMPARISON OF SENTENCE DEPENDENT UPON TYPE OF COUNSEL

	APPOINTED NUMBER OF CASES	RETAINED NUMBER OF CASES	NO COUNSEL NUMBER OF CASES	ROW TOTAL NUMBER OF CASES
Ohio Penitentiary	132(10.7%)	86(7.0%)	2(.2%)	220(17.9%)
Ohio Reformatory	145(11.8%)	79(6.4%)	3(.2%)	227(18.5%)
Lima State Hospital	3(.2%)	2(.2%)	0(.0%)	5(.4%)
Suspended	199(16.2%)	283(23.0%)	1(.1%)	483(39.3%)
Restitution and costs	8(.7%)	3(.2%)	0(.0%)	11(.9%)
Workhouse or county jail	82(6.7%)	95(7.7%)	3(.2%)	180(14.7%)
Workhouse or county jail suspended	21(1.7%)	50(4.1%)	0(.0%)	71(5.8%)
Fine alone	10(.8%)	16(1.3%)	0(.0%)	26(2.1%)
Psychiatric treatment	0(.0%)	5(.4%)	0(.0%)	5(.4%)
Column total	600(48.9%)	619(50.4%)	9(.7%)	1228(100.0%)

TABLE 18. COMPARISON BETWEEN FINAL DISPOSITION DEPENDENT UPON TYPE OF COUNSEL

	APPOINTED NUMBER OF CASES	RETAINED NUMBER OF CASES	NO COUNSEL NUMBER OF CASES	ROW TOTAL NUMBER OF CASES
Pleads guilty as charged	144(9.5%)	158(10.5%)	5(.3%)	307(20.3%)
Pleads guilty to a lesser charge	415(27.5%)	423(28.0%)	5(.3%)	843(55.8%)
Trial by jury, defendant found guilty as charged	19(1.3%)	17(1.1%)	0(.0%)	36(2.4%)
Trial by jury, defendant found not guilty	7(.5%)	12(.8%)	0(.0%)	19(1.3%)
Trial by jury, hung jury	2(.1%)	4(.3%)	0(.0%)	6(.4%)
Trial by jury, defendant found guilty of a lesser charge	5(.3%)	10(.7%)	0(.0%)	15(1.0%)
Trial by judge, defendant found guilty as charged	18(1.2%)	15(1.0%)	0(.0%)	33(2.2%)
Trial by judge, defendant found not guilty	5(.3%)	15(1.0%)	0(.0%)	20(1.3%)
Trial by judge, defendant found guilty of a lesser charge	2(.1%)	2(.1%)	0(.0%)	4(.3%)
Nolle (dismissal by prosecutor)	97(6.4%)	108(7.1%)	9(.6%)	214(14.2%)
Case abated by death	3(.2%)	7(.5%)	1(.1%)	11(.7%)
Referred to medical care	1(.1%)	2(.1%)	0(.0%)	3(.2%)
Column total	718(47.5%)	773(51.2%)	20(1.3%)	1511(100.0%)

TABLE 19. COMPARISON OF DAYS BETWEEN ARRAIGNMENT
AND EITHER PLEA OF GUILTY, DISMISSAL, OR BEGINNING OF
TRIAL DEPENDENT UPON TYPE OF COUNSEL

NUMBER OF DAYS	APPOINTED NUMBER OF CASES	RETAINED NUMBER OF CASES	NO COUNSEL NUMBER OF CASES	ROW TOTAL NUMBER OF CASES
1–3	72(4.8%)	48(3.2%)	1(.1%)	121(8.0%)
4–15	126(8.3%)	63(4.2%)	2(.1%)	191(12.6%)
16–30	90(6.0%)	81(5.4%)	3(.2%)	174(11.5%)
31–60	66(4.4%)	58(3.8%)	2(.1%)	126(8.3%)
61–90	45(3.0%)	32(2.1%)	0(.0%)	77(5.1%)
91–180	107(7.1%)	118(7.8%)	5(.3%)	230(15.2%)
181–270	114(7.5%)	132(8.7%)	4(.3%)	250(16.5%)
271–365	56(3.7%)	156(10.3%)	1(.1%)	213(14.1%)
366–486	33(2.2%)	55(3.6%)	2(.1%)	90(6.0%)
487–605	8(.5%)	18(1.2%)	0(.0%)	26(1.7%)
606–730	1(.1%)	10(.7%)	0(.0%)	11(.7%)
Over 730	0(.0%)	2(.1%)	0(.0%)	2(.1%)
Column total	718(47.5%)	773(51.2%)	20(1.3%)	1511(100.0%)

TABLE 20. COMPARISON OF DAYS BETWEEN INDICTMENT
AND ARRAIGNMENT DEPENDENT UPON TYPE OF COUNSEL

NUMBER OF DAYS	APPOINTED NUMBER OF CASES	RETAINED NUMBER OF CASES	NO COUNSEL NUMBER OF CASES	ROW TOTAL NUMBER OF CASES
1–5	382(25.3%)	152(10.1%)	9(.6%)	543(35.9%)
6–10	176(11.6%)	344(22.8%)	4(.3%)	524(34.7%)
11–20	52(3.4%)	153(10.1%)	2(.1%)	207(13.7%)
Over 20	106(7.0%)	124(8.2%)	5(.3%)	235(15.5%)
Unavailable	2(.1%)	1(.1%)	0(.0%)	3(.2%)
Column total	718(47.5%)	774(51.2%)	20(1.3%)	1512(100.0%)

TABLE 21. COMPARISON OF DAYS BETWEEN ARREST AND
PRELIMINARY HEARING DEPENDENT UPON TYPE OF COUNSEL

NUMBER OF DAYS	APPOINTED NUMBER OF CASES	RETAINED NUMBER OF CASES	NO COUNSEL NUMBER OF CASES	ROW TOTAL NUMBER OF CASES
Waiver	452(42.5%)	371(34.9%)	8(.7%)	831(78.1%)
1–10	36(3.4%)	41(3.9%)	1(.1%)	78(7.3%)
11–25	36(3.4%)	61(5.7%)	0(.0%)	97(9.1%)
26–50	14(1.4%)	29(2.7%)	1(.1%)	44(4.1%)
Over 50	7(.7%)	7(.7%)	0(.0%)	14(1.4%)
Column total	545(51.4%)	509(47.9%)	10(.7%)	1064(100.0%)

TABLE 22. TOTAL NUMBER OF DAYS FROM ARREST TO
DISPOSITION WHEN PRELIMINARY HEARING HELD

NUMBER OF DAYS	NUMBER OF CASES	PERCENTAGE
1–30	3	1.2%
31–60	13	5.1%
61–90	25	9.8%
91–180	47	18.4%
181–210	18	7.0%
211–270	33	12.9%
271–300	15	5.9%
301–365	31	12.1%
366-400	19	7.4%
401–500	31	12.1%
501–600	12	4.7%
601–730	7	2.7%
Over 730	2	.8%
Total	256	100.0%

TABLE 23. DAYS BETWEEN ARRAIGNMENT AND EITHER PLEA
OF GUILTY, DISMISSAL, OR BEGINNING OF TRIAL

NUMBER OF DAYS	NUMBER OF CASES	PERCENTAGE
1–3	17	6.6%
4–15	20	7.8%
16–30	22	8.6%
31–60	23	9.0%
61–90	12	4.7%
91–180	45	17.6%
181–270	37	14.5%
271–365	42	16.4%
366–485	14	5.5%
486–605	6	2.3%
606–730	1	.4%
Unavailable	17	6.6%
Total	256	100.0%

TABLE 24. TOTAL NUMBER OF DAYS WHEN PRELIMINARY HEARING RECORDED AS WAIVED

NUMBER OF DAYS	NUMBER OF CASES	PERCENTAGE
1–30	19	2.1%
31–60	85	9.4%
61–90	64	7.1%
91–180	252	28.0%
181–210	71	7.9%
211–270	94	10.4%
271–300	39	4.3%
301–365	76	8.4%
366–400	55	6.1%
401–500	103	11.4%
501–600	33	3.7%
601–730	5	.6%
Over 730	4	.4%
Unavailable	1	.1%
Total	901	100.0%

TABLE 25. DAYS BETWEEN ARRAIGNMENT AND EITHER PLEA OF GUILTY, DISMISSAL, OR BEGINNING OF TRIAL WHEN PRELIMINARY HEARING RECORDED AS WAIVED

NUMBER OF DAYS	NUMBER OF CASES	PERCENTAGE
1–3	80	8.9%
4–15	126	14.0%
16–30	106	11.8%
31–60	63	7.0%
61–90	47	5.2%
91–180	117	13.0%
181–270	151	16.8%
271–365	98	10.9%
366–485	39	4.3%
486–605	9	1.0%
606–730	4	.4%
Over 730	1	.1%
Unavailable	60	6.7%
Total	901	100.0%

TABLE 26. TOTAL NUMBER OF DAYS FROM ORIGINAL INDICTMENT TO DISPOSITION

NUMBER OF DAYS	NUMBER OF CASES	PERCENTAGE
1–30	25	5.4%
31–60	28	6.1%
61–90	37	8.0%
91–180	96	20.9%
181–210	25	5.4%
211–270	41	8.9%
271–300	28	6.1%
301–365	55	12.0%
366–400	34	7.4%
401–500	51	11.1%
501–600	15	3.3%
601–730	16	3.5%
Over 730	9	2.0%
Total	460	100.0%

TABLE 27. DAYS BETWEEN ARRAIGNMENT AND EITHER PLEA OF GUILTY, DISMISSAL, OR BEGINNING OF TRIAL IN CASES BEGUN BY ORIGINAL INDICTMENT

NUMBER OF DAYS	NUMBER OF CASES	PERCENTAGE
1–3	31	6.7%
4–15	58	12.6%
16–30	46	10.0%
31–60	41	8.9%
61–90	18	3.9%
91–180	68	14.8%
181–270	64	13.9%
271–365	76	16.5%
366–485	37	8.0%
486–605	12	2.6%
606–730	7	1.5%
Over 730	1	.2%
Unavailable	1	.2%
Total	460	100.0%

TABLE 28. COMPARISON OF TOTAL NUMBER OF DAYS AND FINAL DISPOSITION (NUMBER AND PERCENTAGE OF CASES)

NUMBER OF DAYS	PLEADS GUILTY AS CHARGED	PLEADS GUILTY TO A LESSER CHARGE	TRIAL BY JURY, DEFENDANT FOUND GUILTY AS CHARGED	TRIAL BY JURY, DEFENDANT FOUND NOT GUILTY	TRIAL BY JURY, HUNG JURY	TRIAL BY JURY, DEFENDANT FOUND GUILTY OF A LESSER CHARGE	TRIAL BY JUDGE, DEFENDANT FOUND GUILTY AS CHARGED
1–30	11(.7%)	14(.9%)	0(.0%)	0(.0%)	0(.0%)	0(.0%)	0(.0%)
31–60	21(1.4%)	45(2.9%)	0(.0%)	1(.1%)	0(.0%)	0(.0%)	0(.0%)
61–90	23(1.5%)	76(5.0%)	0(.0%)	1(.1%)	1(.1%)	0(.0%)	0(.0%)
91–180	81(5.3%)	238(15.5%)	3(.2%)	7(.5%)	0(.0%)	2(.1%)	4(.3%)
181–210	29(1.9%)	67(4.4%)	4(.3%)	2(.1%)	0(.0%)	0(.0%)	0(.0%)
211–270	39(2.5%)	82(5.3%)	7(.5%)	5(.3%)	1(.1%)	2(.1%)	6(.4%)
271–300	12(.8%)	44(2.9%)	4(.3%)	2(.1%)	0(.0%)	0(.0%)	5(.3%)
301–365	25(1.6%)	86(5.6%)	4(.3%)	5(.3%)	2(.1%)	0(.0%)	3(.2%)
366–400	16(1.0%)	56(3.6%)	4(.3%)	3(.2%)	1(.1%)	4(.3%)	1(.1%)
401–500	34(2.2%)	83(5.4%)	7(.5%)	6(.4%)	2(.1%)	7(.5%)	7(.5%)
501–600	12(.8%)	33(2.1%)	1(.1%)	0(.0%)	0(.0%)	0(.0%)	6(.4%)
601–730	4(.3%)	14(.9%)	2(.1%)	0(.0%)	0(.0%)	0(.0%)	2(.1%)
Over 730	3(.2%)	8(.5%)	0(.0%)	0(.0%)	0(.0%)	0(.0%)	0(.0%)
Column total	310(20.2%)	846(55.1%)	36(2.3%)	32(2.1%)	7(.5%)	15(1.0%)	34(2.2%)

TABLE 28—*Continued*

NUMBER OF DAYS	TRIAL BY JUDGE, DEFENDANT FOUND NOT GUILTY	TRIAL BY JUDGE, DEFENDANT FOUND GUILTY OF A LESSER CHARGE	NOLLE (DISMISSAL BY PROSECUTOR)	CASE ABATED BY DEATH	REFERRED TO MEDICAL CARE	ROW TOTAL
1–30	0(.0%)	0(.0%)	10(.7%)	0(.0%)	1(.1%)	36(2.3%)
31–60	0(.0%)	0(.0%)	13(.8%)	0(.0%)	0(.0%)	80(5.2%)
61–90	0(.0%)	0(.0%)	11(.7%)	1(.1%)	0(.0%)	113(7.4%)
91–180	4(.3%)	0(.0%)	47(3.1%)	1(.1%)	0(.0%)	387(25.2%)
181–210	0(.0%)	0(.0%)	9(.6%)	2(.1%)	1(.1%)	114(7.4%)
211–270	6(.4%)	1(.1%)	16(1.0%)	2(.1%)	0(.0%)	167(10.9%)
271–300	3(.2%)	0(.0%)	11(.7%)	1(.1%)	0(.0%)	82(5.3%)
301–365	4(.3%)	0(.0%)	29(1.9%)	3(.2%)	0(.0%)	161(10.5%)
366–400	2(.1%)	1(.1%)	20(1.3%)	0(.0%)	0(.0%)	108(7.0%)
401–500	3(.2%)	1(.1%)	34(2.2%)	0(.0%)	0(.0%)	184(12.0%)
501–600	0(.0%)	0(.0%)	8(.5%)	0(.0%)	0(.0%)	60(3.9%)
601–730	0(.0%)	1(.1%)	4(.3%)	1(.1%)	0(.0%)	28(1.8%)
Over 730	0(.0%)	0(.0%)	3(.2%)	0(.0%)	1(.1%)	15(1.0%)
Column total	22(1.4%)	4(.3%)	215(14.0%)	11(.7%)	3(.2%)	1535(100.0%)

TABLE 29. COMPARISON OF BAIL STATUS AND FINAL DISPOSITION
(NUMBER AND PERCENTAGE OF CASES)

	PLEADS GUILTY AS CHARGED	PLEADS GUILTY TO A LESSER CHARGE	TRIAL BY JURY, DEFENDANT FOUND GUILTY AS CHARGED	TRIAL BY JURY, DEFENDANT FOUND NOT GUILTY	TRIAL BY JURY, HUNG JURY	TRIAL BY JURY, DEFENDANT FOUND GUILTY OF A LESSER CHARGE	TRIAL BY JUDGE, DEFENDANT FOUND GUILTY AS CHARGED
Defendant detained in jail	49(3.2%)	195(12.7%)	14(.9%)	5(.3%)	1(.1%)	2(.1%)	9(.6%)
Defendant released on bail	181(11.8%)	483(31.5%)	19(1.2%)	24(1.6%)	6(.4%)	11(.7%)	18(1.2%)
Defendant released on personal recognizance	23(1.5%)	43(2.8%)	0(.0%)	2(.1%)	0(.0%)	0(.0%)	1(.1%)
On bail, then returned to jail	6(.4%)	13(.8%)	0(.0%)	0(.0%)	0(.0%)	0(.0%)	0(.0%)
In jail, then released on bail	51(3.3%)	112(7.3%)	3(.2%)	1(.1%)	0(.0%)	2(.1%)	6(.4%)
Total	310(20.2%)	846(55.1%)	36(2.3%)	32(2.1%)	7(.5%)	15(1.0%)	34(2.2%)

TABLE 29—*Continued*

	TRIAL BY JUDGE, DEFENDANT FOUND NOT GUILTY	TRIAL BY JUDGE, DEFENDANT FOUND GUILTY OF A LESSER CHARGE	NOLLE (DISMISSAL BY PROSECUTOR)	CASE ABATED BY DEATH	REFERRED TO MEDICAL CARE	ROW TOTAL
Defendant detained in jail	2(.1%)	2(.1%)	29(1.9%)	1(.1%)	1(.1%)	310(20.2%)
Defendant released on bail	14(.9%)	1(.1%)	132(8.6%)	10(.7%)	2(.1%)	901(58.7%)
Defendant released on personal recognizance	0(.0%)	1(.1%)	12(.8%)	0(.0%)	0(.0%)	82(5.3%)
On bail, then returned to jail	2(.1%)	0(.0%)	1(.1%)	0(.0%)	0(.0%)	22(1.4%)
In jail, then released on bail	4(.3%)	0(.0%)	41(2.7%)	0(.0%)	0(.0%)	220(14.3%)
Total	22(1.4%)	4(.3%)	215(14.0%)	11(.7%)	3(.2%)	1535(100.0%)

TABLE 30. COMPARISON OF DAYS BETWEEN ARRAIGNMENT AND FINAL
DISPOSITION (NUMBER AND PERCENTAGE OF CASES)

NUMBER OF DAYS	PLEADS GUILTY AS CHARGED	PLEADS GUILTY TO A LESSER CHARGE	TRIAL BY JURY, DEFENDANT FOUND GUILTY AS CHARGED	TRIAL BY JURY, DEFENDANT FOUND NOT GUILTY	TRIAL BY JURY, HUNG JURY	TRIAL BY JURY, DEFENDANT FOUND GUILTY OF A LESSER CHARGE	TRIAL BY JUDGE, DEFENDANT FOUND GUILTY AS CHARGED
1–3	51(3.3%)	62(4.0%)	0(.0%)	0(.0%)	0(.0%)	0(.0%)	1(.1%)
4–15	36(2.3%)	142(9.3%)	0(.0%)	0(.0%)	1(.1%)	0(.0%)	1(.1%)
16–30	42(2.7%)	115(7.5%)	0(.0%)	0(.0%)	0(.0%)	0(.0%)	0(.0%)
31–60	30(2.0%)	78(5.1%)	0(.0%)	0(.0%)	0(.0%)	1(.1%)	0(.0%)
61–90	15(1.0%)	44(2.9%)	3(.2%)	1(.1%)	0(.0%)	0(.0%)	1(.1%)
91–180	53(3.5%)	113(7.4%)	9(.6%)	6(.4%)	0(.0%)	1(.1%)	4(.3%)
181–270	36(2.3%)	139(9.1%)	12(.8%)	3(.2%)	1(.1%)	3(.2%)	12(.8%)
271–365	31(2.0%)	103(6.8%)	7(.5%)	5(.3%)	2(.1%)	5(.3%)	8(.5%)
366–486	12(.8%)	39(2.5%)	5(.3%)	3(.2%)	2(.1%)	5(.3%)	2(.1%)
487–605	6(.4%)	10(.7%)	0(.0%)	0(.0%)	1(.1%)	0(.0%)	4(.3%)
606–730	0(.0%)	6(.4%)	0(.0%)	1(.1%)	0(.0%)	0(.0%)	1(.1%)
Over 731	2(.1%)	0(.0%)	0(.0%)	0(.0%)	0(.0%)	0(.0%)	0(.0%)
Column total	314(20.6%)	851(55.6%)	36(2.3%)	19(1.2%)	7(.5%)	15(1.0%)	34(2.2%)

TABLE 30—*Continued*

NUMBER OF DAYS	TRIAL BY JUDGE, DEFENDANT FOUND NOT GUILTY	TRIAL BY JUDGE, DEFENDANT FOUND GUILTY OF A LESSER CHARGE	NOLLE (DISMISSAL BY PROSECUTOR)	CASE ABATED BY DEATH	REFERRED TO MEDICAL CARE	ROW TOTAL
1–3	1(.1%)	0(.0%)	8(.5%)	0(.0%)	0(.0%)	123(8.0%)
4–15	2(.1%)	0(.0%)	13(.8%)	0(.0%)	1(.1%)	196(12.8%)
16–30	0(.0%)	0(.0%)	18(1.2%)	0(.0%)	0(.0%)	175(11.3%)
31–60	1(.1%)	0(.0%)	17(1.1%)	1(.1%)	0(.0%)	128(8.3%)
61–90	0(.0%)	0(.0%)	13(.8%)	1(.1%)	0(.0%)	78(5.1%)
91–180	3(.2%)	0(.0%)	40(2.6%)	3(.2%)	1(.1%)	233(15.2%)
181–270	8(.5%)	1(.1%)	35(2.3%)	2(.1%)	0(.0%)	252(16.4%)
271–365	6(.4%)	2(.1%)	41(2.7%)	3(.2%)	1(.1%)	214(14.2%)
366–486	1(.1%)	0(.0%)	22(1.4%)	0(.0%)	0(.0%)	91(6.0%)
487–605	0(.0%)	1(.1%)	5(.3%)	0(.0%)	0(.0%)	27(1.8%)
606–730	0(.0%)	0(.0%)	3(.2%)	1(.1%)	0(.0%)	12(.8%)
Over 731	0(.0%)	0(.0%)	0(.0%)	0(.0%)	0(.0%)	2(.1%)
Column total	22(1.4%)	4(.3%)	215(14.0%)	11(.7%)	3(.2%)	1532(100.0%)

TABLE 31. COMPARISON OF TOTAL NUMBER OF DAYS AND SENTENCE
(NUMBER AND PERCENTAGE OF CASES)

NUMBER OF DAYS	OHIO PENITENTIARY	OHIO REFORMATORY	LIMA STATE HOSPITAL	SUSPENDED SENTENCE	RESTITUTION AND COSTS	WORKHOUSE OR COUNTY JAIL	WORKHOUSE OR COUNTY JAIL SUSPENDED	FINE ALONE	PSYCHIATRIC TREATMENT	TOTAL
1–30	5(.4%)	8(.6%)	0(.0%)	0(.0%)	0(.0%)	5(.4%)	3(.2%)	2(.2%)	0(.0%)	23(1.9%)
31–60	24(1.9%)	17(1.4%)	0(.0%)	12(1.0%)	0(.0%)	8(.6%)	2(.2%)	3(.2%)	0(.0%)	66(5.4%)
61–90	9(.7%)	37(3.0%)	1(.1%)	27(2.2%)	1(.1%)	17(1.4%)	6(.5%)	0(.0%)	0(.0%)	98(8.0%)
91–180	52(4.2%)	50(4.1%)	1(.1%)	144(11.7%)	4(.3%)	45(3.7%)	24(1.9%)	4(.3%)	0(.0%)	324(26.3%)
181–210	11(.9%)	19(1.5%)	0(.0%)	41(3.3%)	4(.3%)	20(1.6%)	8(.6%)	2(.2%)	1(.1%)	100(8.1%)
211–270	28(2.3%)	23(1.9%)	1(.1%)	50(4.1%)	1(.1%)	17(1.4%)	8(.6%)	4(.3%)	3(.2%)	135(11.0%)
271–300	13(1.1%)	9(.7%)	0(.0%)	26(2.1%)	0(.0%)	14(1.1%)	2(.2%)	0(.0%)	1(.1%)	65(5.3%)
301–365	18(1.5%)	12(1.0%)	0(.0%)	57(4.6%)	1(.1%)	14(1.1%)	6(.5%)	8(.6%)	0(.0%)	116(9.4%)
366–400	15(1.2%)	16(1.3%)	1(.1%)	39(3.2%)	0(.0%)	7(.6%)	2(.2%)	1(.1%)	0(.0%)	81(6.6%)
401–500	23(1.9%)	25(2.0%)	0(.0%)	57(4.6%)	0(.0%)	20(1.6%)	10(.8%)	2(.2%)	0(.0%)	137(11.1%)
501–600	15(1.2%)	8(.6%)	1(.1%)	16(1.3%)	0(.0%)	8(.6%)	3(.2%)	0(.0%)	0(.0%)	51(4.1%)
601–730	4(.3%)	2(.2%)	1(.1%)	11(.9%)	0(.0%)	3(.2%)	2(.2%)	0(.0%)	0(.0%)	23(1.9%)
Over 731	4(.3%)	2(.2%)	0(.0%)	3(.2%)	0(.0%)	2(.2%)	1(.1%)	0(.0%)	0(.0%)	12(1.0%)
Column Total	221(18.0%)	228(18.5%)	6(.5%)	483(39.2%)	11(.9%)	180(14.6%)	71(5.8%)	26(2.1%)	5(.4%)	1231(100.0%)

TABLE 32. SENTENCE DEPENDENT UPON BAIL STATUS

	JAIL	BAIL	PERSONAL RECOGNIZANCE
Ohio Penitentiary	93 cases	81	2
Ohio Reformatory	68	95	2
Lima State Hospital	1	2	0
Workhouse or county jail	38	111	9
Column total	200	289	13
Suspended sentence	58	334	50
Workhouse or county jail suspended	5	55	2
Column total	63	389	52

Appendix B
STATE
PRETRIAL
CRIMINAL PROCEDURE

The following is a state-by-state analysis of the basic procedures applicable to the preliminary stages of criminal prosecutions. The areas covered are bail, preliminary hearing, grand jury, discovery, and speedy trial. These materials were gathered from statutes, criminal rules, and judicial opinions.

ALABAMA

I. BAIL

All charged crimes are bailable, except capital offenses where the proof is evident or the presumption great. Excessive bail is disallowed. ALA. CONST. art. 1, §16. The Alabama Code narrows this by forbidding bail to one charged with a capital offense or charged with personal injury on another which is likely to produce death and which was committed under circumstances such as would constitute murder in the first degree if death should ensue. ALA. CODE tit. 15, §195 (1958). Statute enlarges the constitutional provision by permitting bail to a defendant in a capital case when the state continues a case twice owing to the absence of witnesses. ALA. CODE tit. 15, §197 (1958). A judge may, however, in his discretion, allow bail to one charged with a capital offense. *State v. Massey,* 20 Ala. App. 56, 100 So. 625 (1924).

II. PRELIMINARY HEARING

The magistrate must, "as soon as may be" after arrest, swear and examine first the complainant and prosecution witnesses and then the de-

247

fendant's witnesses. ALA. CODE tit. 15, §133 (1958). He may adjourn examination proceedings after arrest for up to ten days without the defendant's consent. ALA. CODE §129 (1958). Even if defendant waives the preliminary examination, the magistrate may hold it and the evidence obtained may be admitted at trial. *Percy v. State,* 125 Ala. 52 (1899), 27 So. 844 (1900). Defendant has the right to counsel and the magistrate may keep prosecution witnesses separate from defense witnesses. ALA. CODE tit. 15, §134 (1958).

III. GRAND JURY, INDICTMENT, INFORMATION

No person shall, for an indictable offense, be proceeded against criminally, by information, except where such a procedure is constitutionally provided. In misdemeanors, the legislature may by law dispense with a grand jury and authorize proceedings before justices of the peace and other inferior courts. ALA. CONST. art. 1, §8.

Defendant may plead guilty while awaiting grand jury action or preliminary hearing in all except capital cases. When the desire of a defendant to plead guilty is made known to the court, it shall direct a prosecuting officer of the court to prefer and file an information, under oath, accusing the defendant, with the same certainty as an indictment, of the offense for which he is being held. The court shall set a date for the defendant to formally enter a plea of guilty in open court, with counsel present, not fewer than 15 days after arrest nor fewer than 3 days after notice to the court of defendant's intention to plead guilty. ALA. CODE tit. 15, §260–63 (1958).

IV. PRETRIAL DISCOVERY

Absent a statute or court order to the contrary, a defendant has no right to inspection or disclosure of evidence in the possession of the prosecution. The defendant is entitled to inspection of a writing or object in the prosecution's possession when such item is offered in evidence at trial. *Spicer v. State,* 188 Ala. 9, 65 So. 972 (1914). Defendant's own statement or confession to police may be examined before trial, but such examination is discretionary. *Allison v. State,* 281 Ala. 193, 200 So. 2d 653 (1967); *McCants v. State,* 282 Ala. 397, 211 So. 2d 877 (1968); *Sanders v. State,* 278 Ala. 453, 179 So. 2d 35 (1965), (court denied a general demand for production but permitted production of preliminary hearing transcript and defendant's alleged confession). Notes made by the prosecution in preparation of its case are not producible for the defendant's inspection. *Bailey v. State,* 24 Ala. App. 339, 135 So. 407 (1931).

A defendant is not entitled to inspection of a statement of a prosecution witness for purposes of cross-examination or impeachment, even after the witness has testified on direct examination at trial. Whether to grant a defendant the right to inspect a witness's prior statement is discretionary with the trial court. Where there is no showing by the defendant of any inconsistency between the statement and the testimony, production will be denied. *Mabry v. State,* 40 Ala. App. 129, 110 So. 2d 250, *cert. dismissed,* 268 Ala. 660, 110 So. 2d 260 (1959).

A defendant is not entitled to minutes of a state grand jury proceeding, *Gaines v. State,* 146 Ala. 16, 41 So. 865 (1906), nor to a bill of particulars, *Danley v. State,* 34 Ala. App. 412, 41 So. 2d 414, *cert. denied,* 252 Ala. 420, 41 So. 2d 417 (1949). A defendant cannot compel disclosure of the identity of an informer, unless it appears that such disclosure is necessary to show defendant's innocence. *Dixon v. State,* 39 Ala. App. 575, 105 So. 2d 354 (1958).

Depositions of a witness in criminal cases may be taken by a defendant or by the state with defendant's written consent. ALA. CODE tit. 15, §297 (1958). Witness whose deposition is to be taken must be unable to attend court because of infirmity, sickness, out-of-state residence, or residence more than 100 miles from the place of trial, or must be of material importance to the defense. The defendant desiring to take deposition of any witness must also file interrogatories and serve the interrogatories on the prosecution. ALA. CODE tit. 15, §298 (1958).

V. SPEEDY TRIAL

A speedy trial is required by Article 1, §6, of the Alabama Constitution in all prosecutions by indictment. The Alabama Code requires that justice be administered speedily in the Alabama county courts. ALA. CODE tit. 13, §330 (1958). A defendant must affirmatively demand a speedy trial or waive the right thereto.

ALASKA

I. BAIL

All persons charged with offenses are entitled to release on bail, except in capital offenses where the proof is evident or the presumption great. Neither excessive bail nor excessive fines are allowed. ALAS. CONST. art. 1, §11. The judicial officer is required to give a statement of the conditions of bail and to inform the defendant of penalties for violations. ALAS. STAT. §12.30.020(d)(e). The defendant may appeal these conditions. ALAS. STAT. §12.30.030. If bail is denied, the court must state why it was denied. ALAS. R. CRIM. P. 41(a)(1). Determination of the amount of bail is discretionary with the judge or magistrate. ALAS. R. CRIM. P. 41(b).

II. Preliminary Hearing

The arrested person must always be brought before the nearest available committing magistrate within 24 hours. ALAS. R. CRIM. P. 5(a). The committing magistrate must inform the accused of his right to counsel, and that he has the right to have counsel assigned if unable to provide it himself. He shall also tell the defendant of his right to have a preliminary examination and of his right to remain silent. ALAS. R. CRIM. P. 5(c). The Alaska practice is that if the accused waives the preliminary hearing, he is held to answer in the proper court and if the offense is bailable, he may be allowed to provide bail. If the defendant chooses to have a preliminary hearing, he cannot be called upon to plead. The preliminary hearing must be held within a reasonable time. ALAS. R. CRIM. P. 5(d)(1). Sixteen days was held not to be an unreasonable delay where the charge was first degree murder, where the defendant was without counsel and desired counsel, and where the state needed time to prepare its case. *Martinez v. State,* Op. No. 389, 423 P.2d 700 (Alas. 1967).

At the preliminary hearing, the magistrate shall at the request of defendant subpoena the complainant and any witnesses examined before the complaint was filed. ALAS. R. CRIM. P. 5(d)(1)(b). The prosecution must first present evidence in support of its case and all witnesses must be examined in the presence of the defendant and may be cross-examined by him. ALAS. R. CRIM. P. 5 (d)(1)(b). After the prosecution has presented its evidence, defendant is informed by the magistrate that he, the defendant, need not make any statement and that failure to make a statement cannot be used against him at trial. ALAS. R. CRIM. P. 5(d)(1)(d). Then the defendant may present his evidence, produce witnesses, and examine them. Plaintiff may also cross-examine. ALAS. R. CRIM. P. 5(d)(1)(e).

The defendant is held if it appears to the magistrate at the completion of the preliminary examination that a crime has been committed and there is sufficient cause to believe the defendant guilty of the crime. ALAS. R. CRIM. P. (5)(d)(4). It is not a principal function of the preliminary hearing to provide pretrial discovery; its main purpose is to determine whether there is sufficient basis for holding the accused until the grand jury has reviewed the facts. *Martinez v. State,* Op. No. 389, 423 P.2d 700 (Alas. 1967).

III. Grand Jury, Indictment, Information

An offense which may be punished by imprisonment for a term exceeding one year shall be prosecuted by indictment, unless waived. Any other offense may be prosecuted by indictment or information; and information may be filed without leave of court. Offenses punishable by imprisonment for a term exceeding one year may be prosecuted by information if the defendant, after having been advised of the nature of the charge and of his rights, waives prosecution by indictment in open court. ALAS. R. CRIM. P. 7(a)-(b).

The grand jury shall consist of at least twelve citizens, a majority of whom must concur in returning an indictment. The power of grand juries to investigate and make recommendations concerning the public welfare or safety shall never be suspended. ALAS. CONST. art. 1, §8. The grand jury determines whether there is probable cause that the accused is guilty of the offense with which he is charged. ALAS. STAT. §12.40.030. *Brown v. State,* Sup. Ct. Op. No. 89, 372 P.2d 785 (Alas. 1962). Unnecessary delay in presenting the charge to the grand jury or in filing an information against a defendant who has been held to answer to the superior court may result in dismissal of the indictment or information. ALAS. R. CRIM. P. 43(b).

IV. PRETRIAL DISCOVERY

Upon motion of the defendant, the court may order the prosecuting attorney to permit the defendant to inspect and copy designated books, papers, documents, or tangible objects, obtained from or belonging to the defendant or obtained from others by seizure or process upon showing that the items sought may be material to the preparation of his defense, and that the request is reasonable. ALAS. R. CRIM. P. 16. This rule has been held to afford limited discovery in criminal cases. *Martinez v. State,* Op. No. 389, 423 P.2d 700 (Alas. 1967). It is recognized that the accused may be permitted to inspect evidence in the possession of the prosecution where disclosure is necessary to a fair trial. *U.S. v. Rich,* 6 Alas. 670 (1922).

The defendant is entitled by statute to the production of (1) a written and signed statement by a state witness, or (2) a reproduction, which is substantially a verbatim recital of an oral statement made by a prosecution witness to a government agent and recorded contemporaneously with the making of the statement. 1960 LAWS OF ALAS. ch. 103 (practically identical with the Jencks Act, 71 Stat. 595 (1957), 18 U.S.C.A. 3580(a)-(e)(Supp. 1961). When a prosecution witness has testified in court on direct examination, the defendant is entitled to inspect the witness's prior statement for cross-examination or impeachment. The trial court must examine the requested statement to resolve doubt as to defendant's right to inspect it. *Mahle v. State,* 371 P.2d 21 (Alas. 1962).

Granting or denying the defendant's request for disclosure of the grand jury minutes is within the discretion of the trial court. The court has said that the burden is on the defense to show that a particularized need for the grand jury minutes exists which outweighs the policy of secrecy. *Merrill v. State,* Op. No. 392, 423 P.2d 686, *cert. denied,* 386 U.S. 1040 (1967). The right of the defendant to a bill of particulars indicating the place of commission of the alleged crime is recognized where the defendant needs such information to prepare his defense. *U.S. v. Abrahamson,* 10 Alas. 518 (1945).

V. SPEEDY TRIAL

A speedy trial in all criminal proceedings is required. ALAS. CONST. art. 1, §11. Delay of 14 months in bringing defendant to trial was deprivation of right and required dismissal. Failure to demand a speedy trial is not a waiver of the right unless a court finds that the failure was the result of a tactical decision made by the defendant and his attorney. *Glasgow v. State,* 469 P.2d 682 (Alas. 1970). Unnecessary delay in bringing a defendant to trial is one cause for dismissal. ALAS. R. CRIM. P. 43(b); same as FED. R. CRIM. P. 48(b)(4). Unless the resulting delay is purposeful, oppressive, or prejudicial to the defendant, the granting of a continuance is not a violation of the defendant's right to a speedy trial. *Spight v. State,* 450 P.2d 157 (Alas. 1969).

ARIZONA

I. BAIL

Excessive bail shall not be required. ARIZ. CONST. art. 2, §15. All persons charged with crime shall be bailable, except for capital offenses when the proof is evident or the presumption great. ARIZ. CONST. art. 2, §22.

In fixing the amount of bail, the innocence of the accused is presumed. Bail is not necessarily deemed excessive merely because the defendant cannot give the amount required. *Gusick v. Boies,* 72 Ariz. 233, 233 P.2d 446 (1951). The court may impose any conditions of release it deems necessary, including custody, restrictions on travel, associates, or place of abode, the deposit of money, a prohibition against carrying or possessing a dangerous weapon, drinking, or using drugs. ARIZ. REV. STAT. ANN. §13–1577 (Supp. 1956).

II. PRELIMINARY HEARING

Following his arrest an accused, brought before a magistrate not empowered to try the case, must be informed of the charge, of his right to counsel during the preliminary examination, and of his right to waive preliminary examination. ARIZ. R. CRIM. P. 16. The preliminary examination must be completed at one session, but may be postponed upon good cause for up to two days per postponement, not to exceed a total of six days. ARIZ. R.

CRIM. P. 20. If the defendant waives the preliminary examination, he shall be held to answer before the proper court. If the offense is bailable, he may be released until his arraignment. Notwithstanding the waiver, the magistrate or county attorney may examine witnesses for the state. All witnesses shall be examined in the defendant's presence and may be cross-examined. ARIZ. R. CRIM. P. 23. Defendant is permitted, after the state has examined its witnesses, to answer the charge and explain the facts appearing against him. ARIZ. R. CRIM. P. 24.

III. GRAND JURY, INDICTMENT, INFORMATION

There is no grand jury except upon the order of the judge when in his opinion the public interest so demands. ARIZ. R. CRIM. P. 81. The defendant may plead guilty to an indictment or information for any offense, but the court may refuse to accept the plea and may order not guilty to be entered of record. ARIZ. R. CRIM. P. 183. Every felony and misdemeanor of which the superior court has original jurisdiction shall be prosecuted by indictment or information, and every misdemeanor may be prosecuted by indictment or information. ARIZ. R. CRIM. P. 78. No information may be filed against any person charged with an offense punishable by death or imprisonment in a state prison until such person has or waives the preliminary examination. ARIZ. R. CRIM. P. 79.

Grand jury proceedings are conducted in secret and the content of witness's testimony is not to be disclosed unless the trial statements of a witness are in conflict with the statements made before the grand jury. ARIZ. R. CRIM. P. 107.

IV. PRETRIAL DISCOVERY

The accused has no right to inspection or disclosure of evidence, absent a statute or court order to the contrary. *State ex rel. Mahoney v. Super. Ct. of Maricopa County,* 78 Ariz. 74, 275 P.2d 887 (1954). Suppression by the prosecution of evidence favorable to the defense is a violation of due process, however, and a new trial is required. The failure to reveal such evidence is not justified by the fact that the defendant's counsel never requested the evidence. If the defendant does not know of the existence of favorable evidence until after the trial, he has not waived the right of disclosure. *State v. Fowler,* 101 Ariz. 561, 422 P.2d 125 (1967).

The court may deny a vague subpoena duces tecum which it decides is in the nature of a "fishing expedition" into the work product of the county attorney. *State v. Colvin,* 81 Ariz. 388, 307 P.2d 98 (1957). The defendant is entitled to inspection of a writing or object in the possession of the prosecution when the item is offered in evidence at the trial. *Mahoney v. Super. Ct., supra; Corbin v. Super. Ct.,* 103 Ariz. 465, 445 P.2d 441 (1968).

When a police officer has testified in a case, the defendant has the right to examine the notes and reports of the officer regarding matters about which he has testified. The defendant is not, however, entitled to a pretrial examination of the reports of the officers. *State ex rel. Corbin v. Super. Ct.,* 99 Ariz. 382, 409 P.2d 547 (1966). The accused has no right of inspection or disclosure of a document or article in the prosecution's possession which is not admissible in evidence. *State v. McGee,* 91 Ariz. 101, 370 P.2d 261, *cert. denied,* 371 U.S. 844 (1962).

Upon motion of the defendant at any time after the filing of the indictment or information, the court may order the county attorney to permit the defendant to inspect or copy designated books, papers, documents, or tangible objects, obtained from or belonging to the defendant or obtained from others by seizure or by process upon a showing that the items sought may be material to the preparation of his defense, and that the request is reasonable. ARIZ. R. CRIM. P. 195. Under its inherent residual power, the court may allow discovery to the defendant beyond the scope of the rule when such discovery is essential to the sound administration of justice. *State ex rel. Polley v. Super. Ct. of Santa Cruz County,* 81 Ariz. 127, 302 P.2d 263 (1956).

The defendant does not have a right to inspect his own written statement in the hands of the prosecution, whether it is a confession or an admission against interest. An application to do so is addressed to the sound discretion of the trial court and generally speaking such an application should be granted only under exceptional circumstances. *State v. Von Reeden,* 9 Ariz. App. 190, 450 P.2d 702 (1969).

The defendant is entitled to inspect prior statements of a witness for purposes of cross-examination or impeachment when the witness has testified on direct examination at the trial. *State v. Wallace,* 97 Ariz. 296, 399 P.2d 909 (1965); *State v. Green,* 103 Ariz. 211, 439 P.2d 483 (1968). To be granted the right of inspection the defendant is not required to show any inconsistency between the contents of the statement and the testimony of the witness at trial. *State v. Ashton,* 95 Ariz. 37, 386 P.2d 83 (1963).

The accused is not entitled to disclosure of the state grand jury minutes. In order to see the minutes, the accused must show a "particularized need," either before or during the trial. ARIZ. R. CRIM. P. 107. Circumstances which justify the trial court's ordering the disclosure of the grand jury minutes include: (1) after the witness has testified at trial, to determine whether the testimony is consistent, (2) where the witness is charged with perjury, and (3) when permitted by the court in the furtherance of justice. *State ex rel. Ronan v. Super. Ct. of Maricopa County,* 95 Ariz. 319, 390 P.2d 109 (1964).

An information is sufficient where the accused is informed of the name given the offense by statute, and of the specific conduct alleged. If the accused desires further details, he can ask for a bill of particulars to supply them. *State v. Maxwell,* 103 Ariz. 478, 445 P.2d 837 (1968).

The prosecution's right to discovery is limited to being notified of the defendant's intention to interpose insanity or an alibi as a defense to the crime charged. ARIZ. R. CRIM. P. 192.

V. SPEEDY TRIAL

Justice in all cases shall be administered openly and without unnecessary delay. ARIZ. CONST. art. 2, §11. The accused in a criminal prosecution shall have the right to have a speedy public trial by an impartial jury. ARIZ. CONST. art. 2, §24. If within 30 days an information has not been filed against a person held to answer for an offense, or if a person who has been indicted or informed against for an offense is not brought to trial for the offense within 60 days after the indictment information, the prosecution must be dismissed upon application of such person. ARIZ. R. CRIM. P. 236. In all criminal prosecutions the state and the defendant shall each have a right to a speedy trial. ARIZ. R. CRIM. P. 240.

The right to a speedy trial runs from the time the accused is held to answer by a magistrate. The accused need not demand a timely trial to protect his right to a speedy trial when he files a motion to dismiss and to quash. *State v. Pruett,* 101 Ariz. 65, 415 P.2d 888 (1966). It is no denial of a speedy trial when the accused's own action has contributed in part to the running of more than the normal time from the trial's beginning to its end.

ARKANSAS

I. BAIL

All persons shall before conviction be bailable by sufficient sureties, except for capital offenses when the proof is evident or the presumption great. ARK. CONST. art. 2, §8. Justices of the peace have no power to admit to bail in cases of murder, manslaughter, or any other capital offense. ARK. STAT. ANN. §43–622. Those granted bail must be residents of the state. ARK. STAT. ANN. §43–703. One accused of a felony when on bail may remain upon bail or be kept in custody as the court may direct. ARK. STAT. ANN. §43–710 (1947).

II. PRELIMINARY HEARING

An arrested person shall be brought before a magistrate and the charge(s) against him forthwith examined, with a reasonable amount of time allowed for the defendant to procure counsel. If the offense is a felony, the magistrate shall commit, hold to bail, or discharge as is required. If the magistrate himself has jurisdiction of the case, he may proceed to a final determination. The magistrate of the county in which the public offense has been committed may examine the charge. ARK. STAT. ANN. §43–605.

Upon the conclusion of the examination, the defendant may be discharged if the magistrate feels there is not sufficient cause for believing that the defendant has committed a public offense. The accused shall be held for trial or released on bail if the magistrate finds that reasonable grounds exist for believing the defendant guilty of the offense charged or of some other offense. ARK. STAT. ANN. §43–619.

III. GRAND JURY, INDICTMENT, INFORMATION

All offenses previously required to be prosecuted by indictment may be prosecuted either by indictment of the grand jury or upon information filed by the prosecuting attorney. ARK. CONST. amend. 21, §1.

The grand jury must inquire into the cases of all those imprisoned in the county jail or on bail who are to answer a criminal charge in that court and who have not been indicted. ARK. STAT. ANN. §43–907. They must indict persons as they find them guilty of the charge. ARK. STAT. ANN. §43–908.

If an indictment is used, the language of the indictment must be certain as to the title of the prosecution, the name of the court in which the indictment is presented, and the name of the parties. It shall not be necessary to include a statement of the act or acts constituting the offense, unless the offense cannot be charged without doing so. Nor is it necessary to allege that the act or acts constituting the offense were done willfully, unlawfully, feloniously, maliciously, deliberately, or with premeditation, but the name of the offense charged in the indictment must carry with it all such allegations. The state, upon the request of the defendant, must file a bill of particulars, setting out the act or acts upon which it relies for conviction. ARK. STAT. ANN. §43–1006 (1947).

IV. PRETRIAL DISCOVERY DEPOSITIONS

The Arkansas discovery statute does not apply to criminal cases. *Bailey v. State,* 227 Ark. 889, 302 S.W.2d 796, *cert. denied,* 335 U.S. 851 (1957); *Edens v. State,* 235 Ark. 996, 363 S.W.2d 923 (1963).

In *Jones v. State,* 213 Ark. 863, 213 S.W.2d 974 (1948), the trial court denied the defendant's pretrial motion for production by the prosecution of the defendant's confession, which was later introduced as evidence at the trial. The appellate court held that while the motion should have been granted, the denial was not sufficiently prejudicial as to warrant reversal of a conviction. The court noted that copying the confession would have furnished no evidence that the confession was not freely and voluntarily made.

A defendant is not entitled to inspect the statement of a prosecution witness for the purpose of cross-examination or impeachment, even after the witness has testified at the trial. *Bates v. State,* 210 Ark. 1014, 198 S.W.2d 850 (1947).

The accused is not entitled to disclosure of the minutes of the proceedings of the state grand jury. The defendant is entitled to a copy of the indictment, but not to the testimony by which the state at the trial expected to sustain its accusation. *Hofler v. State,* 16 Ark. 534 (1855). Neither is the accused entitled to examine grand jury testimony during the trial to determine whether the trial testimony of the prosecution witness was consistent with his grand jury testimony. *Arnold v. State,* 179 Ark. 1066, 20 S.W.2d 189 (1929).

The bill of particulars now required by law in criminal cases shall state the act relied upon by the state in sufficient detail as was formerly required by an indictment so that the defendant is able to prepare his defense. A supplemental bill of particulars may be required upon order of the trial court, if the bill of particulars filed by the prosecuting attorney is not sufficiently definite to apprise the defendant of the specific crime with which he is charged. ARK. STAT. ANN. §43–804.

The court may authorize a defendant to take depositions of a material witness where there is reason to believe that the witness will die before trial or be incapable of attending trial. Affidavits must show materiality of the testimony and reasons for taking the deposition. ARK. STAT. ANN. §43–2011.

Notice to the prosecution of defendant's intent to plead insanity is required. ARK. STAT. ANN. §43–1304.

V. RIGHT TO A SPEEDY TRIAL

The accused in all criminal prosecutions shall enjoy the right to a speedy and public trial. ARK. CONST. art. 2, §10. If any person indicted for an offense and committed to prison is not brought to trial before the end of the second term of the court having jurisdiction, he shall be discharged so far as relates to the offense for which he was committed, unless the delay happens upon the application of the prisoner. ARK. STAT. ANN. §43–1708. If any person indicted for any offense and held to bail is not brought to trial before the end of the third term after the finding of the indictment, and the holding to bail on indictment of the court in which the indictment is pending, he shall be discharged, so far as relates to such offense, unless the delay happened on his application. ARK. STAT. ANN. §43–1709. If, when application for discharge is made under either of these two statutes, the court is satisfied that there is material evidence on the part of the state which cannot be obtained, that reasonable exertions have been made to procure it, and that there is just ground to believe that the evidence can be obtained at the succeeding term, the case may be continued until the next term, and the prisoner remanded or admitted to bail. ARK. STAT. ANN. §43–1711.

To be entitled to discharge on delay of the trial, the prisoner must demand trial or resist postponement. *Dillard v. State,* 65 Ark. 404, 46 S.W. 533 (1898). A case will not be dismissed for want of prosecution unless the defendant has either demanded a trial or resisted a continuance. *Fox v. State,* 102 Ark. 393, 144 S.W. 516 (1912).

CALIFORNIA

I. BAIL

All persons shall be bailable except for capital offenses when the proof is evident or the presumption great. CAL. CONST. art. 1, §6; CAL. PENAL CODE §1270 (West 1969). If the charge is for any other offense, he may be admitted to bail, before conviction, as a matter of right. CAL. PENAL CODE §1271 (West 1969). Excessive bail shall not be required. CAL. CONST. art. 1, §6. Admittance to bail after conviction is discretionary in all cases except in appeals from judgments imposing (1) a fine or (2) imprisonment in misdemeanors. CAL. PENAL CODE §1272 (West 1969).

In fixing the amount of bail, the judge shall consider: (1) the seriousness of the charge, (2) the defendant's previous criminal record, and (3) the probability of his appearing at the trial or hearing. CAL. PENAL CODE §1275 (West 1969).

When defendant has been held to answer upon an examination for a public offense, admission to bail may be by any magistrate who is empowered to issue a writ of habeas corpus. CAL. PENAL CODE §1277 (West 1969).

After indictment for a capital offense, a defendant must be held in custody unless admitted to bail on examination upon a writ of habeas corpus. CAL. PENAL CODE §1286 (West 1969).

For good cause shown, bail may be increased or decreased by the court. CAL. PENAL CODE §1289 (West 1969). For good cause shown, any court which can release a defendant on bail may release him on his own recognizance if it appears defendant will surrender himself to custody as agreed. CAL. PENAL CODE §1318 (West 1969). This is purely discretionary with the court. CAL. PENAL CODE §1318.2 (West 1969). A defendant charged with a felony and released on his own recognizance who willfully fails to appear as he has agreed is guilty of a felony. CAL. PENAL CODE §1319.4 (West 1969).

II. PRELIMINARY EXAMINATION

When the defendant is brought before a magistrate after arrest, he must be informed of the charge against him, and of his right to counsel in every stage of the proceedings. CAL. PENAL CODE §858, 859 (West 1969). After defendant has appeared before the judge for arraignment, if the public offense is a felony to which the defendant has not pleaded guilty (according to §859a), the judge must set a time for examination of the case, allowing not less than two days, excluding Sundays and holidays, for the prosecutor and defendant to prepare for the examination and must issue subpoenas for witnesses within the state required by prosecution or defense. CAL. PENAL CODE §859b (West 1969; Additional Supp. 1971). A defendant may waive the preliminary examination. CAL. PENAL CODE §860 (West 1969). If the right is not waived, a defendant in custody shall have the right to a preliminary examination within ten court days of the date he is arraigned or pleads, whichever occurs later. CAL. PENAL CODE §859b (West 1969; Additional Supp. 1971). The preliminary examination must be completed at one session unless the judge, for good cause, postpones. Postponement may not be for more than two days at a time, nor for more than six days, unless by defendant's consent or on his motion. CAL. PENAL CODE §861 (West 1969).

During the examination, witnesses must be examined in the defendant's presence and may be cross-examined on his behalf. CAL. PENAL CODE §865 (West 1969). When the state has finished examining its witnesses, any witnesses the defendant may produce must be sworn and examined. CAL. PENAL CODE §866 (West 1969). The defendant may not be examined unless he is represented by counsel or unless he waives his right to counsel. CAL. PENAL CODE §866.5 (West 1969). Witnesses may be separated by the judge and excluded from the examination of other witnesses. CAL. PENAL CODE §867 (West 1969).

In cases of homicide, the testimony of each witness must be reduced to writing, as a deposition, and authenticated. Where a transcript is made and filed, both the prosecuting attorney and the defendant shall receive a copy. The defendant's copy must be delivered to him without cost at least five days before trial or earlier if he demands. CAL. PENAL CODE §869, 870 (West 1969; Additional Supp. 1971).

III. GRAND JURY, INDICTMENT, INFORMATION

Offenses which prior to 1954 had to be prosecuted by indictment are now prosecuted by information, after examination and commitment by a magistrate, or by indictment with or without such examination and commitment, as may be prescribed by law. CAL. CONST. art. 1, §8. Before an information is filed, there must be a preliminary examination, commenced by a written complaint. CAL. PENAL CODE §738 (1969).

The grand jury must be drawn at least once a year in each county. CAL. CONST. art. 1, §8. It may inquire into all public offenses committed or triable within the county and present them to the court by indictment. CAL. PENAL CODE §917 (West 1969).

IV. PRETRIAL DISCOVERY

The civil statute providing for discovery is not applicable to criminal cases. *Ballard v. Super. Ct. of County of San Diego,* 64 Cal. 2d 159, 410 P.2d 838 (1966), 49 Cal. Rptr. 302; *People v. Lindsay,* 227 Cal. App. 2d 482, 38 Cal. Rptr. 755 (1964).

In the absence of a countervailing showing that the information may be used for an improper purpose, discovery is now available not as a matter of discretion but as a matter of right. Traynor, *Ground Lost and Found in Criminal Discovery,* 39 N.Y.U.L. REV. 228, 244 (1964). However, a refusal to permit the defendant to inspect pretrial evidence in the prosecution's possession does not necessarily violate the defendant's constitutional right to due process of law. *People v. Lindsay,* 227 Cal. App. 2d 482, 38 Cal. Rptr. 755 (1964). The motion for production must be timely or the right to production will be waived. *People v. Norman,* 177 Cal. App. 2d 59, 1 Cal. Rptr. 699, *cert. denied,* 364 U.S. 820 (1960). In another case, the court said the defendant was entitled to disclosure of discoverable matters, even though he makes his first demand at trial. *People v. Wilson,* 222 Cal. App. 2d 616, 35 Cal. Rptr. 280 (1963).

The power and jurisdiction of the court to permit the inspection of evidence in the possession of the prosecution is discretionary with the trial court. *People v. Terry,* 57 Cal. 2d 538, 370 P.2d 985, 21 Cal. Rptr. 185, *cert. denied,* 375 U. S. 960 (1962). In a proper case, a person charged with a crime may inspect, before trial, statements of his own in the possession of the prosecution, whether signed, unsigned, or on recording tape. *People v. Lindsay,* 227 Cal. App. 2d 482, 38 Cal. Rptr. 755 (1964). *People v. Super. Ct. of Shasta County,* 264 Cal. App. 2d 694, 70 Cal Rptr. 480 (1968).

A defendant's right to pretrial discovery is well established in California as a corollary to the right to a fair trial and extends to the names of the prosecution's witnesses and reports of expert witnesses for the people. *People v. Morris,* 226 Cal. App. 2d 12, 37 Cal. Rptr. 741 (1964). The courts will permit inspection of evidence in the prosecution's possession if it is relevant and material to his defense. *People v. Riser,* 47 Cal. 2d 566, 305 P.2d 1, *cert.*

denied, 353 U. S. 930, *appeal dismissed,* 358 U. S. 646 (1956). *See* Annot. 7 ALR 3d 8, at 58.

The district attorney is not required to seek out defendant's counsel and present statements to him for inspection; it is the duty of defense counsel to go to the district attorney's office and inspect the statements available to him there. *People v. Crovedi* (Cal. App.) 49 Cal. Rptr. 724, *superseded* 65 Cal. 2d 199, 417 P.2d 868, 53 Cal. Rptr. 284 (1966). Where the defendant's requests are granted, the prosecution is bound to produce only such documents as are in his possession at the time of the order; the order is not a continuing one. Absent a court order, the prosecution is not under a continuing duty to furnish subsequently acquired documents, absent a showing of bad faith. *People v. Briggs,* 58 Cal. 2d 385, 374 P.2d 257, 24 Cal. Rptr. 417 (1962); *People v. Bazaure,* 235 Cal. App. 2d 21, 44 Cal. Rptr. 831 (1965).

California courts have stated that failure to show admissibility of evidence is not a bar to discovery and inspection by the defense. *People v. Curry,* 192 Cal. App. 2d 664, 13 Cal. Rptr. 596 (1961); *Ballard v. Super. Ct. of County of San Diego,* 64 Cal. 2d 159, 410 P.2d 838, 49 Cal. Rptr. 302 (1966).

The defendant is entitled to pretrial discovery of the names and addresses of witnesses. *People v. Lopez,* 60 Cal. 2d 223, 384 P.2d 16, 32 Cal. Rptr. 424 (1963). For purposes of cross-examination or impeachment the defendant is not entitled to production of testimony given by a witness at a prior trial. *People v. Hollander,* 194 Cal. App. 2d 386, 14 Cal. Rptr. 917 (1961). The California courts have taken the view, however, that in order to be granted inspection of the statement of a prosecution witness, the defendant is not required to show some inconsistency between the statement and the trial testimony of the witness; the only requirement is that the information requested be relevant and material to the defense. *People v. Cooper,* 53 Cal. 2d 755, 349 P.2d 964, 3 Cal. Rptr. 148 (1960); *People v. Estrada,* 54 Cal. 2d 713, 355 P.2d 641, 7 Cal. Rptr. 897 (1960).

The court has permitted inspection of relevant material from a police or investigation report, a police record, or an investigation file. *People v. Darnold,* 219 Cal. App. 2d 561, 33 Cal. Rptr. 369, *cert. denied,* 376 U. S. 927 (1963). In a case denying a motion for the production of police records, one California court notes, *inter alia,* that the files in law enforcement agencies relating to the apprehension, prosecution, and punishment of criminals are not subject to public inspection. *People v. Wilkins,* 135 Cal. App. 2d 371, 287 P.2d 555 (1955).

In some cases, the court has refused to permit the defendant to inspect his confession or statement on the ground that there was no showing of circumstances warranting the requested inspection. *Brenard v. Super. Ct.,* 172 Cal. App. 2d 314, 341 P.2d 743 (1959); *People v. Burch,* 196 Cal. App. 2d 754, 17 Cal. Rptr. 102 (1961). Where the accused's statement or conversation was made or had before or during the offense, the defendant could discover recordings or transcriptions of the conversation between himself and a police officer posing as a prospective accomplice. *Cash v. Super. Ct. of Santa Clara County,* 53 Cal. 2d 72, 346 P.2d 407 (1959).

A defendant can inspect a statement or confession made by a co-defendant which is in the prosecution's possession. *People v. Garner,* 57 Cal. 2d 135, 367 P.2d 680, 18 Cal. Rptr. 40, *cert. denied,* 370 U. S. 929 (1961); *People v. Aranda,* 63 Cal. 2d 518, 407 P.2d 265, 47 Cal. Rptr. 353 (1965). The trial court denied access in a situation where, since any statements of the co-defendant were presumably made outside the defendant's presence, such statements would not be admissible against the defendant. *Schindler v. Super. Ct. of Madera County,* 161 Cal. App. 2d 513, 327 P.2d 68 (1958).

The accused is not entitled to inspect the prosecution's private notes or memoranda made a short time after the crime. *People v. Bermijo,* 2 Cal. 2d 270, 40 P.2d 823 (1935).

For the defendant to inspect a prosecution witness's statement for purposes of cross-examination or impeachment after the witness has testified on direct examination, the defendant must "lay a proper foundation." The court requires some specificity when the witness's reports are requested by the defendant. *People v. Carella,* 191 Cal. App. 2d 115, 12 Cal. Rptr. 446 (1961); *People v. Cooper,* 53 Cal. 2d 755, 349 P.2d 964, 3 Cal. Rptr. 148 (1960). The defendant may be permitted to inspect before trial a statement of a prospective prosecution witness for the purpose of cross-examining or impeaching him at the trial in the event that he testifies. *People v. Estrada,* 54 Cal. 2d 713, 355 P.2d 641 (1960), 7 Cal. Rptr. 897; *People v. Renchie,* 201 Cal. App. 2d 1, 19 Cal. Rptr. 734 (1962).

The defendant is entitled to a transcript of the grand jury proceedings before the trial if he is prosecuted by indictment, or to a transcript of the testimony at the preliminary hearing if he is prosecuted by information. CAL. PENAL CODE §938.1 (West 1969). Under the statute permitting the disclosure of the grand jury minutes, the accused is entitled to the testimony of all the witnesses before the grand jury, whether or not such testimony was used as the basis for the indictment. However, the defendant may not inspect exhibits presented before the grand jury. *People v. Pipes,* 179 Cal. App. 2d 547, 3 Cal. Rptr. 814 (1960).

Some California cases have recognized that the prosecution is privileged to withhold from the accused the identity of an informer. *People v. Womack,* 200 Cal. App. 2d 634, 19 Cal. Rptr. 451 (1962); *People v. Fuqua,* 222 Cal.

App. 2d 306, 35 Cal. Rptr. 163 (1963). Disclosure of the identity of an informer is not required absent a timely request for it. *People v. Ker,* 195 Cal. App. 2d 246, 15 Cal. Rptr. 767, *cert. granted,* 368 U. S. 974 (1962); *People v. Escoto,* 185 Cal. App. 2d 599, 8 Cal. Rptr. 488 (1960). *See* Annot. 76 ALR 2d 262, at 299–302. Where identity of the informer is essential, relevant, or helpful to the defense, disclosure will be ordered. *Honore v. Super. Ct. of Alameda County,* 70 Cal. 2d 162, 499 P.2d 169, 74 Cal. Rptr. 233 (1969); *People v. Scott,* 259 Cal. App. 2d 268, 66 Cal. Rptr. 257 (1968). Where the informer is a participant in the offense, disclosure is required. *People v. Scott, supra.* Disclosure is not required where he is not a participant. *People v. Avila,* 222 Cal. App. 2d 83, 34 Cal. Rptr. 677 (1963); *People v. Fuqua,* 222 Cal. App. 2d 306, 35 Cal. Rptr. 163 (1963). Identity must be disclosed where there is no showing of probable cause apart from the informant's communication. *People v. Hammond,* 54 Cal. 2d 846, 357 P.2d 289, 9 Cal. Rptr. 233 (1960).

The court has held that the accused could be denied permission to interview a witness held in custody by the prosecution. The court will not reverse a conviction even if the interview was wrongfully denied, where there is no showing that such denial prejudiced the defendant. *People v. Aadland,* 193 Cal. App. 2d 584, 14 Cal. Rptr. 462 (1961).

The prosecution in a rape case was held entitled to discover the names of witnesses that the accused intended to call, and any x-rays he intended to introduce in evidence to support his affirmative defense of impotency. However, the prosecution was not entitled to the names and addresses of all the physicians who had treated the accused prior to the trial or to all the doctor's reports. A defendant, also, may not be required to produce private documents in his possession. *Jones v. Super. Ct. of Nevada County,* 58 Cal. 2d 56, 372 P.2d 919, 22 Cal. Rptr. 879 (1962).

The defendant is required to give notice of an intention to plead insanity. CAL. PENAL CODE §1016.

V. SPEEDY TRIAL

The accused in all criminal prosecutions, in any court whatever, has the right to a speedy and public trial. CAL. CONST. art. 1, §13. Unless the defendant is brought to trial within 60 days after being charged with a felony, the charge must be dismissed, unless the defendant participates or consents to the delay. CAL. PENAL CODE §1382 (West 1969). Within 90 days after a demand by a prisoner in a state prison, any pending charge against the prisoner must be brought to trial or dismissed. CAL. PENAL CODE §1381 (West 1969); *People v. Godlewski,* 22 Cal. 2d 677, 140 P.2d 381 (1943). The right to a speedy trial will be deemed waived unless the defendant both objects to the date set and thereafter files a timely motion to dismiss. *People v. Wilson,* 60 Cal. 2d 139, 383 P.2d 452, 32 Cal. Rptr. 44 (1963).

COLORADO

I. Bail

All persons are bailable by sufficient sureties except for capital offenses where the proof is evident or the presumption great. COLO. CONST. art. 2, §19. Excessive bail shall not be required. COLO. CONST. art. 2, §20. Any person arrested who is in custody and for whom no bail has been set may advise any county judge by written request to set bail. COLO. R. CRIM. P. 46(a)(1). After conviction in a capital offense, bail may be allowed pending appeal. COLO. R. CRIM. P. 46–1. The amount of bail is up to the discretion of the court. COLO. R. CRIM. P. 46–11.

II. Preliminary Hearing

The accused must be taken without unnecessary delay to the nearest available county judge. If the accused was arrested without a warrant, a complaint must be filed without unnecessary delay in the county court of the county in which the crime was committed. COLO. R. CRIM. P. 5(a)(1). The county judge shall advise the accused of the complaint against him, the amount of bail, of his right to counsel, of his right not to make a statement, and of his right to file a motion requesting a preliminary hearing. COLO. R. CRIM. P. 5(b)(1).

Within ten days after accused is brought before the court, either he or the district attorney may file a written motion for a preliminary hearing to determine whether probable cause exists. Upon such filing, the county judge shall set the date for hearing, which must be within 30 days of setting, unless good cause is shown by the court. COLO. R. CRIM. P. 5(c)(1). The preliminary hearing shall be held before a judge of the court in which the complaint was filed. The accused is not called upon to plead, and may introduce evidence in his own behalf. If the county judge finds such probable cause exists, he will bind the accused over for trial. COLO. R. CRIM. P. 5(c)(2).

If, after expiration of the ten-day period, no motion for preliminary hearing is filed, the accused is bound over for trial. COLO. R. CRIM. P. 5(d).

III. Grand Jury, Indictment, Information

The chief judge of the district court in each county may order a grand jury summoned where authorized by law or required by the public interest.

COLO. R. CRIM. P. 6. In counties with a population in excess of 100,000, a grand jury shall be called at the first term of each court with jurisdiction to make such an order. COLO. REV. STAT. ANN. §78–6–1.

Any offense against the state of Colorado may be prosecuted by indictment or information. COLO. R. CRIM. P. 7(a)–(b). If the accused has either failed to file a motion for preliminary hearing or has had preliminary hearing and has been bound over for trial, the information may be filed without leave of court. COLO. R. CRIM. P. 7(b)(2).

IV. DISCOVERY

The court may, upon motion of accused, order the prosecutor to inspect confessions of accused, pertinent medical or physical examination reports, books, papers, documents, tangible objects, places, or *any other* relevant materials upon a showing of materiality to preparation of the defense. COLO. R. CRIM. P. 16(a)–(c). Upon granting of such motion, the prosecution may inspect certain documents, papers, books, or reports upon a showing that his request is reasonable and the information sought is material. COLO. R. CRIM. P. 16(d). The Colorado rules also provide for protective orders and stipulate that, a motion granting discovery having been obtained, the party from whom discovery is sought is under a continuing duty to disclose new material previously requested. COLO. R. CRIM. P. 16(f),(h).

Both prosecutor and defense counsel may, upon motion, take a deposition of a prospective witness, upon a showing that said witness may be unable to attend a trial or hearing or upon a showing that such deposition is necessary to prevent injustice. COLO. R. CRIM. P. 15(a).

V. SPEEDY TRIAL

In criminal prosecutions, the accused has the right to a speedy public trial. COLO. CONST. art. 2, §16. If a person is committed for a criminal or supposed criminal matter and is not tried on or before the expiration of the second term of the court having jurisdiction of the offense, the defendant must be set at liberty by the court and the case dismissed. This rule does not apply if the delay was caused or requested by the defendant or if the court at the second term is satisfied that attempts have been made to procure the evidence and that there are reasonable grounds to believe that such evidence may be procured at the third term. COLO. REV. STAT. ANN. §39–7–12 (1963).

A delay of two years and eight months in bringing the accused to trial is clearly a violation of the constitutional guarantee of a speedy trial. *In re Miller,* 66 Colo. 261, 180 P. 749 (1919). An overcrowded docket causing a delay longer than three terms of the court prior to trial entitled the accused to a discharge. COLO. CONST., §16; *Rude v. People,* 44 Colo. 384, 99 P. 317 (1908). However, the lapse of three full terms between a defendant's discharge in a preliminary hearing before a justice of the peace and the filing of an information in the district court for the same offense does not entitle him to a discharge under this same section. *In re Snyder,* 110 Colo. 35, 129 P.2d 672 (1942). An accused is not *absolutely* entitled to a final discharge because he has not been brought to trial within two terms after his imprisonment. *Seiwald v. People,* 66 Colo. 332, 182 P. 20 (1919).

A defendant who made no objection to the trial date and requested a continuance to an even later date waived any statutory right to a discharge. *Adargo v. People,* 159 Colo. 321, 411 P.2d 245 (1966). The grant of a continuance to the district attorney which extends the time beyond the second term is within the discretion of the court. *Jordan v. People,* 155 Colo. 224, 393 P.2d 745 (1964).

CONNECTICUT

I. BAIL

The accused must be released on bail upon sufficient security except in capital offenses when the proof is evident or the presumption great. CONN. CONST. art. 1, §8. Each person who is detained in a community correction center pursuant to the issuance of a bench warrant or for arraignment, sentencing, or trial, for an offense which is not punishable by death, is entitled to bail and must be released from such an institution upon entering into a recognizance with sufficient surety or upon the posting of cash bail for his appearance in court. CONN. GEN. STAT. ANN. §54–53, §54–66. The judge sets the conditions of bail and may modify them. One of the following assurances is made upon release of the accused: (1) execution of a written promise to appear, (2) execution of a bond without surety in no greater amount than necessary, or (3) execution of a bond with surety. CONN. GEN. STAT. ANN. §54–53, §54–66.

II. PRELIMINARY HEARING

In a hearing for probable cause, the defendant is called upon to plead. If he waives such examination, he is held to answer forthwith in the appropriate court. If the defendant does not waive examination, the judge must hear the evidence within a reasonable time. The defendant may cross-examine witnesses against him and may introduce evidence in his own behalf. If the judge finds probable cause to believe that an offense has been committed and that defendant has committed it, the defendant is held for trial; if not, defendant is discharged. CONN. GEN. STAT. ANN. §54–76(a). The right to a preliminary hearing is not a constitutional right and is not a matter of right under Connecticut law unless the case remains before the circuit court. *State v. Stallings,* 25 Conn. Supp. 386, 206 A.2d 277 (1964).

III. GRAND JURY, INDICTMENT, INFORMATION

An original information may be filed in the superior court against any person accused of a crime in any case in which an inferior court may, at its discretion, punish or bind him over for trial, and may be filed in any other case upon the order of the superior court. CONN. GEN. STAT. ANN. §54–42. It is necessary for a grand jury to return an indictment for any crime punishable by death or life imprisonment. CONN. GEN. STAT. ANN. §54–45. An information may be used for all noncapital cases. CONN. GEN. STAT. ANN. §54–46.

IV. PRETRIAL DISCOVERY

The rules for civil action apply in criminal cases insofar as they are adaptable to criminal proceedings. *State v. Trumbull,* 23 Conn. Supp. 41, 176 A.2d 887 (1961). The rule applicable in civil actions allows the court, upon the motion of either party, to permit disclosure of facts or documents material to the mover's cause of action or defense and within the knowledge, possession, or power of the adverse party. CONN. GEN. STAT. ANN. §52–197.

In *Trumbull,* the court held that the defendant did not have an absolute right to discovery of his own statements, confessions, or letters that were in the possession of the prosecution.

Whether to grant or deny an accused's right to inspect evidence in the prosecution's possession is in the discretion of the trial court. *State v. Cocheo,* 24 Conn. Supp. 377, 190 A.2d 916 (1963). The court held that denial of a defendant's request, made during cross-examination of the prosecution's witness, for permission to inspect a statement previously made to the police by the witness, was proper, since the defendant had neither stated a reason for the request nor asserted that the witness's testimony and statement were inconsistent.

Information disclosed to a state attorney to enable him to perform the duties of his office is privileged, on the grounds of public policy. *State v. Zimnaruk,* 128 Conn. 124, 20 A.2d 613 (1941); *State v. Roy,* 23 Conn. Supp. 342, 183 A.2d 291 (1962); *State v. Salvatore,* 23 Conn. Supp. 459, 184 A.2d 551 (1962).

However, the court held that the defendant had the right to inspect the coroner's report, including all the testimony of all the witnesses examined before him, after it had been filed with the clerk of the superior court. *Daly v. Dimock,* 55 Conn. 579, 12 A. 405 (1887).

Ordinarily the defendant is not entitled to inspection of prior statements, even after a witness has testified at the trial. *State v. Zimnaruk,* 128 Conn. 124, 20 A.2d 613 (1941); *State v. Pikul,* 150 Conn. 195, 187 A.2d 442 (1962). It is within the discretion of the trial court to grant or deny the defendant the right to inspect a witness's prior statement. *State v. Pikul,* 150 Conn. 195, 187 A.2d 442 (1962). The *Pikul* Court rejected the defendant's suggestion that the court should adopt the rule that pretrial statements, after they are shown to be relevant, are producible as a matter of right.

The defendant must lay a proper foundation for inspection and take the necessary preliminary steps. *State v. Molinar,* 24 Conn. Supp. 160, 188 A.2d 69 (1962). The defendant's request was denied when he gave no reason for wanting to see the prosecution witness's statement except to state that if there was a statement, he should be allowed to cross-examine the witness. *State v. Salvatore,* 23 Conn. Supp. 459, 184 A.2d 551 (1962).

If the prosecution witness uses a paper, memorandum, or statement to refresh his memory while testifying, the defense has the right, on proper demand, to inspect and use it for cross-examination. *State v. Masse,* 24 Conn. Supp. 45, 186 A.2d 553 (1962).

Connecticut subscribes to the rule that ordinarily the accused is not entitled to production of the state grand jury minutes; it is within the discretion of the trial court. *State v. Hayes,* 127 Conn. 543, 18 A.2d 895 (1941).

When the information charges the offense by its common law or statutory name, or by merely stating so much of the definition of the offense as will give the defendant and the court notice of what offense is charged, but fails to inform the defendant of particulars sufficient to enable him to prepare his defense, or fails to give him information to which he is entitled under the state constitution, the accused has the right to a bill of particulars. However, where the information clearly provides the defendant with the information to which he is entitled, the defendant is not entitled to a bill of particulars as a matter of right. *State v. Summa,* 5 Conn. Cir. Ct. 78, 242 A.2d 94 (1968). A bill of particulars which would amount to a disclosure of the prosecution's evidence will generally not be granted. *State v. Miller,* 24 Conn. Supp. 247, 190 A.2d 55 (1962).

The identity of an informer could not be disclosed in a situation in which the informer told the police of the location of illegal liquor sales. *State v. Jackson,* 4 Conn. Cir. Ct. 125, 226 A.2d 804 (1966). Disclosure cannot be required where the legality of a search without a warrant, whether due to probable cause, consent, or some other factor, is established by evidence apart from the informer's communication. *State v. Penna,* 5 Conn. Cir. Ct. 44, 241 A.2d 385 (1967).

When it appears to the judge that a witness whose evidence will be necessary at trial cannot appear at the trial, the judge may order that the deposition of the witness be taken. The deposition may be used at the trial. CONN. GEN. STAT. ANN. §54–86.

V. SPEEDY TRIAL

The accused in all criminal prosecutions is entitled to a speedy public trial. CONN. CONST. art. 1, §8.

"Speedy trial" means that the state must proceed with the prosecution without undue delay. *State v. Saunders,* 2 Conn. Cir. Ct. 207, 197 A.2d 533 (1964). The defendant's right to a speedy trial is not absolute and unyielding, regardless of the circumstances of the delay. The state's right to effective enforcement of the criminal case requires that an allowance be made for a reasonable accommodation to the pressures and needs of those who are charged with administering the law. *State v. Kelley,* 2 Conn. Cir. Ct. 613, 203 A.2d 613 (1964).

The right to a speedy trial may be waived where the defendant consents to the delay or where both the defense and the prosecution agree upon or stipulate for a postponement. Waiver may be implied where the defendant makes no objection in court to a continuance. *State v. Holloway,* 147 Conn. 22, 156 A.2d 466 (1959).

However, an affirmative showing of prejudice is not necessarily required of a defendant who is claiming undue delay in the bringing of his case to trial. Where the defendant had counsel of his own choice, had been released on bail, and had failed to demand a trial, he was not denied his right to a speedy trial. *State v. Orsini,* 155 Conn. 367, 232 A.2d 907 (1967).

DELAWARE

I. BAIL

All prisoners are bailable by sufficient sureties unless charged with a capital offense when the proof is positive or the presumption great. DEL. CONST. art. 1, §12. The Delaware Code was supplemented in 1968 to reform the bail system in the various courts of the state and to empower the courts to permit a system of personal recognizance or an unsecured personal appearance bond to be used whenever feasible and consistent with a reasonable assurance of appearance and the safety of the community. DEL. CODE ANN. 11 §2101.

A capital crime is not bailable, but if the court, after full inquiry, doubts the truth of the accusation, the prisoner may be bailed. The burden is on the defendant to demonstrate such doubt. DEL. CODE ANN. 11 §2103.

II. PRELIMINARY HEARING

Every person arrested must be brought before a magistrate without unreasonable delay and if possible within 24 hours of the arrest. DEL. CODE ANN. 11 §1911. A justice of the peace must conduct a preliminary hearing if it is not waived. DEL. R. CRIM. P. 5(c). In a capital crime, if the justice finds probable grounds for the accusation, he must bind over the accused to the court having the proper jurisdiction over the offense. If it is not a capital offense, the offense may be bailable until the necessary appearance before the court of jurisdiction. DEL. R. CRIM. P. 5(c). The defendant may cross-examine witnesses and may introduce evidence in his behalf at the preliminary hearing. DEL. R. CRIM. P. 5(c).

III. GRAND JURY, INDICTMENT, INFORMATION

Except in special circumstances, no person charged with an indictable offense may be proceeded against criminally by information. DEL. CONST. art. 1, §8. Where jurisdiction with respect to a misdemeanor has been properly conferred upon the inferior courts, prosecutions for the violations of such misdemeanors may be commenced by the filing of an information if the General Assembly so provides. *State v. Cloud*, 52 Del. 439, 159 A.2d 588 (1960). A defendant may knowingly and in open court waive his right to an indictment in all cases except an offense punishable by death. Where an indictment is so waived, the offense may be prosecuted by information. DEL. R. CRIM. P. 7.

IV. PRETRIAL DISCOVERY

Delaware procedure allows the defendant inspection of any relevant: (1) written or recorded statements or confessions made by the defendant or a co-defendant whether or not charged as a principal, accomplice, or accessory in the same or a different proceeding which are known by the attorney general to be in the control of the state; (2) written reports of autopsies, ballistics tests, fingerprint and handwriting analyses, blood, urine, and breath tests, and written reports of physical or mental examination of the defendant or the alleged victim by a physician, dentist, or psychologist made in connection with the particular case or copies thereof, also within the control of the state; and (3) recorded testimony of the defendant before a grand jury. DEL. R. CRIM. P. 16(a). The court may upon motion also grant inspection of other tangible documents, as well as building or places, upon a showing that the items sought may be material to the preparation of his defense and that the request is reasonable. DEL. R. CRIM. P. 16(b).

If the court grants the defendant's request for inspection, it may condition its order by requiring that the defendant permit the state to inspect any similar documents which are under the control of the defendant. Since discovery is not a right, before the court will exercise its discretion to grant discovery it must be satisfied that the defendant has shown good cause, that the items sought are material, that the imposition of any condition is reasonable, and that the best interests of justice will be served thereby. DEL. R. CRIM. P. 16(c).

Depositions may, upon motion of the defendant, be ordered by the court after the filing of an information and indictment. It must appear that a prospective witness may be unable to attend a trial or hearing, that his testimony is material, and that the deposition is necessary to ensure justice. The party taking the deposition must give every other party reasonable written notice of the time and place the deposition will be taken.

V. SPEEDY TRIAL

In all criminal prosecutions the accused has the right to a speedy and public trial. DEL. CONST. art. 1, §7. If a person is committed for treason or a felony and is not indicted and tried at the next term of the court, he must be released on bail, unless it appears by affidavit that the witnesses for the state, who must be named, are unavailable. If the prisoner is not then indicted and tried at the second term after his commitment, he must be discharged from prison. DEL. CODE ANN. 10, §6910.

The exercise of the court's discretionary powers to stay the proceedings does not violate the constitutional provisions guaranteeing justice without unreasonable delay. *Lanova Corp. v. Atlas Imperial Diesel Engine Co.,* 44 Del. 593, 64 A.2d 419 (Super. Ct. 1949). The right to a speedy trial may be waived by the failure of a person arrested to assert his right at the proper time. In determining waiver the court must consider the activities of both the state and the defendant. *Kominski v. State,* 51 Del. 163, 141 A.2d 138 (1958).

FLORIDA

I. BAIL

Every person charged with a crime or with violation of a municipal or county ordinance is entitled to release on reasonable bail supported by sufficient surety unless he is charged with a capital offense or an offense punishable by life imprisonment and the proof of guilt is evident or the presumption great. FLA. CONST. art. 1, §14 (1968 Revision). After conviction, bail may be granted at the discretion of either the trial or appellate court. If the court refuses to lessen the amount of bail the defendant may institute habeas corpus proceedings seeking reduction of bail. FLA. R. CRIM. P. 1.130(a), (b)(3) (1970).

II. PRELIMINARY HEARING

When the defendant is brought before the magistrate upon arrest, he shall be informed (1) of the charge, (2) of the purpose of a preliminary hearing, (3) of his right to counsel during the preliminary hearing, (4) of his right to waive such hearing, and (5) of his right not to testify and that, if he should testify, anything he says may be used against him in a subsequent proceeding. FLA. R. CRIM. P. 1.122(a). Waiver of a preliminary hearing must be in writing. FLA. R. CRIM. P. 1.122(b)(1). If the preliminary hearing is not waived, the hearing shall be completed in one session unless a postponement is ordered by the judge. FLA. R. CRIM. P. 1.122(e). All witnesses shall be examined in the defendant's presence and may be cross-examined. FLA. R. CRIM. P. 1.122(h). If the prosecuting attorney orders that any of the preliminary hearing be transcribed, a copy shall be furnished free to the defendant. FLA. R. CRIM. P. 1.122(k). If it appears from the evidence that there exists probable cause to believe an offense has been committed and defendant has committed it, the defendant shall be held to answer at trial; if not, the defendant shall be discharged. FLA. R. CRIM. P. 1.122 (1970). The magistrate may for good cause postpone the hearing, but no postponement shall be for more than two days, and the total postponements shall not exceed six days, except for exceptional circumstances; if no postponement is ordered, the hearing shall be completed at one session. FLA. R. CRIM. P. 1.122(e)(1970).

III. GRAND JURY, INDICTMENT, INFORMATION

All offenses triable in criminal court must be prosecuted upon information under oath, to be filed by the prosecuting attorney. The grand jury for the county court may indict for offenses triable in the criminal court. Upon the finding of an indictment the circuit judge shall commit or bail the accused for trial in the criminal court. FLA. CONST. art. 5, §9(5) (1968 Revision).

An offense punishable by death must be prosecuted by indictment. The criminal court of record prosecutes solely by information. Other courts prosecute by indictment, information, and affidavit. FLA. R. CRIM. P. 1. 140 (1970).

The grand jury must inquire into every offense triable within the county for which any person is held to answer if no indictment or information has yet been brought, and into all other indictable offenses presented by the prosecutor or in their knowledge. FLA. STAT. ANN. §905.16 (1971). The judge of any circuit court may dispense with the convening of a grand jury at any term of the court by filing a written order. FLA. STAT. ANN. §905.01 (1971).

IV. PRETRIAL DISCOVERY

Upon defendant's motion, the court shall order the prosecuting attorney to permit defendant to inspect and copy defendant's written or recorded statements or confessions, reports of physical or mental examinations and scientific tests, recorded testimony of defendant before the grand jury, and any designated papers or other tangible things. The defendant may have his own expert present at any test made by the state (e.g., ballistics, fingerprints, blood, semen, etc.). If the court grants defendant discovery under this rule, it shall condition its order by requiring that the defendant permit comparable discovery to the state. Upon motion the court shall also order the prosecution to furnish the names of witnesses on whose evidence the indictment or information is based. The defendant may also be required to furnish the names of his witnesses to the state. FLA. R. CRIM. P. 1.220(a), (b),(c),(e)(1970).

Each party is under a continuing duty to disclose any additional material discovered which he would have had to produce at the time of the previous discovery order. FLA. R. CRIM. P. 1.220(g) (1970).

Defendant is not entitled to discovery of material that is not substantive evidence but is clearly the work product of the prosecuting attorney, or of a transcript of the testimony of a state witness. *State v. McCall,* 186 So. 2d 324 (Fla. App. 1966). The statute, FLA. STAT. ANN. §925.05 (Supp. 1970), does not contemplate a fishing expedition but is instead limited to documents or things which are used as "evidence of the State." *Barton v. State,* 193 So. 2d 618 (Fla. App. 1967). The defendant in a criminal case is not entitled to inspect, either before or during the trial, statements of a prosecution witness which were taken by an officer in preparation for the trial, whether or not such statements are sought for the purpose of cross-examination or impeachment. *Adjmi v. State,* 208 So. 2d 859 (Fla. App. 1968).

The defendant is not entitled to examine prior statements of a witness even after the witness has testified on direct examination at the trial. *Colebrook v. State,* 205 So. 2d 675 (Fla. App. 1968). If the prosecution witness's statement is used by the prosecution at the trial, the defendant is entitled to inspection for purposes of cross-examination and impeachment. *Jackman v. State,* 140 So. 2d 627 (Fla. App. 1962).

The accused is not entitled to disclosure of the minutes of the proceedings of the state grand jury. Disclosure of testimony before the grand jury is prohibited by statute except when it is required by the court to determine whether it is consistent with that given by the witness before the court, or to disclose the testimony of one charged with perjury, or when permitted by the court in the furtherance of justice. FLA. STAT. ANN. §905.27 (Supp. 1970). Granting or denying the defendant's request for the grand jury minutes is within the trial court's discretion.

The accused cannot require a bill of particulars if the specifications asked for are within his knowledge or are readily accessible to him. *Tavalaccio v. State,* 59 So. 2d 247 (Fla. App. 1963). A bill of particulars which if furnished would amount to disclosure of the prosecution's evidence will generally not be granted. *Peel v. State,* 154 So. 2d 910 (Fla. App. 1963).

The prosecution is privileged to withhold disclosure of the identity of an informer from the accused. *Decca v. State,* 186 So. 2d 92 (Fla. App. 1966); *Pearson v. State,* 221 So. 2d 760 (Fla. App. 1969). The burden is upon the defendant to show why an exception should be made.

The court has recognized that the right to interview persons having knowledge of the case ordinarily accrues to the defendant. The right is not absolute but is subject to the trial court's discretion. *Baker v. State,* 47 So. 2d 728 (Fla. 1950).

Upon the written demand of the prosecuting attorney, specifying insofar as is known to the prosecuting attorney the place, date, and time of the commission of the crime, the defendant must furnish notice of his intention to claim an alibi, containing specific information as to the place at which the defendant claims to have been at the time of the alleged offense, and, as completely as known to the defendant or his attorney, the names and addresses of the witnesses by whom he proposes to establish such an alibi. The prosecuting attorney must in turn provide the defendant with the names and addresses of the witnesses the state proposes to offer in rebuttal to discredit the defendant's alibi at the trial. Both parties are under a continuing duty to disclose promptly the names and addresses of additional witnesses. If either party fails to disclose either the name or address, the evidence of that party may be excluded at the trial. FLA. R. CRIM. P. 1.200 (1970).

The defendant must also provide notice of his intention to rely upon the defense of insanity, and must file a bill of particulars showing as nearly as he can the nature of the insanity he expects to prove and the names of the witnesses by whom he expects to prove such insanity. The court may require that the defendant be examined by one or more disinterested qualified experts, not exceeding three, in the presence of attorneys for the state and the defendant. Upon good cause shown for the omission of the notice and procedure as to the defense of insanity, the court may in its discretion permit the introduction of the evidence.

V. SPEEDY TRIAL

In all criminal prosecutions the accused is entitled upon demand to have a speedy and public trial. FLA. CONST. art. 1, §16. Every person charged with a felony, noncapital or capital, must be brought to trial without demand within 180 days of the crime charged, and if he is not brought to trial within such time he shall upon motion timely filed be forever discharged from the crime provided that such person has been continuously available for trial during such period of time for trial. The time periods established shall commence when such person is taken into custody as a result of the conduct giving rise to the crime charged. FLA. R. CRIM. P. 1.191(a)(1).

A person charged with a crime shall upon demand filed with the court be brought to trial within 60 days, unless the state is granted a continuance because of exceptional circumstances, and if not brought to trial within such period of time following such demand shall upon motion timely filed with the court be forever discharged from the crime, provided that such person has been continuously available for trial during said period of time. The time period established shall commence when such demand has been properly filed and served. FLA. R. CRIM. P. 1.191(a)(2).

The court may order an extension of time or continuance where exceptional circumstances are shown to exist; exceptional circumstances shall not include general congestion of the court's docket, lack of diligent preparation or failure to obtain available witnesses, or other avoidable or foreseeable delays. FLA. R. CRIM. P. 1.191(f).

GEORGIA

I. BAIL

Excessive bail is not allowed. GA. CONST. art. 1, §2–109. Capital offenses are bailable only before a judge of the superior court; this in every case is a matter of discretion. All other offenses are bailable by the committing court. GA. CODE ANN. §27–901. After indictment, no person can be made to give bail more than twice before trial for the same offense. GA. CODE ANN. §27–903. Any judge having jurisdiction over a person charged with committing an offense against the criminal laws of the state may in his discretion authorize the release of such person on his own recognizance.

II. Preliminary Hearing

A court of inquiry is held to determine the existence of probable cause which, if found, would require the accused to appear before the court competent to try him. GA. CODE ANN. §27–407. Courts of inquiry may be held by any superior or county court judge or by a justice of the peace, or even a town official acting as a justice of the peace. GA. CODE ANN. §27–401. If possible, the accused must be afforded counsel. GA. CODE ANN. §27–403. The commitment hearing may be waived by the defendant only if the decision to waive is a knowledgeable one and free of duress.

III. Grand Jury, Indictment, Information

In all misdemeanor cases and in noncapital felonies in which defendants have been bound over to the superior court or are confined in jail pending commitment trial, or are in jail, having waived commitment trial, the prosecution may prefer accusations. Defendants shall be tried on these accusations provided they have in writing waived indictment by a grand jury. Superior court judges may, without grand jury action, receive and act upon pleas of guilty in misdemeanors and in felony cases not punishable by death or life imprisonment. With the consent of both the judge and the accused, the judge may try issues without a jury. In such cases, counsel must be present in court to defend the accused. GA. CODE ANN. §27–704.

IV. Pretrial Discovery

The accused is not entitled to inspect evidence which is in the possession of the prosecution. Thus, the defendant's request to examine, before trial, statements of witnesses, written reports in the prosecution's possession, and the clothing of the murder victim was denied, the court noting that there was no rule of procedure or statute requiring the prosecution to make his evidence available before trial. *Blevins v. State,* 220 Ga. 720, 141 S.E.2d 426 (1965); *Bryan v. State,* 224 Ga. 389, 162 S.E.2d 349 (1968). However, the defendant is entitled to inspection of a writing or object in the possession of the prosecution when it is offered in evidence at the trial. *Walker v. State,* 215 Ga. 128, 109 S.E.2d 748 (1959).

It was held to be error for the trial court to deny defense counsel the right to interview the only eyewitness to a murder, who was being held incommunicado in jail, since it denied the defendant a fair and impartial trial and the full benefit of counsel. *Wilson v. State,* 93 Ga. App. 229, 91 S.E.2d 201 (1956).

V. Speedy Trial

All persons charged with an offense against the laws of the state must have a public and speedy trial by an impartial jury. GA. CONST. art. 1,

§2–105. The accused may make a demand for trial. If the defendant is not tried within the term of court in which he was indicted or the next succeeding regular term, provided there were juries available at both terms to try him, he must be completely discharged. GA. CODE ANN. §27–1901.

Although an accused was tried ten years after the indictment, there was no unconstitutional denial of the defendant's right to a speedy trial where the defendant was incarcerated in another state during the interval, where the defendant made no demand for a speedy trial, where he made no complaint until after his conviction, and where there was no allegation of purposeful delay on the part of the state. *Malcolm v. State,* 225 Ga. 470, 169 S.E.2d 779 (1969).

HAWAII

I. BAIL

All persons charged with a criminal offense must be bailable by sufficient sureties unless the offense is punishable by imprisonment for life without parole, when the proof is evident and the presumption great. HAWAII REV. STAT. 37, §709–3. If the offense is not for imprisonment for life without parole, the defendant may be admitted to bail before conviction as a matter of right and is entitled to bail after conviction while appealing the decision if the sentence is for less than 20 years. Except in cases of imprisonment for life without parole and imprisonment for 20 years or more it is in the discretion of the trial court to admit the defendant to bail after conviction. HAWAII REV. STAT. 37, §709–4. Excessive bail cannot be required. The court may dispense with bail if it is reasonably satisfied that the defendant will appear when directed, unless the defendant is charged with an offense punishable by life imprisonment. HAWAII CONST. art. 1, §9.

In cases where the punishment for the offense charged may be imprisonment for life without parole, or for a term of more than ten years with or without a fine, only a judge or justice of a court of record is competent to admit the accused to bail. HAWAII REV. STAT. 37, §709–5. Where the offense is the illegal infliction of a wound, or any other injury which may terminate in the death of the person injured, the prisoner cannot be released if it appears probable that death will result from the injury. HAWAII REV. STAT. 37, §709–8.

The amount of bail is discretionary with the judge or justice, but it should be determined so as not to enable the wealthy to avoid punishment of a pecuniary penalty, nor to render the privilege useless to the poor. The officer should consider the financial circumstances of the accused. HAWAII REV. STAT. 37, §709–9.

II. PRELIMINARY HEARING

The magistrate of the district court may try cases if the punishment for the offense is limited to a fine and/or imprisonment of one year. If the accused is entitled to, and requests, trial by jury, the magistrate must examine and either discharge the accused or commit him for trial. HAWAII REV. STAT. 32, §604–8.

If a case must be tried in the first instance before a jury or if it can be tried only on a grand jury indictment, the magistrate of the jurisdiction or the magistrate who issued the arrest warrant must consider whether there is probable cause to believe the accused guilty of the crime charged. If he finds probable cause for guilt, he delivers a mittimus and binds the accused over for a circuit court trial. HAWAII REV. STAT. 37, §710–1.

III. GRAND JURY, INDICTMENT, INFORMATION

All capital or otherwise infamous crimes must be prosecuted on a presentment or indictment of a grand jury. HAWAII CONST. art. 1, §8. In criminal cases which are brought in the first instance in a court of record, but in which a grand jury indictment is not required, the prosecutor may arraign and prosecute the accused upon either an indictment or information. He may prosecute by indictment or information whether or not there has been a previous examination or commitment for trial by a judge or magistrate. HAWAII REV. STAT. 37, §711–8.

IV. PRETRIAL DISCOVERY

The defendant's request to see a copy of his confession during a voir dire examination of a witness-detective's testimony regarding the circumstances surrounding the taking of such defendant's statements to determine the voluntariness of the confession was denied because the contents of the confession were not material to the issue of voluntariness. *State v. Hashimoto,* 46 Hawaii 183, 377 P.2d 728 (1962).

The prosecution is privileged to withhold from the accused disclosure of the identity of an informer. To compel disclosure, the defendant must establish that his right to a fair trial or his constitutional rights have been prejudiced. *State v. Texeira,* 50 Hawaii 138, 433 P.2d 593 (1967).

The accused is entitled to inspection of all depositions taken against him. HAWAII REV. STAT. 37, §711–67.

V. SPEEDY TRIAL

The accused in all criminal prosecutions is entitled to a speedy and public trial. HAWAII CONST. art. 1, §11. No person can be prosecuted for any offense under the laws of the state, with certain exceptions, unless the prosecution is commenced within two years of the commission of the offense. HAWAII REV. STAT. 37, §707–1. The rights of the defendant against a delay in the prosecution, as protected by the criminal rules, are personal to the defendant and may be waived if they are not properly asserted. *State v. Wong,* 47 Hawaii 361, 389 P.2d 439 (1964). HAWAII R. CRIM. P. 48(b).

IDAHO

I. BAIL

All persons are bailable by sufficient sureties except where the charge is a capital offense where the proof is evident or the presumption great. Excessive bail cannot be required. IDAHO CONST. art. 1, §6. Admission to bail is defined as the order of a competent court or magistrate that the defendant be discharged from actual custody upon bail. IDAHO CODE ANN. §19–2901. After the defendant has been admitted to bail upon an indictment, the court may, upon good cause, either increase or reduce the amount of bail. IDAHO CODE ANN. §19–2918.

II. PRELIMINARY HEARING

The accused must be taken before a magistrate without unnecessary delay. IDAHO CODE ANN. §19–515. A preliminary examination is required unless the defendant waives it. IDAHO CODE ANN. §19–514 (Cum. Supp. 1969). Upon the defendant's request, he has a right to counsel. IDAHO CODE ANN. §19–515.

The magistrate determines at the preliminary examination whether there is probable cause to hold the defendant. IDAHO CODE ANN. §19–804 (Cum. Supp. 1969). The examination is conducted in one session unless it is continued for good cause. IDAHO CODE ANN. §19–804 (Cum. Supp. 1969). Upon the request of either party, the magistrate issues subpoenas for witnesses for both parties. IDAHO CODE ANN. §19–807 (Cum. Supp. 1969). The witnesses for the state must be examined under oath in the presence of the defendant and may be cross-examined in his behalf. IDAHO CODE ANN. §19–808 (Cum. Supp. 1969). When the state's witnesses have been examined, the defendant may produce any material witnesses who must be examined and cross-examined in the defendant's presence. IDAHO CODE ANN. §19–809 (Cum. Supp. 1969).

III. GRAND JURY, INDICTMENT, INFORMATION

No person may be held to answer for any criminal offense unless on presentment or indictment of a grand jury or an information of the public prosecutor after a commitment by a magistrate. After a charge has been ignored by a grand jury, no one can be held upon information of the public prosecutor. IDAHO CONST. art. 1, §8. The courts of the state have jurisdiction to hear cases upon information as they do in like prosecutions upon indictments. IDAHO CODE ANN. §19–1301.

The grand jury must inquire into all public offenses committed or triable within the county and present them to the court by presentment or indictment. IDAHO CODE ANN. §19–1101. The grand jury may present or indict without preliminary hearing, arrest, or commitment of the accused. *State v. Taylor,* 59 Idaho 724, 87 P.2d 454 (1939). Informations are of equal dignity with indictments, subject only to constitutional limitation. *In re Winn,* 28 Idaho 461, 154 P. 497 (1916).

IV. PRETRIAL DISCOVERY

The courts have discretion to order or deny inspection of evidence in the possession of the prosecution. The trial court did not abuse its discretion in refusing the disclosure of statements and admissions of certain witnesses, a pistol, a jacket, a watch, and money taken from the victim where the defendant convicted of robbery and kidnapping failed to allege any substantial prejudice resulting from the failure to grant such discovery. *State v. Oldham,* 92 Idaho 124, 438 P.2d 275 (1968).

The defendant has the statutory right to inspect a statement made by or under the direction of a witness and used by him to refresh his memory. IDAHO CODE ANN. §9–1204. Denial of the defendant's request to examine notes made by an officer at the time of and shortly after the defendant's arrest and referred to by the officer during the course of his testimony was "patently erroneous" under the statute, although in this case the error was harmless. *State v. Johnson,* 92 Idaho 533, 447 P.2d 10 (1968).

A defendant may have witnesses examined conditionally on his behalf. IDAHO CODE ANN. §19–3101. When a material witness for defendant is about to leave the state, or may for reasons of health be unable to attend trial, defendant may apply for an order that the witness be examined conditionally. IDAHO CODE ANN. §19–3102.

V. SPEEDY TRIAL

The accused in all criminal prosecutions has the right to a speedy and public trial. IDAHO CONST. art. 1, §13; IDAHO CODE ANN. §19–106. The defendant is entitled to a discharge where the indictment is not found against him at the next term of the court, or when he is not brought to trial at the next term. IDAHO CODE ANN. §19–3501. When a complaint is filed against a person, he becomes the accused and is then guaranteed the right to a speedy trial. *Jacobson v. Winter,* 91 Idaho 11, 415 P.2d 297 (1966).

ILLINOIS

I. BAIL

All persons are bailable by sufficient sureties except on capital offenses where the proof is evident or the presumption great. ILL. CONST. art. 1, §9. When from all the circumstances the court is of the opinion that the accused will appear as required, the accused may be released on his own recognizance. There are criminal sanctions rather than fines for failure to appear. ILL. ANN. STAT. ch. 38, §110–2 (Smith-Hurd 1970).

The amount of bail must be (1) sufficient to assure compliance with the conditions set forth in the bail bond, (2) not oppressive, (3) commensurate with the nature of the offense charged, (4) considerate of the past criminal acts and conduct of the defendant, and (5) considerate of the financial ability of the accused. When a person has been convicted and only a fine has been imposed, the amount of bail shall not exceed twice that fine. ILL. ANN. STAT. ch. 38, §110–5 (Smith-Hurd 1970). The amount of bail may be reduced and contested. ILL. ANN. STAT. ch. 38, §110–6 (Smith-Hurd 1970).

A person for whom bail has been set shall execute the bail bond and deposit with the clerk of the court a sum equal to 10 percent of the bail. When the conditions of the bail bond have been performed and the accused has been discharged from all obligations, the clerk of the court shall return to the accused, unless the court orders otherwise, 90 percent of the sum which was originally deposited and shall retain the remaining 10 percent to cover administrative costs. ILL. ANN. STAT. ch. 38, §110–7 (Smith-Hurd 1970).

II. PRELIMINARY HEARING

The purpose of the preliminary examination is to determine if there is probable cause to hold the accused for trial, to inform him of the charges against him, to fix bail, and to perpetuate testimony. Committee Comments, ILL. ANN. STAT. ch. 38, §109–3 at 294 (Smith-Hurd 1970).

A person arrested with or without a warrant must be taken without any unnecessary delay before the nearest or most accessible judge in the county. At the preliminary appearance the judge must (1) advise the accused of the charge(s) against him, and advise him of his right to counsel, who is appointed if the accused is indigent, (2) hold the hearing if the judge is without jurisdiction to try the case, and (3) tell the defendant of his bail rights. ILL. ANN. STAT. ch. 38, §109–1(b)(Smith-Hurd 1970).

If there is probable cause to believe that the accused has committed an offense, he must be held to answer. The accused may waive the preliminary hearing and will then be held to answer unless the prosecutor or the judge asks for an examination of the state witnesses. If after this testimony probable cause is not established, the accused must be discharged even though he waived the preliminary examination. ILL. ANN. STAT. ch. 39, §109–3 (Smith-Hurd 1970).

III. GRAND JURY, INDICTMENT, INFORMATION

No person shall be held to answer for a crime punishable by death or imprisonment unless the initial charge was brought by indictment of a grand jury or the accused has received a prompt preliminary hearing to determine probable cause. ILL. CONST. art. 1, §7.

Any waiver of indictment must be in open court and will not be permitted by one accused of a crime punishable by imprisonment in the penitentiary unless he is represented by counsel or has waived counsel. Waiver will be valid if the court, addressing the defendant personally in open court, has informed him and determined that he understands the following: (1) the nature of the charge; (2) the minimum and maximum sentences including, when applicable, the penalty to which the defendant may be subjected because of prior convictions or consecutive sentences; and (3) that he can be prosecuted for the offense only after indictment by a grand jury unless he waives indictment. If the state expressly concurs in the waiver in open court, prosecution may then proceed by either waiver or complaint. ILL. ANN. STAT. ch. 110A, §401 (Smith-Hurd 1970).

IV. PRETRIAL DISCOVERY

Except as otherwise provided the state shall, upon written motion of defense counsel, disclose to defense counsel the names and last known addresses of persons whom the state intends to call as witnesses, together with their relevant written or recorded statements, memoranda containing substantially verbatim reports of their oral statements, and a list of memoranda reporting or summarizing their oral statements. ILL. R. CRIM. P. 412(a)(i)(1971). In addition, the state must also disclose any written or recorded statements and the substance of any oral statements made by the accused or by a co-defendant, and a list of witnesses to the making and acknowledgment of such statements; a transcript of those portions of grand jury minutes containing testimony of the accused and relevant testimony of persons whom the prosecuting attorney intends to call as witnesses at the hearing or trial; any reports or statements of experts, made in connection with the particular case, including results of physical or mental examinations and of scientific tests, experiments, or comparisons; any books, papers, documents, photographs, or tangible objects which the prosecuting attorney intends to use in the hearing or trial or which were obtained from or belong to the accused; and any record of prior criminal convictions which may be used for impeachment of persons whom the state intends to call as witnesses at the hearing or trial. ILL. R. CRIM. P. 412(a)(ii),(iii),(iv),(v), (vi)(1971).

The state shall also inform defense counsel if there has been any electronic surveillance (including wiretapping) of conversations to which the accused was a party, or of his premises. ILL. R. CRIM. P. 412(b)(1971).

Except as otherwise provided in these rules, the state shall disclose to defense counsel any material or information within its possession or control which tends to negate the guilt of the accused as to the offense charged or would tend to reduce his punishment therefor. ILL. R. CRIM. P. 412(c)(1971).

The work product is not subject to disclosure, nor is an informant's identity where the failure to do so would not infringe upon the constitutional rights of the accused. ILL. R. CRIM. P. 412 (j)(i), (ii)(1971). Disclosure also will not be required where it involves a substantial risk of grave prejudice to national security and where a failure to disclose would not infringe upon the constitutional rights of the accused. ILL. R. CRIM. P. 412(j)(iii)(1971).

Subject to constitutional limitations, a judicial officer may require the accused, among other things, to appear in a lineup; speak for identification by witnesses to an offense; be fingerprinted; pose for photographs not involving reenactment of a scene; try on articles of clothing; permit the taking of specimens of material under his fingernails; permit the taking of samples of his blood, hair, and other materials of his body which involves no unreasonable intrusion thereof; provide a sample of his handwriting; and submit to a reasonable physical or medical inspection of his body. ILL. R. CRIM. P. 413(a)(1971).

If, subsequent to compliance with these rules, a party discovers additional material or information which is subject to disclosure, he shall promptly notify the other party or his counsel of the existence of such additional material, and if the additional material or information is discovered during trial, the court shall also be notified. ILL. R. CRIM. P. 415(b)(1971).

If it appears to the court in which a criminal charge is pending that the deposition of any other person other than the defendant is necessary for the preservation of relevant testimony because of the substantial possibility it would be unavailable at the time of hearing or trial, the court may, upon motion and notice to both parties and their counsel, order the taking of such person's deposition under oral examination or written questions for use as evidence at a hearing or trial. ILL. R. CRIM. P. 414(a)(1971).

V. Speedy Trial

The accused in all criminal prosecutions has the right to a speedy and public trial. ILL. CONST. art. 1, §8 (1970). If the defendant is held on custody for 120 days without being tried or if the defendant is on bail for 160 days without being tried, and the defendant has demanded a trial, then the charges must be dismissed. However, if the state can show good cause and due diligence in securing material evidence, the court may then grant an extra 60 days to bring the defendant to trial. ILL. ANN. STAT. ch. 38, §103–5 (Smith-Hurd 1970).

Every person not tried in accordance with these provisions shall be discharged from custody or released from the obligations of his bail or recognizance. ILL. ANN. STAT. ch. 38, §103–5(c) (Smith-Hurd 1970).

The constitutional safeguards concerning a speedy trial protect only against arbitrary and oppressive delays. *People v. Nowak,* 45 Ill. 2d 158, 258 N.E.2d 313 (1970). If the defendant is tried within 120 days of his demand for trial, he has not been deprived of his right to a speedy trial. *People v. Baskin,* 38 Ill. 2d 141, 230 N.E.2d 208 (1967). The right to a speedy trial means the right to have speedily heard the charge on which the accused is detained. *People v. Nettles,* 107 Ill. App. 2d 143, 246 N.E.2d 29 (1969). The state, as well as the accused, has a right to a speedy and impartial trial. *People v. Goodrich,* 73 Ill. App. 2d 196, 218 N.E.2d 794 (1966).

Where the defendant requested a continuance and one was granted, he was not denied a speedy trial even though it took place more than 120 days after his arrest. *People v. Rice.* 122 Ill. App. 2d 329, 258 N.E.2d 841 (1970). The right to a speedy trial under this section is waived when the question of undue delay is not presented to the trial court. *People v. Worley,* 45 Ill. 2d 96, 256 N.E.2d 751 (1970).

INDIANA

1. Bail

Offenses other than murder or treason shall be bailable by sufficient sureties. Murder or treason is not bailable when the proof is evident or the presumption strong. IND. CONST. art. 1, §17. Excessive bail cannot be required. IND. CONST. art. 1, §16. The court must fix bail in a reasonable amount considering the nature of the offense and the penalty adjudged. IND. ANN. STAT. §9–2315 (1956). The court will look to the financial ability of the defendant to provide the required amount as well as to the purpose of bail. *Hobbs v. Lindsey,* 240 Ind. 74, 162 N.E.2d 85 (1959).

II. Preliminary Hearing

An arrested accused must be taken before the nearest magistrate, who will immediately docket the cause, hear the cause, and either acquit, convict, or punish or hold for bail as the case may be, unless the offense is not bailable, in which case the defendant may be committed to jail. IND. ANN. STAT. §9–704 (1956). An arrested person who is reasonably believed to have committed a felony may offer an alibi. If the arresting officer still believes that the accused is guilty, an additional pleading and procedure is created, the preliminary charge. Any person so detained must be immediately taken before a magistrate or judge and is entitled to a hearing on the preliminary charge. At this hearing the facts of the felony are presented to the accused, and he is informed of his right to counsel. The court then rules on discharge or commitment. IND. ANN. STAT. §9–704(a)(1956).

III. Grand Jury, Indictment, Information

All public offenses except treason and murder may be prosecuted in the circuit or criminal court by an affidavit filed in term time, except where a prosecution by indictment for the same offense is already pending. IND. ANN. STAT. §9–908 (1956). The grand jury must meet at least once each year in each county. IND. ANN. STAT. §9–803 (1956).

IV. Pretrial Discovery

The accused has no right to inspect evidence in the possession of the prosecution. Where the defendant moved during trial for production of police reports of statements made by prosecuting witnesses, the request was denied on the ground that the defendant's right to a fair trial does not include the right to inspect statements and reports in the prosecution's working files. If they had been part of the public record, the defendant could inspect. *Anderson v. State,* 239 Ind. 372, 156 N.E.2d 384 (1959); *see also Brown v. State,* 241 Ind. 14, 158 N.E.2d 290 (1959).

The judge or court may allow discovery by either party of books, papers, or documents in the possession or control of the other party. IND. ANN. STAT. §9–2407 (1956); IND. R. TRIAL PROC. 34 (A)(1)(Special Supp. 1970). Right to production under the statute is not absolute and is addressed to the court's discretion. *Weer v. State,* 219 Ind. 217, 36 N.E.2d 787, *rehearing denied,* 219 Ind. 229, 37 N.E.2d 537 (1941).

The defendant is not entitled to production, for purposes of cross-examination or impeachment, of prior statements made by a witness even after the witness has testified at the trial. If there is no showing of inconsistency between the contents of the statement and the witness's testimony at the trial, production of the statement is denied. *Anderson v. State,* 239 Ind. 372,

156 N.E.2d 384 (1958); *Brown v. State,* 241 Ind. 14, 158 N.E.2d (1959).

Unless the prosecutor can show a paramount interest in nondisclosure, pretrial statements made by a prosecution witness to either the grand jury or the law enforcement agents of the state are discoverable by the defense. *Antrobus v. State,* 254 N.E.2d 873 (1970). Those statements have as much possibility of being useful for purposes of impeaching the credibility of a witness and should not be treated differently than any other pretrial statement. *Antrobus v. State, supra.* The accused is not entitled to inspection of his own testimony before the grand jury, absent a showing that such testimony is material in preparing his defense. *Porter v. State,* 173 Ind. 694, 91 N.E. 340 (1910).

The defendant must give notice of his intention to use an alibi as a defense not less than ten days before trial. The notice must include specific information regarding the exact place at which the defendant claims to have been at the time stated in the indictment or information as the time of the offense. IND. ANN. STAT. §9–1631 (1956). The defendant may require the prosecution to provide a specific statement of the exact date and place the prosecution proposes to present at the trial as the date and place where the defendant was alleged to have committed or participated in the offense. If the date given by the defendant and that of the prosecution are not the same, the defendant shall, not later than four days after the prosecutor's notice, serve upon the prosecutor defendant's second notice presenting such changed date. IND. ANN. STAT. §9–1632 (1956). In the absence of a showing of good cause for a failure to file notice by either party, the judge may exclude the party's evidence. IND. ANN. STAT. §9–1633 (1956).

The defendant or his counsel must in writing set up a defense of unsound mind at the time the offense charged was committed. The prosecuting attorney may reply by a general denial in writing. IND. ANN. STAT. §9–1701 (1956).

V. SPEEDY TRIAL

The accused in all criminal prosecutions has the right to a public trial. IND. CONST. art. 1, §13. All courts must be open, and every man have a remedy by due course of law; justice must be administered freely and without denial, speedily and without delay. IND. CONST. art. 1, §12.

A defendant cannot be detained in jail on a charge, without a trial, for a continuous period of more than six months from the date the charge was filed against him, or from the date of his arrest, whichever is later, except where a continuance on his motion was granted, or the delay was caused by his act, or where there was insufficient time to try him during such period because of congestion of the court calendar; provided, however, that in the last mentioned circumstance, the prosecuting attorney shall make such statement in a motion for continuance not later than ten days prior to the date set for trial, or if such motion is filed less than ten days prior to trial, the prosecuting attorney shall show additionally that the delay in filing the motion was not the fault of the prosecutor. IND. R. CRIM. P. 4(A) (1970).

If any defendant held in jail on an indictment or an affidavit shall move for an early trial, he shall be discharged if not brought to trial within 50 judicial days from the date of such motion, except where a continuance within said period is had on his motion, or the delay is otherwise caused by his act, or where there was not sufficient time to try him during such 50 judicial days because of the congestion of the court calendar, provided, however, that in the last mentioned circumstance, the prosecuting attorney shall file a timely motion for continuance as under subdivision (A) of this rule. IND. R. CRIM. P. 4(B) (1970).

No person shall be held by recognizance to answer an indictment or affidavit, without trial, for a period embracing more than one year continuously from the date on which a recognizance was first taken therein; but he shall be discharged except as provided by subdivision (A) of this rule. IND. R. CRIM. P. 4(C) (1970).

If application is made for discharge of a defendant under this rule but the court is satisfied that there is evidence for the state which cannot then be had, that reasonable efforts have been made to procure such evidence, and there is just ground to believe that this evidence can be obtained within 90 days, the cause may be continued, and the prisoner remanded or admitted to bail; and if he is then not brought to trial within this additional 90 days, he shall be discharged. IND. R. CRIM. P. 4(D) (1970).

The constitutional right to a trial without delay is a right of equal importance to that of trial by jury; if one of these rights may be waived, so may the other. Where the defendant participated in the trial without objecting to the delay, he waived his rights under the statute. *Randolph v. State,* 234 Ind. 57, 122 N.E.2d 860 (1954). Neither the constitutional article nor the statute is self-executing. While it is true that there is no burden upon the defendant to request a speedy trial, if the terms of the court go by and he is, through no fault of his own, not brought to trial, the burden of invoking the statute falls upon him, and his right thereunder can only be asserted by affirmative action on his part. *Randolph v. State, supra.*

IOWA

I. BAIL

All persons are bailable before conviction by sufficient sureties, except for capital offenses where the proof is evident or the presumption great. IOWA CONST. art. 1, §12. Excessive bail cannot be required. IOWA CONST. art. 1, §17. No defendant convicted of first degree murder or of treason may be admitted to bail. IOWA CODE ANN. §763.2 (1950).

In determining which conditions of release will reasonably assure appearance, the magistrate on the basis of available information may take into account the nature and circumstances of the offense charged, the defendant's family ties, employment, financial resources, character, and mental condition, length of residence in the community, record of convictions, and record of appearance at court proceedings or of flight to avoid prosecution or of failure to appear at court proceedings. IOWA CODE ANN. §763.16 (1950). The defendant must be informed by the judge of the penalties for violation, and may appeal from the conditions of release. IOWA CODE ANN. §§763.16 and 763.17 (1950).

II. PRELIMINARY EXAMINATION

When an accused is brought before a magistrate upon preliminary information, he must be informed immediately of his right to counsel and of his right to waive the examination. The proceedings may be adjourned to give the accused an opportunity to obtain counsel. A waiver does not deprive the accused of a later plea on habeas corpus to show that he is not detained on sufficient evidence to sustain the charge. IOWA CODE ANN. §761.1 (1950). The examination should be terminated in one session and may be adjourned by the magistrate only for good cause. IOWA CODE ANN. §761.4 (1950).

Upon the request of the defendant, the magistrate must grant a private hearing. IOWA CODE ANN. §761.13 (1950). After hearing the testimony at the preliminary hearing, the magistrate must decide whether a public offense has been committed. If sufficient cause exists to believe the accused guilty, the magistrate must commit the defendant to answer for the crime. IOWA CODE ANN. §761.17 (1950).

III. GRAND JURY, INDICTMENT, INFORMATION

All nonfelonies for which the punishment does not exceed a fine of $100, or imprisonment for 30 days, are tried summarily before an officer authorized by law, on information under oath, without indictment or the intervention of a grand jury. The defendant has the right of appeal. No one can be held to answer for a more serious offense except on presentment or indictment by a grand jury. IOWA CONST. art. 1, §11. This constitutional provision has been enlarged by statute, and the defendant may now be prosecuted either upon indictment or information for more serious offenses; the district and supreme courts have now the same power over offenses tried by information as they did for similar prosecutions tried by indictment. IOWA COE ANN. §769.1 (1950). The standard for what is chargeable by the county attorney's information is now controlled by the standard for indictment. If under the Iowa Constitution and Code there can be no indictment there can also be no information. *State v. Wyatt,* 207 Iowa 322, 222 N.W. 867 (1929). Any time that the grand jury is not actually in session, the county attorney may charge an indictable offense by filing an information. IOWA CODE ANN. §769.2 (1950).

IV. PRETRIAL DISCOVERY

The defendant has no right to ask for disclosure of the prosecution's evidence merely in the hope that something may turn up to help him. *State v. Kelly,* 249 Iowa 1219, 91 N.W.2d 562 (1958); *State v. Stump,* 254 Iowa 1181, 119 N.W.2d 210, *cert. denied,* 375 U. S. 853 (1963).

The defendant is not entitled to unrestricted examination of the police records; however, the court has held that the trial judge should have determined in the presence of the county attorney and defense counsel whether there was anything relevant to the issue of entrapment on tapes of police radio calls. If so, they should have been made available to the defendant. *State v. White,* 260 Iowa 1000, 151 N.W.2d 552 (1967).

A defendant charged with intoxication while driving a motor vehicle is entitled to the results of a chemical test but cannot have access to the work sheets or fluid sample used in the test. *State v. Johnson,* 259 Iowa 599, 145 N.W.2d 8 (1966); *see also State v. Dist. Ct. of Delaware County,* 253 Iowa 903, 114 N.W.2d 317 (1962).

Whether to grant or deny the defendant the right to inspection of a statement used by a witness while on the stand to refresh his memory is within the trial court's discretion. *State v. Hodge,* 252 Iowa 449, 105 N.W.2d 613, *cert. denied,* 368 U. S. 402 (1960). The court denied the defendant's request for pretrial inspection of a prosecution witness's statement, notwithstanding the defendant's contention that without such information he could not adequately cross-examine witnesses. *State v. Tharp,* 258 Iowa 224, 138 N.W.2d 78 (1965).

The court held that during a trial in which the prosecution had used parts of the grand jury minutes in connection with his examination of the defendant or witnesses, the defense was not entitled to inspect or use the minutes. The minutes were neither offered into evidence nor shown to the witnesses. *State v. Williams,* 197 Iowa 813, 197 N.W. 991 (1924). The court has held, however, that the trial court has the power to require the prosecution to permit the defense to inspect any and all exhibits used before the grand jury and intended to be offered at the trial. *State v. Burris,* 198 Iowa 1156, 198 N.W. 82 (1924).

Where a crime is charged by its statutory name, the defendant is entitled to a bill of particulars. *State v. Schuling,* 216 Iowa 1425, 250 N.W. 588 (1933). The defendant does not have an absolute right to a bill of particulars if a short form of indictment is used. *State v. Powers,* 239 Iowa 430, 30 N.W.2d 476 (1948). Where there is no request for a bill of particulars, there is no abuse of discretion in the failure of the trial court to order one on its own motion. *State v. Berenger,* 161 N.W.2d 798 (Iowa 1968).

If the defendant pleads not guilty and plans to use insanity or an alibi as a defense, he must file written notice no later than four days before the trial, setting forth the names, addresses, and occupations of the witnesses and a statement of what the defendant expects to prove by the testimony of each witness. IOWA CODE ANN. §777.18 (1950).

A defendant may examine witnesses conditionally or on notice or commission. IOWA CODE ANN. §781.10 (1950). The deponent or party need not produce any writing which reflects an attorney's impressions, conclusions, or opinions. The court may determine that certain matters will not be inquired into, may decide the scope of the examination as well as who may be present. IOWA R. CIV. P. 141 (Supp. 1971).

V. SPEEDY TRIAL

In all criminal prosecutions the accused has the right to a speedy trial. IOWA CONST. art. 1, §10. The accused must be tried within 60 days after the indictment unless good cause is shown. IOWA CODE ANN. §795.2 (1950). If an indictment is not filed against a person held to answer for a public offense at the next regular term of the court or within 30 days, the prosecution must be dismissed. IOWA CODE ANN. §795.1 (1950). If the acts or omissions of the accused are the cause of or a contributing factor in the delay which passes the trial over the second or subsequent term, the defendant is not entitled to a dismissal. Such acts or a failure to act may give rise to an agreed postponement, or to a waiver of the provisions of the state and federal constitution. *McCandless v. Dist. Ct. of Polk City,* 245 Iowa 599, 61 N.W.2d 674 (1954).

KANSAS

I. BAIL

All persons are bailable by sufficient sureties except for capital offenses where the proof is evident or the presumption great. Excessive bail cannot be required. KAN. CONST. art. 1, §9.

Any judge of a court of record, on the application of any prisoner committed for a bailable offense, may inquire into the case and admit the prisoner to bail. KAN. STAT. ANN. §62–628. The court at each term must order the amount in which persons charged by indictment or information are to be held to bail, and the clerk must endorse the amount on the warrant. KAN. STAT. ANN. §62–1207.

II. PRELIMINARY HEARING

If no special provisions apply, every person arrested by warrant for any offense must be brought before a magistrate of the same county. With the defendant's consent, the magistrate may adjourn for a period not exceeding ten days. KAN. STAT. ANN. §62–610. When an accused is brought before a magistrate, the magistrate must examine both the witness and the complaint "as soon as may be." KAN. STAT. ANN. §62–614. The magistrate must determine whether or not an offense has been committed and whether or not there is probable cause to believe the defendant has committed the crime.

III. GRAND JURY, INDICTMENT, INFORMATION

Offenses may be prosecuted in the court having jurisdiction either by indictment or information. KAN. STAT. ANN. §62–801. Informations may be filed with the county prosecuting attorney in any court having jurisdiction of the offense. KAN. STAT. ANN. §62–802. A grand jury must be ordered and summoned to attend a term of the district court of any county when a petition of the taxpayers of the county for a grand jury is presented at least 40 days before commencement of the term at which the grand jury is desired. KAN. STAT. ANN. §62–901.

IV. PRETRIAL DISCOVERY

The defendant is not entitled to inspect evidence in the possession of the prosecution. *State v. Oswald,* 197 Kan. 251, 417 P.2d 261 (1966). The defendant is entitled to inspect a writing or object in the prosecution's possession when it is offered in evidence at the trial. *State v. Stephens,* 168 Kan. 5, 209 P.2d 924 (1949); *State v. Furthmyer,* 128 Kan. 317, 277 P. 1019 (1929). The accused is not entitled to inspect, at least before trial, a statement made by a witness or by anyone else. *State v. Furthmyer,* 128 Kan. 317, 277 P. 1019 (1929).

The report of the coroner's inquest is a public document and is subject to public inspection, but notes taken by an attorney at an inquest are not public and not producible. *State v. Hooper,* 140 Kan. 481, 37 P.2d 52 (1934). The report of the Kansas Bureau of Investigation containing statements of a prosecution witness was made solely for the use of the officers and was of a quasi-private character, and was of no concern to anyone until it was divulged in court. It could not be produced for inspection to be used for cross-examination or impeachment of witnesses. *State v. Hill,* 193 Kan. 512, 394 P.2d 106 (1964). The transcript of a prosecution witness's testimony given at the preliminary examination was not producible even though the prosecuting attorney used the transcript during the trial in his examination of the witness. *State v. Laird,* 79 Kan. 681, 100 P. 637 (1909).

Whether or not to grant the defendant the right to inspect a prosecution witness's statement for cross-examination or inspection lies in the court's discretion. Production of the police investigation report, used by a witness to refresh his memory before trial but not while on the witness stand, was discretionary with the court, and a refusal to produce the report was not prejudicial error. *State v. Oswald,* 197 Kan. 251, 417 P.2d 261 (1966).

The accused is not entitled to a bill of particulars specifying the particular day on which the crime occurred. *State v. Gordon,* 146 Kan. 41, 68 P.2d 635 (1937). Nor is the accused entitled to a bill of particulars setting out specific details as to the place where the alleged crime or some incident connected with it took place. *State v. Eason,* 163 Kan. 763, 186 P.2d 269 (1947).

The defendant must give written notice to the county attorney of his intention to offer evidence of an alibi, stating where the defendant contends he was at the time of the offense and the names of the witnesses which he proposes to use in support of his contention. The court may allow the defendant to endorse additional names of witnesses on such notice. The defendant can compel the county attorney to amend the complaint or information if the time and place of the offense are not specifically stated to enable him to offer evidence of an alibi. If the defendant fails to give notice, he cannot offer evidence of an alibi. KAN. STAT. ANN. §62–1341.

Depositions shall be taken and read in the same manner and with the same effects as in civil actions. Interrogatories shall also follow the civil rules. KAN. STAT. ANN. §62–1314. Deponent may be examined on any relevant, nonprivileged matter. At trial and upon motion, deposition may, if admissible, be used to contradict or impeach the deponent as a witness or may be used if the deponent is dead, outside the county, or unable to testify owing to infirmity, age, or imprisonment. KAN. STAT. ANN. §60–226(d)(1).

V. SPEEDY TRIAL

The accused in all prosecutions must have a speedy public trial. KAN. CONST. art. 1, §10. If the defendant has been indicted and imprisoned he must be brought to trial within two terms of the court. KAN. STAT. ANN. §62–1431. If the defendant is on bail, he must be brought to trial within three terms of the court unless the defendant is the cause of the delay. KAN. STAT. ANN. §62–1432. The court may grant a one-term delay if the prosecution can show that it has been diligent and that there exists a reasonable likelihood of discovery of evidence. KAN. STAT. ANN. §62–1433.

Where the defendant causes the delay, he is not entitled to raise the issue of the right to a speedy trial. *State v. Stanley,* 179 Kan. 613, 296 P.2d 1088 (1956). Consent to a continuance or a failure to object will be deemed a waiver of the right to a speedy trial. *State v. Dewey,* 73 Kan. 735, 88 P. 881 (1907). However, the defendant need not make a demand for a speedy trial, as long as he has not contributed to the delay. *State v. Hess,* 180 Kan. 472, 304 P.2d 474 (1956).

KENTUCKY

I. BAIL

All persons are bailable by sufficient sureties unless the charge is a capital offense where the proof is evident or the presumption great. KY. CONST. §16. Excessive bail cannot be required. KY. CONST. §17. If the offense is nonbailable, or if the person arrested is unable to give bail, he is committed to jail. KY. R. CRIM. P. 3.02. If there are reasonable grounds to believe that the release of the defendant would endanger person or property, the magistrate shall require bail in any sum deemed reasonable to keep the peace and to insure good behavior for one year. The provisions concerning bail apply to bail for good behavior. KY. R. CRIM. P. 3.06.

If the offense is bailable, the magistrate must fix the sum and enter it upon the order of commitment. KY. R. CRIM. P. 3.18. A hearing application for admission to bail is made before or after indictment for a capital offense; the burden of showing that the proof is evident or the presumption great that the defendant is guilty of the offense is on the state. KY. R. CRIM. P. 4.04. If the defendant is admitted to bail, the amount is what in the judgment of the court will insure compliance with the terms of the bond. In determining the amount of bail the court shall consider the ability of the defendant to give bail, the nature and circumstances of the offense charged, the weight of the evidence against him, the character and reputation of the defendant, and the probability of the defendant's complying with the terms of the bond. KY. R. CRIM. P. 4.06.

II. PRELIMINARY HEARING

An arrested person, whether the arrest is under a warrant or without a warrant, must be taken before a magistrate without delay. KY. R. CRIM. P. 3.02. If the magistrate has jurisdiction of the offense, he must proceed with the trial. If he has jurisdiction of the preliminary hearing, he must hold it or order the accused taken before a court of competent jurisdiction to hold the preliminary hearing. KY. R. CRIM. P. 3.04.

When the accused is brought before a magistrate, he must be informed of the charge against him, of his right to a preliminary hearing, of his right to remain silent, and of his right to counsel. The magistrate must allow a reasonable time for the defendant to procure counsel and must allow bail if the offense is bailable. If the offense is punishable by a $500 fine or 12 months' imprisonment, the examining court may provide counsel for the preliminary hearing. KY. R. CRIM. P. 3.08. If the defendant was not provided with counsel at the preliminary hearing, he will be granted a hearing on motion to set aside the conviction even in absence of allegation that meritorious grounds existed for appeal or identification of errors. *Stinnet v. Commonwealth,* 446 S.W.2d 292 (Ky. 1969).

The defendant may waive his preliminary hearing, but upon demand of the state attorney the magistrate may examine some of the witnesses, with the defendant allowed to cross-examine. KY. R. CRIM. P. 3.10. If the defendant waives the preliminary hearing, or if it is found that probable cause exists to believe the defendant has committed the offense, he is held to answer in the circuit court. KY. R. CRIM. P. 3.14.

III. GRAND JURY, INDICTMENT, INFORMATION

No person can be proceeded against criminally by information for an indictable offense. KY. CONST. §12. All crimes except common law crimes, felonies and misdemeanors for which the punishment is infamous, and those offenses required by law to be prosecuted by indictment may be prosecuted by information. KY. R. CRIM. P. 6.02; OP. ATT. GEN. 63-808.

IV. PRETRIAL DISCOVERY

The defendant has no right to inspect evidence in the possession of the prosecution before trial. The court may, on motion of the defendant, order the attorney for the state to permit the defendant to inspect and copy any relevant written or recorded statements or confessions made by the defendant in the possession of the state, and the results of any physical or mental examinations and scientific tests known by the attorney for the state to be in the possession of the state. KY. R. CRIM. P. 7.24. On motion of the defendant, the court may order inspection of books, papers, documents, or tangible objects in the control of the state upon a showing of materiality and reasonableness. Pretrial discovery or inspection of reports made by officers and agents of the state, or of statements made to them by witnesses or prospective witnesses, is not authorized. If the court grants relief to the defendant under this procedure, it may condition its order by requiring that the defendant permit the state to inspect or copy statements, scientific or medical reports, books, papers, documents, or tangible objects which the defendant intends to produce at the trial and which are in his possession.

The court may on sufficient showing order at any time that the discovery or inspection be denied, restricted, or deferred, KY. R. CRIM. P. 7.24(2), (3), (6).

If after complying with an order granting discovery a party discovers additional material previously requested and subject to discovery, he must promptly notify the other party of the material. If discoverable material has not been properly disclosed, the court may prohibit the party from introducing in evidence the material not disclosed. KY. R. CRIM. P. 7.24(8), (9).

After a witness called by the state has testified on direct examination, the court must, on motion of the defendant, order the state to produce any statement of the witness in its possession which relates to the subject matter of the witness's testimony. If the state elects not to comply, the court shall, on defendant's motion, strike the testimony of the witness or, if justice requires, declare a mistrial. KY. R. CRIM. P. 7.26.

Where the prosecution has a document in court during the course of the trial which the accused thinks is relevant and material to his defense, he should not be denied the right to examine it. *Arthur v. Commonwealth,* 307 S.W.2d 182 (Ky. 1957). Where the evidence is offered at the trial, the defendant has the right to inspect it. *Wendling v. Commonwealth,* 143 Ky. 587, 137 S.W. 205 (1911). The defendant also has the right to see and use any writing which is used by the prosecution in cross-examination. *Meadors v. Commonwealth,* 281 Ky. 622, 136 S.W.2d 1066(1940).

Any person indicted by the grand jury is entitled to a transcript of any notes or recordings relating to his indictment by paying the prescribed fee. KY. R. CRIM. P. 5.16(2).

A bill of particulars may be allowed where it appears to the trial court that the accused is entitled to notice of what charges he will be called upon to defend. *Chaplin v. Commonwealth,* 274 S.W.2d 55 (Ky. 1955). An accused cannot ask for a bill of particulars if the specifications asked for are within his own knowledge or are readily accessible to him. *Harris v. Commonwealth,* 285 S.W.2d 489 (Ky. 1956).

If a prospective witness may be unable to attend the trial, or is about to become a nonresident, and if his testimony is material, the court may order his testimony taken by deposition. KY. R. CRIM. P. 7.10. If the witness is dead or out of the state, his deposition may be used at the trial, unless it appears that the witness's absence was procured by the party offering the deposition. KY. R. CRIM. P. 7.20.

V. SPEEDY TRIAL

In all criminal cases the accused has the right to a speedy public trial. KY. CONST. §11. All prosecutions must proceed when the defendant appears or is brought before the court unless postponed for cause. The trials of all persons in custody under arrest must be held as promptly as reasonably possible. KY. R. CRIM. P. 9.02. The accused is entitled to a speedy trial and can secure it by mandamus. *Hoskins v. Wright,* 367 S.W.2d 838 (Ky. 1963). Failure of the accused to demand trial is a waiver of his right to a speedy trial, *Barker v. Commonwealth,* 385 S.W.2d 671 (Ky. 1965). It is not incumbent upon the state to seek out the defendant and ask him if he wants a speedy trial. *LaVigne v. Commonwealth,* 398 S.W.2d 691 (Ky. 1966).

LOUISIANA

I. BAIL

All persons must be bailable by sufficient sureties except: (1) persons charged with a capital offense where the proof is evident or the presumption great; (2) persons convicted of felonies, provided that where a minimum sentence of less than five years at hard labor is actually imposed, bail must be allowed pending appeal until final judgment. Excessive bail cannot be required. LA. CONST. art. 1, §12. The court must order the disposition of security in satisfaction of the bail obligation in cases of forfeiture. LA. REV. STAT. ANN. §15:86 (1967). Bail must be given at the earliest possible time. LA. REV. STAT. ANN. §15:81 (1967).

When a person charged with a capital offense makes application for admission to bail, the judge must hold a hearing, with both the defendant and the state present. Before indictment, the burden is on the state to show that the proof is evident or the presumption great. After indictment, the burden is on the defendant to show that the proof is not evident nor the presumption great. LA. CRIM. PRO. CODE ANN. art. 313 (West 1966).

Factors to be considered in determining the amount of bail are the seriousness of the offense charged, the weight of the evidence against the defendant, his previous criminal record, his ability to give bail, and any other circumstances affecting the probability of the defendant's appearance. LA. CRIM. PRO. CODE ANN. art. 317 (West 1966). There are certain fixed amounts for certain felonies. LA. CRIM. PRO. CODE ANN. art. 316 (West 1966).

A person held may invoke the supervisory jurisdiction of the supreme court on a claim that the trial court had improperly refused bail or a reduction of bail in a bailable case. LA. CRIM. PRO. CODE ANN. art. 322 (West 1966). A person in custody may be released by order of the court on his own personal bail without furnishing a surety. LA. CRIM. PRO. CODE ANN. art. 336 (West 1966).

II. PRELIMINARY HEARING

District courts having criminal jurisdiction may conduct preliminary hearings in all cases of persons accused of felonies; city or parish courts having criminal jurisdiction may conduct preliminary hearings in all non-capital offenses; and justices of the peace may do so in all cases not capital or necessarily punishable at hard labor. LA. CRIM. PRO. CODE ANN. art. 291 (West 1966).

Before filing an indictment or information the court may on its own or upon request either of the state or the defendant immediately order a preliminary examination in felony cases. LA. CRIM. PRO. CODE ANN. art. 292 (West 1966). The examination must be conducted promptly, but the accused must be allowed time to obtain counsel. LA. CRIM. PRO. CODE ANN. art. 293 (West 1966).

At the preliminary examination the state and the defendant may produce witnesses who are examined in the presence of the accused and who are subject to cross-examination. The defendant may also testify subject to cross-examination. LA. CRIM. PRO. CODE ANN. art. 294 (West 1966). If the defendant has not been indicted by the grand jury for the offense charged, he must be released, if it appears there is no probable cause to charge him with the offense. LA. CRIM. PRO. CODE ANN. art. 296(West 1966).

III. GRAND JURY, INDICTMENT, INFORMATION

A prosecution for an offense punishable by death must be instituted by indictment by a grand jury. Each parish within the state must impanel a grand jury of twelve twice a year. A quorum of nine is required to indict. LA. CONST. art. 7, §42. Other criminal prosecutions in district court may be instituted by indictment or by information. LA. CRIM. PRO. CODE ANN. art. 382; *see also* arts. 383, 384(West 1966).

IV. PRETRIAL DISCOVERY

The accused is not entitled to inspection or disclosure of evidence in the prosecution's possession. *State v. Hunter,* 250 La. 295, 195 So. 2d 273 (1967); *State v. Johnson,* 249 La. 950, 192 So. 2d 135, *cert. denied,* 388 U.S. 923(1966). Whether to grant or deny the defendant's motion for discovery of the prosecution's evidence is discretionary with the trial court. *State v. Dowdy,* 217 La. 773, 47 So. 2d 496, *cert. denied,* 340 U.S. 856 (1950).

Except for the defendant's written confession, all evidence relating to a criminal case in the prosecution's possession is privileged and is not subject to inspection by the accused unless and until it is offered in evidence in the trial. *State v. Pailet,* 246 La. 483, 165 So. 2d 294 (1964). However, the defendant is entitled to inspection when an item is offered in evidence at the trial. *State v. Pailet, supra; State v. Michel,* 225 La. 1040, 74 So. 2d 207, *affirmed.* 350 U. S. 91, *rehearing denied,* 350 U. S. 955, *cert. denied,* 355 U. S. 879 (1957).

Denial of the accused's request for a pretrial inspection of his written confession is a denial of his constitutional rights. *State v. Dorsey,* 207 La. 928, 22 So. 2d 273 (1945). *See also State v. Simien,* 248 La. 323, 178 So. 2d 266 (1965); *State v. Hunter,* 250 La. 295, 195 So. 2d 273 (1967). The rule does not apply to oral confessions. *State v. Bickham,* 239 La. 1094, 121 So. 2d 207, *cert. denied,* 364 U.S. 874 (1960); *State v. Lea,* 288 La. 724, 84 So. 2d 169, *cert. denied,* 350 U.S. 1007 (1955). Nor does it apply to written confessions which are not to be offered in evidence by the prosecution. *State v. Labat,* 226 La. 201, 75 So. 2d 333, *aff'd,* 350 U. S. 91, *rehearing denied,* 350 U. S. 955 (1954). The defendant has no right to inspection of a document or article in the prosecution's possession which is not admissible in evidence. *State v. Bankston,* 165 La. 1082, 116 So. 565 (1928).

The accused is not entitled to inspection of a prior statement by a witness even after the witness has testified on direct examination at the trial. The prosecution witness's statement should be produced for the use of the defense where it is shown that the contents are directly relevant to the issue of the defendant's guilt. *State v. Weston,* 232 La. 766, 95 So. 2d 305 (1957). To be granted inspection, the defendant must lay a proper foundation. *State v. Weston, supra; State v. Bonner,* 252 La. 200, 210 So. 2d 319 (1968). The defendant must show some inconsistency between the contents of the statement and the witness's testimony at the trial. *State v. Young,* 249 La. 1053, 193 So. 2d 243 (1967); *State v. Martin,* 250 La. 705, 198 So. 2d 897 (1967).

A bill of particulars which amounts to disclosure of the prosecution's evidence will generally not be granted. *State v. Williams,* 230 La. 1059, 89 So. 2d 898 (1956); *State v. Hudson,* 253 La. 992, 221 So. 2d 484 (1969).

Where a short form of indictment is used, the accused may require the state to furnish him a further bill of particulars if he needs more detailed information in order to prepare his defense; he is entitled to such remedy as a matter of right. *State v. Howard,* 243 La. 971, 149 So. 2d 409 (1963); *State v. Hudson,* 253 La. 992, 221 So. 2d 484 (1969).

The prosecution is privileged to withhold the identity of an informer, especially where such identity does not help the defendant regarding his defense. *State v. Freeman,* 245 La. 665, 160 So. 2d 571 (1964).

The accused can be denied the right to interview a witness; thus the right to interview the witness without the witness's counsel present was denied. *State v. Gosey,* 111 La. 616, 35 So. 786 (1904).

V. Speedy Trial

In all criminal prosecutions the accused has the right to a speedy and public trial. LA. CONST. art. 1, §9. The state and the defendant have the right to a speedy trial. LA. CRIM. PRO. CODE ANN. art. 701 (West 1966).

The law requiring justice without delay means without unreasonable and unnecessary delay. *Ex parte Ryan,* 124 La. 356, 50 So. 385 (1909). The right to a speedy trial does not deprive the state of a reasonable opportunity to fairly prosecute accused persons with all reasonable and necessary delays. *State v. Collins,* 242 La. 704, 138 So. 2d 546 (1962).

When an accused took no steps to secure a speedy trial, and the prosecuting officer for reasons which were found insufficient failed to set the case for trial within a reasonable time, it did not prevent the subsequent trial and conviction of the accused. *State v. Banks,* 111 La. 22, 35 So. 370 (1904).

MAINE

I. Bail

No person before conviction is bailable for any of the crimes which are capital offenses when the proof is evident or the presumption great. ME. CONST. art. 1, §10. Excessive bail shall not be required. ME. CONST. art. 1, §9.

The magistrate before whom the defendant is brought must allow the defendant reasonable time and opportunity to consult counsel and must admit him to bail. ME. R. CRIM. P. 5(b) (1972). Pending sentence the court may commit the defendant or continue or alter the bail. ME. R. CRIM. P. 32(a) (1972). The amount of bail is that which, in the judgment of the person authorized to fix bail, will insure the presence of the defendant, having regard for the nature and circumstance of the offense charged, the financial ability of the defendant to give bail, the character of the defendant, and the policy against unnecessary detention pending trial. The judge may authorize the release of the defendant without security upon conditions as may be prescribed to assure his appearance. ME. R. CRIM. P. 46(a), (c) (1972).

II. Preliminary Hearing

When a person is arrested, either with or without a warrant, and brought before a magistrate, the magistrate must inform him of the complaint against him, of his right to counsel, of his right to assigned counsel, and of his right to a preliminary examination. He must also be informed that he is not required to make a statement, and that if he does, it may be used against him. ME. R. CRIM. P. 5(b)(1972).

At the preliminary hearing, defendant is not called upon to plead. The defendant may, if he does not waive examination, cross-examine witnesses against him and introduce evidence in his behalf. ME. R. CRIM. P. 5(c) (1972). The judge must determine whether there is probable cause to believe that a crime has been committed and that it is probable to believe the defendant guilty of the crime. If he so finds, the accused is committed to await trial. ME. REV. STAT. ANN. tit. 15, §806 (Supp. 1970); ME. R. CRIM. P. 5(c) (1972).

III. GRAND JURY, INDICTMENT, INFORMATION

No person can be held to answer in any court for an alleged offense unless on an indictment found by a grand jury, except for a charge of contempt of court or when prosecutions by information are expressly authorized by statute. ME. REV. STAT. ANN. tit. 15, §701 (1964). All criminal proceedings originating in the superior court and all felonies shall be prosecuted by indictment, unless indictment is waived, in which case prosecution may be by information. Any offense, except one punishable by life imprisonment, may be prosecuted by information upon defendant's request. Defendant must waive his right to an indictment in writing. ME. R. CRIM. P. 7(a),(b) (1972).

IV. PRETRIAL DISCOVERY

Upon timely motion and a showing that the items sought may be material to the preparation of his defense and that the request is reasonable, the court must order the prosecuting attorney to permit the defendant to inspect and copy designated books, papers, documents, or tangible objects in the possession, custody, or control of the state, including written or recorded statements made by the defendant or a co-defendant, written or recorded statements of witnesses, transcripts of the testimony of witnesses before the grand jury, and results of physical examinations and scientific tests. The order must specify the time, place, and manner of taking of the inspection or copying, and may prescribe other conditions. ME. R. CRIM. P. 16(a) (1972).

The accused is not entitled to disclosure of the grand jury minutes. *Brine v. State,* 160 Me. 140, 205 A.2d 12 (1964).

The court may on a motion by the defendant order that an insufficient bill of particulars be amended or made more precise and definite. *State v. Hume,* 146 Me. 129, 78 A.2d 496 (1951). A bill of particulars which would amount to a disclosure of the prosecution's evidence will not be granted. *State v. Hume, supra; State v. Henderson,* 153 Me. 364, 139 A.2d 515 (1958).

No less than ten days before the trial, the attorney for the state may serve upon the defendant or his attorney a demand that the defendant serve a notice of alibi if the defendant intends to rely on the alibi as a defense at the trial. The demand must state the time and place that the attorney for the state proposes to establish at the trial as the time and place where the defendant participated in or committed the crime. If the defendant intends to rely on an alibi, he must, within five days, serve on the state's attorney and file a notice of alibi which states where the defendant claims to have been at the time stated in the demand. If the defendant fails to answer the demand, without notice of his alibi, he is not permitted to produce evidence of the alibi at the trial other than his own testimony, unless the court for cause shown orders otherwise. ME. R. CRIM. P. 16(b) (1972).

Deposition of a prospective witness may be taken if it appears he will be unable to attend trial, his testimony is material, and justice requires it. ME. R. CRIM. P. 15 (1972).

V. SPEEDY TRIAL

In all criminal prosecutions, the accused has the right to have a speedy public and impartial trial. ME. CONST. art. 1, §6. The existence or expiration of a term of court in no way affects the court's power to act in a criminal proceeding. ME. REV. STAT. ANN. tit. 15, §1201 (Supp. 1970).

The right to a speedy trial is necessarily relative and is consistent with delays. The question of whether a speedy trial is afforded must be determined in light of the circumstances of each case, as a matter of judicial discretion. Generally a demand for trial and resistance to postponement, or some other effort to secure a speedy trial, must be made before the defendant is entitled to a discharge on the ground of delay. *Couture v. State,* 156 Me. 231, 163 A.2d 646 (1960). The right to a speedy trial may be waived, and delays caused by acts of the accused constitute such a waiver. *State v. Hale,* 157 Me. 361, 172 A.2d 631 (1961).

MARYLAND

I. BAIL

Prior to or after conviction an accused who is charged with an offense for which punishment is other than capital is entitled to be admitted to bail. In all other cases the accused may be admitted to bail in the discretion of the court. MD. R. P. 777(a). After conviction, if the offense is capital, bail is within the discretion of the court. MD. R. P. 777(b). The court may require a higher bail after conviction pending sentence. MD. R. P. 777(c). Pending appeal, if the court in its discretion refuses to admit the accused to bail or the accused does not furnish bail, the accused must commence serving his sentence. MD. R. P. 777(d).

Excessive bail ought not to be required. MD. CONST. art. 25. Any person having the power to admit to bail may accept the accused as his own recognizor, upon cash or other property owned by him. MD. ANN. CODE art. 26, §34 (1957). This applies before or after conviction to any criminal offense except a case where death or life imprisonment without parole is a possible punishment. It applies to all persons regardless of age. MD. ANN. CODE art. 27, §638 A (Supp. 1970).

II. PRELIMINARY HEARING

There are no code provisions or rules of procedure in this area.

III. GRAND JURY, INDICTMENT, INFORMATION

A person charged with a misdemeanor before indictment by the grand jury may be prosecuted upon an information filed by the state's attorney. A person charged with a felony may not be prosecuted upon an information, unless the grand jury is waived. In such case an information must be filed by the state's attorney against the accused, unless the case originates before the trial magistrate where it is tried upon warrant. MD. R. P. 708–9.

IV. PRETRIAL DISCOVERY

Upon motion of a defendant and upon a showing of materiality and reasonableness, the court, any time after indictment, may order the state's attorney to produce, for inspection and copying by the defense, designated books, papers, documents, or tangible objects obtained from or belonging to the defendant or obtained from others by seizure or process to furnish the defendant the substance of any oral statement made by him which the state proposes to produce as evidence to prove its case in chief, a copy of any written statement made by him, and the substance of any oral confession made by him. The state must also furnish to the defendant a list of names and addresses of the witnesses whom the state intends to call to prove its case in chief. MD. R. P. 782. The court retains its inherent common law power to require or permit discovery. The main objectives of discovery are to assist the defendant in preparing his defense and to protect him from surprise. *Mayson v. State,* 238 Md. 283, 208 A.2d 599 (1965). Whether to grant or deny the accused the right to inspect evidence in the prosecution's possession is discretionary with the trial court. *McKenzie v. State,* 236 Md. 597, 204 A.2d 678 (1964).

Suppression of natural evidence by the state which is exculpatory to the accused is a violation of due process. *Brady v. Maryland,* 373 U. S. 83 (1963), *affirming, Brady v. State,* 226 Md. 422, 174 A.2d 167 (1961). However, the trial court did not abuse its discretion in denying a request for "any evidence of an exculpatory nature that the State has in its possession." *Leyva v. State,* 2 Md. App. 120, 233 A.2d 498 (1967). The court also denied a motion for examination which was actually a request for a general exploratory examination of state files. *Ward v. State,* 2 Md. App. 687, 236 A.2d 740 (1968).

It was not error for the lower court to refuse to permit the defendant to inspect before trial notes made by police officers after their conversations with him. The court held that there was no abuse of the discretion of the trial court, pointing out that the trial court had ordered the prosecution to permit the defendant to inspect at the time of the conversations all memoranda or transcripts of statements made by the defendant, although it had denied inspection of any memoranda or statements after the conversations. *Glaros v. State,* 223 Md. 272, 164 A.2d 461 (1960).

The trial court did not err in denying discovery and inspection of all written statements of three co-defendants charged with the defendant; no rule provides for disclosure of written statements of a co-defendant. The court did not abuse its discretion by refusing to require the state to say when and where the alleged oral statements by the defendant were made, and by refusing to furnish the defendant with the reports of the experts whom the state intended to call at the trial. *Veney v. State,* 251 Md. 159, 246 A.2d 608 (1968).

A defendant is not entitled to inspection of prior statements by a prosecution witness. To grant such inspection is discretionary with the trial court, but the defendant needs to show inconsistency between the testimony given at trial and the prior statements of the witness. *McKenzie v. State,* 236 Md. 597, 204 A.2d 678 (1964).

The defendant is entitled to such information as will enable him to prepare his defense and to avoid surprise. *Shelton v. State,* 198 Md. 405, 84 A.2d 76 (1951). Granting a bill of particulars is discretionary with the trial court. *Veney v. State,* 251 Md. 159, 246 A.2d 608, *cert. denied,* 394 U. S. 948 (1968). A bill of particulars which would amount to disclosure of the prosecution's evidence will not be granted. *Pearlman v. State,* 232 Md. 251, 192 A.2d 767 (1962).

In criminal cases, where the probable cause for a defendant's arrest depends wholly or in part on information received from a nonparticipating informer and if the name of the informer is useful evidence to indicate the innocence of the accused or lessen the risk of false testimony or is essential to a proper disposition of the case, disclosure should be compelled or the evidence obtained from the arrest and search suppressed. *Drouin v. State,* 222 Md. 271, 160 A.2d 85 (1960).

Depositions may be ordered upon motion, if a prospective witness may be unable to attend trial, if his testimony is material, and if necessary to prevent a failure of justice. Production of designated objects may be ordered at the same time. MD. R. P. 727.

V. SPEEDY TRIAL

The accused in all criminal prosecutions has the right to a speedy trial. MD. CONST. art. 21. If the defendant is serving a sentence in a penal or correctional institution and is indicted for another crime in the state, he must be brought to trial within 180 days after he has delivered to the prosecution and the court a written request that final disposition be made of the indictment, or the charges will be dropped. If good cause is shown in open court, the prisoner or his counsel being present, the court having jurisdiction of the matter may grant any necessary or reasonable continuance. MD. ANN. CODE art. 27, §616 D (1957).

Four factors are considered in interpreting the meaning of the words "speedy trial": (1) length of the delay, (2) prejudice to the defendant, (3) reason for the delay, and (4) waiver of the right. *Hall v. State*, 3 Md. App. 680, 240 A.2d 630 (1968). When the accused has demanded a speedy trial and the delay is less than substantial, even if it is purposeful, oppressive, or negligent, at least some showing by him of a strong possibility of prejudice is required. The right to a speedy trial may be waived by failure to demand it, and where a demand has not been made, the accused must show actual prejudice caused by the undue delaying tactics of the state. *King v. State*, 6 Md. App. 413, 251 A.2d 628 (1969). The right to a speedy trial can be waived by failure to demand it or by the conduct of the accused. *Greathouse v. State*, 5 Md. App. 675, 249 A.2d 207 (1969). The essential ingredient of a speedy trial is not mere speed but orderly expedition. *King v. State*, 5 Md. App. 652, 249 A.2d 468 (1969); *Barnett v. State*, 8 Md. App. 35, 257 A.2d 466 (1969).

MASSACHUSETTS

I. BAIL

No magistrate or court of law may demand excessive or unreasonable bail. MASS. CONST. pt. 1, art. XXVI. A justice of the supreme judicial or superior court, or the clerk of courts, may admit people to bail, and may admit to bail any person committed for not finding sureties to recognize him. Before fixing the amount of bail for a prisoner charged with an offense punishable by imprisonment for more than one year, the court shall obtain from its probation officer all available information relative to prior criminal prosecutions, if any, of the prisoner and the disposition of each prosecution. MASS. GEN. LAWS ANN. ch. 276, §57 (Supp. 1971).

A person held in custody or committed upon a criminal charge, if entitled to be released on bail, may, instead of giving sureties, give his personal recognizance to appear before the court and deposit the amount of the bail which he is so ordered to furnish. MASS. GEN. LAWS ANN. ch. 276, §79 (1959). Defendants charged with crimes against nature, unnatural and lascivious acts, rape, or assault with intent to rape must have a mental health report before being bailed. MASS. GEN. LAWS ANN. ch. 276, §57 (1959). Treason is not bailable. MASS. GEN. LAWS ANN. ch. 264, §1 (1959).

II. PRELIMINARY HEARING

If the accused is charged with a misdemeanor, he may be taken before a magistrate in the county of his arrest and enter into a recognizance without a trial or examination. MASS. GEN. LAWS ANN. ch. 276, §29 (1959). If the accused is brought before a district court upon a capital charge, and does not waive the examination, the superior court may assign counsel. MASS. GEN. LAWS ANN. ch. 276, §37A (1959).

If probable cause is found to believe the prisoner guilty of the crime charged, the accused may be admitted to bail or committed to jail until his trial. MASS. GEN. LAWS ANN. ch. 276, §41, 42 (1959).

III. GRAND JURY, INDICTMENT, INFORMATION

No one may be held to answer in any court for an alleged crime, except on a grand jury indictment or upon a complaint before a district court. This requirement may be waived in all cases except for a crime punishable by death. MASS. GEN. LAWS ANN. ch. 263, §4, 4a (1959).

IV. PRETRIAL DISCOVERY

The accused has no right to inspect evidence in the prosecution's possession. The trial court has discretion to permit or deny discovery motions of this kind.

The denial of the defendant's pretrial motion for an order requiring inspection of the autopsy report, a copy of the alleged confession of the defendant, and all weapons, exhibits, and things in the possession of the prosecuting attorney was upheld on the ground that the motion was an attempt to compel the prosecution to disclose at least in part the evidence on which it relied. The court said that any information in the possession of the prosecution that is necessary to enable the defendant to understand the nature of the crime with which he is charged and to prepare his defense can be obtained through a motion for a bill of particulars. There is no rule of law allowing this type of discovery as a matter of right. *Commonwealth v. Jordan*, 207 Mass. 259, 93 N.E. 809, *aff'd*, 225 U. S. 167 (1911).

The defendant is not entitled to a copy of his confession. *Commonwealth v. Chapin*, 333 Mass. 610, 132 N.E.2d 404, *cert. denied*, 352 U. S. 857 (1956); *Commonwealth v. Lundin*, 326 Mass. 551, 95 N.E.2d 661 (1950). He is not entitled to examination of a co-defendant's confession. *Commonwealth v. Giacomazza*, 311 Mass. 456, 42 N.E.2d 506 (1942).

A motion by the defendant in a murder trial that the state furnish all evidence in its possession tending to exonerate the defendant was denied because the motion was not specific and the defendant suggested no evidence that might help him. *Commonwealth v. Sullivan*, 354 Mass. 598, 239 N.E.2d 5 (1968). A defendant charged with perjury before a grand jury or other body is entitled as of right to a complete transcript of his own testimony before the tribunal where the perjury allegedly occurred, sufficiently in advance of the trial to enable the defendant to prepare his defense, without the necessity of showing "any particularized need." *Commonwealth v. Giles*, 358 Mass. 1, 228 N.Ed.2d 70 (1967).

The defendant is not entitled to inspection of prior statements by a witness to prepare for cross-examination or impeachment. A writing used to refresh the recollection of a witness may be used by the opposing party during cross-examination to raise the question whether it is a proper memorandum for the purpose. The defendant is not entitled to inspect the memorandum before it has been shown to the witness. *Commonwealth v. Greenberg*, 339 Mass. 557, 160 N.E.2d 181 (1959).

The accused has no right to disclosure of state grand jury minutes. *Commonwealth v. Abbott Engineering*, 351 Mass. 568, 222 N.E.2d 862 (1967); *Commonwealth v. Cook*, 351 Mass. 231, 218 N.E.2d 393, *cert. denied*, 385 U. S. 981 (1966). It is within the discretion of the trial court to grant or deny the request for such disclosure. *Commonwealth v. Cook, supra; Commonwealth v. Doherty*, 353 Mass. 197, 229 N.E.2d 267 (1967). Where there is an inconsistency alleged between the grand jury testimony and the trial testimony, it is appropriate for the trial judge to read the minutes and, if he finds an inconsistency, to permit defense counsel to examine the minutes. *Commonwealth v. Doherty, supra.*

The prosecution is privileged to withhold disclosure of the identity of an informer. *Commonwealth v. Congdon*, 265 Mass. 166, 165 N.E. 467 (1928).

The accused should be permitted to interview a witness held in custody. Witnesses belong to neither the prosecution nor the defense. If the refusal is prejudicial error, the verdict will be set aside. *Commonwealth v. Balliro,*

349 Mass. 505, 209 N.E.2d 308 (1965).

The court may, on defendant's application, grant a commission to examine and take the deposition of any material witness residing out of state. The prosecution may join in such commission and may name any material witnesses to be examined on the part of the state. MASS. GEN. LAWS ANN. ch. 277, §76 (1959). If the defendant declines to use the deposition, the prosecution may not, without defendant's consent, use any of it for the state's case. MASS. GEN. LAWS ANN. ch. 277, §77 (1959).

V. SPEEDY TRIAL

The right to a speedy trial is personal and may be waived. In the absence of circumstances negating the implication, failure to demand a prompt trial implies a waiver. *Commonwealth v. Needel,* 349 Mass. 580, 211 N.E.2d 335 (1965). Where the defendant's own pretrial motions were responsible for much of the delay, and he had at no time made an unequivocal demand for trial, he suffered no unconstitutional denial of a speedy trial. *Commonwealth v. Chase,* 348 Mass. 100, 202 N.E.2d 300 (1964).

Anyone in custody upon an indictment must be tried at the sitting of the court next after the expiration of six months from the time he was imprisoned, or be bailed upon his own recognizance, unless the court finds that the witnesses on behalf of the government have been kept away or have been prevented from attending court by illness or accident. MASS. GEN. LAWS ANN. ch. 277, §72 (1959). A person held under an indictment must ask for a speedy trial as a condition of being bailed upon his own recognizance. *Commonwealth v. Hanley,* 337 Mass. 384, 149 N.E.2d 608 (1958).

MICHIGAN

I. BAIL

All persons are bailable before conviction except for murder or treason when the proof is evident or the presumption great. MICH. CONST. art. 1, §15. Excessive bail cannot be required. MICH. CONST. art. 1, §16.

The amount of bail is fixed after consideration of the seriousness of the offense charged, the previous criminal record of the defendant, and the probability of his appearing at trial. MICH. COMP. LAWS §765.6 (Supp. 1971). Cash may be posted in lieu of a bond. MICH. COMP. LAWS §765.11 (1948). Any magistrate or judge has authority in his discretion to refuse to accept a surety. MICH. COMP. LAWS §765.9 (1948).

After conviction, a defendant is not necessarily entitled to bail. *People v. Giacalone,* 16 Mich. App. 352, 167 N.W.2d 871 (1969).

II. Preliminary Hearing

Upon filing of any complaint any judge having probable cause to suspect an offense has been committed within his jurisdiction may direct an inquiry to take place. The judge may require all relevant witnesses to appear and testify. Mich. Comp. Laws §767.3 (1948).

All of the testimony or evidence need not be presented at the preliminary examination. *People v. Likely,* 2 Mich. App. 458, 140 N.W.2d 529 (1966).

After the inquiry, the judge may call for apprehension of the accused if he is satisfied that an offense has been committed and there is probable cause to suspect any person. The judge who has conducted the preliminary examination is disqualified from the hearing on the complaint or the indictment or from presiding at any trial. Mich. Comp. Laws §767.4 (1948).

No information can be filed against an accused who has not had a preliminary examination unless the accused has waived his right to an examination. If the accused waives his right to the preliminary examination without counsel, he may be given a preliminary examination at a later date before trial. Mich. Comp. Laws §767.42 (1948).

III. Grand Jury, Indictment, Information

Anyone called before the grand jury shall have full rights to be represented by counsel. Mich. Comp. Laws §767.3 (1948).

Under Michigan law, one accused of a felony may be arraigned upon an information and tried, convicted, and sentenced without indictment by a grand jury. *Horn v. Peck,* 130 F. Supp. 536 (1955); Mich. Comp. Laws §§767.1, 767.2 (1948).

All courts having jurisdiction of criminal cases have the same power to prosecute cases by information as over similar cases prosecuted upon indictments. Mich. Comp. Laws §767.1 (1948). No information can be filed against an accused who has not had a preliminary examination, unless the accused has waived the preliminary examination. Mich. Comp. Laws §767.42 (1948).

A judge may conduct a one-man grand jury investigation, but due process must be observed. *In re Colacasides,* 379 Mich. 69, 150 N.W.2d 1 (1967).

IV. Pretrial Discovery

The accused has no right to compel disclosure of evidence, admissible or not, in the prosecution's possession. It is within the discretion of the trial court to grant or deny the request. Discovery will be ordered in a criminal case when, in the discretion of the trial judge, the item sought to be inspected is admissible in evidence, and a failure of justice may result from its suppression. The moving party must prove that the information is necessary in the preparation of his defense and is not sought as part of a "fishing expedition." *People v. Maranian,* 359 Mich. 361, 102 N.W.2d 568 (1960). The defendant must make a motion for inspection. *People v. Camak,* 5 Mich. App. 655, 147 N.W.2d 746 (1967).

The defendant is entitled to inspect a statement of a prosecution witness where the witness has testified on direct examination at trial. The defendant is not required to show any inconsistency between the statement and the testimony of the witness to be granted inspection of the statement for cross-examination or impeachment. *People v. Salimone,* 265 Mich. 486, 251 N.W. 594 (1933).

The opposing party has the right to inspect any paper or memo used by a witness to refresh his memory while on the stand. *People v. Lyons,* 49 Mich. 78, 13 N.W. 365 (1882); *People v. Schepps,* 217 Mich. 406, 186 N.W. 508 (1922).

The accused has no right to inspect state grand jury minutes. *People v. Pickett,* 339 Mich. 294, 63 N.W.2d 681 (1954). At trial, however, when the prosecution read and used some isolated parts of the defendant's grand jury testimony, the court held that it was error to have denied without good reason the defendant's request to see a copy of the defendant's grand jury testimony. *People v. Karoll,* 315 Mich. 424, 24 N.W.2d 167 (1946).

If the defendant intends to establish the defense of an alibi or insanity either at the time of the alleged offense or at the time of the trial, he must give the prosecution written notice four days before trial of his intention and the names of the witnesses whom he intends to call to establish the defense. Names of other witnesses may be given before or during the trial by leave of the court, on such conditions as the court may determine. If the defendant claims an alibi, the notice must include specific information as to the place at which the accused claims to have been at the time of the alleged offense. MICH. COMP. LAWS §768.20 (1948).

The court, upon defendant's application, may grant a commission to examine any material witness residing out of the state. MICH. COMP. LAWS §767.77 (1948). After an indictment, the defendant may have witnesses examined in his behalf with notice to the prosecution. MICH. COMP. LAWS §767.79 (1948).

V. SPEEDY TRIAL

The accused in all criminal cases has the right to a speedy and public trial. MICH. CONST. art. 1, §20. It is the duty of public officers involved in a case to bring the case to a final determination without delay other than that which is necessary to secure to the accused a fair and impartial trial. MICH. COMP. LAWS §768.1 (1948).

The right to a speedy trial is a constitutional right, but it has no absolute standard. *People v. Spalding,* 17 Mich. App. 73, 169 N.W.2d 163 (1969). Implementation of the constitutional and statutory right to a speedy trial requires no more than good faith and prompt action by the prosecution. *People v. Ferrazza,* 18 Mich. App. 680, 171 N.W.2d 658 (1969). To preserve the right to a speedy trial, the defendant must demand it. *People v. Kennedy,* 23 Mich. App. 6, 178 N.W.2d 144 (1970).

MINNESOTA

I. BAIL

All persons before conviction shall be bailable. MINN. CONST. art. 1, §7. Excessive bail cannot be required. MINN. CONST. art. 1, §5.

Any person charged with an offense punishable by more than seven years' imprisonment shall not be admitted to bail by a justice of the peace. MINN. STAT. ANN. §629.52 (Supp. 1970). In all other cases, bail may be taken in a sufficient sum to secure the appearance of the accused at the trial. MINN. STAT. ANN. §629.52 (1945).

II. PRELIMINARY HEARING

A preliminary examination unless waived is required before an information may be filed. MINN. STAT. ANN. §628.31 (1945). The judge before whom a defendant is brought upon a charge of having committed an offense shall examine under oath and in the defendant's presence the complainant and witnesses. After this, defendant's witnesses may be examined. Defendant may be assisted by counsel. MINN. STAT. ANN. §629.50 (1945).

III. GRAND JURY, INDICTMENT, INFORMATION

No person can be held to answer for a criminal offense without due process of law. MINN. CONST. art. 1, §7. The district courts have the same power and jurisdiction over prosecutions upon information as they do upon grand jury indictment. MINN. STAT. ANN. §628.29 (1945). A preliminary examination unless waived is required before the filing of an information. MINN. STAT. ANN. §628.31 (1945). It is necessary to impanel a grand jury only to consider evidence of the commission of a crime involving punishment by life imprisonment in a state prison. OP. ATT'Y GEN. 260-B. (Oct. 29, 1952).

IV. PRETRIAL DISCOVERY

The accused has no right to inspection or disclosure of evidence in the possession of the prosecution. *State ex rel. Robertson v. Steele,* 117 Minn.

384, 135 N.W. 1128 (1912); *State v. Grunau,* 273 Minn. 315, 141 N.W.2d 815 (1966).

The defendant is entitled to inspection of the statements of witnesses for purposes of cross-examination or impeachment. Oral statements made by a witness to the police were held not producible in the absence of a showing of substantially verbatim reproduction of the statements. Reports made by police to their superiors were held to be producible for use in the cross-examination or impeachment of officers, and the statute providing that a public officer should not disclose communications made to him in official confidence when the public interest would suffer by disclosure does not bar production after the witness has testified on direct examination. The defendant has the right to inspection of a prosecution witness's statement when it was used to refresh his recollection while on the stand. Where doubt exists as to the producibility of the statement, a hearing should be held in camera to determine the question. *State v. Grunau,* 273 Minn. 315, 141 N.W.2d 815 (1966); *see State v. Forichette,* 279 Minn. 76, 156 N.W.2d 93 (1968).

After the witness has testified for the prosecution, the accused has the right to examine unprivileged pretrial statements of the witness for the purpose of determining whether he wishes to use it for impeachment purposes without laying any further foundation than that such a statement has been made. When doubt exists as to the relevancy of a statement of a prosecution witness, the court will decide on the relevancy in camera, and exclude the irrelevant parts. *State v. Thompson,* 273 Minn. 1, 139 N.W.2d 490, *cert. denied,* 385 U. S. 817 (1966).

An indictment so general that it fails to give the defendant adequate notice of the charge should be supplemented by a bill of particulars. Granting such a bill is discretionary with the trial court. *In re Hitzemann,* 281 Minn. 275, 161 N.W.2d 542 (1968).

Upon the application of the county attorney, the district court in which the criminal charge is pending may require the defendant to file notice of an intent to use an alibi, giving the county or municipality in which the defendant claims to have been at the time of the alleged offense. If the defendant fails to file notice, the court in its discretion may exclude evidence of an alibi at the trial. MINN. STAT. ANN. §630.14 (1945).

Upon cause shown, a judge may allow the taking of depositions of witnesses on defendant's behalf. MINN. STAT. ANN. §611.08 (1963).

V. SPEEDY TRIAL

The accused in all criminal prosecutions has the right to a speedy and public trial. MINN. CONST. art. 1, §6. If an indictment is not brought against the accused at the next term of the court where he is held, the court must order that the prosecution be dismissed, unless good cause is shown. If the defendant has been indicted and the trial is not postponed at his request, he must be tried at the next term of court in which the offense is triable, or the indictment must be dismissed unless good cause is shown. MINN. STAT. ANN. §611.04 (1963).

It is the duty of the court, not of the county attorney, to make the decision as to when a criminal matter shall be heard. *State v. Hartman,* 272 Minn. 58, 136 N.W.2d 543 (1965).

It is imperative that criminal cases be prosecuted with the utmost dispatch, whether the accused is incarcerated or not. Generally, however, the accused seeking an absolute discharge because of the state's failure to accord him a speedy trial must establish that demand for trial at an earlier time was made by him or on his behalf, and that he had sustained prejudice because of the lapse of time. *State v. Borough,* 287 Minn. 48d, 178 N.W.2d 897 (1970).

MISSISSIPPI

I. BAIL

All persons are bailable before conviction except for capital offenses when the proof is evident or the presumption great. Excessive bail must not be required. MISS. CONST. art. 3, §29. Any person twice tried for a capital offense, where in each trial the jury has failed to agree on guilt or innocence, shall also be entitled to bail. MISS. CODE ANN. §2485.5 (1942).

The defendant must be committed to jail if he does not give bail. If the defendant gives bail, the court must state in the mittimus the nature of the offense before he may be released. MISS. CODE ANN. §2485 (1942).

II. PRELIMINARY HEARING

Mississippi has no regular preliminary hearing procedure.

III. GRAND JURY, INDICTMENT, INFORMATION

No person charged with a felony may be proceeded against criminally by information for an indictable offense. The legislature may, however, dispense with the grand jury inquest in cases not punishable by death or imprisonment in the penitentiary and may authorize prosecution in inferior courts. MISS. CONST. art. 3, §27.

IV. PRETRIAL DISCOVERY

The defendant has no right to inspect evidence in the prosecution's possession.

The trial court has discretion whether to grant discovery of evidence in the prosecution's possession. The defendant should be able to inspect tangible evidence which may be used against him or which may be useful in his defense. Due process and a fair trial require this. The court has recognized that the defendant's own statement or confession to the police may be examined before the trial. Inspection of photographs, confessions, and tangible evidence should be allowed, although denial of the right to inspection under certain circumstances may not be prejudicial. *Armstrong v. State*, 214 So. 2d 589 (Miss.), *cert. denied*, 395 U. S. 965 (1968).

The defendant is not entitled to inspection of prior statements by a prosecution witness even after the witness has testified on direct examination at trial. Granting or denying the request for inspection lies in the sound discretion of the trial court. In order to sustain a request for production or inspection it must be shown that the statement sought is at variance with the testimony given at trial. *Mattox v. State*, 243 Miss. 402, 137 So. 2d 920 (1962).

The defendant in a criminal case is not entitled to a bill of particulars. *Wilson v. State*, 221 So. 2d 100 (Miss. 1969); *Jones v. State*, 215 Miss. 355, 60 So. 2d 805 (1952).

The accused ordinarily should be permitted to interview a witness held in public custody upon a showing that the person in custody may be a witness, and that his testimony may be relevant to the issues of the case. *White v. State*, 52 Miss. 216 (1876); *Frazier v. State*, 142 Miss. 456, 107 So. 674 (1926).

V. SPEEDY TRIAL

The accused in all criminal prosecutions has the right to a speedy and public trial. MISS. CONST. art. 3, §26. Every offender must be taken before the proper officer for examination of his case without unnecessary delay. MISS. CODE ANN. §2473 (1942). All indictments must be tried at the first term of the court, unless good cause is shown for a continuance. MISS. CODE ANN. §2518 (1942).

The granting of the defendant's motion for a continuance is a matter largely within the sound discretion of the trial court, and a judgment will not be reversed because the continuance is refused unless there has been an abuse of sound discretion. *King v. State*, 251 Miss. 161, 168 So. 2d 637 (1964).

MISSOURI

I. BAIL

All persons are bailable except for capital offenses where the proof is evident or the presumption great. MO. CONST. art. 1, §20. Excessive bail cannot be required. MO. CONST. art. 1, §21. If the jury fails to render a verdict, the court may, in its discretion, discharge the jury and commit or bail the prisoner for trial at the same or next term of the court. MO. CONST. art. 1, §19.

If the offense charged is bailable, the judge shall admit the accused to bail upon request, in such a sum as seems to be sufficient and proper. MO. R. CRIM. P. 21.12. All persons arrested and held for the alleged commission of a criminal offense must be discharged within 20 hours of the time of the arrest unless a warrant is subsequently obtained. MO. R. CRIM. P. 21.14.

II. PRELIMINARY HEARING

No information charging the commission of a felony may be filed unless the accused has first been accorded the right to a preliminary examination. No preliminary examination is required where an information has been substituted for an indictment. The accused may waive the right to a preliminary examination after being accorded the right of consultation with counsel. MO. R. CRIM. P. 23.02.

The magistrate must advise the accused of the charge against him and, if requested, read him the complaint. As soon as possible, he must examine the complainant and other prosecution witnesses under oath, and in the presence of the accused. MO. R. CRIM. P. 23.03.

If the magistrate determines either that no crime has been committed, or that there is no probable cause to believe the accused guilty, he must discharge the accused. MO. R. CRIM. P. 23.08.

III. GRAND JURY, INDICTMENT, INFORMATION

No one shall be prosecuted for a felony or misdemeanor except upon an indictment or information. MO. CONST. art. 1, §17. No information charging the commission of a felony may be filed unless the accused has first been given a preliminary examination before a magistrate. The accused may waive his right to preliminary examination after being given the right to consult with his attorney. No preliminary examination is required where an information has been substituted for an indictment. MO. R. CRIM. P. 23.02.

IV. PRETRIAL DISCOVERY

The defendant is not entitled to inspection or disclosure of evidence in the prosecution's possession. *State v. Engberg,* 377 S.W.2d 282, (Mo. 1964); *State v. Aubuchon,* 381 S.W.2d 807 (Mo. 1964); *State v. Spica,* 389 S.W.2d 35 (Mo. 1965). Whether to grant or deny the inspection is within the discretion of the trial court, but the accused may be permitted to inspect evidence to protect his constitutional rights. *State v. Aubuchon, supra; State v. Spica, supra.* If there is no showing that inspection of the requested items is necessary to make the trial fundamentally fair, the motion for production will be denied. *State v. Spica, supra.* Good cause for production should appear from the motion, evidence, or admissions of the parties that the documents contain relevant and material evidence. *State ex rel. Phelps v. McQueen,* 296 S.W.2d 85 (Mo. 1956).

The trial court does not have the authority to order production of irrelevant and immaterial matter which is not admissible in evidence, even though such matter might aid in the preparation for trial. *State v. Hinojosa,* 242 S.W.2d 1 (Mo. 1951); *see State v. Gilliam,* 351 S.W.2d 723 (Mo. 1961).

Upon application of either party in a criminal case, a subpoena duces tecum may be issued commanding the production of books, papers, documents, or other objects, and the court may direct that the objects designated in the subpoena be produced before the court prior to the trial or prior to when they are to be offered in evidence. The court may, upon their production, permit them or portions thereof to be inspected by the parties and their attorneys. MO. R. CRIM. P. 25.19.

A report or statement of a witness in the hands of the prosecution should be produced only if there is a satisfactory showing that the requested report or statement is of such a nature that, without it, the defendant's trial would be fundamentally unfair, as where a material witness previously made a statement of facts which completely exonerates the defendant or which would totally change the degree of a crime. *State v. Aubuchon,* 381 S.W.2d 807 (Mo. 1964).

Defense counsel should be permitted to examine a paper or document from which a witness has refreshed his recollection while on the stand, but this is not required where the paper is not used at the trial. *State v. Smith,* 431 S.W. 2d 74 (Mo. 1968); *State v. Gadwood,* 342 Mo. 466, 116 S.W.2d 42 (1938).

No disclosure can be made of any grand jury deliberations, nor of the statement or vote of any grand juror. The transcripts or minutes of testimony of witnesses before the grand jury may be made available to the attorney general, prosecuting attorneys, circuit attorneys, and their assistants for use in the performance of their duties. Matters occurring before the grand jury may be disclosed only on direction of the court, upon a finding of necessity to meet the ends of justice, in connection with a judicial proceeding, or when permitted by the court upon a particularized showing by the defendant that grounds may exist for a motion to dismiss the indictment because of matters occurring before the grand jury. Disclosure is not permitted by inspection of transcripts of testimony for purposes of discovery or as a substitute for taking depositions of witnesses enforced on an indictment. Mo. R. Crim. P. 24.24.

If the indictment fails to inform the accused of particulars sufficiently to prepare his defense, the court may direct the filing of a bill of particulars. *State v. Frankum,* 425 S.W.2d 183 (Mo. 1968). A bill of particulars which would amount to disclosure of the prosecution's evidence will not be granted. *State v. Mace,* 357 S.W.2d 923 (Mo. 1962). Failure to move for a bill of particulars within the required time constitutes a waiver of the right to such a bill. *St. Louis v. Capitol Vending Co.,* 374 S.W.2d 519 (Mo. App. 1964).

The disclosure of the identity of an informer is in the discretion of the trial court. *State v. Redding,* 357 S.W.2d 103 (Mo. 1962); *State v. White,* 408 S.W.2d 31 (Mo. 1966). The general rule is that the prosecution is privileged to withhold from the accused disclosure of the identity of the informer; however, this privilege is qualified.

Where, aside from the information supplied by the informer, the police have no reason to suspect the defendant of committing a crime, the privilege against nondisclosure is qualified. For the trial court to treat the privilege of nondisclosure as unqualified is an abuse of discretion and constitutes reversible error. *State v. Cookson,* 361 S.W.2d 683 (1962).

A defendant in any criminal case may obtain the deposition of any witness to be used conditionally. Mo. R. Crim. P. 25.10. Depositions shall be taken as in civil cases, except that the notice to the prosecuting attorney shall state the names of the prospective deponents. Mo. R. Crim. P. 25.11. A deposition, if otherwise admissible, may be used at trial if the witness is dead, out of state, or unable to testify owing to sickness or infirmity. Mo. R. Crim. P. 25.12.

V. Speedy Trial

In all criminal prosecutions, a defendant has the right to a speedy trial. Mo. Const. art. 1, §18(a).

If the defendant, free on bail during the time in question, contributed to the cause of the delay, he was not in any way prejudiced thereby. *State v.*

Brown, 445 S.W.2d 647 (Mo. App. 1969). Where the defendant requested a continuance, he cannot complain that he was denied a speedy trial. *State v. Harris,* 425 S.W.2d 148 (1968).

MONTANA

I. BAIL

Except in the case of a capital offense, when the proof is evident or the presumption great, all persons must be bailable. MONT. CONST. art. III, §19. If the defendant is eligible for bail, he may be released on his own recognizance, subject to conditions which the court may, with reason, prescribe. MONT. REV. CODE tit. 95, §1106 (1947). Bail must be reasonable in amount and commensurate with the nature of the offense charged. MONT. CONST. art. III, §19 (Cum. Supp. 1971). When determining the amount of bail, the court takes into account the defendant's financial ability, his prior record, his employment status, and his family background. MONT. REV. CODE tit. 95, §1110 (1947).

II. PRELIMINARY HEARING

The defendant must be taken before the judge who issues the warrant "without unnecessary delay." MONT. REV. CODE tit. 95, §901 (1947). The purpose of this examination is to determine whether there is probable cause to believe a felony has been committed by the defendant. MONT. REV. CODE tit. 95, §1201 (1947). At the preliminary hearing the judge must inform the accused of the charge against him, of his right to counsel, of his right to assigned counsel should he be indigent, and of his right to remain silent. MONT. REV. CODE tit. 95, §902 (1947). The defendant does not plead to the charge at this time. He may introduce his own witnesses and may conduct cross-examination of witnesses for the prosecution. All persons are interrogated in the presence of the accused. If probable cause exists, the defendant will be bound over to the proper court.

III. GRAND JURY, INDICTMENT, INFORMATION

The county attorney may apply directly to the district court for permission to file an information against a named defendant. The application must be by affidavit, supported by such evidence as the judge may require. If it appears that there is probable cause to believe that an offense has been committed by the defendant, the judge shall grant leave to file the information; otherwise, the application will be denied. MONT. REV. CODE tit. 95,

§1301 (1947). The grand jury may inquire into all public offenses committed, or triable within the county, and present them to the court by indictment. MONT. REV. CODE tit. 95, §1405 (1947).

IV. PRETRIAL DISCOVERY

The accused is not entitled to the inspection or disclosure of evidence in the prosecution's possession. To allow inspection under the civil discovery statute, the material sought must be admissible in evidence. The right to inspection is discretionary with the judge, and cannot be used to conduct a "fishing expedition." *State ex rel. Keast v. Dist. Ct. of Fourth Judicial Dist.*, 135 Mont. 545, 342 P.2d 1071 (1959). The accused is not entitled to inspect, before trial, a statement made by a witness or any other person. *State v. Hall*, 55 Mont. 182, 175 P. 267 (1918).

A defendant is not entitled to inspect statements made by the prosecution's witnesses for the purpose of cross-examination or impeachment, even after the witness has testified on direct examination at the trial. *State v. Arnold*, 84 Mont. 348, 275 P. 757 (1929). Upon showing that the person in custody is or may be a witness on the case and that this testimony may be relevant or material to the case, a defendant may be permitted to interview him. *State v. Gangner*, 73 Mont. 187, 235 P. 703 (1925).

An accused cannot require a bill of particulars where the defendant is fully advised of the nature of the offense charged. *State v. Robinson*, 109 Mont. 322, 96 P.2d 265 (1939).

For purposes of notice only, and to prevent surprise, the prosecution must furnish defendant with a list of the witnesses it intends to call. MONT. REV. CODE ANN. tit. 95, §1803 (1947). Within a reasonable time before trial, any party may move to have produced all documents or things the opposing party intends to introduce in evidence. However, upon a sufficient showing, the court may deny inspection. MONT. REV. CODE ANN. tit. 95, §1803(c) (1947).

The defendant must furnish the prosecution with a statement of his intention to interpose a defense of insanity, self-defense, or alibi, along with the name of all witnesses to be called by defense in support of such a defense. MONT. REV. CODE ANN. tit. 95, §1803(d) (1947).

Before trial, the defendant can be furnished with a copy of any written confession or admission and a list of witnesses. The state will be required to furnish a list of witnesses if the confession was oral. MONT. REV. CODE ANN. tit. 95, §1804 (1947).

If a prospective witness is unable to attend the trial and his testimony is material, the court may, after indictment or information, or after the preliminary hearing, order his testimony to be taken by deposition. Any designated, nonprivileged tangible objects or papers may be produced. The party requesting the deposition shall give all parties reasonable written notice of the time and place of the taking of the deposition. MONT. REV. CODE ANN. tit. 95, §1802 (1947).

V. SPEEDY TRIAL

Persons have the right to a speedy public trial in all criminal prosecutions. MONT. CONST. art. III, §16.

NEBRASKA

I. BAIL

A person accused of committing a crime can be free on bail unless he is charged with treason or murder and the proof of guilt is evident or the presumption of guilt is great. NEB. CONST. art 1, §9. If the district court recommends a specific amount or quality of bail, the judge must be governed by this recommendation when he subsequently sets bail. NEB. REV. STAT. §29–903 (1964).

II. PRELIMINARY HEARING

A magistrate proceeds "as soon as may be" to inquire into a complaint. This is done in the presence of the accused. NEB. REV. STAT. §29–504 (1964). The magistrate may, at his own discretion, order separation of the witnesses for both parties. NEB. REV. STAT. §29–505 (1964). The defendant will be discharged if it appears that no offense has been committed or that there is no probable cause to believe the accused has committed an offense. NEB. REV. STAT. §29–506 (1964).

III. GRAND JURY, INDICTMENT, INFORMATION

Nebraska courts possess, and may exercise, the same power and jurisdiction to hear, try, and determine a prosecution for a crime, misdemeanor, or offense that has been prosecuted by an information as they may exercise if the prosecution had been commenced by a grand jury indictment. NEB. REV. STAT. §219–1601 (1964).

IV. PRETRIAL DISCOVERY

An accused has no right to discover evidence in the possession of the prosecution. *Cramer v. State,* 145 Neb. 88, 15 N.W.2d 323 (1944). A defendant needs a valid reason to compel the prosecution to disclose its evidence. *Cramer v. State, supra.* Inspection may be permitted if the interests of justice so demand. *Hameyer v. State,* 148 Neb. 798, 29 N.W.2d 458 (1947). The court will not grant permission to discover evidence if that evidence would not be admissible at the trial. *Cramer v. State, supra.* The defendant does not have an absolute right to examine the confession he made which is now in the possession of the prosecution; however, it would be proper to order inspection of a written confession if the interests of justice so require. If the only reason for ordering production is generally to aid the defendant in the preparation of his defense, the prosecution will not be required to produce such evidence. *Cramer v. State, supra.* In *Cramer,* a prosecution witness was examined by the prosecuting attorney and the statement he made was later reduced to writing. This memorandum was not viewed as a proper subject for the defense to discover.

A defendant is not entitled for the purpose of cross-examination or impeachment to inspect statements which the prosecution's witnesses made. *Erving v. State,* 174 Neb. 90, 116 N.W.2d 7, *cert. denied,* 375 U. S. 876 (1962). Statements which the prosecution has in its file are nothing more than memoranda or work product of the attorney, and consequently the defendant has no right to inspect them. *Erving v. State, supra.*

A bill of particulars is properly denied where an information adequately informs the defendant of the crime with which he was charged. *Jungclaus v. State,* 170 Neb. 704, 104 N.W.2d 327 (1960).

V. Speedy Trial

In all criminal prosecutions the accused has the right to a speedy trial. NEB. CONST. art. 1, §11. With certain exceptions such as treason and murder, no person can be prosecuted for a felony unless the indictment is found by a grand jury within three years after the offense is committed. An indictment must be found within one year and six months of the time a misdemeanor is committed. NEB. REV. STAT. §29–110 (1964). If a person is jailed, and charged with an indictable offense, and not indicted at the term of court at which he is held to answer, he will be discharged or bailed on his own recognizance. NEB. REV. STAT. §29–1201 (1964).

Every person indicted or informed against for any offense shall be brought to trial within six months. NEB. REV. STAT. 29–1207 (1)(1971 Supp.). Such six-month period shall commence to run from the date the indictment is returned or the information filed. NEB. REV. STAT. 29–1207 (2)(1971 Supp.). In computing the time for trial, the period of time resulting from a continuance granted at the request or with the consent of the defendant or his counsel shall be excluded. NEB. REV. STAT. 29–1207 (4)(b)(1971 Supp.). Continuances granted at the request of the prosecuting attorney will also be excluded in computing the six-month period if such continuance is granted because of the unavailability of evidence material to the state's case, when the prosecuting attorney has exercised due diligence to obtain such evidence and there are reasonable grounds to believe that such evidence will be available at the later date; or if such continuance is granted to allow the prosecuting attorney additional time to prepare the state's case and additional time is justified because of the exceptional circumstances of the case. NEB. REV. STAT. 29–1207(4)(c)(i)(ii)(1971 Supp.). A court may also exclude the period of delay from the six-month period for other reasons not specifically noted in this section upon a showing of good cause. NEB. REV. STAT. 29–1207(4)(f)(1971 Supp.). If the delay was pursuant to an agreement between the defendant's counsel and the state, the defendant will not be discharged. *State v. Lewis,* 177 Neb. 173, 128 N.W.2d 610(1964). For the accused to be discharged, he must show that he has not been responsible for the delay and that time was available to try the case. *Korth v. State,* 46 Neb. 631, 65 N.W. 792(1895).

NEVADA

I. BAIL

A person may be free on bail, unless he is accused of a capital offense when the proof of guilt is evident or the presumption of guilt is great. NEV. CONST. art. 1, §7. The amount of bail is based on a number of factors, including the following: the nature and circumstances of the offense charged; the financial ability of the defendant to give bail; and the character of the defendant. NEV. REV. STAT. §178.498. The defendant may be released on his own recognizance. NEV. REV. STAT. §178.502.

II. PRELIMINARY HEARING

After arrest, a defendant must be taken without unnecessary delay before a magistrate. NEV. REV. STAT. §171.178. Prior to a preliminary examination, the defendant must be informed of the charges against him, of his right to counsel, and of his right to remain silent. NEV. REV. STAT. §171.186. Where an offense is not triable in the justice's court, the defendant will not be called upon to plead. If the defendant does not waive the preliminary examination, the magistrate will hear the evidence within 15 days unless just cause is shown for delay. The defendant may cross-examine adverse witnesses and may introduce evidence on his own behalf. NEV. REV. STAT. §171.196. If it appears that there is probable cause to believe that an offense has been committed, and that the defendant has committed it, he will be bound over to the district court. NEV. REV. STAT. §171.206.

III. Grand Jury, Indictment, Information

The Nevada court has, and may exercise, the same power and jurisdiction to try and determine prosecutions upon an information for crimes, misdemeanors, and offenses, to issue writs and process, and do all other acts as it has in the case of a like prosecution under an indictment. NEV. REV. STAT. §173.025.

IV. Pretrial Discovery

The trial court has the discretion to decide whether or not to order production, for the accused, of evidence in the possession of the prosecution. *Pinana v. State,* 76 Nev. 274, 352 P.2d 824 (1960). It may deny inspection where the basic rights of a defendant are not prejudiced. The accused may, however, be permitted inspection where such is necessary for a fair trial. *Pinana v. State, supra.* After a prosecution witness has testified on direct examination at the trial, the defendant ordinarily is entitled to inspect prior statements that the witness made in order to later cross-examine or impeach him. *Walker v. State,* 78 Nev. 463, 376 P.2d 137, *cert. denied,* 375 U. S. 882 (1962).

Nevada courts have explicitly recognized that an accused, under proper circumstances, may be permitted to inspect grand jury minutes before trial for the purpose of making a motion to dismiss or set aside an indictment. *Ivey v. State,* 82 Nev. 448, 420 P.2d 853 (1966). A transcript of grand jury testimony must be furnished to accused if, by habeas corpus, he challenges probable cause to hold him for trial. *Ivey v. State, supra.*

The identity of an informer need not be disclosed if the defendant is not on trial because of information the informer supplied. *Adams v. State,* 81 Nev. 524, 407 P.2d 169 (1965).

At the defendant's request, the court may order the state to permit the defendant to inspect and copy or photograph any relevant written or recorded statements or confessions made by the defendant. NEV. REV. STAT. §174.235. The defendant may also be allowed to inspect books, papers, documents, tangible objects, or copies or portions thereof which are in the custody of the state. NEV. REV. STAT. §174.245. If the court grants such relief to the defendant, it may, upon the state's motion, condition its order by requiring that the defendant permit the state to inspect similar evidence in its control. NEV. REV. STAT. §174.255.

The results of scientific or medical tests conducted by the state on the defendant in preparation for trial are beyond the scope of discovery. NEV. REV. STAT. §174.235. Internal state documents, memoranda, and statements by prospective state witnesses to state agents which constitute prosecutional work product are also not discoverable by the defendant. NEV. REV. STAT. §174.245.

V. SPEEDY TRIAL

After a person is held to answer for a public offense, he must be indicted or an information must be filed against him within 15 days. Provided that the defendant has not caused a delay, after the finding of the indictment or the filing of the information the defendant must be tried within 60 days. The court may dismiss the indictment, information, or complaint if the state fails to proceed with the prosecution within the required time-frame. NEV. REV. STAT. §178.556. If the action is dismissed for lack of prosecution, the defendant may not be prosecuted for the same offense at a later time. NEV. REV. STAT. §178.562(1). If a defendant is not brought to trial within the time required, the burden is on the prosecution to show good cause for the delay. *In the Matter of Hansen,* 79 Nev. 492, 387 P.2d 659 (1963).

NEW HAMPSHIRE

I. BAIL

Except for capital offenses where the proof is evident or the presumption great, a person who is arrested can be released on either personal recognizance or bail. N.H. REV. STAT. ANN. §597.1 (Supp. 1970). If a person is charged with having committed an offense which is punishable by more than 20 years in prison, life imprisonment, or death, the superior court may release the person on personal recognizance or may determine an amount of bail. N.H. REV. STAT. ANN. §597.4 (Supp. 1970). A person is eligible for, and in the case of one accused of having committed a misdemeanor, entitled to release on personal recognizance if the court is satisfied with the following: that his physical and mental condition will not jeopardize the public or himself; that his employment, family ties, and residence within the state or other sufficient connection with the state make his failure to appear unlikely; that he has not failed to appear in any court when required to do so; that no special circumstance exists creating a likelihood that he would fail to appear. N.H. REV. STAT. ANN. §597.6–a (Supp. 1970). The court, in no event, can require excessive bail. N.H. CONST. pt. 1, art. 33.

II. PRELIMINARY HEARING

It is the responsibility of a police officer who has made an arrest to bring the accused before the court without unreasonable delay. N.H. REV. STAT.

ANN §594.19–a (Supp. 1970). The accused must be brought before a magistrate within 24 hours of his arrest. N.H. REV. STAT. ANN. §594.20–a (Supp. 1970). The court reads the complaint to the accused and informs him of his right to counsel and to a preliminary examination. N.H. REV. STAT. ANN. §596–A:3 (Supp. 1970). An accused may waive the preliminary examination. N.H. REV. STAT. ANN. §596–A:4.

III. GRAND JURY, INDICTMENT, INFORMATION

In order to proceed against a person accused of having committed a crime, the punishment for which may be death or imprisonment for a period in excess of one year, the grand jury must indict him. N.H. REV. STAT. ANN. §601.1 (1955). If a person has been charged with a crime not punishable by death he may waive the indictment. N.H. REV. STAT. ANN. §601.2 (1955).

IV. PRETRIAL DISCOVERY

The trial court, in exercise of reasonable discretion and to prevent injustice, may permit the accused to inspect specific objects or writings in the possession of the prosecution. *State v. Super. Ct.,* 106 N.H. 228, 208 A.2d 832 (1965). Consequently, a defendant may be permitted to inspect guns, bullets, clothing of defendant's victim, knife, hair specimen taken from defendant's body, defendant's car, vacuum sweepings. The court may deny the defendant the right to discover laboratory and chemical reports made as part of the state's investigation. *State v. Super. Ct., supra.* Inspection of the prosecution's evidence may be granted to avoid a delay in the trial. *State ex rel. Regan v. Super. Ct.,* 102 N.H. 224, 153 A.2d 403 (1959). Medical reports of a hospital relating to the defendant's confinement for observation as to his sanity could be produced for inspection by the defense. *State v. Healey,* 106 N.H. 308, 210 A.2d 486 (1965).

The state need not disclose the identity of an informer except for good cause. *State ex rel. Childs v. Hayward,* 109 N.H. 228, 248 A.2d 88 (1968). The respondent in a criminal case may take the deposition of any person in his defense. N.H. REV. STAT. ANN. §517.13 (1955).

V. SPEEDY TRIAL

Every person is entitled to obtain justice promptly and without delay. N.H. CONST. pt. 1, art. 14. An accused is entitled to be free from capricious and oppressive delays; the procedural safeguards afforded him, however, necessitate a deliberate pace. A delay which is neither purposeful nor unreasonable, resulting from diligent and careful consideration of issues potentially decisive of the course of the trial and protection of the rights of both the defendant and the state, is not a denial of the right to a speedy trial. *State v. Coolidge,* 109 N.H. 403, 260 A.2d 547 (1969).

NEW JERSEY

I. BAIL

All persons are bailable by sufficient sureties before conviction, except for capital offenses where the proof is evident or the presumption great. N.J. CONST. art. 1, §11 (1947). Excessive bail shall not be required. N.J. CONST. art. 1, §12 (1947). Excessive bail is not a ground for appeal from conviction. N.J. CONST. art. 1, §12 (Supp. 1971–72). If a person committed for a capital offense punishable by death is not indicted within three months of his commitment, a judge of the superior court or the county court, for cause shown, may admit him to bail. N.J.R. CRIM. P. 3:26–1(b) (1971). If an indictment or accusation is not moved for trial within six months after arraignment, a judge of the supreme court or county court, for cause shown, may discharge the defendant upon his own recognizance. N.J.R. CRIM. P. 3:26–1(c)(1971). All persons charged with bailable offenses shall be bailable before conviction on such terms as will insure their presence in court when required, having regard for their background, residence, employment, and family status and, particularly, the general policy against unnecessary sureties and detention. In its discretion the court may order the release of a person on his own recognizance and may impose terms or conditions appropriate to such release. N.J.R. CRIM. P. 3:26-1(a)(1971).

II. PRELIMINARY HEARING

At the defendant's first appearance before the court following the filing of a complaint, the judge shall inform the defendant (1) of the charge against him, and furnish him with a copy of the complaint if not previously furnished; (2) of his right not to make a statement, and that any statement made may be used against him; and (3) of his right to counsel, or if indigent and entitled to counsel, of his right to have counsel furnished without cost. If the defendant is indigent, the judge shall provide him with counsel unless he affirmatively and with understanding waives this right. The court shall allow the defendant a reasonable time and opportunity to consult counsel before proceeding further. If the defendant is charged with an indictable offense, the court shall inform him of his right to have a hearing as to probable cause and of his right to indictment by the grand jury and trial by jury. If the offense may be tried by the court upon waiver of indictment and trial by jury, the court shall so inform the defendant. All such waivers shall be in writing, signed by the defendant. If the complaint charges an indictable offense which cannot be tried by the court on waiver, it shall not ask for or accept a plea to the offense. The court shall admit the defendant to bail as provided in Rule 3:26 and Rule 7:5. N.J.R. Crim. P. 3:4–2 (1971).

III. Grand Jury, Indictment, Information

The assignment judge of each county shall order and organize one or more grand juries for the county, not exceeding 23 members each, to be summoned at such times as the public interest requires. At least one grand jury shall be serving in each county at all times. N.J.R. Crim. P. 3:6–1 (1971).

A crime punishable by death shall be prosecuted by indictment. Every other offense shall be prosecuted by indictment unless the defendant, after having been advised of his right to indictment, has in writing waived the right, in which case he may be tried on accusation. N.J.R. Crim. P. 3:7–2 (1971).

The indictment or accusation shall be a written statement of the essential facts constituting the offense charged. It need not contain a formal commencement and shall be signed by the prosecuting attorney. N.J.R. Crim. P. 3:7–3(a)(1971).

IV. Pretrial Discovery

Upon defendant's motion, the court shall order the prosecution to permit defendant to inspect and copy or photograph any relevant (1) designated books, objects, papers, obtained for or belonging to him; (2) records of statements or confessions by the defendant or copies thereof; (3) defendant's grand jury testimony; (4) results or reports of physical or mental examinations and of scientific tests or experiments made in connection with the case and known to be in possession of the prosecution; and (5) reports or records of prior convictions of the defendant. N.J.R. Crim. P. 3:13–3(a)(1971).

On defendant's specific motion and absent a showing of good cause to the contrary, the court shall order production by the prosecution of relevant books, papers, documents, and objects and inspection of buildings or places which are within the custody and control of the state. N.J.R. Crim. P. 3:13-3(b)(1971).

The court may also, on defendant's motion, order the prosecution (1) to disclose to the defendant the names and addresses of any persons whom the prosecuting attorney knows to have any relevant evidence or information and to indicate which of those persons he may use as witnesses; (2) to permit defendant to inspect and copy any relevant records of statements by such persons or by co-defendants which are within the custody or control of the prosecuting attorney and any relevant records of prior convictions of prosecuting attorney; and (3) to permit the defendant to inspect and copy any relevant grand jury testimony of such persons or co-defendants. N.J.R. CRIM. P. 3:13–3(c)(1971).

If there is not disclosure before trial, the court shall, on defendant's motion made at trial, order the prosecution to produce any prior statement in its possession made by a witness who is about to testify on direct examination for the state, provided the statement is relevant. N.J.R. CRIM. P. 3:17–1 (1971). If there is a dispute as to relevance, the court shall inspect the statement, in camera, and decide what parts the defendant may inspect. N.J.R. CRIM. P. 3:17–2 (1971).

If any party discovers additional material previously requested or ordered, he shall promptly notify the other party or the court of its existence. If the court discovers that any party has not done so, it may order discovery, grant a continuance, or prohibit the party from introducing the undisclosed material in evidence. N.J.R. CRIM. P. 3:13–3(i)(1971).

A bill of particulars shall be ordered by the court if the indictment or accusation is not sufficiently specific to enable the defendant to prepare his defense. Further particulars may be ordered when a demand therefor is promptly made. N.J.R. CRIM. P. 3:7–5 (1971).

If the court grants discovery to a defendant, it may condition its order by requiring defendant to permit the state to inspect any materials which the defendant intends to use at trial and which are within defendant's possession or control. The state must show that the discovery is material to the preparation of its case and that its request is reasonable. The court may also order the defendant to disclose to the prosecution the names and addresses of those persons whom the defendant intends to use as witnesses at trial and any written statements made by them. N.J.R. CRIM. P. 3:13–3(d)(1971). The state may not obtain discovery of records of statements made by a defendant to his attorney. N.J.R. CRIM. P. 3:13-3(e)(1971).

If the defendant intends to plead an alibi or insanity, he must notify the prosecution of such intent. In the case of alibi, the defendant must also furnish to the prosecution a list of the names and addresses of the witnesses on whom he intends to rely. N.J.R. CRIM. P. 3:11–1, 3:11–2, 3:12(1971).

If the judge decides that a witness may be unable to attend trial, he may upon motion and notice to the parties order that the testimony of such witness be taken by deposition as in civil actions, and that any designated nonprivileged books, papers, or objects be produced at the same time. N.J.R. CRIM. P. 3:13-2(a)(1971).

V. SPEEDY TRIAL

In all criminal prosecutions, the accused shall have the right to a speedy and public trial by an impartial jury. N.J. CONST. art. 1, §10(1947). The right to a speedy trial is the right to move for such trial and to have the indictment dismissed if the state fails to prosecute it at the time for trial fixed by the court. *State v. Coolack*, 43 N.J. 14, 202 A.2d 422 (1964).

At any time after six months following the return of an indictment or the filing of an accusation, the assignment judge may, on his or on defendant's motion, direct that the trial be set for a specified day. Upon failure of the prosecuting attorney to proceed at that time, the assignment judge may order the indictment or accusation dismissed, and such dismissal shall be the equivalent of a judgment of acquittal. N.J.R. CRIM. P. 3:25–2(1971). The right to a speedy trial is waived if the defendant does not demand it. *State v. Hulsizer*, 42 N.J. Super. 224, 126 A.2d 47 (1956).

NEW MEXICO

I. BAIL

Except for capital offenses when the proof is evident or the presumption great all persons may be released on bail. N.M. CONST. art. II, §13. After a person has been indicted, he is entitled to bail if the offense is bailable. N.M. STAT. tit. 41, §4–1.

The court, in its discretion, may admit to bail a person indicted on a capital crime where the proof is evident or the presumption so great that the accused was not initially entitled to bail, if he has been imprisoned for two consecutive terms of court and has not yet been tried. N.M. STAT. tit. 41, §4–5.

After a mistrial, a person tried for a crime punishable by death may be bailed if six members of the jury voted to acquit. N.M. STAT. tit. 41, §4–6.

II. PRELIMINARY HEARING

A magistrate must immediately inform the defendant of the charge which has been brought against him, of his right to counsel, and of his right to waive a preliminary examination. N.M. STAT. tit. 41, §3–1.

At the preliminary examination, the defendant may be sworn and may testify in his own behalf. N.M. STAT. tit. 41, §3–2. The state need only produce evidence sufficient to establish reasonable grounds for the magistrate's exercise of judgment; it is not required to produce all of its evidence. For instance, the complaining witness need not appear at the preliminary hearing. *State v. Selgado*, 78 N.M. 165, 429 P.2d 363 (1967). Witnesses are examined in the presence of the defendant and may be cross-examined by the defendant. N.M. STAT. tit. 41, §3–8.

After the preliminary examination, if it appears to the magistrate that no offense was committed, or that probable cause for charging this defendant was not established, the defendant must be discharged. N.M. STAT. tit. 41, §3–12. One accused of having committed a misdemeanor is not entitled to a preliminary examination. N.M. STAT. tit. 41, §3–8(4).

III. GRAND JURY, INDICTMENT, INFORMATION

Prosecution of any crime, including murder, may be initiated by information set out by the district attorney. *State v. Roy,* 40 N.M. 397, 60 P.2d 646(1936).

IV. PRETRIAL DISCOVERY

In order to be granted the right to inspect the prosecution's evidence, the defendant must show something more than the mere desire to obtain all the prosecutor's information. At any time during the pendency of the action, upon request of the defendant and for good cause shown, the magistrate in actions within his trial jurisdiction may order the prosecution to produce for inspection and copying any records, papers, documents, or other tangible evidence in its possession or available to it. No other discovery proceedings shall be permitted. N.M. STAT. tit. 36, §21–30. If the accused wants to inspect the evidence in the possession of the prosecution for exploratory purposes, or for prying into the state's preparation of the case, the request will be denied. *State v. Tackett,* 78 N.M. 450, 432 P.2d 415(1967).

The defendant is not entitled to inspect, at trial, the transcript of preliminary hearing testimony. *Territory v. McFarlane,* 7 N.M. 421, 37 P. 1111(1894). Defendant may be allowed to inspect a supplemental police report which is referred to by an officer while he is testifying at trial. *State v. Gomez,* 75 N.M. 545, 408 P.2d 48(1965).

Suppressing material evidence that is favorable to the accused denies him of due process. *State v. Morris,* 69 N.M. 244, 365 P.2d 668(1961). Ordinarily, an accused is not entitled to inspect state grand jury minutes. *State v. Tackett, supra.* However, if the prosecution uses grand jury testimony during the trial, the defendant will then be granted inspection. The defendant may examine, however, only those portions of the grand jury testimony which relate to testimony given by the witness at the trial. *State v. Morgan,* 67 N.M. 287, 354 P.2d 1002(1960). A bill of particulars may be required, even though the information supplied the defendant as to the charge is valid under constitutional and statutory requirements. *State v. Graves,* 73 N.M. 79, 385 P.2d 635(1963).

V. SPEEDY TRIAL

One accused of having committed a crime has a right to a speedy trial. N.M. CONST. art. II, §14. Whenever a person is charged with the commission of a felony, the district court shall fix a date for commencement of the trial, which date shall be within 90 days from the time of the person's arrest, and the trial shall begin on that date unless postponed by the court upon a showing of good cause. If not brought to trial within six months from the date of the person's arrest, and if the six-month period has not been extended by the Supreme Court of New Mexico for good cause shown, the felony charge shall be dismissed with prejudice and shall not thereafter be filed in any court. N.M. STAT. tit. 41, §11–4.1(1971 Supp.). A party seeking an extension beyond the six-month period must, within the six-month period, file with the clerk of the supreme court a verified petition for extension concisely stating the facts he deems to constitute good cause and serve a copy on opposing counsel. A hearing, upon five days' notice, will be had on the petition at Santa Fe or such other place designated by the supreme court. N.M. STAT. R. 95(3)(1971 Supp.).

NEW YORK

I. BAIL

When the defendant is charged by information or misdemeanor complaint with an offense of less than felony grade, the court must order recognizance or bail. N.Y. CRIM. PROC. L. §§530.20, 530.40(McKinney 1971). A local criminal court has discretion to allow a suspected felon release on recognizance or bail after affording an opportunity to the district attorney to be heard in opposition to such an order. A local criminal court may not, however, order recognizance or bail when the defendant is charged with a class A felony or the defendant has two previous felony convictions. N.Y. CRIM. PROC. L. §530.20(2)(McKinney 1971). Superior court judges may order recognizance or bail to any person charged with a felony after the district attorney has had an opportunity to be heard on the matter. N.Y. CRIM. PROC. L. §530.40 (McKinney 1971).

To the extent that the issuance of an order of recognizance or bail is a matter of discretion, the court must consider the kind and degree of control or restriction that is necessary to secure the defendant's court appearance when required. N.Y. CRIM. PROC. L. §510.30(McKinney 1971). Excessive bail may not be required. N.Y. CONST. art. 1, §5.

Effective May 1, 1972, any criminal, except one being prosecuted for homicide, shall be released on bail or on his own recognizance, if he is in jail awaiting trial more than 90 days. Administrative Board of the Judicial Conference of the State of New York, Rule 29.1.

II. PRELIMINARY HEARING

The court must immediately inform the defendant of the charges against him and must furnish him with a copy of the accusatory instrument. The defendant has the right to counsel at this hearing and the court will assign counsel if the defendant is indigent. The court must do more than merely inform the defendant of his rights; it must itself take affirmative action to effectuate them. N.Y. CRIM. PROC. L. §§170.10, 180.10(McKinney 1971).

All witnesses called at the preliminary hearing must be sworn and may be cross-examined. The state must offer testimony and evidence in support of the charge. The defendant is entitled to testify in his own behalf and the court has discretion to permit him to call other witnesses and produce other evidence in his behalf. Only non-hearsay evidence is admissible to demonstrate reasonable cause to believe that the defendant committed a felony. The hearing should be completed at one session. In the interest of justice, it may be adjourned by the court, but, absent a showing of good cause, no such adjournment may be for more than one day. N.Y. CRIM. PROC. L. §180.60(McKinney 1971).

After this initial hearing, the court must issue a securing order either releasing the defendant on his own recognizance or fixing bail for his future appearance in the action. N.Y. CRIM. PROC. L. §§170.10, 180.10(McKinney 1971).

If a defendant waives a preliminary hearing, the court must either order that the defendant be held for the action of a grand jury or inquire into the felony charge for the purpose of determining whether a reduction in the charge to a nonfelony is appropriate. N.Y. CRIM. PROC. L. §180.30(McKinney 1971).

III. GRAND JURY, INDICTMENT, INFORMATION

A district attorney must submit to a grand jury evidence concerning a felony allegedly committed by a defendant who, on the basis of a felony complaint, has been held for the action of a grand jury. The district attorney must also submit to the grand jury evidence concerning a misdemeanor allegedly committed by a defendant in any case where the superior court has ordered that such misdemeanor charges be prosecuted by indictment. A district attorney may submit to a grand jury any available evidence concerning any prosecutable offense or any evidence of misconduct on the part of public officials. N.Y. CRIM. PROC. L. §190.55(McKinney 1971).

IV. PRETRIAL DISCOVERY

The court acting on a defendant's motion must order discovery for the defendant of testimony given by the defendant before the grand jury and must order discovery of statements given by the defendant to law enforcement agencies. Discovery may be ordered with respect to property specifically designated by the defendant, except for prosecutorial work product, where the request is reasonable and the property sought is material to the preparation of a defense. The defendant may also discover reports of medical and physical examinations or scientific reports which are within the possession of the state. The court may condition its order of discretionary discovery on the allowance of discovery by the state of property of the same kind or character as that authorized to be inspected by the defendant upon a showing by the state that its request is reasonable and that the items sought would be material to the preparation of the prosecution's case. N.Y. CRIM. PROC. L. §240.20(McKinney 1971).

If after complying with an order of discovery a party finds additional property which is subject to or covered by the order, he must promptly notify the other party or the court of the existence thereof. N.Y. CRIM. PROC. L. §240.40(McKinney 1971).

Evidence of mental disease or defect of the defendant is not admissible as a defense to criminal responsibility unless the defendant notifies both the prosecution and the court of his intention to rely upon such a defense. N.Y. CRIM. PROC. L. §250.10(McKinney 1971). At any time before trial, the state may serve upon the defendant a demand that if the defendant intends to offer at trial an alibi defense the prosecution must be informed of the place where the defendant claims to have been at the time in question and the names and addresses of persons who will testify in support of the alibi. The testimony of witnesses not so specified may be excluded or the state may be allowed an adjournment not to exceed three days. N.Y. CRIM. PROC. L. §250.20(McKinney 1971).

V. SPEEDY TRIAL

The defendant is entitled to a speedy trial. N.Y. CRIM. PROC. L. §30.20(McKinney 1971). Upon defendant's motion, the appropriate court may dismiss an information or an indictment on the grounds that the defendant has been denied the right to a speedy trial. N.Y. CRIM. PROC. L. §§170.30, 210.20(McKinney 1971).

One may waive the right to a speedy trial by one's conduct. *People v. Piscitello*, 7 N.Y. 2d 387, 198 N.Y.S. 2d 273, 165 N.E. 2d 849(1960). Since the burden is on the state to insure that the defendant is arraigned and speedily brought to trial, his failure to take affirmative action to prevent delay may not be construed or treated as a waiver of his right to have a speedy trial. *People v. Prosser*, 309 N.Y. 353, 130 N.E. 2d 891(1955).

Effective May 1, 1972, the prosecution must be ready for trial within six months. If not, charges must be dismissed. A defendant must be freed on bail or on his own recognizance if he is not brought to trial within three months of arrest. In misdemeanor cases with a possible sentence of more than three months, the prosecution must be ready for trial within 90 days, and on other misdemeanor charges the prosecution must be ready for trial within 60 days, or the charges will be dismissed. The provision does not apply to a defendant charged with homicide or to one who is serving a sentence for another crime.

NORTH CAROLINA

I. BAIL

Any justice or judge of the general court of justice can fix and take bail for a person who has been committed to prison, regardless of the crime with which he has been charged. N.C. GEN. STAT. §15–103(Supp. 1969). The judge may, in his discretion, release from custody any person charged with a noncapital felony. In determining the amount of bail and whether or not the defendant should be released on his own recognizance or upon the execution of an unsecured appearance bond, the court takes into account the accused's background, period of residence, employment, and family situation. N.C. GEN. STAT. §15–103.1(Supp. 1969).

II. PRELIMINARY HEARING

The defendant may waive the preliminary examination and give bail. N.C. GEN. STAT. §15–85(Supp. 1969). The magistrate must examine the complainant and the prosecution's witnesses in the presence of the prisoner. N.C. GEN. STAT. §15–87. The magistrate informs him of the charges filed against him and that he may refuse to answer any question. The magistrate then examines the defendant. The defendant is not sworn at this time. N.C. GEN. STAT. §15–89. Defendant may be aided by counsel. N.C. GEN. STAT. §15–87. If he desires he may cross-examine witnesses. N.C. GEN. STAT. §15–88. After the defendant is questioned, he may have his own witnesses sworn and questioned. N.C. GEN. STAT. §15–92.

III. GRAND JURY, INDICTMENT, INFORMATION

An accused may waive the indictment in any case in which he is charged, with the exception of a capital felony. N.C. GEN. STAT. §15–140.1(Supp. 1969).

IV. PRETRIAL DISCOVERY

A defendant has no right to inspect evidence held by the prosecution. In order for such a request for inspection to be granted, the accused would have to first show facts justifying disclosure. *State v. Goldberg,* 261 N.C. 181, 134 S.E.2d 334, *cert. denied,* 377 U. S. 978(1964). The accused has no absolute right to view documents or articles which, though in the possession of the prosecution, are not admissible into evidence. *State v. Hamilton,* 264 N.C. 277, 141 S.E.2d 506(1965). There is some indication that documents and papers which are the "subject" of the charge, or the "very essence" of the case, may be produced for the defendant. *State v. Goldberg, supra.*

Generally, the defendant is allowed to look at notes used by a state's witness to refresh his memory while testifying on the stand. *State v. Peacock,* 236 N.C. 137, 72 S.E.2d 612(1952).

Subject to certain limitations, the prosecutor need not divulge to the accused the identity of an informer. *State v. Bales,* 246 N.C. 83, 97 S.E.2d 476(1957).

If the exact place where the crime was allegedly committed is an essential element of the offense, the accused may obtain further information by a bill of particulars, *State v. Eason,* 242 N.C. 59, 86 S.E.2d 774(1955). The court may, in its discretion, grant a bill of particulars to the defendant if the indictment needs additional information so that the accused is better able to defend himself. N.C. GEN. STAT. §15–143. Records, books, papers, documents, or tangible things may be subpoenaed in a criminal action in the same manner as is provided for in civil actions. N.C. GEN. STAT. §8–61.

A defendant in a criminal action, upon showing that a person the defense might eventually call as a witness is a nonresident of North Carolina or is so physically incapacitated that his attendance at the trial or hearing could not be procured, may be granted permission to take the deposition of that person. N.C. GEN. STAT. §8–74 (as amended by Sess. Laws 1971, ch. 381, §6).

V. SPEEDY TRIAL

Justice is supposed to be administered without delay. N.C. CONST. art 1, §18. If a person who has been charged with a felony asks to be brought to trial and is not indicted during the next term of court after he was confined, the court may allow such a prisoner to be free on bail, unless it appears that witnesses for the state could not be produced at the same term. If the prisoner is not subsequently indicted and tried at the second term of court, he will be discharged from prison. N.C. GEN. STAT. §15–10. Even though the prisoner might be discharged from custody, the state is not barred from prosecuting him for the same offense at a later time. *State v. Patton,* 260 N.C. 359, 132 S.E.2d 891(1963). The right to a speedy trial is waived if the accused fails to demand it. *State v. Hollars,* 266 N.C. 45, 145 S.E.2d 309(1965).

NORTH DAKOTA

I. Bail

A person may be admitted to bail as a matter of right unless the crime he is accused of having committed is a capital one for which the proof is evident or the presumption great. N.D. Const. art. 1, §6. If a person is charged and tried for first degree murder, and there is a hung jury, the accused may then be bailed unless the court believes that the jury was unable to reach an agreement because of misconduct on the part of the jurors, the defendant, or the defendant's counsel. N.D. Cent. Code tit. 29–08–05. If the court is convinced that continued incarceration will cause permanent or serious injury to the defendant's health or endanger his life, the court either may remove the accused to another place of confinement or bail him. N.D. Cent. Code tit. 29–08–10.

II. Preliminary Hearing

If the magistrate before whom the accused is brought does not have the authority to try him, he must immediately inform him of the charges which have been filed against him and of the following rights: to remain silent; to counsel; to assigned counsel if he is without funds; to a preliminary examination; and to waive the preliminary examination. N.D. Cent. Code tit. 29–07–01. If the defendant does not waive his right to a preliminary examination, the magistrate must proceed to evaluate the case. N.D. Cent. Code tit. 29–07–05. If the defendant waives the preliminary examination, the state's attorney may still take witness's testimony. N.D. Cent. Code tit. 29–07–03. Witnesses may be subpoenaed to appear at the preliminary examination. N.D. Cent. Code tit. 29–07–10. Witnesses may be examined in the presence of the defendant, and they may be cross-examined. N.D. Cent. Code tit. 29–07–12.

III. Grand Jury, Indictment, Information

A person can be prosecuted for commission of a felony only after a grand jury has come forth with an indictment. N.D. Const. art. 1, §8. All other offenses may be prosecuted either by indictment or by information.

IV. Pretrial Discovery

When an indictment or information fails to sufficiently inform the defendant of the particulars of the offense so that he is able to prepare his defense, the court can order the state's attorney to furnish a bill of particulars to the defendant. N.D. Cent. Code tit. 29–11–11. In general, the rules of evidence in civil cases are applicable also to criminal cases, including those rules which pertain to depositions and discovery. N.D. CENT. CODE tit. 29–21–12. The court may, therefore, allow the defendant to discover documents, papers, books, accounts, letters, photographs, and objects not privileged. N.D.R. CIV. P. 30.

Whenever a defendant in a criminal case intends to rely upon an alibi as a defense he must give the prosecution at least five days before trial written notice setting forth with particularity the following information: the place or places where he claims to have been when the crime was committed and the names and addresses of the witnesses to his alibi. N.D. CENT. CODE tit. 29–12–28(1971 Supp.).

V. SPEEDY TRIAL

One accused of having committed a criminal act has the right to a speedy trial. N.D. CONST. art. 1, §13. Unless good cause is shown, the court will dismiss the prosecution if a person has been held to answer for a public offense and an information is not filed or an indictment found against him at the next general term of the court. The defendant will also be discharged if he has not caused the postponement of his trial and yet is not tried at the next term after the information is filed or the indictment found. N.D. CENT. CODE tit. 29–18–01. If, for some justifiable reason, the defendant is not prosecuted or tried within the required time period, the court may have the case continued. The defendant may, at this time, be discharged from custody on his own recognizance or he may be bailed. N.D. CENT. CODE tit. 29–18–02. The only time a defendant would be discharged because of delay would be in the situation where he resisted postponement and demanded a trial. *State v. Dinger*, 51 N.D. 98, 199 N.W. 196(1924).

OHIO

I. BAIL

A person who has been accused of committing a crime may be free on bail unless the crime is a capital offense where the proof is evident or the presumption great. OHIO CONST. art. 1, §9. The judge or magistrate fixes bail for felonies. There is to be some correlation between the amount of bail and the seriousness of the offense, the previous criminal record of the defendant, and the probability that he will appear at trial. OHIO REV. CODE §2937.24 (Page 1955). If the court is convinced that the accused will appear, he may be released on his own recognizance. OHIO REV. CODE §2937.29 (Page 1955).

II. Preliminary Hearing

A person charged with a felony must be informed of the right to a preliminary examination. OHIO REV. CODE §2937.02(D)(Page Supp. 1970). The examination may be waived by the defendant but will still be held if the court refuses to accept such waiver. OHIO REV. CODE §2937.10(Page Supp. 1970). No continuance at any stage of the proceeding, however, shall extend for more than ten days unless the state and the accused agree to a further delay. OHIO REV. CODE §2937.21 (Page Supp. 1970).

III. Grand Jury, Indictment, Information

A prosecution may proceed by an information, if the punishment for the offense charged is other than death or life imprisonment and the accused has waived his right to prosecution by indictment. OHIO REV. CODE §2941.021 (Page Supp. 1970). Effective January 1, 1972, if the grand jury does not take final action within 60 days of the bind over, charges will be dismissed unless the prosecutor can show good cause. OHIO SUP. R. 8A.

IV. Pretrial Discovery

A defendant is not entitled to inspect or have disclosed to him evidence which the prosecution has in its possession. *State v. Hahn,* 10 Ohio Op. 29, 25 Ohio L. Abs. 449(1937). Whether or not the accused is allowed to inspect the state's evidence is largely a matter of the trial court's discretion. *State v. Corkran,* 3 Ohio St. 2d 125, 32 Ohio Op. 2d 132, 209 N.E.2d 437(1965).

Statements which were made by the prosecution's witnesses are ordinarily not the subject of defendant's inspection if the purpose of the inspection is for use during cross-examination or to impeach a witness. *State v. Thomasson,* 46 Ohio Op. 402, 58 Ohio L. Abs. 402, 97 N.E.2d 42(1950). The defendant may inspect a writing or object that has been in the state's possession after it is offered into evidence at trial. *State v. Sharp,* 162 Ohio St. 173, 122 N.E.2d 684(1954).

The defendant may not inspect grand jury minutes before trial if the reason for such inspection is preparation for trial or ascertainment of evidence in the hands of the prosecution. *State v. Selby,* 69 Ohio L. Abs. 481, 126 N.E.2d 606(1955).

A defendant is ordinarily allowed to interview one who is being held in public custody if he shows that this person is or may be a witness in the case and that his testimony may be relevant or material to the issues which will be tried. *Atkins v. State,* 115 Ohio St. 542, 155 N.E. 189, *cert. denied,* 274 U. S. 720(1926).

Inspection by the defendant of his own statements or confession is discretionary with the trial court. *State v. Hill*, 23 Ohio Op. 2d 255, 191 N.E.2d 235(1963); *State v. Potts*, 69 Ohio L. Abs. 77, 124 N.E.2d 180(1953).

A defendant may request, and the court may order, a bill of particulars setting out specifically the nature of the offense charged. OHIO REV. CODE §2941.07(Page 1955). If a defendant pleads guilty, he waives his right to a bill of particulars. *Foutty v. Maxwell*, 174 Ohio St. 35, 21 Ohio Op. 2d 288, 186 N.E.2d 623(1962). In a misdemeanor action before a municipal court or a justice of the peace, the defendant is not entitled to a bill of particulars. *Cincinnati v. McKinney*, 101 Ohio App. 511, 1 Ohio Op. 2d 434, 137 N.E.2d 589(1955).

The prosecution need not disclose the identity of an informer to the defendant. *State v. Viola*, 51 Ohio L. Abs. 577, 82 N.E.2d 306, *cert. denied*, 334 U. S. 816(1947). However, if knowing the identity of the informer is essential to the accused's defense, the state will have to come forward with such information. *State v. Beck*, 175 Ohio St. 73, 23 Ohio Op. 2d 377, 191 N.E.2d 825(1963).

After an issue of fact is joined upon an indictment, information, or affidavit, the prosecution or defendant may apply in writing to the court for a commission to take depositions of any witness. OHIO REV. CODE §2945.50 (Page Supp. 1970).

If the defendant in a criminal case intends to offer an alibi in his defense, he must, not less than three days before trial, file and serve upon the prosecuting attorney a written notice to that effect. OHIO REV. CODE §2945.58 (Page 1955).

V. SPEEDY TRIAL

One accused of committing a crime is guaranteed a speedy trial. OHIO CONST. art. 1, §10. Even though the constitution guarantees the defendant a speedy trial, the defendant is expected to demand of the court that this right be satisfied; without such a demand the right is waived. *State v. Doyle*, 11 Ohio App. 2d 97, 40 Ohio Op. 2d 251, 228 N.E.2d 863(1967). If a trial is free from vexatious, capricious, and oppressive delays, then the constitutional provisions granting a speedy trial are considered fulfilled. *State v. Reardon*, 28 Ohio Op. 2d 394, 95 Ohio L. Abs. 56, 201 N.E.2d 818(1964).

No continuance at any stage of the preliminary hearing shall extend for more than ten days unless the state and the accused agree otherwise. OHIO REV. CODE §2937.21 (Page Supp. 1970). Any continuance or delay contrary to this provision, unless procured by defendant or his counsel, is grounds for dismissal. OHIO REV. CODE §2937.21 (Page Supp. 1970). A discharge under this section, however, will not bar a subsequent prosecution for the same offense. *Columbus v. Nappi*, 5 Ohio St. 2d 99, 34 Ohio Op. 2d

222, 214 N.E.2d 83(1966). Unless a continuance is had on the defendant's motion or he has otherwise caused the delay he must be discharged. OHIO REV. CODE §2945.71 (Page 1955).

Effective January 1, 1972, all criminal cases shall be tried within six months of the date of the arraignment on an indictment or information. The chief justice is empowered to take the required action to bring a delinquent case to trial. OHIO SUP. R. 8B.

OKLAHOMA

I. BAIL

A person charged with a criminal offense may be free on bail, providing the crime he has been accused of committing is not a capital offense when the proof of guilt is evident or the presumption of guilt is great. OKLA. CONST. art. 2, §8. The sole guide to determining the amount of bail should be whether it will insure the defendant's appearance to answer the charge against him. *Ex parte Sanders,* 289 P.2d 155 (Okla. 1955). Excessive bail must not be required. OKLA. CONST. art. 2, §9. If the accused was tried by a jury which was unable to reach a verdict, the defendant is then entitled to bail unless it appears that inability to reach an agreement was caused by misconduct on the part of the jurors. OKLA. STAT. ANN. tit. 22, §1102.

II. PRELIMINARY HEARING

At the preliminary examination, witnesses must be questioned in the presence of the defendant. Either the prosecuting attorney or the defendant may request that the testimony be recorded in written form. The convening of a grand jury does not dispense with the prosecution's right to conduct a preliminary hearing. In felony cases the prosecution may have witnesses subpoenaed to appear at the preliminary hearing. There is no preliminary examination in a misdemeanor case. OKLA. STAT. ANN. tit. 22, §258. If the accused fails to cross-examine witnesses at the preliminary hearing this may be viewed as a waiver of the right to confront these witnesses at trial if the witnesses are unable to testify at the later date. *In re Bishop,* 443 P.2d 768 (Okla. 1968).

III. GRAND JURY, INDICTMENT, INFORMATION

Both felonies and misdemeanors may be prosecuted by presentment, indictment, or information. One can be prosecuted for a felony by information, however, only if one has first had a preliminary examination. If one has waived his right to a preliminary examination, the state may commence the prosecution by an information. OKLA. CONST. art. 2, §17. Felonies are prosecuted in the district superior court. Although misdemeanors are generally prosecuted by information, the court may order that the case be presented to a grand jury and consequently be prosecuted by indictment. OKLA. STAT. ANN. tit. 22, §301.

IV. PRETRIAL DISCOVERY

An accused is not entitled to inspect evidence which is in the possession of the prosecution. *Melchor v. State,* 404 P.2d 63 (Okla. 1965). Inspection may be allowed if it will avoid delaying the trial, *Layman v. State,* 355 P.2d 444 (Okla. 1960); or will further the interests of justice, *Application of Killion,* 338 P.2d 168 (Okla. 1959). If objects in the state's possession would not be admissible in evidence, the accused has no right to inspect them. *Application of Killion, supra.* The court may require that documents or papers which are the subject of the charge, or the "very essence" of the case, or which form the "basis" of the charge be produced for the defense to inspect. *Application of Killion, supra.*

Whether to allow inspection of statements made by possible prosecution witnesses for the purpose of later cross-examination or impeachment must be determined by the facts of each case; for instance, where the defendant gave statements to the police without counsel present and subsequently could not recall what she had said, justice would require that she see such statements prior to trial. *Doakes v. Dist. Ct. of Oklahoma City,* 447 P.2d 461 (Okla. 1968).

With certain exceptions the rules of evidence in civil cases are applicable also in criminal cases. OKLA. STAT. ANN. tit. 22, §702. Upon a showing of good cause, the court may order that the defendant be allowed to inspect documents, papers, books, accounts, letters, photographs, objects, or tangible things which contain evidence relating to any of the matters within the scope of examination which are in the state's possession, custody, or control. OKLA. STAT. ANN. tit. 12, §548 (Supp. 1970). Interrogatories also may be taken. OKLA. STAT. ANN. tit. 12, §549 (Supp. 1970).

In general, if a material witness is in jail, the defendant may be permitted to interview him. *Exelton v. State,* 30 Okla. Crim. 224, 235 P. 627(1925). One case, however, held that such interrogation can only be made in the presence of the sheriff. *Robinson v. State,* 8 Okla. Crim. 667, 130 P. 121(1913).

V. SPEEDY TRIAL

The right to speedy trial is assured. OKLA. CONST. art. 2, §20. If one is to answer for a public offense, an indictment or information must be filed at the next term of court after he is held to answer. Absent a showing of good cause, the prosecution will be dismissed if it does not proceed within the time required. OKLA. STAT. ANN. tit. 22, §811. If a defendant is being prosecuted for a public offense and he has not caused a postponement, yet he is not tried at the next term of court in which the indictment or information is triable, the prosecution will be dismissed, unless good reason is shown. OKLA. STAT. ANN. tit. 22, §812.

In *Brown v. State,* the court held that a defendant who is imprisoned need not demand a speedy trial because the law makes that demand for him. *Brown v. State,* 384 P.2d 54(1963). Subsequent cases have taken the view that the accused must make a demand for trial, resist postponement, or make some other effort to secure a speedy trial to entitle him to dismissal of the charge. *Bell v. State,* 430 P.2d 841 (Okla. 1967). When out on bail, defendant must make a written demand for a speedy trial. Where this is not done, his right to a speedy trial is considered to have been waived. *Killian v. Page,* 427 P.2d 442 (Okla. 1967).

OREGON

I. BAIL

If one has been charged with any offense other than murder or treason he may be freed on bail. ORE. CONST. art. I, §14. One accused of murder or treason will not be bailed when the proof is evident or the presumption strong. ORE. REV. STAT. 140.020.

II. PRELIMINARY HEARING

In all cases, a defendant must first be taken before the magistrate and informed of his right to counsel, his right to remain silent, and his right to a preliminary examination. The preliminary examination must be held within five days if the defendant so requests. ORE. REV. STAT. §133.610. At the preliminary examination, witnesses are questioned in the presence of the defendant and may be cross-examined by him. ORE. REV. STAT. §133.670.

III. GRAND JURY, INDICTMENT, INFORMATION

No person can be charged with committing a "crime or misdemeanor" except upon an indictment found by a grand jury. The right to a grand jury investigation may be waived and the prosecution then may proceed after an information is filed. ORE. CONST. art. VII, §20.

IV. Pretrial Discovery

In the absence of a statute or court rule to the contrary, a person who is accused of having committed a crime is not entitled to inspection or disclosure of the evidence which is in the possession of the prosecution. *State v. Tranchell,* 243 Ore. 215, 412 P.2d 520(1966). The defendant, as well as the district attorney, may inspect statements and depositions taken on the information. ORE. REV. STAT. §133.750. A defendant may inspect books, papers, documents, or tangible objects taken from him, including written statements of confessions which he made, upon showing the items sought are material to preparation of defense. ORE. REV. STAT. §133.755.

The state is not required to disclose to the defendant what witnesses said before a grand jury. Nor is the accused authorized to look behind the indictment to evaluate the evidence given before a grand jury. *State v. Guse,* 237 Ore. 479, 392 P.2d 257(1964). If a witness possesses an independent recollection of events, the prosecution cannot be required to produce a writing which he previously used to refresh his memory before entering the witness stand. *State v. Kader,* 201 Ore. 300, 270 P.2d 160(1954).

If the defendant intends to come forth with a plea of insanity as a defense he must file a written notice of that intention at the time he pleads to the charge. ORE. REV. STAT. §135.870.

V. Speedy Trial

Justice must be administered "without delay." ORE. CONST. art. I, §10. If a person is held to answer for a crime, and an indictment is not found within 60 days after he was held to answer, the prosecution must be dismissed, unless good cause to the contrary is shown. ORE. REV. STAT. §134.110. After indictment, a person must be brought to trial within a reasonable period of time or the indictment will be dismissed, provided, however, that the defendant is not responsible for any delay which has occurred. ORE. REV. STAT. §134.120. If sufficient reason is shown for one's not being indicted or tried within a reasonable amount of time a continuance may be ordered. The defendant at that time may be discharged from custody on his own undertaking of bail. ORE. REV. STAT. §134.130.

The defendant is under no duty to demand a speedy trial. *State v. Dodson,* 226 Ore. 458, 360 P.2d 782(1961). There is a duty to demand a speedy trial if the person is serving in a penitentiary for another offense. *Oregon v. Vawter,* 236 Ore. 85, 368 P.2d 916(1963). The defendant must, however, assert his right to be indicted. *Bevel v. Gladden,* 232 Ore. 578, 376 P.2d 117(1962). In spite of the fact that the defendant must assert his right to be indicted, the duty to provide him with a speedy trial lies with the state. *Bevel v. Gladden, supra.*

PENNSYLVANIA

I. Bail

Anyone who is accused of committing a crime may be free on bail, unless the crime with which he is charged is a capital one and the proof is evident or the presumption great. PA. CONST. art. 1, §14. Persons accused of murder or manslaughter may be bailed only by a judge of the supreme court, or by the president or associate law judge of the common pleas court. PA. STAT. ANN. tit. 19, §51. The amount of bail is determined by taking into account many factors, including the following: the nature and circumstances of the offense; the stage of the prosecution; the age, residence, employment, financial standing, family status, character, reputation, previous criminal history, and mental condition of the defendant. The court may, for cause, increase or reduce the amount of bail. PA. R. CRIM. P. 4005(b). Excessive bail, however, cannot be required. PA. CONST. art. 1, §13. The burden is on the state to show that a defendant accused of committing a capital offense has no right to bail. PA. R. CRIM. P. 4002(b)(3). In the discretion of the issuing authority, or the court, a defendant may be released on nominal bail. PA. R. CRIM. P. 4007.

II. Preliminary Hearing

Preliminary procedures differ in Pennsylvania according to the offense charged in the complaint. In general, however, the defendant must be present at the preliminary hearing and may be represented by counsel. If the offense charged is not murder, voluntary manslaughter, kidnapping, arson, robbery, or burglary, the defendant can testify and call witnesses. He also may cross-examine witnesses and inspect physical evidence which has been entered against him. PA. R. CRIM. P. 120. When the preliminary hearing discloses that the prosecution does not appear to be well founded, the defendant is discharged. PA. STAT. ANN. tit. 19, §22.

III. Grand Jury, Indictment, Information

The Pennsylvania Constitution guarantees to each citizen the right to indictment by a grand jury. PA. CONST. art. 1, §10. A defendant may waive action by the grand jury in all cases except those punishable by death or life imprisonment. PA. R. CRIM. P. 215(a). If he is not represented by counsel, the waiver shall take place in open court and can be made at any time before he makes his plea.

IV. Pretrial Discovery

In general, the accused does not have a right to inspect, before trial, the evidence in the possession of the prosecution. In order to be given the privilege of inspecting the prosecution's evidence, one is required to present exceptional circumstances and compelling reasons; a mere allegation that the indictment did not set forth facts with sufficient particularity is not a sound basis on which to grant unlimited discovery. *Commonwealth v. Caplan,* 411 Pa. 563, 192 A.2d 894(1963). A defendant may be permitted to inspect the evidence in the possession of the prosecution if it appears that such would be necessary for a fair trial. *Commonwealth v. Kotch,* 22 Pa. D. & C.2d 105, 51 Luzerne Leg. Reg. R. 59(1960). Under certain circumstances, however, the defendant may be allowed to inspect a statement which was made by one of the prosecution's witnesses and which is now in the prosecution's possession. *Commonwealth v. Smith,* 417 Pa. 321, 208 A.2d 219(1965). The accused has no absolute right to inspect his own confession. *Commonwealth v. Hoban,* 54 Lack. Jur. 213(1952). Neither does he have an absolute right to inspect a statement or confession made by his co-defendant. *Commonwealth v. Graham.* 42 Del. Co. 313 (Pa. 1955). A defendant has also been denied the privilege of inspecting a psychiatrist's report where physicians were employed by the prosecution to determine the defendant's sanity. *Commonwealth v. Wable,* 382 Pa. 80, 114 A.2d 334(1955). The prosecution does not have to make available for the defendant photos of fingerprints, if any, found on a weapon allegedly used in the commission of a crime, nor any picture of the place where the murder allegedly took place. *Petition of Di Joseph,* 394 Pa. 19, 145 A.2d 187(1958).

Ordinarily, a defendant is entitled to inspect prior statements of a witness for the purpose of cross-examining or impeaching him. *Commonwealth v. Carey,* 201 Pa. Super. 292, 191 A.2d 730(1963).

Disclosure of an informer's identity is not required where the informer was not a participant in the offense although the informer was the only material witness to an alleged narcotics transaction besides the police and the accused. *Commonwealth v. Crawley,* 209 Pa. Super. 70, 223 A.2d 885(1967). However, a defendant was entitled to know the identity of informer when the informer was an eyewitness to a heroin purchase made by a narcotics agent. *Commonwealth v. Lloyd,* 427 Pa. 261, 234 A.2d 423(1967).

A defendant does not have an absolute right to discover minutes of a grand jury investigation. *Commonwealth v. Nelson,* 172 Pa. Super. 125, 92 A.2d 431(1952).

A defendant may request that a bill of particulars be furnished him. PA. R. CRIM. P. 221(b). However, if the indictment is reasonably specific, a bill of particulars will not be granted. *Commonwealth v. Evans,* 190 P. Super. 179, 154 A.2d 157(1959).

If a defendant intends to offer the defense of alibi at trial, he must notify the attorney for the state no later than five days before the trial. The notice must specify his intention to claim such a defense. It must also give the place where the defendant will claim to have been at the time of the alleged offense and the names and addresses of witnesses he intends to call in support of his claim. PA. R. CRIM. P. 312(a).

V. SPEEDY TRIAL

An accused has a right to a speedy trial. PA. CONST. art. 1, §9. If a defendant is not tried within six months of his arrest and he was not instrumental in causing the delay, the charges against him will be dismissed. PA. CODE ANN. tit. 19, §781. Upon application and on showing that an indictment has not been found against a defendant within a reasonable time, the court may order dismissal of the prosecution and make such other order as shall be appropriate in the interests of justice. PA. R. CRIM. P. 316(a). The attorney for the state shall be afforded opportunity to show cause why the relief sought should not be granted. PA. R. CRIM. P. 316(b)(1971). The only time that delay caused by the prosecution can be considered reasonable is if the delay was for proper preparation or to secure attendance of witnesses. *Commonwealth v. Gant,* 213 Pa. Super. 427, 249 A.2d 845(1968).

RHODE ISLAND

I. BAIL

Any person who is imprisoned is bailable unless he is charged with having committed an offense punishable by death or by life imprisonment, when the proof of guilt is evident or the presumption is great. R.I. CONST. art. 1, §9. The amount of bail is determined by the justice according to his idea of what is reasonable. R.I. CONST. art. 1, §8. Excessive bail is not allowed. R.I. CONST. art. 1, §8. A person who is accused of having committed murder, robbery, rape, arson, burglary, or treason against the state may be bailed only by a justice of the supreme or superior court. R.I. GEN. LAWS ANN. §12–13–5(1956). If such a person is not indicted within six months, he must either be bailed or discharged. R.I. GEN. LAWS ANN. §12–13–6(1956).

II. PRELIMINARY HEARING

When an accused is brought before a district court, it first determines if it has jurisdiction to hear the case, and then whether or not there is probable cause that the defendant is guilty of the offense with which he has been charged. R.I. GEN. LAWS ANN. §12–10–5,6(1956). Within 24 hours of being arrested, an accused must either be bailed or brought before a judge of the district court. A 24-hour extension may be ordered by the court. R.I. GEN. LAWS ANN. §12–7–13(1956).

III. GRAND JURY, INDICTMENT, INFORMATION

No one may be held to answer for a capital or other infamous crime, unless on presentment or indictment by a grand jury. R.I. CONST. art. 1, §7. An infamous crime is one for which the penalty is imprisonment in a state prison for a minumum of one year. *State v. Nichols,* 27 R.I. 69, 60 A. 763(1905). When a person charged with an offense other than murder is bound over to the superior court, he may waive a grand jury indictment and instead plead to the charge. R.I. GEN. LAWS ANN. §12–12–19(1956).

IV. PRETRIAL DISCOVERY

A defendant has no right to inspect the prosecution's evidence, except in special and unusual circumstances such as where his constitutional rights would be denied by not allowing him such inspection. *State v. DiNoi,* 59 R.I. 348, 195 A. 497, *retrial denied,* 60 R.I. 37, 196 A. 795(1937).

For the purposes of cross-examination, the defendant does have the right to inspect papers or memoranda used by a witness to refresh his memory while testifying at trial. *State v. Deslovers,* 40 R.I. 89, 100 A. 64(1917).

If an indictment fails to inform the defendant of the particulars of the offense with which he has been charged in such a way as to enable him to prepare his defense, the prosecution may be ordered to furnish him with a bill of particulars. Although the prosecution may have to prepare a bill of particulars for the defendant, the prosecution need not disclose either its witnesses or its evidence, nor need it do anything more than furnish the defendant with such facts as fairly disclose the actual charge with which he is accused. R.I. GEN. LAWS ANN. §12–12–9(1956).

V. SPEEDY TRIAL

The Rhode Island Constitution guarantees the defendant the right to a speedy trial. R.I. CONST. art. 1, §10. Any person who is indicted for a serious crime, and is subsequently imprisoned, must be brought to trial or bailed within six months after he has pleaded to the indictment, providing he has demanded a trial. The state is excused from not having proceeded with the trial, though six months have passed, if a material witness for the state has been enticed away or is prevented from appearing at court because of an unavoidable accident. R.I. GEN. LAWS ANN. §12–13–7(1956). The right to a speedy trial is a qualified one and can be waived if the accused fails to assert it. Despite a demand for a speedy trial, there is no guarantee that it will be granted. The court looks at all the circumstances in order to ascertain whether the delay was unreasonable. *Ramsdell v. Langlois,* 100 R.I. 468, 217 A.2d 83(1966).

SOUTH CAROLINA

I. BAIL

Before conviction, all persons are bailable except for those accused of having committed capital offenses when the proof is evident or the presumption great. S.C. CONST. art. 1, §20. Excessive bail shall not be required. S.C. CONST. art. 1, §19.

Any person charged with a noncapital offense may be released on his own recognizance or on an amount of bail specified by the court, unless the court is of the opinion that the accused will not appear or that his being bailed would constitute an "unreasonable" danger to the community. S.C. CODE 17, §300 (Supp. 1969).

The court takes into consideration the following factors when determining whether or not the accused should be bailed: the risk to the community of release; the nature and circumstances of the offense charged; the accused's family ties, employment status, financial resources, mental condition, and length of residence in the community; and past criminal record. S.C. CODE 17, §300.2 (Supp. 1969).

II. PRELIMINARY HEARING

South Carolina has no statutory provision for a preliminary hearing; however, it is required that every person arrested be advised of the true ground on which his arrest was made. S.C. CODE 17, §255(1962).

III. GRAND JURY, INDICTMENT, INFORMATION

If punishment for the offense committed exceeds a fine of $200 or imprisonment for more than 30 days, a person must be prosecuted on a presentment or indictment of a grand jury with two exceptions: time of public danger, and when prosecution by information is expressly authorized by statute. S.C. CONST. art. 1, §17.

IV. PRETRIAL DISCOVERY

The prosecution need not disclose the identity of an informer to the accused. *State v. Hill,* 245 S.C. 76, 138 S.E.2d 829(1964).

V. SPEEDY TRIAL

A person accused of a crime has the right to a speedy and public trial. S.C. CONST. art. 1, §18.

A person accused of having committed a felony may demand a prompt trial; however, he must on the first week of the term ask to be tried promptly. He then must be indicted by the end of that term and tried by the following term. If the defendant is not tried, he is then bailed, and if not tried the following term, then he will be discharged. S.C. CODE 17, §509.

The right to a speedy trial is necessarily relative and may be consistent with delays; consequently the right depends upon individual circumstances. The right is personal and may be waived by the defendant's conduct. Waiver may be inferred where an accused has failed to demand that he be either tried or discharged or where a continuance has been granted on defendant's motion or with his consent, or where he has voluntarily entered a plea of guilty without raising the question of denial of a speedy trial. *Wheeler v. State,* 247 S.C. 393, 147 S.E.2d 627(1966).

SOUTH DAKOTA

I. BAIL

With the exception of capital offenses when the proof is evident or the presumption great, all offenses are bailable. S.D. CONST. art. VI, §8. A person accused of a capital offense can be bailed only at the discretion of the supreme court or the circuit court. S.D. CODE §23–26–3(1967).

II. PRELIMINARY HEARING

The magistrate before whom an accused is brought must at once inform the accused of the charges brought against him, of his right to counsel at every stage of the proceeding, and of his right to waive an examination. S.D. CODE §23–27–1(1967). The examination must be completed at one session unless adjourned for good cause by the magistrate and cannot be postponed for more than two days each time up to a total of six days, unless by consent or motion of the defendant. S.D. CODE §23–27–5(1967). Prior to the entry of an order, either party may move to transfer to the municipal or county court; the receiving court would then continue the hearing. S.D. CODE §23–27–11(1967).

III. GRAND JURY, INDICTMENT, INFORMATION

No person can be held for a criminal offense unless there has been either a presentment or indictment of a grand jury, or an information of the public prosecutor, except in cases of impeachment, in cases recognizable by county courts and justices of the peace. S.D. CONST. art. VI, §10. Unless the accused has waived his right to a preliminary examination, an information cannot be filed against a person until a preliminary examination is held before a magistrate. S.D. CODE §23–20–2(1967).

IV. PRETRIAL DISCOVERY

The defendant is not, as matter of right, entitled to the inspection or disclosure of evidence in the possession of the prosecution. *State v. Wade,* 83 S.D. 337, 159 N.W.2d 396(1968).

The accused has no right to inspect documents or articles in the possession of the prosecution which would not be admissible into evidence. *State ex rel. Wagner v. Cir. Ct. of Minnehaha County,* 60 S.D. 115, 244 N.W. 100(1932).

Subject to certain exceptions and limitations, the prosecution is privileged to withhold from the accused the identity of an informer. *State v. Martin,* 55 S.D. 594, 227 N.W. 66(1929).

A defendant who raises mental illness as a defense is required, at his arraignment, to specially plead "not guilty by reason of mental illness" in addition to the general plea of "not guilty." S.D. CODE §23–37–1(1967).

V. SPEEDY TRIAL

All those accused of having committed a crime have the right to a speedy and public trial. S.D. CONST. art. VI, §7. Unless a criminal action is postponed upon the defendant's application, trial must occur during or before the second term after the one at which the indictment or information is filed. If this is not done, the court will order the prosecution dismissed. S.D. CODE §23–34–2(1967). In order for the prosecution to be dismissed, the lapse of time between indictment and trial would have had to prejudice the accused. *State v. Opheium,* 84 S.D. 227, 196 N.W.2d 716(1969). An order for the dismissal of the action, however, does not bar another prosecution for the same offense. S.D. CODE §23–34–6(1967).

The right to a speedy trial may be waived. Where the accused's own acts have delayed the trial, or where he has not made an affirmative demand for a speedy trial, the right will be considered to have been waived. *State v. Harrison,* 83 S.D. 440, 160 N.W.2d 415(1968).

TENNESSEE

I. BAIL

Unless a person is accused of having committed a capital offense, when the proof is evident or the presumption great, he is bailable. TENN. CONST. art. 1, §15. Only one application for bail may be made; if that is denied, no subsequent request may be made unless new evidence material to the defense is alleged. TENN. CODE ANN. §40–1205(1955). The trial court in its discretion decides the amount of bail. TENN. CODE. ANN. §40–1213(1955). Bail cannot be excessive. TENN. CONST. art. 1, §16. Bail is $1,000 for an offense greater than petit larceny. TENN. CODE ANN. §40–1212(1955). Whether or not a person appealing a felony conviction may be released on bail is a matter left to the discretion of the trial judge. TENN. CODE ANN. §40–3406(1955).

II. PRELIMINARY HEARING

The defendant is brought before the magistrate after his arrest. He then must be informed immediately of the charges which have been filed against him and of his right to counsel. TENN. CODE ANN. §40–1101(1955). At the preliminary hearing witnesses are examined in the presence of the defendant. TENN. CODE ANN. §40–1109(1955).

III. GRAND JURY, INDICTMENT, INFORMATION

All criminal prosecutions must proceed by a presentment, indictment, or impeachment. TENN. CONST. art. 1,§14.

IV. PRETRIAL DISCOVERY

A defendant is not entitled to inspect evidence in the possession of the prosecution. Whether or not inspection of the prosecution's evidence is permitted is a matter of the court's discretion. *Ivey v. State,* 207 Tenn. 438, 340 S.W.2d 907(1960). In order to gain inspection the defendant would have to show the court the purpose for which the inspection is sought. *Anderson v. State,* 207 Tenn. 486, 341 S.W.2d 385(1960).

A criminal defendant may obtain his own written statements and also a list of witnesses who were present at the time the defendant made any oral statement which was against his interest. *Bolin v. State,* 219 Tenn. 4, 405 S.W.2d 768(1966); TENN. CODE ANN. §40–2441 (Supp. 1970). Statements or confessions an accused made to the police may be examined before trial. *Bolin v. State, supra.* However, inspection of a letter written by the accused which later came into the possession of the prosecution is not allowed. *Witham v. State,* 191 Tenn. 115, 232 S.W.2d 3(1950). The defendant cannot inspect notations made by the state's officers in the course of their investigation. *Bolin v. State, supra.*

If proper cause is shown, an accused may be permitted to inspect statements written by a witness or another person. *Anderson v. State,* 207 Tenn. 486, 341 S.W.2d 385(1960).

The prosecution need not divulge the identity of an informer. *Simmons v. State,* 198 Tenn. 587, 281 S.W.2d 487(1955).

V. SPEEDY TRIAL

An accused has the right to a speedy and public trial. TENN. CONST. art. 1, §9; TENN. CODE ANN. §40–2001(1955). If a defendant is charged with an offense and is not indicted at the term in which he was bound, or the trial has not been postponed by the defendant's application and he is not brought to trial at the next regular term of the court in which the indictment is triable, the charges may be dismissed, unless good cause to the contrary is shown. TENN. CODE ANN. §40–2102(1955). One must raise the question of being denied a speedy trial at the time of trial. *State ex rel. Underwood v. Brown,* 193 Tenn. 113, 244 S.W.2d 168(1951). An accused cannot claim that he was denied this right if he either acquiesced in or requested a delay. *King v. State,* 432 S.W.2d 490 (Tenn. 1968). The defendant's right to a speedy trial is a personal one and it may be waived. *State ex rel. Lewis v. State,* 447 S.W.2d 42 (Tenn. 1969).

TEXAS

I. BAIL

A defendant is bailable unless the crime of which he is accused is a capital offense when the proof is evident. TEX. CONST. art. 1, §11. The burden of proof is upon the state to show that the proof is evident that the accused is guilty of an offense for which the death penalty will most likely be inflicted. If the state meets its burden, the accused is not entitled to bail. *Ex parte Tindall,* 111 Tex. Crim. 444, 15 S.W.2d 24(1929). The court may, in its discretion, release the defendant on his personal bond. TEX. CODE CRIM. PROC. art. 17.03(1966). If a defendant in a capital case demands a trial, and it appears that more than one continuance has been granted to the state and that the defendant has not applied for a continuance, he will be entitled to be set free on bail, unless the court is convinced that the continuance was caused by some act on the part of the defendant. TEX. CODE CRIM. PROC. art. 29.12(1966). Excessive bail cannot be required of a defendant. TEX. CONST. art. 1, §13.

II. PRELIMINARY HEARING

If the accused is being tried for a felony, he has a right to a preliminary examination. TEX. CODE CRIM. PROC. art. 16.01(1966). Either party may postpone the examination. TEX. CODE CRIM. PROC. art. 16.02(1966). At the preliminary examination both the state and the defendant have the right to examine and to cross-examine witnesses. TEX. CODE CRIM. PROC. art. 16.06(1966). The accused must be present when a witness is being interrogated. TEX. CODE CRIM. PROC. art. 16.08(1966). After the examination the judge decides whether the accused will be discharged or committed to jail. TEX. CODE CRIM. PROC. art. 16.17(1966).

III. GRAND JURY, INDICTMENT, INFORMATION

No person can be held to answer for a capital offense unless the grand jury has come forth with an indictment. In all other cases the accused shall be charged by information. TEX. SESS. LAWS art. 1.141(1971).

IV. PRETRIAL DISCOVERY

The defendant does not have a right to inspect evidence in the possession of the prosecution. Whether or not such inspection will be granted lies within the discretion of the trial court. *Hanes v. State,* 170 Tex. Crim. 394, 341 S.W.2d 428(1960). The court has denied the defendant, before trial, the right to inspect a confession he allegedly made. *Davis v. State,* 99 Tex. Crim. 517, 270 S.W. 1022(1925). The right of inspecting statements made by a witness or other persons which the prosecution has in its possession has also been denied. *Hill v. State,* 167 Tex. Crim. 229, 319 S.W.2d 318(1958).

Ordinarily, the defendant is allowed to interview a person who is in the custody of the prosecuting authorities if he can show that this person is, or may be, a witness in the case, and that his testimony may be relevant or material to the issues which will be tried. *Bullock v. State,* 73 Tex. Crim. 419, 165 S.W. 196(1914).

The prosecutor can, in most instances, withhold the identity of an informer. *Sikes v. State,* 169 Tex. Crim. 443, 334 S.W.2d 440(1960). The defendant would have to benefit from the disclosure in some apparent way to be granted such disclosure. *Brown v. State,* 135 Tex. Crim. 394, 120 S.W.2d 1057(1938).

Grand jury minutes are generally not a subject for the inspection of the defense. *Sanders v. State,* 402 S.W.2d 735 (Tex. 1966). Whether to grant or deny such a request is within the discretion of the trial court. Where, during the course of the trial, the prosecuting attorney uses or introduces parts of the grand jury minutes in connection with the examination of the defendant or witnesses, the defendant may then inspect and use the grand jury minutes to the extent that they covered the same subject matter that was involved in the portions used or introduced by the prosecution. *Kirkland v. State,* 86 Tex. Crim. 595, 218 S.W. 367(1920). In general, the civil rules of evidence apply also in criminal actions. TEX. CODE CRIM. PROC. art. 38.02(1966).

V. SPEEDY TRIAL

A defendant in any criminal prosecution has the right to have a speedy and public trial. TEX. CONST. art. 1, §10. Unless good cause is shown, the prosecution will be dismissed and the bail discharged if an indictment or information is not presented against the defendant at the term of court which follows his commitment or admission to bail. TEX. CODE CRIM. PROC. art. 32.01(1966). If the defendant does not request a speedy trial, he will be considered to have waived the right. *Hudson v. State,* 453 S.W.2d 147 (Tex. 1970). If a defendant's own actions cause the trial to be delayed or he does not make a request for a speedy trial, the defendant cannot later claim he was denied his right to a speedy trial. *Johnson v. State,* 453 S.W.2d 828 (Tex. 1970).

UTAH

I. BAIL

All prisoners may be bailed except a defendant who has been accused of having committed a capital offense and the proof is evident or the presumption strong. UTAH CONST. art. 1, §8. In the case of an offense punishable by death, a defendant may be bailed only by a judge of the supreme or district court. When, however, the proof of his guilt is evident or the presumption is strong, he cannot be bailed. UTAH CODE ANN. §77–43–3(1953). If a person is charged with an offense other than a capital one, he may be bailed as a matter of right. UTAH CODE ANN. §77–43–4(1953). If a person is convicted of an offense other than one punishable by death, and he has appealed his conviction, he may be admitted to bail. UTAH CODE ANN. §77–43–5(1953).

II. PRELIMINARY HEARING

After arrest, a defendant is brought before a magistrate and informed of the charges against him. The defendant is also told of his right to counsel at every stage of the proceedings. UTAH CODE ANN. §77–15–1(1953). The preliminary examination is conducted by the district judge and is a "substantial right" of one accused of a felony; however, this right may waived. *State v. Overson,* 55 Utah 230, 185 P. 364(1919). At the preliminary hearing, the complaining witness is examined and in the presence of the defendant. The accused may cross-examine the complaining witness. UTAH CODE ANN. §77–15–10(1953). The defendant may also produce his own witnesses. UTAH CODE ANN. §77–15–11(1953).

III. GRAND JURY, INDICTMENT, INFORMATION

After the preliminary examination has been held and the defendant is committed by a magistrate, the prosecution proceeds on an information. UTAH CONST. art. 1, §13. Cases appealed from justices and city courts are prosecuted by either information or indictment. UTAH CODE ANN. §77–16–1(1953).

IV. Pretrial Discovery

The right to inspect evidence held by the prosecution is within the discretion of the court. *State v. Lack,* 118 Utah 128, 221 P.2d 852(1950).

A defendant may be permitted, at the discretion of the trial court, to inspect grand jury minutes before trial for possible impeachment of prosecution's witnesses. *State v. Harries,* 118 Utah 260, 221 P.2d 605(1950).

Where an indictment informs the accused of the crime sufficiently to enable him to prepare his defense, he cannot require a bill of particulars. *State v. Jameson,* 103 Utah 129, 134 P.2d 173(1943).

The rules of evidence used in civil proceedings are applicable to criminal cases with certain exceptions. UTAH CODE ANN. §77–44–2(1953). A deposition may be used for the purpose of contradicting or impeaching the testimony of deponent as a witness. Depositions may be used if the witness is dead, is out of the country, or is unable to attend or testify because of sickness, age, infirmity, or imprisonment. UTAH CODE ANN. §26(d)(1953).

V. Speedy Trial

Charges against a defendant will be dismissed if the defendant is held to answer and is not indicted by the next term of the court or if the defendant is not brought to trial by the next term of the court after having been indicted, unless there is good cause to the contrary. UTAH CODE ANN. §77–51–1(1953). The court must hold at least three terms of the district court per year. UTAH CODE ANN. §78–3–6(1953). The defendant must make a demand for trial. *State v. Bohn,* 67 Utah 362, 248 P. 119(1926). When a defendant has been committed, the district attorney has to move forward by information or indictment within 30 days. If this is not done, the district attorney may be prosecuted for neglect of duty; however, tardy indictment does not automatically justify a ruling that the accused has been denied a speedy trial. *State v. Rutledge,* 63 Utah 546, 227 P. 479(1924).

VERMONT

I. Bail

All crimes are bailable unless the crime charged is a capital offense when the proof is evident or the presumption great. VT. CONST. ch. II, art. 32. In determining the amount of bail, the court considers the accused's ability to furnish bail, the nature of the offense, the penalty for the offense charged, the character and reputation of the accused, the health of the accused, and the character and strength of the evidence. *State v. Toomey,* 126 Vt. 123, 223 A.2d 473(1966). In proceedings against more than one defendant, the standards for fixing bail are applied to each defendant individually. *State v. Toomey, supra.*

II. PRELIMINARY HEARING

Vermont makes no specific mention of any preliminary proceedings.

III. GRAND JURY, INDICTMENT, INFORMATION

Crimes punishable by death or by life imprisonment must be initiated by an indictment by a grand jury. VT. STAT. ANN. tit. 13, §5651 (Supp. 1968). Crimes not punishable by death or by life imprisonment may be prosecuted by an information. VT. STAT. ANN. tit. 13, §5652.

IV. PRETRIAL DISCOVERY

The cases vary as to whether an accused may inspect pretrial statements of prosecution witnesses. In *State v. Martel,* 122 Vt. 491, 177 A.2d 236(1962), after concluding that the statements were relevant and material for use in cross-examination, the defendant was allowed to inspect properly authenticated pretrial statements of a prosecution witness for the purpose of cross-examining the witness after he had testified on direct examination. However, in *State v. Skagen,* 122 Vt. 215, 167 A.2d 530(1961), the defendant was not allowed to examine such statements for the purpose of cross-examination.

The prosecution need not produce statements made by an accomplice of the accused. *State v. Anair,* 123 Vt. 80, 181 A.2d 61(1962). Police and investigatory reports are also beyond the reach of defendant's discovery. *State v. Lavellee,* 122 Vt. 75, 163 A.2d 856(1960).

Upon showing that the items sought may be material to the preparation of the defense, and that the request is reasonable, the court may order the prosecuting attorney to produce for the defendant requested books, papers, documents, statements, and other objects which were initially obtained from the accused. *State v. Lavellee, supra.*

Inspection by the defendant of grand jury minutes is not a matter or right, but rather a matter of the trial court's discretion. *State v. Goyet,* 119 Vt. 167, 122 A.2d 862(1956).

A defendant in a criminal prosecution may at any time after the filing of an indictment, information, or complaint take the deposition of a witness upon a showing that such witness's testimony may be material or relevant. VT. STAT. ANN. tit. 13, §6681. However, depositions in criminal cases are to taken only in exceptional situations where it is necessary to prevent a failure of justice. *Hackel v. Williams,* 122 Vt. 168, 167 A.2d 364(1960).

V. Speedy Trial

One accused of having committed a crime has a right to a speedy trial. VT. CONST. ch. 1, art. 10.

An accused may waive his constitutional right to a prompt trial. A waiver will be implied from actions of the accused which cause the trial to be delayed. *State v. Mahoney,* 124 Vt. 488, 207 A.2d 143(1965).

VIRGINIA

I. Bail

Excessive bail ought not be required. VA. CONST. art. 1, §9. Any judge of a court not of record and any clerk of any county court may admit to bail, upon proper recognizance with surety, a person charged with a crime. VA. CODE §19.1-111. The bail commissioner, clerk, or judge to whom application is made shall hear testimony and admit the accused to bail or remand him to jail. VA. CODE §19.1-122.

II. Preliminary Hearing

The accused must be brought before a judge who must, "as soon as may be," examine, on oath, the witnesses for and against the accused. VA. CODE §19.1-101.

After commitment, the accused may be called for further examination at the discretion of the judge. VA. CODE §19.1-107. The preliminary hearing may not be used by the defendant as a device to discover evidence which will ultimately be used against him at trial. *Foster v. Commonwealth,* 209 Va. 297, 163 S.E.2d 565(1968).

III. Grand Jury, Indictment, Information

An information may be filed upon presentment or indictment by a grand jury, or upon a complaint, in writing, verified by the oath of a competent witness. Unless the accused has waived the right, no person will be tried for a felony without an indictment or presentment first having been found by a grand jury. VA. CODE §19.1-162.

IV. Pretrial Discovery

A person accused of crime is not entitled to the inspection or disclosure of evidence which the prosecution has in its possession. *Abdell v. Commonwealth,* 173 Va. 458, 2 S.E.2d 293(1939).

Statements made by prosecution witnesses which are directly relevant to the issue of defendant's guilt or degree of his crime may be produced for use by the defense in cross-examination or impeachment. *Ossen v. Common-*

wealth, 187 Va. 902, 48 S.E.2d 204(1948). Subject to certain exceptions and limitations the prosecution is privileged to withhold from the accused the identity of an informer. *Webb. v. Commonwealth,* 137 Va. 833, 120 S.E. 155(1923).

A person accused of a crime has the right to call for, and be furnished with, a bill of particulars. *Pine v. Commonwealth,* 121 Va. 812, 93 S.E. 652(1917).

V. SPEEDY TRIAL

A man in a criminal prosecution has a right to demand a speedy trial. VA. CONST. art. 1, §8. If an accused is not tried within three regular terms of court, he will be forever discharged from prosecution for the offense, unless failure to try him was justified. VA. CODE §19.1–191.

The right to have a speedy trial may be either claimed or waived by the accused. *Brooks v. Peyton,* 210 Va. 318, 171 S.E.2d 243(1969). A prisoner who consented to a continuance which prevented his obtaining a speedy trial waived his right to a speedy trial. *Flanary v. Commonwealth,* 184 Va. 204, 35 S.E.2d 135(1945). The mere silence of the accused, or his failure to demand a speedy trial, does not act as a waiver or stop him from claiming his right to a speedy trial. *Howell v. Commonwealth,* 186 Va. 894, 45 S.E.2d 165(1947).

WASHINGTON

I. BAIL

Every person who is charged with an offense, except for capital offenses where the proof is evident or the presumption great, may be bailed. WASH. CONST. art. 1, §20. The amount of bail is determined by the judge in his discretion. WASH. REV. CODE tit. 10, §19.010(1962). In determining the amount of bail, the judge takes into account the defendant's past criminal record. WASH. REV. CODE tit. 10, §19.020 (Additional Supp. 1970).

II. PRELIMINARY EXAMINATION

A magistrate hears the complaint and may adjourn the hearing for up to ten days after the defendant has been brought before him. WASH. REV. CODE tit. 10, §16.040(1962). A preliminary hearing is not necessary to due process of law in a criminal prosecution. *State v. Robinson,* 61 Wash. 2d 107, 377 P.2d 248(1962). The preliminary hearing serves to determine whether the state is justified in proceeding further against the person then before it. *Summers v. Rhay,* 67 Wash. 2d 898, 410 P.2d 608(1966). The prosecutor may charge a defendant in a justice court, where a preliminary hearing is required, or in a superior court, where an information alone will suffice. *State v. Kanistanaux,* 68 Wash. 2d 652, 414 P.2d 784(1966). The accused has a right to confront witnesses at the preliminary hearing. *In re Pettit,* 62 Wash. 2d 515, 383 P.2d 889(1963).

III. GRAND JURY, INDICTMENT, INFORMATION

All public offenses may be prosecuted in the superior courts by an information. WASH. REV. CODE tit. 10, §37.026(1962).

IV. PRETRIAL DISCOVERY

Whether or not the defendant is allowed to inspect the prosecution's evidence is a matter of the trial court's discretion. *State v. Beard,* 74 Wash. 2d 335, 444 P.2d 651(1968). An accused is not entitled to inspect the minutes of the proceedings of a state grand jury. At the trial court's discretion, such inspection may be allowed. *State v. Beck,* 56 Wash. 2d 474, 349 P.2d 387, *aff'g* 369 U. S. 541(1961). One generally cannot obtain a transcript that was made of one's own testimony before a grand jury. *State v. Bell,* 59 Wash. 2d 338, 368 P.2d 177, *cert. denied,* 371 U. S. 818(1962). However, if the defendant was charged with perjuring himself while testifying before the grand jury, then he is entitled to inspect that portion of the transcript which contains his testimony. *State v. Ingels,* 4 Wash. 2d 676, 104 P.2d 944, *cert. denied,* 311 U.S. 708(1940). An accused may be permitted to inspect grand jury minutes before the trial has begun, if such inspection is for the purpose of making a motion to dismiss or set aside the indictment. *State v. Ingels, supra.*

The accused may interview one who is in the custody of the prosecuting authorities if he shows that this person is, or may be, a witness in the case, and that his testimony may be relevant or material to the issues which will be tried. *State v. Susan,* 152 Wash. 365, 278 P. 149(1929).

Ordinarily, a defendant is not allowed to inspect statements made by the prosecution's witnesses for the purpose of cross-examination or impeachment, even after the witness has testified at trial on direct examination. *State v. Robinson,* 61 Wash. 2d 107, 377 P.2d 248, *cert. denied,* 375 U. S. 846(1962). However, at the discretion of the trial court, this may be permitted. *State v. Robinson, supra.*

Although the court would not allow the defendant to examine typed exhibits or a recording of a confession made by the defendant to police, *State v. Clark,* 21 Wash. 2d 774, 153 P.2d 297, *cert. denied,* 325 U. S. 878(1944), nor statements held by the state, officers' reports, and statements of complaining witnesses, *State v. Beard, supra,* the state was required to produce reports of blood tests which were made on both the defendant and the victim, and also clothing and personal effects of both the defendant and the victim. *State v. Thompson,* 54 Wash. 2d 100, 338 P.2d 319(1959).

The prosecution need not disclose to the accused the identity of an informer. *State v. Kittle,* 137 Wash. 173, 241 P. 962(1926). If the accused shows that circumstances justify disclosing the identity of the informer, the court may exercise its discretion and order disclosure. *State v. Malone,* 69 Wash. 2d 872, 420 P.2d 676(1966).

The defendant has no right to inspect statements made by the prosecution's witnesses which the witness uses to refresh his recollection while testifying. *State v. Little,* 57 Wash. 2d 516, 358 P.2d 120(1961).

If the defendant intends to plead insanity by way of defense, he must, at the time of pleading to the information or indictment, file a plea in writing setting up such a defense. WASH. REV. CODE tit. 10, §76.020(1962). Five days before trial, the defendant must file a list of the witnesses he intends to call at the trial. *State v. Sickles,* 144 Wash. 236, 257 P. 385(1927).

V. SPEEDY TRIAL

Justice in all cases shall be administered openly and without unnecessary delay. WASH. CONST. art. 1, §10. After a person has been charged with a criminal offense, an indictment must be found or an information filed against him within 30 days or the court will order the prosecution to dismiss its charge unless good cause to the contrary is shown. WASH. REV. CODE tit. 10, §37.020(1962). A person who has been indicted or against whom an information is filed must be brought to trial within 60 days after the indictment is found or the information filed or the case will be dismissed, unless good cause to the contrary is shown. WASH. REV. CODE tit. 10, §46.010(1962).

The right to be tried without unreasonable delay may be waived. *Stiltner v. Rhay,* 258 P. Supp. 487(1966).

In order to assert one's right to have a trial within 60 days after an information is filed, defendant's request or demand for speedy trial must be certain and explicit. *State v. Christensen,* 75 Wash. 2d 678, 453 P.2d 644(1969). If the defendant claims his right to speedy trial was violated because neither an information nor indictment was filed within 30 days of his arraignment, this right will be waived unless it is raised before appeal. *State v. Eastland,* 77 Wash. 2d 823, 467 P.2d 300(1970).

In order to show that delay has prejudiced his defense, the defendant must show specific prejudice: the delay must have impaired his defense by permitting evidence to be lost or witnesses to become unavailable. *State v. Christensen,* 75 Wash. 2d 678, 453 P.2d 644(1969).

The fact that the trial docket was completely filled is sufficient good cause for delay of trial. *State v. Dunn,* 70 Wash. 2d 572, 424 P.2d 897(1967).

The fact that the accused was discharged for want of prosecution because the trial was delayed does not bar his being prosecuted at a later time on the same charge. *State v. Unrein,* 60 Wash. 2d 168, 372 P.2d 547(1962).

WEST VIRGINIA

I. BAIL

A person arrested for any offense not punishable by death or life imprisonment is bailable; however, those arrested for capital offenses may be bailed at the discretion of the court. W. VA. CODE ANN. §62–1c–1(1966). Excessive bail shall not be required. W. VA. CONST. art. 3, §5. When determining the amount of bail, consideration is given to the seriousness of the offense charged, the defendant's previous criminal record, his financial situation, and the probability of his appearing at trial. W. VA. CODE ANN. §62–1c–3(1966).

II. PRELIMINARY HEARING

The arresting officer must take the accused "without unnecessary delay" before a justice of the county where the arrest was made. W. VA. CODE ANN. §62–1–5(1966). The purpose of the preliminary examination is to determine whether there is probable cause. The examination is available to the accused only if the case is to be presented to a grand jury for indictment. *Guthrie v. Boles,* 261 F. Supp. 852 (N.D. W. Va. 1967).

III. GRAND JURY, INDICTMENT, INFORMATION

If one is charged with a felony, that prosecution must always be by indictment. W. VA. CODE ANN. §62–2–1(1966). Misdemeanors may be initiated either by indictment or by presentment. *State v. Lucas,* 129 W. Va. 324, 40 S.E.2d 817(1946).

IV. PRETRIAL DISCOVERY

Unless required by the court, counsel has the right to refuse to disclose the evidence they expect to introduce at trial. *State v. Paun,* 109 W. Va. 606, 155 S.E. 656(1930).

The court may order the disclosure of certain materials which are known by the prosecuting attorney to be in the possession, custody, or control of the state. For instance, the court may allow the defendant to examine and copy or photograph any relevant written or recorded statements or confessions made by the defendant; results of reports of physical or mental examinations; results of scientific tests or experiments made in connection with the particular case; and books, papers, or tangible objects belonging to or seized from the defendant. W. VA. CODE ANN. §62–1b–2(1966).

The court, for cause, may direct the prosecuting attorney to file a bill of particulars which may be amended at any time, subject to such conditions as justice requires. W. VA. CODE ANN. §62–1b–1(1966). An accused cannot get a bill of particulars if specifications asked for are within his own knowledge, or are readily accessible to him. *State v. Pietranton,* 140 W. Va. 444, 84 S.E.2d 774(1954).

The prosecution need not divulge to an accused the identity of an informer. *State v. Paun,* 109 W. Va. 606, 155 S.E. 656(1930).

V. SPEEDY TRIAL

Persons charged with having committed a crime are to be tried "without unnecessary delay." W. VA. CONST. art. 3, §14. Trials for felonies are to be had at the same term as the indictment is found, "unless good cause be shown for a continuance." W. VA. CODE ANN. §62–3–1 (Supp. 1968). Unless there was good cause for delay, one accused of having committed a felony will be discharged from prosecution if three regular terms of the court have passed without the accused's being tried. W. VA. CODE ANN. §62–3–21(1966). The right of speedy trial is necessarily relative. It is consistent with delays and depends on circumstances. *Wright v. Boles,* 275 F. Supp. 571 (N.D. W. Va. 1967).

WISCONSIN

I. BAIL

All cases are bailable. *In re Perry,* 19 Wis. 711(1865). The court can fix the amount of bail and later increase it if such seems justified. WIS. CONST. art. 1, §8. Before conviction, a defendant arrested for a criminal offense shall be admitted to bail, except as provided in §971.14(1). WIS. STAT. ANN. §969.01(1)(1971). The court in setting bail must consider the ability of the arrested person to give bail, the nature and gravity of the offense and the potential penalty the defendant faces, the defendant's prior criminal record, if any, the character, residence, and reputation of the defendant, his health, the character and strength of the evidence which has been presented to the judge, whether the defendant is already on bail in other pending cases, whether the defendant has in the past forfeited bail or was a fugitive from justice at the time of his arrest, and the policy against unnecessary detention of defendants pending trial. WIS. STAT. ANN. §969.01(4)(1971).

II. PRELIMINARY HEARING

When any person is arrested he shall be taken within a reasonable time before a judge in the county in which the offense is alleged to have been committed. WIS. STAT. ANN. §970.01(1)(1971). The appearance before the magistrate is not to determine whether the accused is guilty but rather to determine whether the accused wishes to exercise his right to have a preliminary examination. *Stecher v. State*, 237 Wis. 587, 297 N.W. 391(1941). At the preliminary examination the state's witnesses are sworn and examined in the presence of the defendant, who may cross-examine them. The defendant has the opportunity to present his own witnesses. WIS. STAT. ANN. §970.03(5)(1971). If probable cause is found that the defendant has committed the named offense, the defendant will then be bound over for trial. *Montgomery v. State,* 128 Wis. 183, 107 N.W. 14(1906).

Upon motion and for cause shown, the trial court may remand the case for a preliminary examination. "Cause" means that the preliminary examination was waived, that defendant did not have advice of counsel prior to such waiver, that he denies that probable cause exists to hold him for trial, and that he intends to plead not guilty. WIS. STAT. ANN. §971.02(2) (Supp. 1971).

III. GRAND JURY, INDICTMENT, INFORMATION

The trial of a felony shall be either by information or by indictment. WIS. STAT. ANN. §967.05(3)(1971).

No information shall be filed until the defendant has had a preliminary examination, unless he waives the examination; but informations may be filed without an examination against defendants who are involuntarily returned to the state under chapter 976 and against corporations. The omission of the preliminary examination does not invalidate any information unless the defendant moves to dismiss prior to the entry of a plea.

IV. PRETRIAL DISCOVERY

A person who is accused of having committed a crime is not entitled to the inspection or disclosure of evidence in the possession of the prosecution. *State ex rel. Spencer v. Freedy,* 198 Wis. 388, 223 N.W. 861(1929). Unless the circumstances are unusual, the general rule is that a defendant is not entitled to inspect statements made by witnesses or other persons, at least until such are offered into evidence. *State v. Herman,* 219 Wis. 267, 262 N.W. 718(1935). The defendant has no right to inspect statements or a confession made by an accomplice. *Santry v. State,* 67 Wis. 65, 30 N.W. 226(1886). The prosecution need not disclose to the defendant notes made by a sheriff, *Ramer v. State,* 40 Wis. 2d 79, 161 N.W.2d 209(1968), nor need it disclose the transcript of a preliminary hearing, *State v. Herman, supra.*

Ordinarily, a defendant is entitled to inspect prior statements made by a prosecution witness at trial for the purpose of cross-examining or impeaching such witness. *State v. Richards,* 21 Wis. 2d 622, 124 N.W.2d 684(1963). Only those portions of the witness's previous testimony which relate to the subject matter of his testimony at trial may be inspected. *State v. Richards, supra.* The portions of testimony that a defendant may inspect must relate directly to the issue of his guilt or the degree of his crime. *Alto v. State,* 215 Wis. 141, 253 N.W. 777(1934). An accused ordinarily is not entitled to inspect the minutes of a state grand jury; however, inspection of minutes may be allowed in instances provided for by legislation and permitted by the court as necessary to protect rights of citizens in administration of justice. *Steensland v. Hoppmann,* 213 Wis. 593, 252 N.W. 146(1934).

If it appears that a prospective witness will be unable to appear at either the trial or a hearing, and that his testimony is material, his testimony may be taken by deposition. Books, papers, documents, or tangible objects which are not privileged may be produced at the same time and place. WIS. STAT. ANN. §887.06(1)(1971).

V. SPEEDY TRIAL

One accused in a criminal prosecution has the right to have a speedy trial. WIS. CONST. art. 1, §7. The trial of a defendant charged with a felony shall commence within 90 days of the date trial is demanded by any party in writing or on the record. The demand may not be made until after the filing of the information or indictment. WIS. STAT. ANN. §971.10(1), (2)(1971).

A case may be continued by the court on its motion, on application of any party, for cause, or by stipulation of the parties, but a continuance cannot be made for more than 60 days. WIS. STAT. ANN. §971.10(3)(a), (b)(1971). A defendant not tried in accordance with the provisions of §971.10 shall be discharged from custody or released from the obligations of his bond. WIS. STAT. ANN. §971.10(4)(1971).

If the defendant's conduct contributed to the trial's delay, he cannot later complain that he was denied his right to a speedy trial. *McGrath v. State,* 42 Wis. 2d 292, 166 N.W.2d 172(1969). Although a defendant is entitled to dismissal without prejudice if his right to a speedy trial is violated, that right only accrues after the defendant has taken affirmative steps to bring his case to trial. *State v. Stoeckle,* 41 Wis. 2d 378, 164 N.W.2d 303(1969). Mere lapse of time does not constitute denial of the right to a speedy trial. *Johnson v. State,* 39 Wis. 2d 415, 159 N.W.2d 48(1968).

WYOMING

I. BAIL

With the exception of those charged with capital offenses when the proof is evident or the presumption great, all persons are bailable. WYO. CONST. art. 1, §14. Any person arrested for an offense not punishable by death must be bailed, and even those accused of capital offenses may be bailed at the discretion of the judge. WYO. R. CRIM. P. 8. Factors to be taken into consideration by the judge in determining bail are the nature and circumstances of the offense charged, the weight of the evidence, the accused's family ties, his employment situation, financial resources, character, and mental condition, his length of residence in the community, and his prior record of convictions and court appearance.

II. PRELIMINARY HEARING

A person who is arrested must be taken "without unnecessary delay" before the nearest available commissioner. WYO. R. CRIM. P. 5(a). The commissioner has the duty of informing the defendant of the complaint that has been brought against him, of his right to a preliminary examination, and of his right to counsel. WYO. R. CRIM. P. 5(b). The defendant has a right to a preliminary examination in all cases which are triable in the district court. This right may be waived. WYO. R. CRIM. P. 7(a). The accused may cross-examine witnesses and introduce evidence at the preliminary examination. WYO. R. CRIM. P. 7(b).

III. GRAND JURY, INDICTMENT, INFORMATION

All prosecutions shall be by indictment or information. WYO. R. CRIM. P. 9.

IV. PRETRIAL DISCOVERY

A defendant is not entitled to the inspection or disclosure of evidence in the possession of the prosecution. *Coca v. State,* 423 P.2d 382 (Wyo. 1967).

The court may order the state's attorney to permit the defendant to inspect and copy or photograph any relevant written or recorded statements or confessions made by the defendant which are in the possession, custody, or control of the state. WYO. R. CRIM. P. 18(a)(1). Reports of results of physical or mental examinations and of scientific tests or experiments made in connection with the case may be produced for the defendant, WYO. R. CRIM. P. 18(a)(2), as may the defendant's testimony taken before a grand jury, WYO. R. CRIM. P. 18(a)(3). The defendant may also inspect photographs, books, papers, documents, tangible objects, building or places, or copies or portions thereof which are in the possession of the state, if he shows that such inspection is material to the preparation of his defense.

After a state's witness has testified on direct examination, the defendant may gain production of those statements the witness made which relate to the testimony he gave on direct examination. WYO. R. CRIM. P. 18(c)(1).

The defendant will not be able to discover reports, memoranda, or other internal governmental documents made by governmental agents in connection with the investigation or prosecution of the case, or of statements made by state witnesses or prospective state witnesses to governmental agents. WYO. R. CRIM. P. 18(b).

If it appears that a prospective witness whose testimony is material will be unable to appear at trial, or at a hearing, his deposition may be taken. WYO. R. CRIM. P. 17(a). Books, papers, documents, or tangible objects which are not privileged may be produced at the time of the deposition. WYO. R. CRIM. P. 17(a).

If the court grants discovery to the defendant, the defendant in turn may be required to allow the state to inspect or copy or photograph scientific or medical reports, books, papers, documents, tangible objects, or copies or portions thereof, which the defendant intends to produce at trial. The state is not authorized, however, to discover reports, memoranda, or other internal defense documents made in connection with the investigation or defense of the case, or of statements made by the defendant, or by state or defense witnesses, or by prospective witnesses which were made to the defendant or to his agents or attorneys.

V. SPEEDY TRIAL

An accused has a right to a speedy trial in all criminal prosecutions. WYO. CONST. art. 1, §10. If there is an unnecessary delay in presenting the charge to the grand jury or in filing an information against the defendant, or if there is unnecessary delay in bringing the defendant to trial, the court may dismiss the indictment, information, or complaint. WYO. R. CRIM. P. 45(b). However, if the court is convinced that the state has made a reasonable effort to procure evidence and that such evidence will be available at the succeeding term, the case may be continued. WYO. STAT. ANN. §7–236.

BIBLIOGRAPHY

BOOKS

Alexander, James. *A Brief Narrative of the Case and Trial of John Peter Zenger.* Cambridge: Belknap Press, 1963.

Beaney, William. *The Right to Counsel in American Courts.* Ann Arbor: University of Michigan Press, 1955.

Beeley, Arthur. *The Bail System in Chicago.* Chicago: University of Chicago Press, 1966.

Black, Henry. *Black's Law Dictionary.* St. Paul: West Publishing Company, 1968.

Blackstone, William. *Commentaries on the Law of England.* 4 vols. Portland: T. B. Wait, 1807.

Chevigny, Paul. *Police Power—Police Abuses in New York City.* New York: Pantheon, 1969.

Coke, Edward. *The Second Part of the Institutes of the Laws of England.* 5th ed. London: 45 Brooke, 1797.

Downie, Leonard, Jr. *Justice Denied: The Case for Reform of the Courts.* New York: Praeger, 1971.

Foote, Caleb. *Studies on Bail.* Philadelphia: University of Pennsylvania Law Review, 1966.

Freed, Daniel J., and Patricia M. Wald. *Bail in the United States: 1964.* Washington, D.C.: U.S. Government Printing Office, 1964.

Goldfarb, Ronald. *Ransom: A Critique of the American Bail System.* New York: Harper and Row, 1965.

Hall, Jerome. *Theft, Law, and Society.* Boston: Little, Brown and Company, 1935.

Hall, Livingston, Yale Kamisar, Wayne LaFave, and Jerold Israel. *Modern Criminal Procedure.* 3rd ed. St. Paul: West Publishing Company, 1969.

Heller, Francis. *The Sixth Amendment to the Constitution of the United States: A Study in Constitutional Development.* New York: Greenwood Press, 1969.

Holdsworth, William S. *A History of English Law.* 3rd ed. London: Methuen and Company, 1922.

Institute on the Operation of Pretrial Release Projects. *Bail and Summons: 1965.* New York, 1965.

367

Karlen, Delmar. *Anglo-American Criminal Justice.* Oxford: Clarendon Press, 1967.

Lafave, Wayne. *Arrest: The Decision to Take a Suspect into Custody.* Boston: Little, Brown and Company, 1965.

Meador, Daniel. *Habeas Corpus and Magna Carta: Dualism of Power and Liberty.* Charlottesville: University of Virginia Press, 1966.

Menninger, Karl. *The Crime of Punishment.* New York: Viking Press, 1968.

Miller, Frank. *Prosecution: The Decision to Charge a Suspect with a Crime.* Boston: Little, Brown and Company, 1969.

Moley, Raymond. *Our Criminal Courts.* New York: Minton, Balch, and Company, 1930.

Morris, Pauline. *Prisoners and Their Families.* New York: Hart Publishing Company, 1965.

Moynihan, Daniel P. *The Report of the National Commission on the Causes and Prevention of Violence.* New York: G. Braziller, 1969.

Newman, Donald. *Conviction: The Determination of Guilt or Innocence Without Trial.* Boston: Little, Brown and Company, 1966.

Oaks, Dallin, and Warren Lehman. *A Criminal Justice System and the Indigent.* Chicago: University of Chicago Press, 1968.

Orfield, Lester. *Criminal Procedure from Arrest to Appeal.* New York: New York University Press, 1947.

Pollock, Frederick, and Frederic Maitland. *The History of English Law: Before the Time of Edward I.* 2 vols. Boston: Little, Brown and Company, 1895.

Ragland, George, Jr. *Discovery Before Trial.* Chicago: Callaghan and Company, 1932.

Remington, Frank, Donald Newman, Edward Kimball, Marygold Melli, and Herman Goldstein. *Criminal Justice Administration.* New York: Bobbs-Merrill Company, Inc., 1969.

Schlesinger, Arthur M. *Birth of a Nation.* New York: Alfred A. Knopf, Inc., 1968.

Scott, Arthur. *Criminal Law in Colonial Virginia.* Chicago: University of Chicago Press, 1930.

Skolnick, Jerome. *Justice Without Trial.* New York: Wiley, 1966.

Stephen, James. *A History of the Criminal Law of England.* 3 vols. London: Macmillan and Company, 1883.

Story, Joseph. *Commentaries on the Constitution of the United States.* Boston: Little, Brown and Company, 1905.

Subin, Harry I. *Criminal Justice in a Metropolitan Court: The Processing of Serious Criminal Cases in the District of Columbia Court of General Sessions.* Washington, D.C.: Office of Criminal Justice, U. S. Dept. of Justice, 1966.

Swift, Zephaniah. *A System of the Laws of the State of Connecticut.* 2 vols. Windain: John Byrne, 1796.

Westley, William. *Violence and the Police.* Cambridge: Massachusetts Institute of Technology Press, 1970.

Wigmore, John H. *Evidence.* 10 vols. Boston: Little, Brown and Company, 1940.

ARTICLES

"A Riot Against the Law's Delay." 76 *Newsweek* (August 24, 1970), 19.

Alschuler, Albert. "The Prosecutor's Role in Plea Bargaining." 36 *University of Chicago Law Review,* 50 (1968–1969).

American Bar Association Special Committee on the Administration of Criminal Justice. "Criminal Justice: The Vital Problem of the Future." 39 *American Bar Association Journal,* 743 (1953).

Amsterdam, Anthony, Bernard Segal, and Martin Miller. "Entrance into the Criminal Case—Representing the Client Shortly After Arrest." 14:1 *Practical Lawyer,* 19 (1968).

Arnold, Thurman, "Law Enforcement—An Attempt at Social Dissection." 42 *Yale Law Journal,* 1 (1932).

Banfield, Laura, and C. David Anderson. "Continuances in the Cook County Criminal Courts." 35 *University of Chicago Law Review,* 259 (1968).

Botein, Bernard. "The Manhattan Bail Project: Its Impact on Criminology and the Criminal Law Processes." 43 *Texas Law Review,* 323 (1964–1965).

Bowman, Charles. "The Illinois Ten Per Cent Bail Deposit Provision." 1965 *University of Illinois Law Forum,* 35.

Boyle, John. "Bail Under the Judicial Article." 17 *DePaul Law Review,* 267 (1968).

"Breakdown of the Courts in America." 66, *U. S. News and World Report* (March 10, 1969), 58.

Breitel, Charles. "Controls in Criminal Law Enforcement." 27 *University of Chicago,* 427 (1960).

Brezner, Samuel. "How the Prosecuting Attorney's Office Processes Complaints." 27 *The Detroit Lawyer,* 3 (1960).

Bunce, J. Elliot, and Eric Youngquist. "Discovery and Disclosure: Dual Aspects of the Prosecutor's Role in Criminal Procedure." 34 *George Washington Law Review,* 92 (1965–1966).

Burger, Warren E. "Paradoxes in the Administration of Criminal Justice." 58 *Journal of Criminal Law,* 428 (1967).

"Burger's Role." 66 *U. S. News and World Report* (January 14, 1969), 14.

Byrn, Robert. "Urban Law Enforcement: A Plea from the Ghetto." 5 *Criminal Law Bulletin,* 125 (1969).

Calkins, Richard. "Grand Jury Secrecy." 63 *University of Michigan Law Review,* 455 (1965).

Cannon, David. "Prosecutor's Duty to Disclose." 52 *Marquette Law Review,* 516 (1969).

Cavalluzzo, Paul. "Marijuana, The Law and the Courts." 8 *Osgoode Hall Law Journal,* 215 (1970).

Coates, Walton. "The Grand Jury, the Prosecutor's Puppet: Wasteful Nonsense of Criminal Jurisprudence." 33 *Pennsylvania Bar Association,* 311 (1962).

Cohen, Maxwell. "Habeas Corpus Cum Causa—the Emergence of the Modern Writ." 18 *Canadian Bar Review,* 10 (1940).

Comment. "Criminal Discovery." 10 *St. Louis Law Journal,* 518 (1965–1966).

Comment. "Developments in the Law—Discovery." 74 *Harvard Law Review,* 940 (1961).

Comment. Justice Walter V. Schaefer. 54 *Kentucky Law Journal,* 521 (1966).

Comment. "Preliminary Hearings in Pennsylvania: A Closer Look." 30 *University of Pittsburgh Law Review,* 481 (1968–1969).

Comment. "Prosecutorial Discretion in the Initiation of Criminal Complaints." 42 *Southern California Law Review,* 519 (1969).

Comment. "The Influence of the Defendant's Plea on Judicial Determination of Sentence." 66 *Yale Law Journal,* 204 (1957).

Comment. "The Self-Incrimination Privilege: Barrier to Criminal Discovery?" 51 *California Law Review,* 135 (1963).

"Crime Expense: Now Up to 51 Billions a Year." 69 *U. S. News and World Report* (October 26, 1970), 30.

Dash, Samuel. "Cracks in the Foundation of Criminal Justice." 46 *University of Illinois Law Review,* 385 (1952).

Davidson, William. "The Worst I've Ever Seen." 241 *Saturday Evening Post* (July 13, 1968), 17.

Davis, Samuel. "Bail—an Examination of Release on Recognizance." 39 *Mississippi Law Journal,* 303 (1967–1968).

Dawson, Robert, and Frank Miller. "Non-use of the Preliminary Examination: A Study of Current Practices." 1964 *Wisconsin Law Review,* 252.

Ervin, Samuel. Foreword to "Preventive Detention: A Step Backward for Criminal Justice." 6 *Harvard Civil Rights—Civil Liberties Law Review,* 291 (1971).

Everett, Robinson. "Discovery in Criminal Cases—in Search of a Standard." 1964 *Duke Law Journal,* 477.

Flannery, Thomas A. "Prosecutor's Position on Discovery in Federal Criminal Cases." 33 *Federal Rules Decisions,* 47 (1963).

Foote, Caleb. "The Coming Constitutional Crisis in Bail." Parts I & II. 113 *University of Pennsylvania Law Review,* 959, 1125 (1965).

Gentile, Carmen. "Fair Bargains and Accurate Pleas." 49 *Boston University Law Review,* 514 (1969).

Ghent, Jeffrey F. "Annotation: Development, Since Hickman v. Taylor, of Attorney's 'Work Product' Doctrine." 35 *American Law Reports,* 412 (3rd ed. 1971).

Goldstein, Joseph. "Police Discretion Not to Invoke the Criminal Process: Low Visibility Decisions in the Administration of Justice." 69 *Yale Law Journal,* 543 (1960).

———. "The State and the Accused: Balance of Advantage in Criminal Procedure." 69 *Yale Law Journal,* 1149 (1960).

Gross, Thomas, and Murray Rosenthal. "Bringing the Systems Approach to Criminal Justice." 9:6 *Nation's Cities* (June, 1971), 27.

Hellman, Peter. "Stealing Cars Is a Growth Industry." *New York Times Magazine* (June 20, 1971), 42.

Hruska, Roman. "Preventive Detention: The Constitution and the Congress." 3 *Creighton Law Review,* 36 (1969).

Jenks, Edward. "The Story of Habeas Corpus." 18 *Law Quarterly Review,* 64 (1902).

Johnson, Phillip. "Multiple Punishment and Consecutive Sentences: Reflections on the 'Neal' Doctrine." 58 *University of California Law Review,* 357 (1970).

Junker, John. "The Right to Counsel in Misdemeanor Cases." 43 *Washington Law Review,* 685 (1968).

"Justice on Trial." 77 *Newsweek* (March 8, 1971), 16.

Kadish, Sanford. "Legal Norm and Discretion in the Police and Sentencing Processes." 75 *Harvard Law Review,* 904 (1962).

Kahn, E. J., Jr. "Annals of Law." *New Yorker* (February 6, 1971), 76.

Kaiser, R. Lamont. "The Bail System: Is It Acceptable?" 29 *Ohio State Law Journal,* 1005 (1968).

Kaplan, John. "The Prosecutorial Discretion." 60 *Northwestern Law Review,* 174 (1965–1966).

Katz, Lewis R. "Gideon's Trumpet: Mournful and Muffled." 55 *Iowa Law Review,* 523 (1970).

———. "Municipal Courts—Another Urban Ill." 20 *Case Western Reserve Law Review,* 87 (1968–1969).

Kaufman, Irving. "The Grand Jury: Its Role and Its Powers." 17 *Federal Rules Digest*, 331 (1955).

Kennedy, Robert F. "Crime in the Cities Improving the Administration of Criminal Justice." 58 *Journal of Criminal Law*, 428 (1967).

King, Maxwell. "Four Inmates Speak." 163 *New Republic* (July 4, 1970), 23.

Kuh, Richard. "The Grand Jury Presentment: Foul Blow or Fair Play?" 55 *Columbia Law Review*, 1103 (1955).

LaFave, Wayne. "Alternatives to the Present Bail System." 1965 *University of Illinois Law Forum*, 8.

———. "Detention for Investigation by the Police: An Analysis of Current Practices." *Washington University Law Quarterly*, 331 (1962).

———. "The Prosecutor in the United States." 18 *American Journal of Comparative Law*, 532 (1970).

Levin, Gerald. "The San Francisco Bail Project." 55 *American Bar Association Journal*, 135 (1969).

Livermore, Joseph. "Policing." 55 *Minnesota Law Review*, 649 (1971).

Londin, James. "Bail or Jail." *The Record of the Association of the Bar of the City of New York* (1964).

Louisell, David W. "Criminal Discovery and Self-Incrimination: Roger Traynor Confronts the Dilemma." 53 *California Law Review*, 89 (1965).

McIntyre, Donald, and David Lippman. "Prosecutors and Early Dispositions of Felony Cases." 56 *American Bar Association Journal*, 1154 (1970).

Miller, Edwin. "The Omnibus Hearing—an Experiment in Federal Criminal Discovery." 5 *San Diego Law Review*, 293 (1968).

Miller, Paul. "Preventive Detention—a Guide to the Eradication of Individual Rights." 16 *Howard Law Journal*, 1 (1970).

Mills, James. "I Have Nothing to Do with Justice." 70 *Life* (March 12, 1971), 62.

Mitchell, John. "Bail Reform and the Constitutionality of Pretrial Detention." 55 *University of Virginia Law Review*, 1223 (1969).

Murphy, John. "State Control of the Operation of Professional Bail Bondsmen." 36 *University of Cincinnati Law Review*, 375 (1967).

Note. "A Study of the Administration of Bail in New York City." 106 *University of Pittsburgh Law Review*, 693 (1958).

Note. "Bail: An Ancient Practice Reexamined." 70 *Yale Law Journal*, 966 (1961).

Note. "Bail in the United States: A System in Need of Reform." 20 *Hastings Law Journal*, 380 (1968).

Note. "Bailbondsmen and the Fugitive Accused—the Need for Formal Removal Procedures." 73 *Yale Law Journal*, 1098 (1964).

Note. "Guilty Plea Bargaining: Compromises by Prosecutors to Secure Guilty Pleas." 112 *University of Pennsylvania Law Review,* 865 (1964).

Note. "Preliminary Hearing in the District of Columbia—an Emerging Discovery Device," 56 *Georgetown Law Journal,* 191 (1967).

Note. "The Duty of the Prosecutor to Disclose Exculpatory Evidence." 60 *Columbia Law Review,* 858 (1960).

Note. "The Grand Jury as an Investigatory Body." 74 *Harvard Law Review,* 590 (1961).

Note. "The Legal Status of Convicts During and After Incarceration." 37 *Virginia Law Review,* 105 (1951).

Note. "The Preliminary Hearing—an Interest Analysis." 51 *Iowa Law Review,* 164 (1966).

Note. "The Unconstitutionality of Plea Bargaining." 83 *Harvard Law Review,* 1387 (1970).

Oaks, Dallin. "Habeas Corpus in the States 1776–1865." 32 *University of Chicago Law Review,* 243 (1965).

Parnas, Raymond. "The Police Response to the Domestic Disturbance." 1967 *Wisconsin Law Review,* 914.

Ploscowe, Morris. "The Development of Present-Day Criminal Procedures in Europe and America." 48 *Harvard Law Review,* 443 (1935).

Polstein, Robert. "How to 'Settle' a Criminal Case." 8 *Practical Lawyer,* 35 (1962).

"Prisons in Turmoil." 76 *Newsweek* (September 14, 1970), 42.

Ralls, William. "Bail in the United States." *Michigan State Bar Journal,* 28 (1969).

Rankin, Anne. "The Effect of Pretrial Detention." 39 *New York University Law Review,* 641 (1964).

Recent Cases. 22 *Case Western Reserve Law Review,* 119 (1971).

Recent Cases. 46 *Virginia Law Review,* 1002 (1960).

Roberts, John, and James Palermo. "A Study of the Administration of Bail in New York City." 106 *University of Pennsylvania Law Review,* 693 (1958).

Schoenfeld, C. G. "Psychoanalysis, Criminal Justice Planning and Reform, and the Law." 7 *Criminal Law Bulletin,* 313 (1971).

Schwartzwald, Martin. "Our Bail System—Instrument of Injustice?" 35 *Manitoba Bar News,* 209 (1965).

Scigliano, Robert. "The Grand Jury, The Information and the Judicial Inquiry." 38 *University of Oregon Law Review,* 303 (1958).

Snepp, Frank. "A Procedure for Negotiated Pleas." 9 *Trial Judges' Journal,* 80 (1970).

Stein, Melvin. "Preliminary Hearings in Pennsylvania: A Closer Look." 30 *University of Pittsburgh Law Review,* 481 (1969).

"The High Cost of Criminal Laws." 123 *America* (October 24, 1970), 310.

"The Shame of the Prisons." 97 *Time* (January 18, 1971), 48.

Trammell, George, III. "Control of System Policy and Practice by the Office District Attorney in Brooklyn and Los Angeles." 5 *The Prosecutor,* 242 (1969).

Tribe, Lawrence. "An Ounce of Detention: Preventive Justice in the World of John Mitchell." 56 *University of Virginia Law Review,* 371 (1970).

Tydings, Joseph. "Improving Archaic Judicial Machinery." 57 *American Bar Association Journal,* 154 (1971).

Vetri, Dominick. "Guilty Plea Bargaining: Compromises by Prosecutors to Secure Guilty Pleas." 112 *University of Pennsylvania Law Review,* 865 (1964).

"What's Wrong with the Courts: The Chief Justice Speaks Out." 69 *U. S. News and World Report* (August 24, 1970), 69.

White, Welsh S. "A Proposal for Reform of the Plea Bargaining Process." 119 *University of Pennsylvania Law Review,* 439 (1971).

Whyte, James. "Is the Grand Jury Necessary?" 45 *University of Virginia Law Review,* 461 (1965).

Willis, Hugh. "Constitution Making by the Supreme Court Since March 29, 1937." 15 *Indiana Law Journal,* 179 (1939–1940).

Wittner, Dale. "Logjam in Our Courts." 69 *Life* (August 7, 1970), 18.

Work, Charles, and Frederick Watts. "Developing an Automated Information System for the Prosecutor." 9 *American Criminal Law Quarterly,* 164 (1970).

"Workshop: Establishing Bail Projects." 1965 *University of Illinois Law Forum,* 42.

Younger, Richard. "The Grand Jury Under Attack." 46 *Journal of Criminal Law, Criminology, and Police Science,* 26 (1955–1956).

MISCELLANEOUS REPORTS

Administrative Board of the Judicial Conference of the State of New York. Statement of John Lindsay (October 9, 1970).

American Bar Association Project on Minimum Standards for Criminal Justice. "Standards Relating to Pretrial Release" (approved draft, 1968). "Standards Relating to Discovery and Procedure Before Trial" (tentative draft, May, 1969).

American Bar Association Project on Standards for Criminal Justice. "Standards Relating to the Prosecution Function and the Defense Function" (tentative draft, March, 1970).

American Bar Foundation. *The Administration of Criminal Justice in the United States, Pilot Project Report:* Vol. 2, *Detroit, Michigan;* Vol. 5, *Milwaukee County, Wisconsin* (1961).

Brief for the Association of the Bar of the City of New York and the Lawyers Committee for Civil Rights Under Law as Amicus Curiae, *United States ex rel. Frizer v. McMann* (2d Cir. 1971).

Columbia Broadcasting System and Eric Sevareid (CBS correspondent). "Justice in America, Part III: Crime and the Courts" (transcript of June 15, 1971, program).

Committee on Rules of Practice and Procedure. Alternative Drafts of Proposed Amendment to Rule 45 Federal Rules Criminal Procedure (March, 1971).

Court of Common Pleas of Allegheny County, Pennsylvania. Sixth Annual Report: July 1, 1969–June 30, 1970. Pittsburgh, 1970.

Edelhertz, Herbert. *The Nature, Impact and Prosecution of White-Collar Crime.* National Institute of Law Enforcement and Criminal Justice, U. S. Department of Justice. Washington, D. C.: U. S. Government Printing Office, 1970.

Jennings, John B. *The Flow of the Arrested Adult Defendants Through the Manhattan Criminal Court in 1968 and 1969.* New York City Rand Institute. New York: Rand Corporation, 1971.

Judicial Council of California. *Annual Report of the Administrative Office of the California Courts.* Sacramento, 1971.

League of Women Voters of Minneapolis. *Hennepin County Municipal Court* (April, 1971, study).

Molleur, Richard. *Final Report of the D.C. Bail Project: Bail Reform in the Nation's Capital,* II. Washington: Georgetown University Law Center, 1966.

National Conference on Bail and Criminal Justice. Proceedings of May 27-29, 1964. Washington, D.C., 1965.

President's Commission on Law Enforcement and Administration of Justice. Task Force Reports: *Science and Technology; The Challenge of Crime in a Free Society; The Courts.* Washington, D.C.: U. S. Government Printing Office, 1967.

Report of the President's Commission on Crime in the District of Columbia. Washington, D.C.: U. S. Government Printing Office, 1966.

State of Ohio Department of Mental Hygiene and Correction. *Ohio Judicial Criminal Statistics: 1969.* Columbus, 1969.

United States Senate, Hearings Before the Subcommittee on Constitutional Rights of the Committee on the Judiciary. *Preventive Detention.* 91st Cong., 2d sess., 1970. Washington, D.C.: U. S. Government Printing Office, 1970.

NEWSPAPER ARTICLES

New York Times

July 30, 1971, p. 37, col. 2.
July 13, 1971, p. 1, col. 5.
July 11, 1971, §1, p. 36, col. 3.
July 9, 1971, p. 1, col. 2-3.
July 7, 1971, p. 1, col. 2; p. 3, col. 3.
July 4, 1971, §1, p. 1, col. 5, col. 7;
       §1, p. 31, col. 2.
July 3, 1971, p. 5, col. 1.
June 17, 1971, p. 45, col. 4.
June 15, 1971, p. 39, col. 1.
June 11, 1971, p. 1, col. 7;
       p. 39, col. 1.
June 10, 1971, p. 22, col. 3.
June 9, 1971, p. 1, col. 2.
June 1, 1971, p. 27, col. 1.
May 31, 1971, p. 17, col. 5.
May 28, 1971, p. 37, col. 4.
May 24, 1971, p. 35, col. 4.
May 23, 1971, §1, p. 46, col. 1
May 14, 1971, p. 20, col. 7.
May 7, 1971, p. 25, col. 1.
April 25, 1971, §4, p. 8, col. 1.
March 18, 1971, p. 26, col. 1.
March 15, 1971, p. 28, col. 1.
March 14, 1971, p. 1, col. 6.
March 12, 1971, p. 1, col. 1;
       p. 12, col. 5
       p. 18, col. 1.
March 8, 1971, p. 1, col. 3, col. 7.
February 22, 1971, p. 33, col. 6.
February 21, 1971, p. 27, col. 1.
February 9, 1971, p. 38, col. 3.
February 4, 1971, p. 1, col. 3;
       p. 31, col. 2.
February 2, 1971, p. 46, col. 8.
January 31, 1971, p. 67, col. 5.
January 7, 1971, p. 1, col. 4.
December 12, 1970, p. 31, col. 3;
       p. 32, col. 2.
December 6, 1970, §1A, p. 1, col. 1;
       p. 24, col. 6.
November 18, 1970, p. 1, col. 7;
       p. 52, col. 1, col. 6.

October 28, 1970, p. 43, col. 4;
       p. 47, col. 4.
October 11, 1970, p. 9, col. 1;
       p. 80, col. 2, col. 6.
October 6, 1970, p. 1, col. 2.
October 4, 1970, p. 1, col. 8;
       p. 77, col. 5.
October 2, 1970, p. 1, col. 3.
September 17, 1970, p. 49, col. 1;
       p. 80, col. 1.
August 23, 1970, §4, p. 10, col. 1.
August 11, 1970, p. 1, col. 6.
June 19, 1970, p. 1, col. 1.
June 15, 1970, p. 35, col. 2.
November 11, 1969, p. 49, col. 8.
July 13, 1969, §4, p. 13, col. 4.
July 12, 1969, p. 1, col. 6.
February 11, 1969, p. 24, col. 1.
January 30, 1969, p. 1, col. 6.
August 25, 1968, p. 47, col. 1.
April 28, 1968, p. 48, col. 1.

Cleveland Plain Dealer

July 12, 1971, p. 1, col. 2.
July 5, 1971, §A, p. 20, col. 2.
June 17, 1971, p. 2, col. 1.
June 11, 1971, p. 9, col. 1.
June 8, 1971, §B, p. 2, col. 3.
June 6, 1971, §A, p. 12, col. 3.
June 1, 1971, §D, p. 20, col. 1.
May 13, 1971, §A, p. 7, col. 3.
April 12, 1971, §B, p. 2, col. 5.
April 1, 1971, §D, p. 2, col. 3.
March 29, 1971, p. 1, col. 2.
March 28, 1971, p. 11, col. 1.
March 13, 1971, §A, p. 12, col. 2.
March 12, 1971, §A, p. 11, col. 1.
February 3, 1971, p. 2, col. 1.

Cleveland Press

March 18, 1971, §F, p. 5, col. 3.
February 23, 1971, §A, p. 5, col. 5.
November 23, 1970, §A, p. 9, col. 1;
       §B, p. 1, col. 1.

New York Law Journal

April 30, 1971, p. 1, col. 1, col. 6.
March 29, 1971, p. 1, col. 4.
February 8, 1971, p. 1, col. 6.
February 5, 1971, p. 1, col. 4.

San Francisco Examiner

January 21, 1971, p. 6, col. 4.

San Francisco Chronicle

April 4, 1971, p. 2, col. 1.
January 21, 1971, p. 8, col. 1.

The Village Voice

February 18, 1971, p. 1, col. 1.

Wall Street Journal

August 20, 1970, p. 10, col. 3.
July 17, 1968, p. 14, col. 4.

The Washington Post

March 27, 1971, §A, p. 1.

TABLE OF CASES

UNITED STATES SUPREME COURT CASES

Adderly v. Florida, 385 U. S. 39 (1966).
Alderman v. United States, 394 U. S. 165 (1969).
Argersinger v. Hamlin, 401 U. S. 908 (1971).
Baldwin v. New York, 399 U. S. 66 (1970).
Boykin v. Alabama, 395 U. S. 238 (1970).
Brady v. Maryland, 373 U. S. 83 (1963).
California v. Byers, 91 S. Ct. 1535 (1971).
California v. Green, 399 U. S. 149 (1970).
Cincenia v. Lagay, 357 U. S. 504 (1958).
Coleman v. Alabama, 399 U. S. 1 (1970).
Dennis v. United States, 384 U. S. 855 (1966).
Draper v. United States, 358 U. S. 307 (1958).
Duncan v. Louisiana, 391 U. S. 145 (1968).
Feiner v. New York, 340 U. S. 315 (1951).
Gideon v. Wainwright, 372 U. S. 335 (1963).
Giles v. Maryland, 386 U. S. 66 (1967).
Griffin v. Illinois, 351 U. S. 12 (1956).
Hickman v. Taylor, 329 U. S. 495 (1947).
Hurtado v. California, 110 U. S. 516 (1884).
Jones v. Florida, 394 U. S. 720 (1969).
Klopfer v. North Carolina, 386 U. S. 213 (1967).
Mallory v. United States, 354 U. S. 449 (1957).
Miranda v. Arizona, 384 U. S. 436 (1966).
Mooney v. Holohan, 294 U. S. 103 (1934).
North Carolina v. Alford, 400 U. S. 25 (1970).
NLRB v. Jones & Laughlin Steel Corp., 301 U. S. 1 (1937).
Oyler v. Boles, 368 U. S. 448 (1962).
Parker v. Ellis, 362 U. S. 574 (1959).
Ponzi v. Fessenden, 258 U. S. 254 (1922).
Schecter Poultry Corp. v. United States, 295 U. S. 495 (1935).
Stack v. Boyle, 342 U. S. 1 (1951).
Ungar v. Sarafite, 376 U. S. 575 (1964).

United States v. Butler, 297 U. S. 1 (1936).

Weeks v. United States, 232 U. S. 383 (1913).

Williams v. Florida, 399 U. S. 78 (1970).

Wong Son v. United States, 371 U. S. 471 (1963).

FEDERAL COURT CASES

Bandy v. United States, 278 F.2d 214 (Douglas, Circuit Justice, 1960).

In re Lamar, 294 F.688 (D. N.J. 1924).

Pannell v. United States, 320 F.2d 698 (D.C. Cir. 1963).

Scott v. United States, 419 F.2d 264 (D.C. Cir. 1969).

Shores v. United States, 174 F.2d 838 (8th Cir. 1949).

United States v. Dilliard, 101 F.2d 829 (2nd Cir. 1938).

United States v. Garsson, 291 F.646 (2nd Cir. 1923).

United States v. Rumrick, 180 F.2d 575 (6th Cir. 1950).

United States v. Muraskin, 99 F.2d 815 (2nd Cir. 1938).

Moore v. Carroll, 315 F. Supp. 1129 (E.D. Pa. 1970).

STATE CASES

Adargo v. People, 159 Colo. 321, 411 P.2d 245 (1966).

Altobella v. Priest, 385 P.2d 585 (Colo. 1963).

Autrey v. State, 44 Ala. App. 53, 202 So. 2d 88 (1967).

Barker v. Commonwealth, 385 S.W.2d 671 (Ky. 1965).

Bell v. State, 430 P.2d 841 (Okla. Ct. App. 1967).

Bevel v. Gladden, 232 Ore. 578, 376 P.2d 117 (1962).

Colebrook v. State, 205 So. 2d 675 (Fla. 1968).

Commonwealth v. Chase, 348 Mass. 100, 202 N.E.2d 300 (1964).

Commonwealth v. Needel, 349 Mass. 580, 211 N.E.2d 335 (1965).

Couture v. State, 156 Me. 261, 163 A.2d 646 (1960).

Dillard v. State, 65 Ark. 404, 46 S.W. 533 (1898).

Glasgow v. State, 469 P.2d 682 (Alas. 1970).

Greathouse v. State, 5 Md. App. 675, 249 A.2d 207 (1969).

Hudson v. State, 453, S.W.2d 147 (Tex. Cr. App. 1970).

In re Camden County Grand Jury, 10 N. J. 23, 89 A.2d 416 (1952).

Johnson v. State, 453 S.W.2d 828 (Tex. 1970).

Jones v. Super. Ct., 58 Cal. 2d 56, 372 P.2d 919, 22 Cal. Rptr. 879 (1962).

King v. State, 432 S.W.2d 490 (Tenn. 1968).

Kominski v. State, 51 Del. 163, 141 A.2d 138 (1958).

Loy v. Grayson, 99 So. 2d 555 (Fla. 1957).

Malcolm v. State, 225 Ga. 470, 169 S.E.2d 779 (1969).

McCandless v. Dist. Ct. of Polk City, 245 Iowa 599, 61 N.W.2d 674 (1954).

McGrath v. State, 42 Wis. 2d 292, 166 N.W.2d 172 (1969).

People v. DiCarlo, 161 Misc. 484, 292 N.Y.S. 252 (1932).

People v. Kennedy, 23 Mich. App. 6, 178 N.W.2d 144 (1970).

People v. Piscitello, 7 N.Y.2d 387, 198 N.Y.S.2d 273, 165 N.E.2d 849 (1960).

People v. Prosser, 309 N.Y. 353, 130 N.E.2d 891 (1955).

People v. Schade, 161 Misc. 212, 229 N.Y.S. 612 (Queens Cty. Ct. 1936).

People v. Vanderhoof, 71 Mich. 158, 39 N.W. 28 (1888).

People v. Witenski, 15 N.Y.2d 392, 207 N.E.2d 358, 259 N.Y.S.2d 413 (1965).

People v. Worley, 45 Ill. 2d 96, 256 N.E.2d 751 (1970).

Raburn v. Nash, 78 N.M. 385, 431 P.2d 874 (1967).

Ramsdell v. Langlois, 100 R.I. 468, 217 A.2d 83 (1966).

Randolph v. State, 234 Ind. 57, 122 N.E.2d 860 (1954).

State v. Banks, 111 La. 22, 35 So. 370 (1904).

State v. Bohn, 67 Utah 362, 248 P. 119 (1926).

State v. Borough, 178 N.W.2d 897 (Minn. 1970).

State v. Brown, 445 S.W.2d 647 (Mo. App. 1969).

State v. Christensen, 75 Wash. 2d 678, 453 P.2d 644 (1969).

State v. Dinger, 51 N.D. 98, 199 N.W. 196 (1924).

State v. Dodson, 226 Ore. 458, 360 P.2d 782 (1961).

State v. Dorsey, 207 La. 928, 22 So. 2d 273 (1945).

State v. Doyle, 11 Ohio App. 2d 97, 40 Ohio Op. 2d 251, 228 N.E.2d 863 (1967).

State ex rel. Underwood v. Brown, 193 Tenn. 113, 244 S.W.2d 168 (1951).

State v. Hale, 157 Me. 361, 172 A.2d 631 (1961).

State v. Harrison, 83 S.D. 440, 160 N.W.2d 415 (1968).

State v. Holloway, 147 Conn. 22, 156 A.2d 466 (1959).

State v. Hulsizer, 42 N.J. Super. 224, 126 A.2d 47 (1956).

State v. Johnson, 28 N.J. 133, 145 A.2d 313 (1958).

State v. Johnson, 3 N.C. App. 420, 165 S.E.2d 27 (1969).

State v. Konigsberg, 33 N.J. 367, 164 A.2d 740 (1960).

State v. Lindhoff, 161 N.W.2d 741 (Iowa 1968).

State v. Mahoney, 124 Vt. 488, 207 A.2d 143 (1965).

State v. Stoeckle, 41 Wis. 2d 378, 164 N.W.2d 303 (1969).

State v. Tune, 13 N.J. 209, 98 A.2d 894 (1953).

Thies v. State, 178 Wis. 98, 189 N.W. 539 (1922).

ENGLISH CASES AND STATUTES

Darnel's Case, 3 How. St. Tr. 1 (1627).

Jenkes Case, 6 How. St. Tr. 1190 (1676).

3 Hen. 7, c. 3 (1486).

1 & 2 Phil. & M., c. 13 (1554).

3 Car. 1, c. 1 (1627).

31 Car. 2, c. 2 (1676).

31 Car. 2, c. 2 (1679).

1 W. & M. Sess. 2, c. 2 (1689).

7 & 8 W. 3, c. 3, Sess. 1 (1695).

6 & 7 W. 4, c. 114, Sess. 1 (1836).

20 & 21 Geo. 5, c. 32 (1930).

12 & 13 Geo. 6, c. 51 (1949).

Various state and federal statutes, rules of criminal procedure, and constitutions were used throughout the study.

INDEX

Accusations, types of, 15 – 17. *See also* Charging process; Indictment

Addicts, 108

Alibi, statutes on, 189 – 90

American Bar Association: Pretrial Release Report, 144n*23;* recommendation on discovery, 187

American Bar Foundation, 119

Arraignment (preliminary appearance), 25 – 27, 116, 155; expanded booking procedure proposed as substitute for, 127 – 29

Arrest: police discretionary power in, 95 – 103, 120n*120;* as selective law enforcement, 114 – 15

Attorneys, role of in deterioration of criminal justice system, 219. *See also* Defense attorneys; Prosecutor

Bail: historical development of, England, 18 – 20; U.S., 20 – 21; distinction between statutory right and constitutional protection with regard to, 21, 137 – 39; effect of on attorney and case, 21; as factor in delaying case, 38 – 39, 51; and further offenses, 61 – 62, 142n*18;* preliminary determinations of, 128; right to, 137 – 41; Eighth Amendment intent unclear regarding, 137 – 39; and use of 1789 Judiciary Act, 138; *Stack v. Boyle* as Supreme Court interpretation of Eighth Amendment's intent, 138 – 39; denial of, and preventive detention, 139 – 40; use of as delay tactic, 147 – 48; use of in plea bargaining, 148; use of in securing witnesses, 149; statistics on pleas and sentences of bailed versus jailed de-

fendants, 151 – 53; in-jail hearings on, 153; standards for determination of, 155; and judges' practices, 155 – 59; high amount of, 158 – 59; securing of, 159 – 60; bondsmen's fees, 160; burden of on poor, 160, 163 – 64; treatment of jumpers, 162 – 63; alternatives to monetary, 164 – 67; reformed systems of to aid poor, 168 – 71; Illinois 10 percent deposit program, 168 – 70, 173; recommendations regarding, 171 – 75

Bail bondsmen, 159 – 64; fees, 160; power of in criminal justice system, 161; decisions of on bonding, 161 – 62; treatment of bail jumpers by, 162 – 63; opposition of to 10 percent bail deposit program, 168 – 70 *passim*

Bail Reform Act of 1966, 171

Bentham, Jeremy, 14

Blacks: police attitudes toward, 100 – 102; as target of preventive detention act, 145

Booking, 103; expanded procedure proposed, 127 – 29, 173

Botein, Bernard (Judge), 91n*8*

Brennan, William J. (Justice), 181n*8*

Burger, Warren E. (Chief Justice), 2n*7,* 77n*130,* 79n*135,* 82, 173n*131*

Charging process: overcharging as cause of trial delay, 72 – 75; complexity of, 92; prosecutor's role in, 104 – 15; importance of screening, 105 – 6; use of misdemeanor process, 106 – 7; prosecutor's options in, 106 – 8; court diversion programs, 108; screening practices,

193-?..

This book was set in ten point TIMES ROMAN via IBM-MTST input and RCA Videocomp. It was composed by Auto-Graphics, Monterey Park, California, and printed and bound by Benson Printing Company, Nashville, Tennessee. The paper is Jackson Offset 60 pound, manufactured by Allied Paper Incorporated. The design is by LaWanda McDuffie with Edgar J. Frank.